STEPPING STONES TO NOWHERE

Galen Roger Perras

STEPPING STONES TO NOWHERE

The Aleutian Islands, Alaska, and American Military Strategy, 1867–1945

Naval Institute Press
Annapolis, Maryland

First published in 2003 in Canada by UBC Press,
University of British Columbia, 2029 West Mall,
Vancouver, British Columbia V6T 1Z2

Published and distributed in the United States of America
by Naval Institute Press, 291 Wood Road,
Annapolis, Maryland 21402-5034

Library of Congress Catalog No. 2002114070

ISBN 1 59114 836 7

Contents

Maps and Illustrations

Acknowledgments

This book is the culmination of a very long road. It originated in the mid-1980s at the Royal Military College of Canada, where I completed my master's thesis, "An Aleutian Interlude: Canadian Participation in the Recapture of the Island of Kiska," under the skilful direction of Dr. Ronald Haycock. Upon entering the doctoral program at the University of Waterloo in 1989, I opted to expand that earlier project by delving far more deeply into the American side of the Aleutian campaign. Almost six years later, with the greatly appreciated assistance of Dr. John English and the other members of my doctoral committee, I completed and defended my dissertation, "Stepping Stones to Nowhere? The United States, Canada, and the Aleutian Island Campaign, 1942-1943."

My exceptional friend Colinda Clyne applied her keen editorial skills to the original dissertation and to an early manuscript incarnation, and provided much appreciated personal support for more than a decade. I also wish to thank Emily Andrew and Camilla Jenkins of UBC Press both for recruiting this manuscript and for skilfully shepherding it through the tricky reefs and shoals of the academic publishing world. Thanks are also due to copyeditor Darcy Cullen, proofreader Judy Phillips, indexer Patricia Buchanan, and cartographer Eric Leinberger. The Aid to Scholarly Publishing Programme kindly provided funds to publish this book. Much of the research for the original doctoral dissertation, on which this book is based, was made possible by a grant from the Social Sciences and Humanities Research Council of Canada. A special round of applause is due the four anonymous reviewers, who provided much useful advice.

My parents, Roland and Dolores Perras, despite reservations about their oldest son's fixation with "that history thing," also provided much needed support, for which I thank them.

The editors of *The Northern Mariner* and *the Journal of Military History* graciously allowed me to use material from my previously published articles: "'The Defence of Alaska Must Remain a Primary Concern of the United States': Canada's Contribution to the Defence of Midway, May-June 1942," *The Northern Mariner* 7 (October 1997); "'We Know Damn Well that the Only Asiatic Enemy We Are Guarding against Is Russia': The Kurile Islands in American Pacific Strategy, 1943-1945," *The Journal of Military History* 61, 1 (January 1997); and "Canada As a Military Partner: Alliance Politics and the

Campaign to Recapture the Island of Kiska," *The Journal of Military History* 56, 3 (July 1992). Professor Larry Black kindly allowed me to quote from his father's privately held diary.

The following archives, libraries, and institutions did much to ensure that this project finally came to fruition: the Air Force History Support Office, Bolling Air Force Base, Washington, DC; Amherst College Archives, Amherst; the Australian War Memorial, Canberra; the National Archives of Australia, Canberra; the British Columbia and Archives Service, Victoria; the Directorate of History and Heritage, Department of National Defence, Ottawa; Duke University Archives, Durham; Durham University Archives, Durham; the Dwight D. Eisenhower Presidential Library, Abilene; the Green Library, Stanford University; the Hoover Institution on War, Revolution and Peace, Stanford University; the Library of Congress, Washington, DC; the Marine Corps Historical Center, Washington, DC; the George C. Marshall Library, Lexington; the Massey Library, Royal Military College of Canada, Kingston; the Military History Institute Archives, Carlisle Barracks; the National Archives of Canada, Ottawa; the Naval Historical Center, Washington, DC; Queen's University Archives, Kingston; the Public Record Office, Kew; the Rasmussen Library, University of Alaska, Fairbanks; the Franklin Delano Roosevelt Library, Hyde Park; the United States Military Academy Archives, West Point; the National Archives and Records Administration, College Park and Washington, DC; the Naval Historical Institute Library, Annapolis; the United States Air Force Academy Library, Colorado Springs; and the Yale University Library, New Haven.

Introduction

In the year 2000 a series of network television news items drew attention to a distant dot on the globe that few Americans knew even existed. That dot was the barren and windswept island of Shemya in the north Pacific, one of the westernmost portions of the elongated Aleutian archipelago. Home already to a top secret military listening post, Shemya briefly came to public prominence because it was chosen as the site for an advanced radar facility that would form part of a national anti-ballistic missile system. However, once President Bill Clinton decided to postpone the development of that complex and controversial system in late 2000, Shemya and the remainder of the Aleutians fell back into well-accustomed obscurity. It was not the first time that the Aleutians chain, in whole or in part, had received attention for its purported strategic military value. In the following pages, we shall see how a variety of Americans, some renowned, others obscure, viewed the Aleutian Islands as a potential strategic asset from the moment they were acquired in 1867, only to see those hopes fade into the strategic mists for over sixty years before their dramatic re-emergence in the Second World War.

Stretching westward from the rugged Alaskan mainland like a dagger stabbing at the distant vastness of northeast Asia, the nearly 300 islands in the bleak archipelago are devoid of trees but boast a surfeit of mountains and several dozen active volcanoes. The Aleutians rarely experience prolonged periods of sub-zero arctic temperatures but the chain's position between the volatile north Pacific Ocean to the south and the frigid Bering Sea to the north renders it vulnerable to some of the world's most extreme weather changes. Rain or snow falls more than 200 days a year, dense fog and thick mists are all too common, and severe gale-force winds, known locally as "williwaws," occur frequently.

The Aleutian Islands might seem to be an exceedingly unlikely battlefield. Yet on 11 May 1943, thousands of heavily armed American soldiers stormed the Aleutian island of Attu. Determined to wrest the isolated place from the Japanese troops who had seized it in June 1942, the Americans became embroiled in a bitter struggle that ended three weeks later – once they had completely exterminated the obdurate and impossibly brave Japanese garrison. Confronted, then, with what they believed to be a much larger enemy force on Kiska Island, the Americans assembled a massive army and naval task force of 35,000 men (including 5,000 Canadians) for an assault.

But when that vast armada invaded Kiska on 15 August, it discovered that the Japanese had slipped away covertly several weeks earlier. Having suffered heavy casualties on Attu, the heavily laden soldiers were relieved to have met no opposition on Kiska. C.P. Stacey, Canada's official army historian, labels the attack a "fiasco" and a "ridiculous anti-climax," while Walter A. McDougall describes the retaking of a deserted Kiska by a "bloated" force as a "farce." Similarly, Jonathan M. Nielson argues that, while Attu "had been a grim soldiers' battle fought with courage, albeit poor-to-dismal strategic insight and tactical direction," Kiska "had been a tragic mistake that tied down enormous resources that could have been better used elsewhere." Finally, in his sweeping and definitive study of the Second World War, Gerhard Weinberg avers that "the United States insistence on retaking Kiska and Attu was almost as unwise as the Japanese insistence on trying to hold on to these indefensible outposts which led to nowhere for either side."[1]

Such harsh retrospective critiques have tended to apply to the Aleutian campaign as a whole. Describing the Aleutians as a theatre of military frustration, renowned naval historian Samuel Eliot Morison avers that "no operations in this region of almost perpetual mist and snow accomplished anything of great importance or had any appreciable effect on the outcome of the war." British strategist Basil H. Liddell Hart's opinionated, but immensely readable, history of the Second World War contends that employing over 100,000 servicemen "in this trivial task" in the north Pacific was "a flagrant example of bad economy of force, *and* a good example of the distraction that can be caused by a diversionary initiative with slight expenditure."[2] Few familiar with Japan's unhappy role in the bitter Aleutian campaign would disagree with such negative assertions. Historian Takahashi Hisashi states unequivocally that Japan's invasion of the Aleutians in 1942 "was a sheer waste of ships, men, and vital supplies that could have been better used elsewhere than in this near-arctic wasteland." Vice Admiral Takijiro Onishi complains that Japan's military "took a foolish liking to the place and poured in too much material and unnecessary personnel, making it impossible to leave."[3]

Blessed by the powers of hindsight, these critical assessments are mostly valid. The recapture, first of Attu and then of Kiska, had come in a decisive year of combat that had witnessed the brutal jungle and naval battles of attrition for Guadalcanal in the south Pacific, the loss of over 300,000 German soldiers in Stalingrad's desolate frozen ruins, the surrender of the tattered remnants of General Erwin Rommel's fabled Afrika Korps in Tunisia, and history's largest tank battle on the vast Russian steppe at Kursk. But while a significant body of literature discusses the Aleutian campaign in some manner or another, many analyses start with Japan's occupation of the western Aleutians in 1942 and end with the triumphant American return to those islands fifteen months later. That is not so say that many of these works lack merit. Indeed, John Haile Cloe's detailed description of the Aleutian air war and Brian Garfield's gripping popular history of the entire campaign are particularly engaging accounts of the very real hardships faced by brave warriors fighting and dying in an unforgiving and harsh combat environment.[4]

Yet most Aleutian discussions miss the point. The Aleutian campaign certainly did little to ensure Japan's ultimate defeat – the awful battles for the Philippines, Saipan, Iwo Jima, and Okinawa in 1943-5 loom far larger in that regard. Far more interesting is the fact that the campaign for the Aleutians was the culmination of decades of debate about the potential strategic value – or lack thereof – of that isolated and windswept archipelago. From the time Alaska was controversially acquired by an expanding United States from a declining Russian empire in 1867, a fair number of Americans, many of whom held prominent political and military positions, believed fervently that the Aleutians were the strategic key in a long-term and potentially bitter struggle to dominate the north Pacific. Wartime commanders General Simon Bolivar Buckner Jr. and General John L. DeWitt, for example, were ardent advocates of an offensive across the north Pacific towards Japan itself, and they represented a persistent strand of American strategic thought dating back decades to noted luminaries such as Admiral Alfred Thayer Mahan and General William (Billy) Mitchell. Furthermore, like Mahan and Mitchell, Buckner and DeWitt faced determined opponents who maintained that the Aleutians could not support major operations and that the supporters of a northern route to Japan failed to recognize that the targets of any real strategic significance lay in the central Pacific.

Unfortunately, even among studies that focus on the pre-war strategic situation confronting the United States in the Pacific, the Aleutians are rarely given the attention they deserve. In his very detailed official army history of pre-war plans and preparation, Mark S. Watson, maintaining that the "defense of the extreme north Pacific was not a major anxiety of the War Department in 1939," devotes just four pages to Alaskan defence prior to the Second World War.[5] In his exceptional analysis of the US Army's role in the

Pacific from 1902 to 1940, Brian McAllister Linn argues that army attempts to defend the territory against Japanese aggression were limited not so much by its strategic ineptitude but by the American leadership's failure to take sensible precautions and to discern the nation's true strategic interests.[6] Not surprisingly, his analysis focuses on Hawaii and the Philippines. Alaska is mentioned only very briefly in the context of its role as the mostly forgotten northern anchor of the Alaska-Hawaii-Panama strategic triangle concept that emerged during attempts to revise the United States Navy's (USN) "Orange" battle plan for Japan. On the other hand, Edward S. Miller's impressive study of Plan Orange includes an extensive discussion of the Aleutians prior to the Second World War but sums up their wartime role in paragraph.[7]

I hope that this book will rectify the most glaring omission – the absence of a comprehensive work that explains just how the Aleutian Islands became "a lodestone for strategists who had never been there"[8] and for some who had. It is a story of strong personalities seeking to up-end or disregard the unbending dictates of geography and climate, the vagaries of domestic and international politics, the often acrimonious arguments over strategic principles, intense inter-service rivalry and personal animosities, and the development of a Canadian-American military alliance. My approach to this case study is threefold. First, I examine military politics, focusing on the ways in which the Joint Chiefs of Staff (JCS), the Combined Chiefs of Staff (CCS), and their various attendant advisory bodies dealt with north Pacific strategy during the Second World War. I identify the persistent problems that plagued the formulation of a grand strategy intended to satisfy fully each American service and its political masters, as well as public opinion and America's most important allies, namely Britain, the Soviet Union, and Canada. In a sense, I hope to expose the nature of campaign making, revealing the lengthy and sometimes virulent debates, the unforeseen wrong turns, the strategic blind alleys, the mistaken assumptions, and dangerous misperceptions. The American military often had great difficulty setting its strategic priorities, a problem due to pre-war battles over resources, the nature of the Pacific theatre, as well as inter-service rivalry. Such problems were exacerbated by the very nature of the American federal system of governance, insofar as competing centres of power were deliberately built into it. Perhaps such a system ensured a more democratic political process but it rendered war-making problematic, at best.

Second, I extensively analyze proposals to follow up America's victory in the Aleutians with major offensives against the Kurile Islands and, possibly, the Japanese home islands themselves. Those proposals have generally received short shrift from historians for the simple reason that American forces never tried to occupy the Kuriles, preferring instead to operate in the more temperate and more accommodating central Pacific. Had that northern attack gone forward, however, America's postwar relations with the Soviet Union may have become more confrontational. Unfortunately, many of the strongest advocates of a drive across the north Pacific, most notably generals John DeWitt and Simon Buckner, wholly failed to comprehend the potentially vast implications of their grand schemes. Beyond the situation with the Soviets, a major American offensive against the Kuriles would have substantially altered the thrust of the Pacific conflict, if not the entire global Allied war effort. Moreover, as in the Aleutian campaign, advocates for a Kurile attack tended to ignore considerations of weather and logistics, as well as the capabilities of the various services and the complex organizational dynamics at work in American strategy making in the Second World War.

Finally, I discuss the intermittent presence of Canada in north Pacific and Aleutian military affairs from the 1920s to 1943. For Billy Mitchell, Canada seemed a natural ally against a potentially hostile and alien Japan. And, while Canadian forces played an important role in rolling back the Japanese presence in the Aleutians in the Second World War, that role was not inevitable. Many senior Canadian officers in the interwar period feared being dragged into a conflict involving the United States and Japan, and saw a belligerent and politically aggressive America as the greatest threat to Canadian sovereignty. Once war came, Canada's intensively Eurocentric military, fixated on Germany's destruction, initially opposed any contribution to the Pacific that might damage its effort in Europe. In the end, however, Canadian domestic political concerns and worries about declining ties with America would drive Canada's military contribution to the Aleutians.

A word of warning to some readers. In recent years, it has become quite fashionable in some historical and academic circles to pooh-pooh the value of "top-down" history, with its "great man" at the top of the social or political pyramid, in favour of a focus on the masses below. I do not wish to disparage broad-based social history, which has much of value to contribute on a variety of topics, both societal and military. However, my particular interest and expertise lie with those men at the top of the political/military hierarchy, men who had the power (or wished that they had) to make key strategic decisions about the Aleutians and the north Pacific. Certainly some will argue, perhaps with justification, that I have glossed over the harsh realities faced by the men who actually fought and died in the Aleutians in the Second World War. For those who crave such experiences, I heartily recommend the books of Cloe and Garfield; they provide a real flavour of the daily struggle in the Aleutians. The battle for the Aleutians is truly the stuff of history, and I embarked upon this quest for answers with the humbling words of a nineteenth-century *Times* editorialist ringing in my ears. Historians, he argued, "know about as much of real cause and consequence as postmen, porters and footmen do of their masters' private affairs."[9] Let us hope that I can do a little better than postmen, porters, and footmen in discussing Aleutian affairs.

Abbreviations

AAF	army air force
ADC	Alaska Defense Command
ALCOM	Alaskan Command
AWC	Army War College
AWPD	Air War Plans Division
BLG	battalion landing groups
CCS	Combined Chiefs of Staff
CGS	Chief of the General Staff (Canada)
CIC	Combined Intelligence Committee
CINCPAC	Commander-in-Chief, Pacific
CNO	Chief of Naval Operations
CSP	Combined Staff Planners
CWC	Cabinet War Committee (Canada)
DEA	Department of External Affairs (Canada)
DND	Department of National Defence (Canada)
IJA	Imperial Japanese Army
IJN	Imperial Japanese Navy
JANPC	Joint Army and Navy Planning Committee
JCS	Joint Chiefs of Staff
JIC	Joint Intelligence Committee (United States)
JPS	Joint Planning Staff
JSPC	Joint Strategic Plans Committee
JSSC	Joint Strategic Survey Committee
JWPC	Joint War Plans Committee
MID	Military Intelligence Division
NWB	Naval War Board
NWC	Naval War College
OPD	Office of the Director of Plans and Operations
PBY	patrol boatplane
PHPS	Post Hostilities Planning Staff (Britain)
PJBD	Permanent Joint Board on Defence
PWAC	Post-War Advisory Committee
PWC	Pacific War Council
RCAF	Royal Canadian Air Force
RMS	Revenue Maritime Service

SPD	Strategic Plans Division
SPG	Strategy and Policy Group
SSF	Special Service Force
USN	United States Navy
USSEA	Under-Secretary of State for External Affairs
WDC	Western Defense Command
WPD	War Plans Division

One of Our Great Strategic Points:
Alaskan Defence, 1867-1934

On 18 October 1867, to the resounding accompaniment of salvoes of cannon fire echoing over the nearby sea and mountains, Russia's small garrison on the island of Sitka formally handed over the Russian colony of Alaska to 250 blue-clad American soldiers. The rather short official ceremony was delayed briefly when the Russian flag became entangled as it was being lowered from its twenty-five-metre pole. The problem was resolved only when some sailors jury-rigged a special rope that permitted an adept soldier to shinny up the mast to untangle the snarled colours. After raising America's Stars and Stripes, General Lovell H. Rousseau accepted the formal transfer from the Russian military commander, and the officers sat down with the Russian governor to thrash out some minor, but perplexing, private property issues.[1]

With this brief, if flawed, rite, the vast Alaskan territory passed quietly from a declining autocratic old-world empire to a younger and rising new-world democratic power. One determined man, Secretary of State William Henry Seward, had acted as a catalyst to the controversial purchase of the distant territory. As a senator in the 1850s, an energetic Seward had become convinced that future American greatness would depend on his country's ability to fully exploit Asia's incredible potential, "the chief theatre of events in the world's great hereafter." Having noted as early as 1846 that the United States should expand "to the icy barriers of the North," Seward openly asserted seven years later that he truly welcomed Russia's continued development of Alaska, certain that facilities built there would inevitably "become the outposts of my country – monuments of the civilization of the United States in the northwest."[2]

Russia's imperial masters had been surprisingly amenable to Seward's desires. After decades of rapacious and brutal economic exploitation that had led to the deaths of thousands of Alaskan natives at the hands of Russian troops or from foreign diseases, by the 1840s Russian Alaska had ceased to be profitable, as its fur trade had languished while administrative costs had soared. Moreover, as American power inexorably expanded across the North American continent, in 1853 eastern Siberian Governor Nikolai Murav'ev pessimistically predicted, "We can expect that sooner or later we will have to cede our North American possession to them." Four years later, Grand Duke Konstantin warned that "the United States, striving constantly to round out its possessions and desiring to dominate North America undividedly, will take the said colony from us and we will be unable to regain it." But the immediate threat had been Britain, the global power controlling most of the territory abutting Alaska.

In 1854 Russia had found itself at war with Britain, France, Sardinia, and the Ottoman Empire – a war Russia did not win. When the United States warned the Russians that a British attack on Alaska might be forthcoming, Czar Nicholas I hurriedly raised the notion of selling Alaska to the Americans before the asset was lost. Britain, however, did not attack Alaska and the United States's rapidly burgeoning domestic crisis and subsequent bloody Civil War aborted any American purchase in the 1850s. Once that divisive conflict had ended and America had been reunited in 1865, most pleased that Russia had backed the Union cause and angry with perfidious Albion for its support of the vanquished Confederacy, Seward viewed Alaska's purchase as

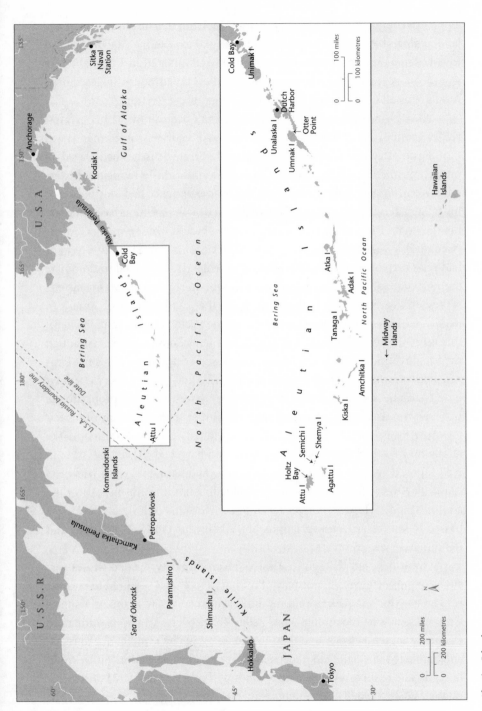

Aleutian Islands

a potent geopolitical instrument, allowing the United States to squeeze England's vulnerable colony of British Columbia and to obtain a vital bridgehead to Asian markets. His strenuous efforts finally culminated in a formal treaty signed on 20 June 1867. For $7.3 million, the United States had acquired Alaska plus all of the "uncivilized tribes" living in the territory.[3]

Although Seward rightfully ranked Alaska's acquisition as his greatest achievement in a long public life, he ruefully and accurately noted that "it will take the country a generation to appreciate it." Strategic issues had played an important role in pushing the deal through a notoriously recalcitrant Congress. According to Seward's son, the Civil War experience had only bolstered his father's fervent desire to possess Alaska: a dearth of Union bases bordering the north Pacific had made it difficult to chase down the many Confederate raiding vessels that plagued vulnerable Union ships. Therefore, Seward had reasoned, his nation had to possess Greenland and Iceland to dominate the north Atlantic, and Alaska to dominate the north Pacific. Massachusetts representative Nathanial P. Banks declared that, with Alaska in American hands, "we have in our grasp the control of the Pacific Ocean, and may make this great theater of the future whatever we may choose it to be." Although the Senate quickly ratified the deal, unimpressed critics in the House of Representatives, who described the deal as "Seward's folly" and Alaska as "a polar bear's garden," sought to block the purchase by refusing to appropriate the necessary funds. Representative Benjamin F. Butler spoke for many of his fellow Americans when he averred that, if the United States had wanted Alaska at any time in the last twenty years, "we could have had [it] for the asking." He proposed giving Russia the purchase price and letting it keep a worthless Alaska, if Russian friendship was so valuable to Andrew Johnson's struggling administration. However, Butler failed to convince his colleagues; the House passed the necessary appropriations bill, albeit reluctantly, in July 1868 and the purchase was complete.[4]

Seward believed that, given Alaska's racial disparity – 2,000 whites versus 25,000 Aboriginals – "a display of military force" was required to cow the restless natives. The American army, however, faced severe manpower shortages. Its vast wartime strength had fallen from over 1.5 million soldiers to 57,000 by September 1867 and then to a mere 27,442 by 1876, thanks to rising anti-military sentiment and a focus on domestic reconstruction. Sitka would host Alaska's main army base, and a handful of other tiny isolated posts were established by 1869. The Aleutians, however, did not garner a garrison; the closest troops were placed at Kodiak Island, east of the island chain, in June 1869. Military government in the territory proved quite unpopular, both in Alaska and in Washington's distant halls of power. As the army struggled, with rather little success, to constrain widespread illegal trade in alcohol and guns to local Natives, its soldiers were frequently and often justly accused by white settlers and politicians of idleness, bootlegging, and frequenting prostitutes. These practices led to the court-martialling of over 20 percent of Alaska's garrison in 1868-9 alone. Then, after an unsympathetic Congress drastically cut the military budget in 1870, the army scrambled to find resources to wage protracted Indian wars in the American west, and shut down every Alaskan post except Sitka, leaving just 121 troops in the territory. In 1877 Sitka too was mothballed and Alaska went without a permanent army garrison until the Klondike gold rush twenty years later.[5]

Still, the army was not entirely absent from Alaska after 1877. Numerous small military expeditions criss-crossed the vast unformed territory, exploring deep river valleys, mapping the boundless interior, and tracing its harsh Arctic shoreline. After a lull, the discovery of substantial gold deposits in Canada's nearby Yukon Territory in the late 1890s brought thousands of prospectors and settlers flooding into the region, and induced another brief upsurge in army exploration. By 1900, however, the army was forced to give way to the United States Geological Survey and the Smithsonian Institution, the military's expeditionary activities being labelled inefficient, expensive, and scientifically unprofessional. The army, however, had shown no interest in the Aleutians, leaving that archipelago to the navy. Compelled to take up the army's police function in Alaska after 1877, the navy also manifested little enthusiasm for the Aleutians. It had sent a schooner, the USS *Fenimore Cooper,* to the Aleutians in 1853. Commanded by Acting Lieutenant William Gibson, the ship's mission was a simple one: to locate suitable harbours, undertake some soundings and topographical studies, and find useable coal deposits. Further, Gibson had been instructed to pay particular attention to the island of Adak, as "this is the point through which the great circle passes between San Francisco and Shanghai." The mission's results, however, were disappointing. No coal was located, though the ship did study Adak, as well as Atka, Tanaga, and especially Attu. The USN preferred to concentrate its constrained efforts and limited resources on southeast Alaska, while the Revenue Maritime Service (RMS) operated small cutters in Aleutian waters after 1867, making use of a small facility on Unalaska, an island in the eastern

Aleutians. Unalaska assumed modest military importance for a brief period in the late 1880s, thanks to a remarkably fractious and long-standing sealing dispute in the Bering Sea. Unhappy that foreign sealers, mostly Canadian and Japanese, were refusing to acknowledge American sovereignty in the region and relentlessly harvesting valuable fur seals at an unsustainable pace, in 1888 the USN dispatched a small squadron to Unalaska to show the flag and round up offending sealers and their vessels. It took another three years to strike a tenuous diplomatic accord, and American and British ships, supplemented by 138 marines, remained at Unalaska for some time to police the fragile sealing deal.[6]

Soldiers finally came back to Alaska in 1897, their belated return having been prompted by growing concerns about civil disorder and violence engendered by the fortuitous discovery of gold in the Yukon. By 1900 the army had established more than a dozen posts in the vast territory, and the War Department had designated Alaska a full-fledged military department as troops settled again into a mostly humdrum policing role.[7] The outbreak of the Russo-Japanese War in February 1904 then threatened to greatly complicate matters. America's relations with Japan had generally been good since Commodore Matthew Perry's "Black Ships" had firmly dragged a xenophobic and unwilling Japan into the wider world in 1853. America's subsequent acquisition of the Philippines and Hawaii in the 1890s – the first by force of arms, the second via some political chicanery – also brought significant changes. Some British officers feared that America's newfound imperialist tendencies could endanger Britain's interests in the Pacific and in China (both Britain and Canada had cast covetous eyes upon Hawaii). But more important, Japanese-American relations, "hitherto almost exclusively concerned with such matters as tariff revision and extraterritoriality would now be those between rival empires."[8] Still, when a Japanese staff officer in 1901 appraised the possibility of foreign power intervention were Japan and Russia to come to blows, he thought the United States would remain neutral. Two years later, the rapidly expanding and improving Imperial Japanese Navy (IJN) believed that, while America was an emerging major naval power, it likely would not deploy the USN's bulk in the Pacific.[9]

Although noted strategist Admiral Alfred Thayer Mahan had warned Assistant Secretary of the Navy Theodore Roosevelt in 1897 that "we have much more likelihood of trouble on [the Pacific] side rather than the Atlantic," the ever confident Roosevelt thought differently. That year, he ordered the Naval War College (NWC) to plan for a potential conflict with Japan, but as president, in March 1904 Roosevelt warned that Japan's victory over Russia would see the rise of "a great new force in eastern Asia." A Russophobe, Roosevelt firmly believed Japan would play "our game" by balancing Russian power in Asia.[10] Congress also appeared to share Roosevelt's benign view of Japan. In March 1904 the navy set aside Kiska as a naval reservation; three months later, the army-navy Joint Board ruled that Kiska's retention would be vital in a major war with Japan. For several years, though, a parsimonious Congress stubbornly declined to appropriate any money for Kiska's military development. Even when Roosevelt suggested in 1907 that the Japanese, "their heads ... swollen to a marvellous degree," might take advantage of a diplomatic crisis, brought on by the ill treatment of Japanese immigrants in the United States, to attack Alaska, he found little domestic support. British officials in Washington reported that the president could call upon few allies in the American military, thanks to his frequent and unhelpful interference in promotions of officers to senior ranks, and they doubted whether the American population or major capitalists would fully support a war with Japan. Such views gained credence when Congress again pointedly refused to loosen tightly held purse strings, forcing the navy to build a badly needed wharf and coaling station on Kiska from pre-existing funds.[11]

Secretary of War Elihu Root did his best to spark some interest in the Japanese threat. In an alarmist memorandum written in October 1906, Root averred that Japan, "ready for war," could take the "Philippines, Hawaii, and probably the Pacific coast" of the United States. And while Root predicted American forces would eventually recover those territories, "the loss suffered by us would probably be permanent and irrevocable" given that there would be little or no prospect of inflicting any effective reprisals against Japan. Roosevelt and the USN, though obviously frustrated by congressional parsimony, did little to help Root's position. Admiral Charles Sperry had enthusiastically greeted the 1905 renewal of the Anglo-Japanese alliance as the best "guarantee of peace both in Europe and in the East." And even if Japan, concerned by the poor treatment some of its nationals were experiencing in the western United States – San Francisco had banned Japanese children from public schools in 1907 and Japanese adults faced considerable discrimination – wanted to act, the NWC believed that Japan was far too busy absorbing its recent gains in Korea and Manchuria to want trouble with the United States. If trouble did start, few in the USN thought that the Aleutians would play a prominent role in any war in the Pacific. In 1896 the Naval War Board (NWB) formulated a war plan that envisaged the main fleet waiting for the Japanese navy at Hawaii; the Aleutians would host only a few cruiser scouts searching for the approaching enemy armada.[12]

Little changed over the next two decades. Alaska's garrison amounted to a mere 1,000 soldiers, scattered among several isolated posts far from the Aleutians. The considerably more valuable Philippines and Hawaii were so poorly defended that the British feared they might prove all-too tempting as targets for their increasingly aggressive Japanese ally. NWC planners agreed. Convinced that Japan could easily grab Guam, Hawaii, and the Philippines by striking first, in 1911 they contended that all those places would be vital for any successful American counterattack. Three approaches were considered: a northern route via the Aleutians to Okinawa Island; an attack via Hawaii and Guam; or a northward route from the Philippines. Rejecting the Aleutian option because of the region's notoriously dismal climate, the NWC also dismissed a central Pacific operation for fear of prohibitive shipping losses. Arguing that advancing via the Philippines would take too long and call for too many warships, a semi-retired Mahan proposed basing nearly all the USN's Pacific fleet at Kiska. Dismissing weather concerns because he found it "difficult to admit that for white men climatic inconveniences of an over-cold climate can equal in effect those of one constantly over-warm," Mahan noted that Kiska-based vessels would be only 1,800 and 2,700 miles from Japan and Guam respectively, well within the fleet's 4,000-mile cruising radius. More important, shifting ships to Kiska would compel the IJN to retreat hastily to its home bases. Judging Kiska's harbour to be too small to shelter the entire fleet and too remote to easily stock with coal, the USN declined to place valuable vessels so close to Japan at a conflict's outset, adding that a Kiska-based offensive would expose American forces to harassment on both flanks. Mahan admitted that stocking coal was a costly and intricate problem but one that was "not insoluble to money and brain," and he argued instead for the audacity that he maintained could "be found in every great military achievement."[13]

Mahan failed to change many minds. Although the admiral was highly regarded in many other nations with blue water naval ambitions, particularly Germany and Japan, where his seminal 1891 study, *The Influence of Sea Power upon History, 1660-1783*, was well received, Mahan's influence at home had been fading for some time. In 1892, while desperately seeking to avoid sea service – he suffered terribly from sea sickness – Mahan had been roundly criticized by the chief of the Bureau of Navigation, who declared that it was "not the business of a naval officer to write books." The American public too, Mahan had admitted in 1907, "viewed his promotion of a military spirit as the obtrusion of an alien temperament." Thus, in 1911 while the navy promised to make Kiska a great strategic point, given "the possible complications that may arise between ourselves and Asia," it selected Hawaii's Pearl Harbor as its main Pacific anchorage; Kiska's proximity to the Kuriles rendered it too vulnerable to a surprise assault.[14]

A subsequent 1913 war scare prompted the Army War College (AWC) to warn that the Japanese potentially could seize parts of Alaska; two years later, they added that Japan could even occupy bases throughout southeast Alaska and British Columbia. Any serious hopes that Alaska's security needs would be speedily addressed faded quickly, though. First, as the British had noted in 1908, the American army, "unfit to invade Japan," did not seriously consider that Japan could assault North America. Second, the fantastic eruption of general war in Europe in 1914 put Alaska's needs very much on the strategic backburner, much to R.M. Johnston's chagrin. Professor at Harvard and at the AWC, and an ardent propagandist for military preparedness, Johnson advocated placing 20,000 soldiers in Hawaii and Alaska to ensure their retention, for he feared a Japanese conquest of those territories.[15] Although the British agreed that the Japanese could seriously threaten American security, only once the First World War had ground to its bloody conclusion did Johnston's suggestions receive a cursory hearing. In late 1919 the Joint Board confirmed that the main navy anchorage would remain in Hawaii, but recommended the establishment of a small scout force for Alaskan waters. Four months later the Joint Army and Navy Planning Committee (JANPC) endorsed an Alaskan base to support the operations of destroyers, submarines, and small craft in Alaskan waters, with a provision for enlargement for capital ships at some later, unspecified time. But Alaska's base still ranked last on a long list of strategic priorities. Further, a shortage of funds militated against fuel depots at Kiska and at the town of Dutch Harbor on Unalaska, although the navy gave its moral support for the establishment of commercial Aleutian coaling stations. Two submarine chasers and two Coast Guard survey vessels provided Alaska with a scouting force in 1919 but only two small cutters lingered forlornly in Alaskan waters a year later; the other ships had been sent elsewhere.[16]

The American military had even more bitter pills to swallow. Successive postwar Republican administrations, responding to intense public isolationism and dramatically altered postwar strategic circumstances, repeatedly rejected large defence expenditures throughout the 1920s. Although the National Defense Act of 1920 had set its strength at 280,000 troops, by the early 1930s the army could muster only 118,750 soldiers, far short of the 165,000 men it believed were absolutely required to adequately meet its many responsibilities.[17] Though this state of affairs led some American officers to complain vociferously in 1921 to a visiting Canadian about the "attitude of the small army men" in Congress,[18] the navy felt even more aggrieved, especially after the promulgation of the 1922 Washington Naval Treaty. Concluded after protracted and at times bitter negotiations between the United States, Britain, Japan, France, and Italy, the complex pact imposed a warship tonnage ratio, set a ten-year moratorium on naval construction, and established maximum tonnages for many ship classifications. Article XIX, its most controversial provision, banned new bases and forbade the improvement of existing Pacific facilities. Japan, Hawaii, Australia, New Zealand, and Singapore were exempted; Alaska and the Aleutians were not.

Getting all of the signatories to accept Article XIX had been no easy task. Seeking to effectively bridle the Japanese military's ability to operate in the south Pacific, Britain suggested that Japan move to disarm the central Pacific island possessions it had acquired from a defeated Germany after 1918. Badly in need of a respite from a prohibitively expensive naval arms race, Japan's increasingly fragile democratic government was unwilling to see the talks collapse, even though the IJN vociferously viewed any shipping cuts as a bitter negation of its goal of complete naval parity with the Anglo-Saxon powers. Therefore, Japan's initial price for demilitarizing its Pacific possessions was steep: the United States would have to stop work on defences on Guam, Hawaii, and the Philippines. When the Americans categorically refused to agree to Hawaii's inclusion, the British managed to convince the wary Japanese to accept Britain's proposal, with the proviso demanded by Japanese domestic opinion – that the Aleutians be included within Article XIX. To sweeten the deal, Japan pledged to demilitarize the Kuriles. The American delegation, with ready access to decrypted Japanese message traffic, was happy to accept for, as Colonel Theodore Roosevelt Jr. crowed, the deal left America "in a slightly better position than Japan. We trade certain fortifications, which we would never have completed, for fortifications which they would unquestionably have completed. We retain one outpost in the Pacific of great importance [Hawaii] and they give up all but their mainland."[19]

Many American isolationists warmly embraced the Washington Naval Treaty as a welcome, if overdue, curtailing of the USN's dangerous navalist ambitions. Admiral William Veazie Pratt, a naval non-conformist in that he favoured aircraft carriers over battleships and worried that constant predictions of a war with Japan could be self-fulfilling, defended the deal on the grounds that his service would be wise not to ignore international political relations and domestic public opinion. But most of Pratt's fellow sailors believed that Article XIX had seriously weakened the navy's ability to properly preserve the nation's interests in the western Pacific. Far more dangerous, many hard-core Japanese nationalists felt they had traded away valued and long-standing security ties with Britain for a vague arms-limitation agreement that endangered their national security. In May 1921 the British Embassy in Japan reported that an increasingly anti-American IJN appeared to regard the United States as a potential foe intent on dictating political terms to Japan. After the Washington Treaty was concluded, the IJN's anti-treaty faction claimed that war with America over China had become inevitable; two years later Japan's general staff formed the Committee for the Research of Military Preparations against the United States.[20] The IJN's complaints soon evaporated, not only because subsequent increasingly nationalist Japanese governments circumvented treaty obligations, but because, in the western Pacific at least, the Washington agreement had rendered the IJN the far superior fleet.[21] The general anti-Western hostility, however, remained and flourished over the next two decades.

Surprisingly, the USN began to show the Aleutians some attention after the Washington agreements came into effect. Strictly forbidden from fortifying the archipelago, the navy could study the islands for military use at some unspecified date when treaty restrictions would no longer apply. In 1923 two ships investigated possible anchorages throughout the chain. The mission report advised that, while some good harbours could be developed after considerable dredging work, they would be useful only in fine weather, a somewhat rare commodity in the region. Despite this pessimistic finding, the navy opted to retain its options on Alaskan naval reservations and then suggested that the army hand over its Alaskan facilities to USN control. Claiming that

Alaska was now an integral part of national security, the navy wanted to study additional base sites, and advocated placing a defence installation as close to the Aleutians as was permissible under treaty obligations.[22]

This proposal went nowhere, as most American navy officers were obsessed with the need to confront Japan only in the central Pacific. Some prominent individuals sought to change this. The first was Hector C. Bywater. Credited by some with giving Admiral Yamamoto Isoroku the idea to attack Pearl Harbor, by 1921 the British-born Bywater, who wrote on naval matters for several American newspapers, thought the Aleutians might play a key role in a war between America and Japan. Contending initially that Dutch Harbor on Unalaska should be properly fortified to oppose a potential Japanese incursion, in 1925 Bywater published a speculative account of a future conflict between America and Japan. Criticizing America's dismal level of defence preparedness, Bywater still predicted that the United States could defeat Japan, but only after a bitter two-year struggle. He also gave the Aleutians a prominent role in that speculative American triumph, postulating that the USN would send decoy ships to Dutch Harbor to draw IJN attention while the main fleet struck elsewhere.[23]

Bywater exercised no real influence on formal American military strategy making but Brigadier General William (Billy) Mitchell of the army air service was much better placed. A vehement air power advocate, he believed future conflicts would be extinguished quickly and decisively by massed aircraft raining destruction upon an opponent's cities and industries. As a newly minted lieutenant, Mitchell had helped build a vital telegraph system in Alaska, an assignment that had invoked a life-long love for the region. In 1919 Mitchell posited a triangular defensive flyway system anchored on Alaska, the Panama Canal, and Canada. Intent on capitalizing on the growing airmindedness of an American public apparently enthralled by the airplane's almost messianic promise,[24] Mitchell had organized a four-plane flight from New York City to Alaska to aid the dispatch of warplanes to Asia, and to ensure that the great airways of the future would be controlled "by the two great English speaking races."[25] The Canadian government had permitted the flight but the extensive logistical effort required to ensure the mission's successful completion demonstrated that, while Mitchell's flyway theories were theoretically sound, they were, for the moment at least, technically unachievable.[26]

Rarely discouraged and frequently undiplomatic – Britain's Lord Hugh Trenchard had said Mitchell would go far if he could "break the habit of trying to convert his opponents by killing them" – Mitchell saw his cherished air service lose 95 percent of its enlisted manpower and $485 million in congressionally approved appropriations by mid-1920.[27] Desperate to demonstrate bombing's efficacy against land and sea targets, and to form a strategic air force absolutely independent of meddlesome army or navy control, Mitchell focused on Japan. Indeed, that obsession marked a return of sorts, as an extensive 1912 tour of Asia had convinced him that growing American commercial activity in Asia and rampant discrimination against Japanese immigrants in the United States had made inevitable a war with Japan. Mitchell had strongly opposed the Washington Treaty, arguing that waves of warplanes flying from Aleutian bases "could reduce Tokyo to powder." If America refused to prepare itself for an inevitable conflict, the martial Japanese "would take [Alaska] away from us, first by dominating the sky and then creeping up the Aleutians" and down Canada's west coast; "we would be in for it."[28] After visiting Asia again on his honeymoon, Mitchell warned in December 1923 that Japan might construct "the greatest military machine the world ever saw, such as the armies of Genghis Khan and Tamerlane." Believing

General Billy Mitchell, aerial warfare prophet and Alaskan defence advocate, undated.

the likely point of contact would be the north Pacific, echoing Mahan, Mitchell opined that a northern advance, either Japanese or American, could neither be flanked nor taken in reverse. His October 1924 report thus recommended initiating a decisive bombing offensive by 300 planes, operating from Alaska, against congested Japanese cities built from flammable products – the type of attack certain Japanese officials had feared for some time.[29] Concerned that Japan would seek to pre-empt such a devastating assault by attacking Alaska first, Mitchell wanted to ensure his aerial armada could get to Alaska quickly. That required Canadian cooperation, and Mitchell felt certain Canada would be quite eager to help. First, Canada had permitted Mitchell's 1919 flight and had provided considerable logistical support. Then, unwilling to be a "partner to an arrangement ... that could by any possibility be said to be directed against the United States or that might endanger the good relations between" the empire and the United States, Canadians had helped destroy the Anglo-Japanese alliance in 1922. Furthermore, after visiting Canada briefly in 1923, Mitchell had come away firmly convinced that "in their tastes, ideas, and manners of living," Canadians were far more American than British. He was certain too that a Japanese invasion of Alaska would threaten Canada and the United States equally: thus "a distinct understanding with Canada is a perfectly logical and sensible thing, one in accordance with all our traditions and our position in the Northern Hemisphere."[30]

Mitchell got an opportunity to test his notions in 1924, when the army air service dispatched four planes on a round-the-world flight. Predictably Mitchell took credit for the voyage, having told a reporter in late 1922 that he "was arranging for a 'round the world' trip with a squadron of six planes." It was Major General Mason Patrick, chief of the air service, who authorized the trip, however, ostensibly to demonstrate the feasibility of long-range air travel and the value of aircraft to global commerce, and to "bring to the United States, the birthplace of the airplane, the signal honor of being the first nation to successfully circumnavigate the globe by air." Certainly prestige was at stake as British military pilots were also seeking to make such an historic flight, but there was more to the American excursion. With a flight plan that would take the planes along the Great Circle Route via the Aleutians, the Kurile Islands, and then Japan itself, one of the American logistical officers attached to the mission, Lieutenant Clayton Bissell, admitted to some Canadian counterparts that the flight's main object "was to test the air-route from the U.S. to Japan via the Aleutians and Kurile Islands, and to obtain first hand knowledge of any possible air or seaplane bases along this route." But while the flight was successful, poor weather and mechanical problems besetting the planes in the north Pacific had left the crews doubtful that much could be done militarily in the Aleutians. As Lieutenant L.P. Arnold had noted on 7 May 1924, "the Aleutians have but two kinds of weather it seems – bad and worse."[31]

Finding the military generally unsympathetic to his contentions, in 1925 Mitchell published *Winged Defense*. It was not Mitchell's finest effort. Though he hoped that its value lay in the ideas and theories that he had advanced, Mitchell admitted that the book had "been thrown together hastily." Described by a charitable biographer as repetitious and disorganized, the book argued that air power had produced a new war doctrine that had completely rearranged existing systems of national defence, "and a new doctrine of peace which eventually will change the relations of nations with each other due to the universal application and rapidity of aerial transport." Asserting again that 300 aircraft should be based in central Alaska, Mitchell wanted some of those planes to be based as far west as Attu. Mitchell further expounded on his notions in October 1925 before the Board of Aeronautic Inquiry. Predicting that Japan could seize the Aleutians and convinced that only air power could adequately secure Alaska, Mitchell announced that Canadian cooperation would be forthcoming, since Canada was "as much exposed to this danger as we are ourselves and Canada looks to this country for protection in an eventuality of this kind, rather than to Great Britain."[32]

But Mitchell had once again miscalculated. Although Canada and the United States had cooperated in the First World War to jointly produce munitions and to collect intelligence, postwar military collaboration had not amounted to much beyond a 1926 agreement requiring Canada to reply to specific requests for information, which the War Department might make, albeit via British offices. Furthermore, although Canada had feared that a renewal of the increasingly contentious Anglo-Japanese alliance might dramatically harden American attitudes towards Canada and the empire, relatively few Canadians viewed Americans as their natural allies. Instead, when they pondered the strategic situation in the Pacific in the 1920s, which they did only rarely, Canadians worried less about an aggressive Japan than about an America that could become "an uncommonly ugly neighbour" were Canada to fail to safeguard its neutrality against Japanese forces seeking to use Canadian territory to attack American targets.[33]

Mitchell's ideas attracted little support at home either. He was lobbying President Calvin Coolidge's administration, whose "attitude of opposition to possibly expensive innovation [had] permeated all the executive departments." In addition, he had managed to alienate many potential supporters through his vociferous advocacy and his stubborn refusal to concede that his opponents might be making valid points. After Mitchell's planes sank a captured German battleship in 1921, his blatant public attempts to capitalize on that success at the expense of the navy had prompted an exasperated Coolidge to remark that Mitchell "has talked more in the last three months than I have in my whole life." Mitchell's subsequent appearance before the Board of Aeronautic Inquiry in 1925, which should have been a shining moment, was ruined by his perplexing insistence on spouting forth with long-winded recitations from *Winged Defense,* a distressing performance that frustrated even Mitchell's friends.[34] And after years of constantly criticizing hidebound army and navy attitudes about aviation, Mitchell had few service allies left. Not only was America's military generally uninterested in any Canadian alliance, much of the army's planning focused on the need to prosecute a war with Britain by invading Canada. General Malin Craig, the army's assistant chief of staff for operations, dismissed Mitchell's proposal to militarize the Aleutians, averring that Mitchell had ignored both the region's dismal climate and limited aircraft technical capabilities. Contending that Mitchell "so notoriously overestimates what could be done with air power by the United States," army planners concluded, in November 1925, that he had also "grossly overestimated what Japan could and would be able to accomplish with air power." Judging Mitchell's conclusions to be unsound militarily, they labelled his many reports simple propaganda for a unified air service. By February 1926, Mitchell had resigned his military commission following an insubordination conviction. Condemned to live out his remaining days in an increasingly bleak civilian wilderness, the air power prophet often used his martyr status to press his case even as his predictions "became progressively inflated and less realistic."[35]

While Mitchell had fallen victim to the "casual fascination and easy hopes" offered by strategic bombing,[36] realism also seemed conspicuously absent from American planning for conflict with Japan. Although the JANPC had predicted, in October 1919, that Japan and America were on a collision course to war, given Japan's increasingly desperate need for foreign markets and resources, the Joint Board, charged with formulating the "color" plans against potential foes, had great difficulty with the "Orange" plans dealing with Japan. The board dutifully produced various Orange incarnations, all of which shared one basic unshakeable assumption – that Japan, striking first, would conquer the western Pacific, thus compelling the USN to undertake a lengthy campaign culminating in a decisive naval engagement and blockade that would force Japan's capitulation.[37] With no major American bases west of Hawaii and because the USN would confront a quite formidable IJN operating close to its home facilities, many army strategists saw little chance for success. While Orange plans may have been "the product of the best minds of a whole generation of planners," from an army point of view they had set clearly unattainable tasks and had sharply illustrated "the failure of political-military coordination."[38]

Most Orange plans had rather little to say about Alaska. The 1928 scheme classified Alaska as a possession, which, while it could be subjected to either minor or major attacks, could not be provided with adequate defence forces. Six months later, the Joint Board reluctantly accepted that Kiska and Unalaska offered potential base sites. However, it stressed that their military usefulness would be badly constrained by a severe climate, and that they were too far from Japan to allow for the effective cutting of Japanese sea communications. Judging a Japanese assault on the Aleutians to be improbable, and citing poor weather and hazardous navigation, the board opined that an Aleutian-based American offensive could not effectuate decisive strategic results without giving Japan an undesirable and dangerous free hand in the Philippines; thus, a southern advance was infinitely preferable.[39]

The Aleutians merited little attention after 1928. Part of the reason was President Herbert Hoover. A Quaker and a former secretary of commerce under Coolidge, Hoover had an innate suspicion of the military and an abiding conviction that economic growth could solve nearly all problems. Told by his military advisers that the nation's defensive assets were sufficient to protect the Western hemisphere against hostile incursions, Hoover sought additional arms control agreements rather than new weapons. In 1930 President Herbert Hoover's naval aide, without specifically mentioning the Aleutians, dismissed concerns that islands near North America could be captured by an enemy unless two things occurred: the USN were overcome, and both Canada and Mexico took sides against America – scenarios he viewed as highly improbable. Two years later, after Japan grabbed the resource-rich Chinese province of Manchuria, thereby initiating a major diplomatic crisis,

Britain's naval attaché in Washington revealed that many USN officers believed that continued exertions to preserve the "Open Door" to China might bring on a war with Japan "at no distant date." On the other side of the Pacific, an American army officer attached to the Tokyo embassy attested that many Japanese were convinced America sought absolute control of the Far East, and reported a surge of popular publications postulating preemptive Japanese assaults on such varied targets as the Philippines, the Panama Canal, and Alaska. Then, in June 1933 a Japanese ship, purportedly carrying forestry and farming specialists, made three unauthorized visits to Attu. Given that Alaska was situated on the shortest route from eastern Asia, Alaskan Governor John W. Troy was convinced that it was an obvious target for any enemy navy, and he therefore lobbied hard for air and naval bases. In response, air corps commander Major General B.D. Foulois suggested providing a composite air group, two coastal patrol units, and infantry supported by rail-mounted artillery to prevent any foe from grasping a foothold in the resource-rich strip stretching northward from Anchorage to Fairbanks. But that was all Foulois was willing to support, as there was "nothing in southeastern Alaska or along the Aleutian Islands, which is worth making an effort to defend, nor is it believed that there is sufficient strategic value to the Seward Peninsula, or the Alaskan territory west of the 154th meridian to warrant an enemy invasion and seizure of such territory."[40]

Given the army's ongoing and difficult struggle to properly garrison the Philippines and Hawaii "against a strong and aggressive regional power,"[41] Foulois's tentative offer was at least a modest step in the right direction. But, in July 1933 the air corps omitted Alaska from a list of critical areas needing bases (the continental United States, the Philippines, Hawaii, and the Panama Canal) until the Drum Board, established a month later to determine air field priorities, added the Caribbean possessions, Guam, and Alaska. Unable to properly provision every critical region, the board assigned top priority to New England and Seattle. Alaska came firmly in last place, as it was deemed unlikely to be affected by operations anytime in the near future. This decision left Lieutenant Colonel C.H. Mason profoundly unsatisfied. Having served in Alaska, Mason asserted that even a small Japanese force could skilfully employ Alaska's formidable terrain to successfully fend off much larger American formations. Alaska's garrison consisted of two under-equipped and understaffed infantry companies based at Skagway in the Alaskan Panhandle. It could not be expected to foil such an assault, and Mason predicted that disaster would ensue unless two infantry battalions, artillery, a composite air force, and some patrol boats were placed in Alaska before any conflict began.[42]

Although the War Plans Division (WPD) predicted, in February 1934, that a Japanese capture of eastern Siberia could pose a threat to Alaska and Hawaii, the army declined to accept either Foulois's or Mason's modest proposals. According to Harry H. Woodring, assistant secretary of the War Department, by the mid-1930s the army "existed in little more than name only"; territorial posts were dangerously under-garrisoned, and equipment and weaponry were both badly outmoded and in short supply. When a new Plan Orange was finalized in February, the army pledged to dispatch to Alaska a single infantry battalion and a few artillery pieces – but only once war had broken out.[43] One WPD officer admitted that it was inexpedient to expand Alaska's garrison, given deep spending cuts and the need "to avoid the appearance of a menacing political gesture." Nevertheless, he argued that Alaska's proximity to Japan and the threat that Japanese bases in the Aleutians would pose to American interests dictated that a mobile force and some aircraft be located at Fairbanks. This call too went unheeded, as the assistant chief of staff of personnel thought it would be pointless to dispatch any troops to Alaska: "If the war is won, we can dictate the fate of Alaska; if it is lost, the opponents will dictate its fate." Brigadier C.E. Kilbourne, the WPD's assistant chief of staff, declined to garrison Fairbanks, although he held out the slim possibility that some troops might be sent there if the Far East remained unstable – recommendations approved by Chief of Staff General Douglas MacArthur and Secretary of War George H. Dern.[44]

The War Department's efforts to keep Alaskan security deliberations far from the public eye were foiled by one persistently stubborn man. Elected in 1932 as Alaska's delegate to the House of Representatives, Anthony J. Dimond had arrived in Washington downright determined to persuade his fellow Americans that Japan posed a severe threat to Alaska. The dogged, New York-born Dimond grandly viewed himself as a modern-day Cato, "the ancient Roman who was so much alarmed about the danger to his country by the strength and power of Carthage that he never ended a speech without saying ... 'Carthage must be destroyed.'" Arguing that Japan could employ numerous unguarded Alaskan harbours to assail the continental United States, in March 1934 Dimond presented HR 9524, a bill to establish a military facility at Fairbanks (including 100 aircraft) at an estimated cost of $16 million.[45] The bill died a quick and dismal death in committee, as Dimond could muster few allies in the halls of Congress. Alaska's wartime governor, Ernest Gruening, compared Dimond to Cassandra, the mythical Greek woman cursed with a gift for unheeded prophecy. Even Dimond's biographer admits that Dimond's requests for improving territorial and national defence "received so little attention that he had few active opponents to argue against." Many political operatives scornfully viewed Dimond's bill as simply a cynical political attempt to funnel New Deal money to Alaska. For his part, Kilbourne opposed the project, as he believed the facility's construction would require $23 million plus $6 million annually to keep it operational.[46]

Nevertheless, concerned that an increasingly strident Japan might soon renounce the Washington Treaty and openly rearm, the services began taking tentative steps towards a reassessment of north Pacific security. In May 1934 the USN undertook two separate initiatives, one minor, the other more substantive. First, it dispatched Edwin T. Layton to Dutch Harbor to investigate allegations of a Japanese spy operating there. Layton's investigation led him to arrest the only Japanese man in the area, along with his suspected confederate, the town's sole prostitute, an act that rendered Layton exceedingly unpopular with sailors seeking sexual relief on shore leave.[47] Then, having previously sent a few vessels to the Aleutians in 1931-2 to check for evidence of covert Japanese incursions, the USN dispatched seven ships and six planes to undertake a more comprehensive series of Aleutian soundings and obtain more detailed topographical photographs. The mission's chief aviation officer came away unimpressed. Poor weather, frequent high winds, mountainous terrain, and soft mossy ground made the construction of good landing fields anywhere in the Aleutians unlikely. Dutch Harbor, Kiska, and especially Adak Island offered better prospects for seaplane bases. Yet as the expedition's leader pointed out, although ships could operate safely in the short Aleutian summer, they could not do so in the region's harsh winter. Thus, he opined, the strategic situation did not justify a permanent naval base in the archipelago.[48]

The air corps, however, had plans of its own – plans that had some potentially serious long-term implications. On the surface the matter seemed simple enough. In early June 1934, the air corps briefly informed the State Department that it intended to send ten new B-10 bombers across western Canada "to further diplomatic relations with Canada and to conduct a goodwill flight to Alaska."[49] The matter was far from simple, though, as the air corps desperately needed a successful mission. It had serious concerns about its future budgets after Franklin Roosevelt's 1932 election. In December 1932, just weeks after winning the presidential election over Hoover, Franklin Roosevelt had told the outgoing president that he approved of Hoover's "clear and satisfactory" disarmament policy, adding that success in that area would "have a very positive and salutary influence on debt and economic discussions." Concentrating on badly needed social and employment programs at the cheerless height of the dismal Great Depression, President Roosevelt had slashed the army's 1934 appropriation by $144 million. Facing the impending demise of numerous key programs, MacArthur had managed to restore most of the cuts but only after initiating a bitter personal confrontation with Roosevelt. Despite those efforts, the military's budget fell to its lowest outlay since before the First World War.[50] The military's standing with the new president had also taken a beating, thanks to an airmail fiasco. Unhappy with airmail contracts awarded by Hoover to politically connected friends, Roosevelt had voided those tainted deals in February 1934 and then ordered the air corps to take up the job. Using planes ill-equipped to operate in inclement weather or at night, employing inexperienced pilots, and beset by awful weather, by 1 June the army had lost twelve pilots in sixty-six crashes. Called to task by a livid president for this shabby performance, Foulois withstood the "worst" tongue-lashing of his military career. Even Billy Mitchell bleated sorrowfully from the sidelines that "if any army aviator can't fly a mail route in any sort of weather, what would we do in a war?"[51]

For the air corps, already enmeshed in an acrimonious struggle with the USN over the control of coastal defence,[52] the airmail fiasco could not have been more badly timed, casting as it did serious doubts about its ability to sustain long-distance operations. More than the air corps's tattered reputation was at stake with the Alaskan flight. Although the mission's stated aim was the furthering of relations with Canada, in truth, the army very much wanted to survey potential Alaskan airfield sites. Far more ominously, the flight's secret orders referred to the need to test "the practicability of despatching an air force to Alaska should necessity therefor [sic] arise."[53] Given Japan's increasing aggressiveness, the fact that the War Department was paying more attention to Alaskan security was not surprising. The rub, however, was that the most expedient method of moving aircraft quickly and safely to Alaska meant overflying Canadian territory. And while Canadian-American military overflight agreements had been in place since the 1920s (and renewed by Canada in early June 1934[54]), those accords applied to short flights of convenience in eastern North America, not to major cross-continent excursions. The air corps sincerely desired to investigate the technical efficacy of an Alaskan air route, but clearly it intended also to test Mitchell's more controversial notion of a Canadian-American military alliance against Japan.

Canadian Chief of the General Staff (CGS) Major General A.G.L. McNaughton thought that any political estrangement from America unfortunately bolstered those Canadians opposed to cooperation with Britain in wartime. However, he concurred with a 1933 tri-service report indicating that the greatest threat to Canada's sovereignty stemmed from American military intervention, were Canada unable to stop Japanese incursions. Having noted in 1933 that Canada could find itself "in an invidious and even dangerous position" if it could not defend its neutrality,[55] McNaughton charged that the War Department mission constituted "nothing more than a military reconnaissance designed to open an air route from the United States to Alaska which would facilitate reinforcing that territory in the event of war between the United States and Canada." Thus, acquiescence would set an unfortunate precedent that "might make it very difficult to maintain our neutrality or to terminate the custom" in a crisis, and might encourage Japan to seek similar aerial privileges.[56]

McNaughton's concerns could not be taken lightly. Desperately keen to recast the moribund and cash-starved Canadian army into a professional force capable of directing Canada's security policy and playing a meaningful role in another European conflict, McNaughton "had made himself very strong with the Government, particularly with [Prime Minister] R.B. Bennett."[57] The general's complaints, however, carried relatively little weight with the one civil servant whose influence exceeded even his in Ottawa's intimate halls of power. Recruited directly from academia's ivory tower to head the tiny Department of External Affairs (DEA) by Prime Minister W.L.M. King in 1925, hardworking and incisive Under-Secretary of State for External Affairs (USSEA) O.D. Skelton had speedily made himself absolutely indispensable to his political masters. Described by one American diplomat "as a man who has always been a friend of the United States and an advocate of more confident relations with us," the strongly anti-imperialist Skelton believed Canada's security lay "in her own reasonableness, the decency of her neighbour, and the steady development of friendly intercourse, common standards of conduct, and common points of view."[58] He doubted whether allowing American planes to occasionally overfly British Columbia would commit Canada to a more permanent arrangement, and reminded McNaughton that America's position was unique, "as it alone possesses territories on this continent between which a route through Canada is a natural one." Still, as a sop to Department of National Defence (DND) concerns, Skelton thought that the mission should avoid the commercially promising Mackenzie Valley aerial route.[59]

DND had asked Skelton not to reveal its military rationale for rejecting the Mackenzie flight plan,[60] and a puzzled State Department protested that American aircraft had taken the Mackenzie route twice before without problems or Canadian objections. The American minister in Ottawa responded that Canadians sincerely feared that America was preparing to militarize Alaska to support bombing raids against Japan or the Soviet Union. Thus, Warren Robbins concluded, "They may feel that it is in the interest of Canadian neutrality not to facilitate any flights which might contribute to develop this route for this purpose." When Skelton officially informed the American legation of Canada's objections to the Mackenzie Valley flight path, Pierre de la Boal made it very clear that the said refusal "was likely to be looked upon on both countries as a measure prompted by military considerations quite unusual in the existing relations between Canada and the United States and reminiscent of the inhibitions which exist in other parts of the world." This unsubtle threat did its job. If Canada declined America's overflight request, Skelton had told Bennett, it would be preferable to say that the desired route was unavailable, rather than discuss any defence issues. Despite McNaughton's renewed objections, the prime minister allowed the Americans to employ the Mackenzie route.[61]

This covenant very nearly unravelled several days later when the *Washington Herald* claimed that the mission aimed to test the route's ability to concentrate air power in Alaska in wartime. Robbins was called on the carpet by an enraged Skelton, and his attempts to cast the newspaper report as sensationalist were only partially successful. Skelton decided not to revoke permission for the Alaska flight, but he averred that the *Herald's* claims would likely stir up an already suspicious Japan and make it "impossible for us to permit any more passages from the United States to Alaska." Robbins thought the short-lived contretemps had inflicted only limited damage to Canadian-American relations. But the all-too-public disclosure had offended tender Canadian sensibilities and had hurt American interests because the hand of those in DND "who were inclined to view our military operations with some suspicion" had been strengthened. This was a significant consideration and Robbins had no doubt that some Canadian officers wanted to put in place policies that would "render any incursions from the United States in time of war as difficult as possible."[62]

The ten bombers left Washington, DC, on 19 July 1934. Ostentatiously stopping at various western Canadian cities (where they attracted large and enthusiastic crowds and numerous high-profile official receptions from local Canadian politicians), they arrived safely in Alaska five days later. Although mission commander Colonel H.H. Arnold reported that Alaska would require the installation of a considerable infrastructure to render it a suitable military staging area, he thought Canada's military element had gained a very favourable impression of the army air corps. Edmonton's American Consul entertained similar hopes. While an unsympathetic local press had played up the flight's military rationale, the consul happily noted that Canadian servicemen had indicated their pleasure "over what they regard as a symbol of identity between the interests of Canada and the United States in the matter of Alaskan defense." Foulois, too, was greatly pleased. He had hoped the B-10 bomber would be able to reinforce such disparate and distant key points such as Alaska, Hawaii, and the Panama Canal without recourse to intermediate refuelling facilities. As Arnold's fliers had managed to cover 18,000 miles at an average rate of 820 miles per day, Foulois thought the mission had clearly proven the value of the new plane.[63]

Others were less content. Believing the army flight had violated its shaky coastal defence truce, the navy opted for one-upmanship. On the day Arnold's planes had left Washington, six USN seaplanes, accompanied by four supply ships, had departed for Alaska along a flight line up the Pacific coast towards Alaska. (The navy mission took twenty-eight days to get to Alaska and eighteen days to return – a less than stellar accomplishment.) MacArthur too was very displeased. Having negotiated the shaky coastal defence truce with the navy after some considerable effort, he angrily denied Arnold's fliers any decorations after they took a thousand-mile ocean detour on the return trip to demonstrate army capabilities to counter seaborne threats.[64] The response from Ottawa was not particularly warm either. McNaughton complained that the flight's success would lead to "the gradual establishment of a practice of dispatching aircraft to Alaska over Canadian territory that might give rise to a rather awkward situation on some future occasion." He hoped, just as Robbins had feared, to prevent American intervention by completing Defence Scheme No. Two, a plan to ensure Canada's neutrality in any war between America and Japan. Moreover, other Canadian military and foreign policy officials viewed the USN's Aleutian survey, the Alaskan flight, and USN plans for north Pacific exercises in 1935 as evidence that America would militarize the Aleutians once the Washington Treaty had lapsed.[65] If the Alaskan flight had intended to test Mitchell's claim that Canada and the United States were natural allies against Japan, the test had failed: the flight had left Canada's military even more determined to avoid potentially dangerous American entanglements. Far more dangerous complications, however, were on the immediate horizon.

2

He Who Holds Alaska Will Hold the World:
Alaskan Security, 1934-41

The debate about Aleutian security after 1921 had been largely academic, for as long as the Washington Treaty remained intact and unamended, the American military could do nothing about perceived problems beyond keeping various studies on file for future reference. But matters became far more dangerous and far less conjectural in December 1934 when Japan declared that after 31 December 1936 it would no longer be bound by the Washington Treaty. Japan had accepted that pact in 1922 in the hope that substantial arms reductions and closer political cooperation with the West would allow it to dominate China. But after Japan's invasion of Manchuria had embittered relations with Washington and London, in early 1934 Tokyo sought a more advantageous naval tonnage deal. When Roosevelt showed no desire to consider anything of the sort and dissuaded Britain from granting the IJN any naval concessions, Japan promptly abandoned the Washington Treaty.[1]

A stunned State Department sought to play down the move, maintaining that the treaty would continue in force until the end of 1936, and asserting its complete willingness to enter into any new arms control negotiations. A sympathetic *New York Times* agreed much could happen in the next two years to "keep sensible men from immediately surrendering to the darkest forebodings about what 'must' come after the 31st December, 1936," but State Department Asia expert Stanley K. Hornbeck welcomed Japan's decision. In his considered opinion, Japan might renegotiate the arms deal as long as the United States "*may* build an unquestionably superior Navy and *may* construct fortifications in the Philippine Islands, in the Aleutian Islands, and even at Guam, those facts will exercise a restraining influence upon Japan." But when a deeply shaken Roosevelt queried him about the significance of Japan's action, Kilbourne grimly replied that war had become more probable and the army was ill prepared to fight since it had "neither a single complete infantry division, a complete cavalry division nor an adequate air force." Japan could attack Hawaii, the Panama Canal, and Alaska – and perhaps America itself. Losing the Philippines, Guam, and the Aleutians would be "a grave blow to our prestige and pride," even if they were retaken; Kilbourne therefore wanted to fortify those possessions by substantially increasing garrisons in Hawaii, the Panama Canal, and Alaska and creating an expeditionary force. Agreeing that the preservation of the Hawaii-Alaska-Panama Canal strategic triangle would deter aggression and allow for the successful prosecution of any ensuing war, Secretary of War George H. Dern faced a critical conundrum. America could not bolster its Pacific possessions before 31 December 1936 without risking conflict. Yet if it waited, Japan might strike pre-emptively before proper defences could be mounted; Dern therefore endorsed Kilbourne's recommendations at a cost of $360 million.[2]

Would some of that money be Alaska-bound? In May 1934 J.J. McSwain, chair of the House Committee on Military Affairs, proposed that $150 million dollars be allocated to the construction of seven major coastal air bases. That initiative had gone nowhere as the Baker Board, established to review air corps capabilities, attested in July 1934 that air power lacked strategic decisiveness and America should therefore not fear an aerial assault.[3] Subsequently, in February 1935 Florida representative Mark Wilcox asked for $190 million to finance ten massive airfields capable of defeating attacks launched from aircraft carriers, Newfoundland, eastern Canada, or Caribbean islands. One base, Wilcox argued, should be in Alaska not only to protect its vast mineral wealth but also because Alaska was "closer to Japan than it is to the center of [the] continental United States." Unimpressed, Kilbourne noted that only the secretary of war had the power to delineate the number and location of army facilities. Moreover, Wilcox's bill also outlined specific installation sizes, something Kilbourne doubted would gain War Department approval, given concerns about concentrating too many planes at any one base. He did think that a central Alaskan airfield "would have an extensive effect on [Japanese] diplomatic relations and their conversations," but also believed that the creation of an Aleutian base would be unlikely given the region's poor weather.[4]

House Representative Anthony J. Dimond had sought to grasp this new opportunity firmly. While admitting that the Aleutians were ill suited for land-based aviation, he had felt certain amphibious planes could operate along the archipelago year-round. Billy Mitchell had then reappeared. Mounting his last hurrah before his imminent, untimely death, Mitchell had told McSwain's committee in February 1934 that "air power can neutralize anything standing still or moving on the surface of the earth or the water" – a direct assault on the hidebound army and navy. The retired air prophet had described the Japanese as "our dangerous enemy in the Pacific," declaring with certainty that they "won't attack Panama. They will come right here to Alaska. Alaska is the most central place in the world for aircraft, and that is true either of Europe, Asia, or North America. I believe in the future he who holds Alaska will rule the world, and I think it is the most important strategic place in the world."[5]

Mitchell's testimony may have prompted Congress to pass a revised Wilcox National Defense Act in August 1935 but it then curiously sabotaged the legislation by failing to provide any funding. Dern's proposals to expand the army and strengthen Pacific garrisons also went unheeded despite a January 1935 State Department assessment indicating that, because Japan respected only military strength, America could prevent war only by fielding much larger forces than Japan. Dominated by liberal New Dealers "disenchanted with the insurance theory of defense," Roosevelt's administration posited that increased military expenditures would only provoke additional international crises. So, the amount of money dedicated to defence was a paltry 1.2 percent of the Gross National Product (GNP) in 1935, compared with

2.8 percent in 1920 and 0.9 percent in 1930. It amounted to only 14 percent of federal expenditures, down from 37 percent in 1920 and 25 percent in 1930.[6] Hoping that money for an Alaskan base might become available, the air corps's Tactical School recommended a composite air group for Fairbanks and secondary landing fields throughout Alaska but not in the Aleutians.[7]

The government's failure to fund Pacific defensive improvements adequately left unresolved the question of how to deal with the Japanese threat. Although army planners had demanded that Plan Orange be substantially revised, the United States Navy (USN) and General Douglas MacArthur had blocked attempts at reform. Once MacArthur stepped down in October 1935 to assume an uncommonly lucrative sinecure in the distant Philippines, the army had a chance to face down the navy – no easy job, for, as one army air corps officer famously put it, "there are two governments in Washington, the Government of the United States, and the United States Navy."[8] MacArthur's hard-headed and "uncommonly foresighted and capable" replacement, General Malin Craig, seeking to focus on hemispheric security, wanted to alter Plan Orange drastically.[9] Brigadier General Stanley D. Embick, the new director of the War Plans Division (WPD), concurred. "Conceiving of the continental United States as a citadel and its overseas possessions as outposts of the main fortress,"[10] Embick, as the commander of the Manila fortress in 1933, had thought that implementing Plan Orange would be an act of madness. Thus, he had wanted to neutralize the Philippines immediately and to protect the Alaska-Hawaii-Panama Canal strategic triangle as America's peacetime Pacific frontier. It would be non-provocative, less draining financially, and would leave the Americans "free to take the offensive at our own volition," rather than compel them to undertake premature military operations for the relief of distant and embattled outposts of dubious value. Embick sought to undo MacArthur's acceptance of a new Plan Orange that proposed a USN advance to the western Pacific via Japan's Mandated Islands. This acceptance demonstrated MacArthur's "complete lack of strategic consistency or total misunderstanding" of the situation. A cynical Embick asserted in December 1935 that retaining bases in an independent Philippines would invite war. He feared that European powers would try to manoeuvre the United States into bearing the full brunt of armed resistance to Japan. In addition, dispatching forces into the heart of enemy defences would in all likelihood end in a "national disaster." Therefore, he again recommended neutralizing the Philippines and safeguarding the Alaska-Hawaii-Panama Canal triangle.[11]

Embick had the full support of an army that, as Henry Stimson later put it, disparaged "the peculiar psychology of the Navy Department, which seemed to retire from the realm of logic into a dim religious world in which Neptune was God, Mahan was his prophet, and the United States Navy the only true Church." More important, he had the president's backing. Roosevelt was concerned about the USN's ongoing obsession with retaining "an offensive mission ... notwithstanding the fact that greater navy advocates point[ed] out that the fleet [was] maintained primarily as our first line of defense." And, increasingly inclined to see continued American presence in the Philippines as shaped by an outdated Open Door imperialism, the usually pro-navy president considered bases in an independent Philippines to be a military liability rather than an asset.[12] Jonathan Utley argues that Roosevelt was a poor strategic manager prior to 1941, an opinion shared by the USN in this case. Convinced that Embick's plan could relegate it to a permanent defensive role in the eastern Pacific, the navy argued that a strongly defended Philippines would force Japan to divert scarce resources there and thus weaken its ability to counter a central Pacific thrust. Moreover, adroitly playing the ever-useful race card, the navy maintained that abandoning the western Pacific would "yield our nation's geographical barrier against the usurpation by the yellow race of the place of the white man in the Far East." Unable to reach a compromise, in early 1936 the services presented separate reports.[13]

The army and navy finally came to an understanding in February 1938, a concocted and fragile compromise arising from a determined army assault on Plan Orange. The army outlined the following Orange fallacies: it offered of only one course of action; it insisted on defeating Japan by naval action alone, "in spite of the fact that history does not record a single instance of any first-class military-naval power having ever been subdued primarily by such actions"; and it involved a risky offensive across many thousand of miles of water, irrespective of the issues involved, international and domestic conditions, or the consequences of defeat. The army demanded the promulgation of flexible strategic alternatives in harmony with national interests and policy. That meant rejecting any war plan that went beyond "the necessity of defense and provision for contingencies," that is, any plan emphasizing solely the preservation of the Alaska-Hawaii-Panama Canal strategic triangle.[14] The USN insisted that the army should continue to defend the Philippines so that decisive offensive operations could be mounted in the western Pacific. The February 1938 compromise managed to mollify both sides. In return for retaining its plans to send its main fleet to the west Pacific, the USN pledged to defend the eastern Pacific strategic triangle and to acknowledge the possibility of involvement in a European conflict.[15]

Both services could agree that Alaska was unimportant strategically, a consensus resulting partly from a lack of knowledge about the north Pacific. The WPD had admitted, in 1937, that it had never thoroughly studied Alaska's military possibilities, while Chief of Naval Operations (CNO) Admiral W.D. Leahy said, in August of that year, that inaccurate information about the Aleutians had concerned him for some time. The army had made a start, creating the Alaskan Mapping Project in 1936, a ten-year program to produce navigational and strategic maps for Alaskan air operations.[16] As for the navy, in May 1935 Secretary of the Navy Claude Swanson had told Roosevelt that Kiska, Guam, and Samoa would be developed in an emergency. Then, after Dimond had asked in April 1936 for the creation of an Alaskan naval base once Japan abandoned the Washington Treaty, the navy's Strategic Plans Division (SPD) had remarked that an unfavourable climate had been the principal reason for the navy's general unwillingness to develop Alaskan bases. However, as some officers contended that Aleutian air operations were feasible, the SPD recommended building naval air facilities at Dutch Harbor, Kodiak, and Sitka. As for surface ships, the SPD only suggested that sending a few vessels to Alaskan waters for winter exercises might be useful. Rear Admiral Ernest J. King agreed that the navy should immediately select and equip naval air bases in the Alaskan area. He suggested putting airboat facilities at Sitka and Kodiak, creating a fuel dump on Unalaska, and assigning an airboat squadron and a tender to Alaskan waters in the summer months as a small step towards permanently assigning at least two airboat squadrons to Alaska.[17]

Further support for action came from a major study of the Aleutians filed with the Navy Department in late August 1936. Probably compiled by an officer at the Naval War College, the document proved rather prescient. If Japan and the United States came to blows, the author asserted, cooperation with the Soviets and Canadians could be vital to hold and reinforce the Aleutians and Alaska. Furthermore, he outlined the military capacity of various Alaskan points, paying particular attention to the islands of Unalaska, Umnak, Adak, Amchitka, and Kiska. The study conceded that Japan might grab the Aleutians to prevent them from being used to support American aerial operations against the Japanese home islands; it maintained that no one harbour in the region could be used as a "fleet base" and drew particular attention to the north Pacific's dismal climate. At the same time, it downplayed the archipelago's value for offensive operations for either Japan or America: "In any campaign in the Western Pacific therefore, the probable purpose of Japan regarding the Aleutian Islands might be to prevent their occupation by the United States. To the United States, they are primarily a defensive area and as such, must be made secure against aggression from the west."[18]

Yet when these assessments came to the attention of USN commander-in-chief Admiral A.J. Hepburn, he was very reluctant to take any action, fearing that major Alaskan programs would be needlessly provocative to Japan. However, as the navy could clearly benefit from north Pacific training exercises, Hepburn authorized a patrol base for Kodiak, on condition that it not absorb funds needed elsewhere or require congressional approval (and no doubt, scrutiny). Told only that naval facilities would probably have high priority in 1939, a frustrated Dimond introduced yet another bill calling for an Alaskan naval base. But, although Swanson acknowledged that Alaska's growing strategic importance would soon require naval facilities capable of supporting at least a limited naval presence, he opposed Dimond's proposal because other projects had higher priority. Thus, the bill died.[19]

Political considerations had also curtailed enthusiasm for improving Alaskan defences. Seeking to determine whether Japan had fortified its Pacific possessions in violation of a 1921 pact with the United States, in mid-1936 Secretary of State Cordell Hull decided to permit Japanese vessels to visit Alaska. Few Japanese vessels took up this offer, and Hull's fervent, if naïve, hopes for a reciprocal response were dashed when no American ships were allowed near Japan's Pacific holdings – no great surprise to Leahy and the USN.[20] Far more worrisome was Roosevelt's attitude. In 1934 the president peppered Arnold with "about 100 questions about Alaska." Furthermore, Democratic ward-heeler James Farley claimed that Roosevelt had expressed interest in 1933 in using Aleutian bases to bomb Japan. Then in November 1936 Roosevelt proposed neutralizing the Pacific – excepting only Japan, Australia, New Zealand, Singapore, and Hawaii – and stated his willingness to demilitarize "that portion of Alaska nearest Japan."[21] Roosevelt often floated policy trial balloons only to lose interest later as something else captured the attention of his elusive and restless mind. But this time he ordered the State Department to study his proposal in some detail.

The State Department saw definite advantages in Roosevelt's approach, since many Americans would undoubtedly back a moral initiative that added no practical burden; moreover, Japan might welcome the removal of western militaries from the west Pacific. The department, however, doubted whether such a complex arrangement was achievable and whether Japan would adhere to any bargain. An unhappy Roosevelt then dispatched an aide to Britain, only to discover that the wary British thought it pointless to seek any agreement unless Japan modified its very aggressive policies towards China. Although London did offer to reconsider its position if Roosevelt presented a more concrete proposal, the outbreak of the Sino-Japanese War in July 1937 ended further talk about neutralizing the Pacific. Then, when the president asked the military in November 1937 to address Alaska's security needs, the Subcommittee on National Defense saw no need to increase the territory's paltry two-company garrison. The army wanted only an air station placed at Fairbanks and navy plans were equally unambitious. Seaplane stations at Sitka and Kodiak would be ready before long, but the USN believed it was undesirable and unnecessary to assign warships to Alaska in peacetime.[22]

The military soon had another chance to demonstrate its indifference to Alaskan security, thanks to a presidential tour planned for September 1937. Roosevelt greatly enjoyed taking extended sea cruises that blended politics and personal recreation (especially deep-sea fishing), but his decision to visit Alaska and then British Columbia briefly had definite political aims. He had briefly considered forging defensive alliances with British dominions in 1934 after London had pondered allowing Japan to build more warships; once Britain had backed down, Roosevelt had let the idea lapse. Still, Canada remained on the president's mind, although he encouraged Canada to defend itself, perhaps because he feared American isolationists would charge "that we are proposing an offensive and defensive alliance with the British Empire." So, when Roosevelt visited Canadian prime minister W.L.M. King in Quebec City in July 1936, he mentioned that, while some American senators favoured military intervention if Japan attacked British Columbia, he thought a highway across Canada would suffice as an important means to reinforce Alaska in a crisis.[23]

Roosevelt's conversation with King, followed by his 14 August 1936 speech averring that Americans "can and will defend ourselves and defend our neighborhood,"[24] convinced many Canadians that they needed defence against American military intervention. On 30 September 1936 Canadian army intelligence, confronting press rumours that the American military was constructing an air base at Fairbanks and possibly "a large underground air base on one of the Aleutian Islands," contended the American military might be fortifying the Aleutians "with unprecedented secrecy." Also that month, the Canadian army stated that although Canada faced three alternatives if Japan and the United States engaged in battle – siding with America regardless of Britain's position, joining an Anglo-American coalition, or declaring itself neutral – only the last two seemed really possible. If Canada opted for neutrality and Japan invaded British Columbia or used Canadian waters to attack American targets, then, the army warned, the American public might demand military occupation of British Columbia by American forces. The Canadian military's prescription was extensive, as its existing forces were incapable of adequately supervising the west coast, let alone fighting a major war; the Department of National Defence (DND) wanted six destroyers (rather than two) plus four minesweepers, twenty-three air force squadrons, new coastal and anti-aircraft guns, sixty-four west coast observation posts, and six mechanized army divisions, at a cost of $200 million over five years. While a deeply distrustful Department of External Affairs (DEA) officer, Loring Christie, insisted that this program was much better suited for combat in Europe than on Canada's mountainous west coast, the prime minister favoured enhancing Canada's ability to guard its neutrality and sovereignty, "being certain that British protection means less and less," while relying on America could mean "losing our independence." Ergo, when the program's first year cost was cut back, meaning that there would be money only to fortify one coast and certainly not for a politically dangerous expeditionary force, the Cabinet and the military agreed virtually without discussion to strengthen the Pacific frontier.[25]

Canadian concerns appeared overstated when King and Roosevelt met at the White House in early 1937. Discussing Pacific neutrality, Roosevelt added again that building an Alaska highway could be advantageous militarily in the event of trouble with Japan. Having been warned by Skelton and Christie that Canada risked becoming a mere protectorate if it relied too much on American military assistance (Skelton had argued that Canada was "still the most secure, the least exposed of all countries"[26]), King pointed out that, while some Canadians believed the 1823 Monroe Doctrine safeguarding the Western hemisphere from external interference provided for their defence, "no self-respecting Government could countenance such a view." Roosevelt's response, King thought, was significant. Declaring that Canada should not worry about its Atlantic seaboard, the president simply said that he would like Canada to add a few patrol boats on the Pacific coast and properly fortify the city of Vancouver. Profoundly relieved that Roosevelt discussed Canadian defences so nicely and without "suggesting how Canada should handle its affairs," King nevertheless rejected the notion of a common Canadian-American political or military point of view. That was all right up to a certain point, King said before visiting Roosevelt, but it "should never be permitted to run counter to the advantages" Canada gained from its British connection. He was content to be the bridge linking America and Britain and to modestly rearm.[27]

As Skelton acidly remarked to a visiting American, a bridge was meant "to be walked on." With the international situation worsening, a frustrated Roosevelt told Hull on 4 August that he wanted an Alaskan highway completed speedily, and his mood improved little when Hull responded that Canada had shown little inclination to even discuss the matter.[28] Roosevelt gained a clear opportunity to demonstrate his continued interest in the highway, thanks to his minister in Ottawa. Noting Roosevelt's plan to stop in Seattle on his way back from Alaska, Norman Armour thought a brief presidential debarkation in British Columbia would demonstrate solidarity between the American northwest and western Canada.[29] Hull fully backed the Canadian detour, but Assistant Secretary of State for Western European Affairs J. Pierrepont Moffat (who shared Under Secretary of State Sumner Welles's "Europhobic hemispherism"[30]) did not. He was concerned that Canadians might misinterpret an Alaskan highway proposal as indicative of something formal and permanent. He was also under the impression that only the Interior Department and a few congressmen were keen to see the road come to fruition; he was unaware that the American military had demonstrated "the slightest interest in this matter."[31]

Certainly no stranger to the grand public gesture, Roosevelt shunned Moffat's circumspect advice. Met by boisterous crowds in British Columbia, Roosevelt gathered considerable local journalistic praise for his bonhomie but no Canadian promise regarding an Alaskan route was forthcoming. Canada would consider the road, Skelton said, but constructing internal east-west communications would remain the top priority. Worried that that response would displease Roosevelt and desirous to keep the discussion firmly on an economic plane that avoided the road's military potential,

Christie suggested a joint examination of the project's feasibility.[32] He had reason to be worried. Roosevelt believed Canada's west coast defences were "not only inadequate, but almost non-existent." When reminded by Armour on 9 November that Canada was trying to remedy those clear deficiencies, the president, doubting the effort would suffice, requested a coordinated defence plan for the territory lying between northern Washington state and the Alaskan Panhandle, and a formalized means to exchange military information with the Canadian authorities. Recalling that America and Britain had struck a deal to jointly defend the north Pacific in the First World War (when Roosevelt had been assistant secretary of the navy in the Woodrow Wilson administration), the president thought the USN should quietly dispatch an officer to Ottawa to explore the matter. Armour felt that Prime Minister King should be sounded out before anything was initiated, and he convinced Roosevelt to let him handle the matter as he saw fit.[33]

Armour then met immediately with Sumner Welles, for far more than Canada was on the agenda. Urged by Hull to take a major foreign policy initiative in such troubled times, on 5 October Roosevelt issued his infamous "Quarantine" speech. Cleverly employing the analogy of a medical quarantine to isolate aggressors and claiming that America could not hope to remain safe by blithely ignoring dangerous realities, Roosevelt struck a nerve even though he fatally undermined his message by stating, shortly thereafter, that he had been thinking of only a general treaty rather than direct political and military sanctions. The speech impressed Britain's notoriously distrustful Prime Minister Neville Chamberlain to such an extent that his ambassador in Washington approached Welles on 27 November about naval staff talks. That initial offer was declined. However, after Japanese aircraft sank the hapless USS *Panay* as it patrolled China's Yangtze River on 12 December, Roosevelt, considering a blockade of Japan, sent USN Captain Royal E. Ingersoll to London to determine what might be done to restrain Tokyo.[34]

While the Ingersoll talks had not been proposed when Armour discussed the Canadian proposal with Welles on 9 November, Welles feared the initiative's potentially stunning political implications. Thus, when Armour suggested having King visit Washington rather than sending an officer to Ottawa, Welles, worried that Canadian ties would leave Roosevelt exceedingly vulnerable to charges of brokering a secret alliance with Britain, wanted to ascertain personally Roosevelt's "more considered views on the advisability of approaching the Canadians at this time." On 20 December Roosevelt told Welles he wanted King and two dominion officers to come to Washington as soon as possible for frank, off-the-record discussions. King did not want to make the trip, concerned that his presence in the American capital might somehow derail ongoing Anglo-American trade talks. But Major General E.C. Ashton and Commodore Percy Nelles could go, as Skelton saw great advantages flowing from military exchanges with Washington, adding that there "was much to be said for getting our defence programme on a realistic North American basis."[35]

DEA staffer Hugh Keenleyside had advocated Canadian-American staff talks the previous May, but had reluctantly concluded that practical politics would probably make it impossible to reach any "serious and well-thought out defensive agreement between Canada and the United States." Roosevelt's proposed talks seemed to offer effective cooperation, except that the Canadian army's support for the discussions had far more to do with settling domestic political scores than creating new ties with the United States. Colonel H.D.G. Crerar, who had written the September 1936 appreciation, firmly hoped that security collaboration with America would "knock the feet from under" subversive Canadians who opposed military ties to Britain. Pointing to frequent difficulties experienced by DND "in the pursuit of its approved objectives through obstruction or, at least, lack of sympathetic action, elsewhere," Ashton vigorously attacked the ultra-isolationist view that Canada should not fight at Britain's side. Charging that that option would be tantamount to secession from the Commonwealth and pointedly noting that a defenceless Canada would concern Washington, Ashton favoured talking only if America "would safeguard Canada's situation and would not force her into a serious situation."[36]

Ashton and Nelles arrived at the expensively fashionable Canadian Legation in northwest Washington, DC, on 19 January for two days of conversations with Craig and Leahy. Ashton opened the discussions by announcing that, while he could give and receive information, he lacked the authority to make any commitments. Craig then outlined defence arrangements for Washington state, and Ashton reciprocated with some general details concerning Canada's west coast. Craig then stunned the Canadians by offering to incorporate British Columbia into the American army's operational command structure and by requesting details about airfields in British Columbia capable of handling bombers. Ashton sought to avoid addressing Craig's staggering offer by discussing whether Canada might join a war against Japan with or without British participation, might support Britain without American assistance, or might opt for neutrality. Although Craig thought only an Anglo-American alliance against Japan merited serious consideration, he declined to discuss his offer further, preferring to focus on landing fields and coastal defences.[37] To Ashton's considerable relief, Leahy demonstrated a marked disinterest in Canadian security. Accustomed to wielding considerable power given Secretary Swanson's frequent illnesses and long acquainted with Franklin Roosevelt,[38] Leahy was far more concerned with defeating the IJN in the western Pacific. While Japan might raid North America, such raids would not presage invasion. Even if Japan used Canadian territorial waters to attack American targets, Leahy averred that those forces could easily be found and promptly disposed of. And with that, the Americans concluded that they could offer no formal security commitments, an assertion the Canadians were keen not to dispute.[39]

Ashton and Nelles may not have realized that the contradictory comments made by the Americans reflected the ongoing Plan Orange dispute, but they clearly recognized the many dangers inherent in Craig's proposal. Two seemingly contradictory responses then emerged. First, scrambling to complete Defence Scheme No. Two, the Canadian army warned King that extensive military contacts with the United States could be most discomfiting if Britain opted for neutrality in a Japanese-American conflict – a risk that hardly seemed commensurate with the subservient role Canada might have at America's side. Contending that a Pacific strategy could not be seen in isolation from dangers elsewhere, the Canadian general staff advised King to offer "no military commitments in advance of an actual crisis developing." Second, in July Canada's military chiefs, reassured that America would safeguard British Columbia, thought that Atlantic defences should receive prior consideration because the menace there was "now fully equal, if not considerably greater than, that which exists on the Pacific."[40]

This conclusion ignited a major row between DND and the DEA – an isolationist Christie demanded the army be stripped "to the bone, excepting those [units] designed for coast defence" – but the legation discussions went unnoticed in America. When AWC officers presented their Canadian theatre study on 28 January, the document failed to mention that the dominion might ally itself with America. Instead, it noted that even a limited American ground offensive would greatly cripple Canada's economy. The fact that the Canadian initiative had become linked to the Ingersoll mission probably dampened any enthusiasm Roosevelt had felt for a defence pact with Canada. Moreover, while Ingersoll had agreed only to some nebulous plans to deter Japan and to keep communication channels open, press leaks compelled Leahy (directed by Roosevelt) to say Ingersoll had only discussed naval tonnage ratios.[41]

Plan Orange's newest incarnation, ready in February 1938, also said little about any vital strategic role for or threat to Alaska. Both services pledged to defend the territory, yet the army promised to send only 7,000 soldiers to Unalaska and only after war had broken out. Recalling a 1936 estimate that said Japan would be able to occupy the Aleutians and the Alaska Peninsula with only a reinforced brigade, Colonel Sherman Miles argued that troops should be promptly dispatched to Unalaska. Miles believed that talks should be initiated with the USN because its plans would have direct bearing on the problem, and if the navy proved uncooperative, the WPD alone should study Alaska. When the navy proved unable to discuss Alaskan security in much detail, the Fourth Army in San Francisco had to field War Department inquiries about its ability to reinforce Dutch Harbor speedily in a crisis. As considerable time would be required to assemble special equipment needed to operate in Alaska, the Fourth Army would not be able to move troops within fifteen days of a war's outbreak, as called for in Plan Orange. Accepting that a sufficiently strong Alaskan garrison had to be maintained to deter an attack and to delay any invader until adequate help could arrive, the WPD was reluctant to garrison Kodiak and Unalaska because they were minor and unfinished navy installations, remote in both distance and time from Alaska's developed centres. In addition, they lacked air support, would be expensive to build and maintain, and would subject soldiers to difficult living conditions. Thus the WPD rejected Miles's Unalaska recommendation, plumping instead for Anchorage as the ideal spot for a permanent garrison.[42]

The navy had different ideas. In late January 1938 Roosevelt gave the navy new ships, noting that "our national defense is inadequate for purposes of national security"; the army received only an additional $17 million. Certain that this was an insufficient sum, Congress established the National Resources Commission to study the nation's economic assets on a state-by-state basis. Directed to examine Alaska's potential, Ingersoll and the WPD's Lieutenant Colonel B.P. Hartle determined that Alaska required little local defence; instead, "like all other parts of our possessions, Alaska receives its initial measure of protection from the U.S. fleet." But as the USN had stated in February 1937, establishing adequate Alaskan bases would require at least $100 million, money that was clearly not available.[43] Congress then set up a new board, led by Hepburn, in May 1938 to examine total defence needs. Presenting its findings on 1 December, the Hepburn Board advocated spending $326 million to build or improve twenty-six bases in the United States, the Caribbean, and the Pacific. Although Alaskan naval bases would be necessary links for the defence of Alaska and the Pacific northwest, the board thought poor weather militated against creating an Aleutian seaplane base. Determining that Unalaska was the westernmost point that could be inexpensively maintained in peacetime, the board desired that a patrol squadron be placed there. Kodiak would get three patrol squadrons, and Sitka would be expanded to handle a full squadron. Hepburn also cited Kodiak and Unalaska as suitable for two submarine divisions.[44]

Unfortunately the navy, which was keenly interested in putting a $200 million advanced base on Guam, had played its political cards badly. Hepburn maintained that the recommended program was intended to provide bases that could support "vital" defensive patrols at the outbreak of war. Concerned that the USN was seeking to make Guam a major facility for offensive operations and aware that the House of Representatives had voted 205 to 168 in January 1939 to block any spending on Guam for fear of antagonizing Japan, Roosevelt mocked the navy's "beautiful idea" of spending $500 million to defend America's outlying possessions. He offered only $65 million for base improvements, none of which was earmarked for Guam. The Alaskan installations, a definite afterthought, got some money. The army, which Hepburn also had not consulted, viewed the sudden interest in Alaska as unwelcome. Retired marine corps major general Smedley D. Butler spoke for some in the army when he told Congress that a vulnerable Alaska should be abandoned in the event of war. Quite unable to reinforce the Aleutians in a timely fashion, the army wanted to amend the joint army-navy war plan in May 1939 to compel the USN to secure its own installations.[45]

Sparked by Roosevelt's November 1938 statement that the United States had to be prepared to defend all of North and South America, the Joint Board ordered the JANPC to study options in the event that the revisionist powers sought to simultaneously violate the Monroe doctrine and grab the Philippines.[46] The JANPC's findings, ready in April 1939, classified Germany as the major threat, followed by Italy and lastly Japan. Predicting that the

Fascist powers would seek to acquire Latin American bases, the JANPC was willing to accept early Pacific defeats in order to properly secure the Atlantic and the Panama Canal. It also wanted to substantially increase the navy and the marine corps, to create a three-division army expeditionary force, and to enhance defences in Hawaii, Panama, Puerto Rico, other Pacific possessions, and finally Alaska.[47]

The Joint Board instructed the services to use the JANPC conclusions to design plans addressing various strategic alternatives ranging from hemispheric defence to offensive operations in Pacific and European waters. Five "Rainbow" plans emerged by 1940, covering various offensive and defensive schemes for wars in Europe and the Pacific. Rainbow 1, which assumed America would have to fight Japan and Germany simultaneously on its own, gained approval from the Joint Board on 14 August 1939 and formal acceptance from Roosevelt in October. Rainbow 1 averred acting defensively in the Pacific until the war with Germany improved enough to shift major forces against Japan. Both services were charged with defending Alaska as far west as Unalaska. Committed to safeguarding Kodiak and Unalaska, the army also promised to dispatch 6,600 soldiers to Alaska no later than a month after hostilities had been initiated.[48] The ink was barely dry on Rainbow 1, though, when the army handed responsibility for Unalaska's security back to the navy. What did not change was Alaska's defence rating. Although Japan was capable of seizing undefended positions in the Aleutians and coastal Alaska, the WPD thought that "a successful defense and retention of our holdings at Sitka-Kodiak-Unalaska and Anchorage will render hostile establishment and operation in Alaska impracticable."[49]

Germany's massive invasion of Poland on 1 September 1939 and the subsequent belligerence of France, Britain, and the British dominions birthed alarming new complications. Roosevelt stated on 1 September that "we are not going to get in to this war," adding two days later that while he could not "ask that every American remain neutral in thought," he would seek to avoid a "black-out of peace in the United States." General George C. Marshall, the army's new head, hoped so too. A veteran of the First World War and numerous unglamorous postings in the interwar period, Marshall had earned a reputation for speaking his mind, no matter the cost. Indeed, as the army's deputy chief, when casually asked by the president on 14 November 1938 if he agreed with Roosevelt's proposal to send warplanes to European democracies, Marshall icily responded, "I am sorry, Mr. President, but I don't agree at all." Although Roosevelt never again referred to the general by his given name after this rebuff, on 1 September 1939 he personally selected Marshall to head the army even though far more senior officers were available. Marshall regarded the interwar period as the army's "Dark Ages."[50] Believing that far too many Americans (including Roosevelt) "expect too much of machines" and that talk about air power's efficacy "staggers the imagination," he wanted 250,000 soldiers for the army. Roosevelt agreed only to 227,000 and Marshall's attempts to gain the secretary of war's intervention were fruitless. Harry Woodring thought that a small force capable of expansion best served national interests and discouraged domestic militarism.[51]

The army tried to bolster Alaska's pitiful defences: 300 soldiers at Skagway and a navy tug so old and decrepit it could not prevail against strong headwinds or tides. Having decided in August 1939 that Anchorage should host Alaska's main airfield and that Dutch Harbor and Kodiak needed secondary bases, the air corps planned to assign twenty-five bombers and twenty-seven pursuit planes to Alaska. Once Europe plunged into madness, the air corps spared fifty-eight aircraft, a rather modest supplement.[52] By November the army had finally settled on Anchorage as the most suitable location for a small mobile ground force as well.[53] Still, getting money for the Anchorage facility proved far more difficult than Marshall had anticipated. When the army's budget request of $853 million came before Congress in April 1940, the politicians slashed $67 million, including the Anchorage base allocation, despite Europe's widening war. Dimond apocalyptically described the cut as economy by annihilation, and after considerable lobbying by Marshall and rumours of an impending Soviet attack on Alaska, the House restored the money by month's end. Roosevelt had told Prime Minister King in late April that he might find it desirable to send some ships across the Atlantic to help the allies without formally declaring war. Despite that, he was worried that giving more money to the army might lead some Americans to believe that it would fight overseas, and as a result, suggested cutting the army's 1941 appropriation. Forced to battle for the bare minimum to ready the army for what might come, Marshall cleverly recruited influential Democratic party financier Bernard Baruch to press his case. Germany's invasion of France on 10 May helped too, as the president reinstated the money on 13 May. By October 1940 the army had received over $8 billion, a sum that exceeded its cumulative budgets over the previous twenty years, as it set out to enrol 1.5 million men by autumn 1941.[54]

The tough fight to fund Anchorage left the army quite disinclined to voluntarily widen its Alaskan responsibilities. As early as February 1940 the USN asked the Joint Board to study how it could protect its new Alaskan bases. When the army did not respond to that request by April, the navy suggested shifting some troops from Anchorage to Sitka, Kodiak, and Unalaska. The army was deliberately dragging its feet, partially because it did not know whether Anchorage would be funded, but also because it could not defend Unalaska. Further, if the navy completed its Alaskan installations before the army could garrison them, those bases might become tempting targets for pre-emptive Japanese or Soviet aggression. Unwilling to see its Anchorage force scattered, the army offered only three combat teams for Sitka, Kodiak, and Unalaska once war began.[55]

The army had little support. After visiting Alaska in July 1940, air corps commander Major General H.H. Arnold, "a relentless prophet and proponent of the most terrifying technologies of war, a master of lurid prophecy and alarmist prose," wanted the USN to help the army establish emergency landing strips, communications facilities, and weather stations throughout the Aleutians.[56] Unable to present a united front against such demands, the army agreed to defend navy installations and ordered that "the governing principle for the defense of Kodiak, Sitka and Unalaska should be that Army forces should be on the ground *before* an enemy strikes, and in sufficient *strength* to repel the likely hostile effort, and to maintain a self-sustained defense until reinforcements can arrive. The first reserve for necessary reinforcement of holding detachments at Kodiak, Sitka and Unalaska should be the garrison of the Army's main base at Anchorage."[57]

The job of organizing the army's new Alaskan roles promised to be no simple task. But the army had chosen a new Alaskan commander, a man who would play an absolutely key role in Alaskan defence until late 1943. Simon Bolivar Buckner Jr., the silver haired Kentucky-born progeny of an aging Confederate general and his much younger wife, descended upon Anchorage in July 1940. Fifty-four-year-old Buckner was exceptionally outgoing and tactless, and possessed a booming voice. In fact, local legend alleged that a bearskin in his office had come from an animal that had "just up and died of fright" after the general had yelled at it.[58] Buckner had been personally chosen for his new post by Fourth Army commander Lieutenant General John L. DeWitt, the officer responsible for the security of the entire American west coast stretching from Alaska southwards to Mexico. A controversial figure who would be slain by a Japanese artillery shell while commanding Okinawa's invasion in 1945, Buckner is praised as a rugged disciplinarian who revelled in the outdoors, and condemned as both an unimaginative tactician who wasted American lives at Okinawa and an incorrigible racist who openly despised African and Native Americans.[59] At first glance Buckner seemed a less than ideal choice for any senior command. A 1907 West Point graduate, he had earned his pilot's wings in the First World War but had seen no combat in that awful conflict. Eminently erudite, sometimes to his own disadvantage in a service that distrusted glibness, Buckner's most prominent posting prior to the Second World War had been as the commandant of cadets at West Point, where he had rightly earned a reputation as a harsh and unforgiving taskmaster who had forgotten "that cadets are born, not quarried."[60]

Wasting no time at all in establishing his command presence, Buckner spent his first three weeks on the job flying to distant and sometimes dismal army posts scattered willy-nilly throughout his new bailiwick. No fan of the USN, and doubtful the navy could or would render him much assistance in a crisis, he insisted that Alaska's isolated garrisons had to be able to act without outside support. He thus requested land-based aircraft to hold hostile forces at a sufficient distance until an adequate force could arrive and destroy or drive off the enemy. Moreover, demonstrating a substantial strategic debt to Mahan and Mitchell, Buckner wanted his command suitably equipped to undertake and support aggressive warfare onto the Asiatic mainland via the shortest route. He also desired an infantry regiment plus artillery at Dutch Harbor and a nearby airfield, and ceaselessly promoted the creation of air strips in western Alaska to "provide the structure for a powerful air defense permitting aggressive action by bombers and facilities for fighters to accompany them on almost every mission." Buckner's self-supporting garrison notion persuaded the army to form largely autonomous Alaskan air-ground teams, a practice that "guided the subsequent expansions of garrisons throughout the territory and into the Aleutian chain during the [world] war."[61]

Buckner did not always get what he wanted, nor did he always offer constructive criticism. DeWitt, eventually an ardent advocate himself of an Alaskan-based offensive against Japan, was initially reluctant to support Buckner's notion of Alaska as a departure point for aggressive warfare without further exhaustive study.[62] Frustrated by what he perceived as roadblocks after touring the Aleutians in a destroyer in September 1940, Buckner recklessly alleged, "Naval officers had an instinctive dread of Alaskan waters, feeling that they were a jumping-off place between Scylla and Charybdis and inhabited by a ferocious monster that was forever breathing out fogs and coughing up williwas [ferocious winds] that would blow the unfortunate mariner onto uncharted rocks and forever destroy his chances of becoming an admiral."[63] This willingness to bait the navy publicly would nearly cost Buckner his job in 1942.

Buckner's request for a sizeable Dutch Harbor garrison was accepted, although it sparked an argument about the nature of the threat faced by Alaska. In January 1941 the army's Military Intelligence Division (MID) felt that Japan's primary martial aim would be to safeguard itself against attack. The Japanese therefore would not move in force against Alaska, as that would endanger their home islands without the prospect of any significant strategic gain. However, in a war's initial phase, and "if unopposed," Japan could occupy the Aleutian Islands, the Alaska Peninsula, and other undefended portions of Alaska. Employing a division supported by aviation and surface ships, the Japanese could then seek to prevent the Americans from using the Aleutians as a jumping-off point for an offensive against Japan. Similarly, bases in the islands would permit the Japanese to assail vulnerable American shipping. Worried that this assessment would buttress the navy's continued demands for more substantial Alaskan army garrisons, the WPD grew even more concerned when discussions in February 1941 revealed the disquieting news that the navy could neither prevent a hostile surprise landing in Alaska nor even warn the army that such an assault was coming. Seemingly unconcerned, the navy judged such an attack unlikely, given that the Japanese would be more interested in other regions, especially as objectives in Alaska were far less important than those in Hawaii or on the west coast. If the Japanese did attack, USN strength would be sufficient to render any enemy movement towards Alaska extremely dangerous. Although that admission badly damaged the navy's relentless case for a larger army garrison, the War Department nonetheless promptly raised the territory's troop allotment to 19,000, including 5,000 men for Dutch Harbor alone, for it feared that unforeseen shipping shortages might severely limit its ability to reinforce Alaska quickly.[64]

Persuading the air corps to establish a base in the Aleutians proved more difficult. After discussing the matter with Arnold on 8 January 1941, the WPD decided that Unalaska could not support an airfield. When the army re-affirmed that judgment in April, Buckner angrily viewed Arnold's refusal to amend the decision as a personal betrayal. Recalling that Arnold had stated in Fairbanks in July 1940 that Alaska should be given great air bases to protect America from attack, Buckner averred that Arnold possessed "an undue degree of optimism" if he believed aircraft could be rushed to Alaska in a crisis. Buckner's solution was to seek another more suitable Aleutian base location. By May he had found Otter Point on Umnak Island, just over 100 kilometres west of Dutch Harbor. Arguing that Japan could seize Umnak with airborne troops and then threaten Dutch Harbor, DeWitt was so con-vinced of Otter Point's strategic importance that he described the scheme "as the most important piece of paper I now have to act upon in connection with the defense of Alaska."[65]

Captain R.C. Parker of the Thirteenth Naval District's Alaskan Sector doubted whether the navy had the resources needed to defend Umnak, while Otter Point's lack of a sheltered anchorage would require an expensive break-water and pier. The WPD thought even less of the idea, arguing that bad weather, poor communications, mountainous terrain, and the fact that Umnak and Unalaska were not mutually supporting positions all militated against putting an air strip at Otter Point.[66] Despite Buckner's incautious accusations to the contrary, Arnold was not averse to doing more in Alaska. In his postwar memoirs Arnold maintained that, while Alaskan defence had always been a high priority for him, he could never acquire the money or aircraft "really needed there to give us the kind of bases we required then." Although these comments suggest retrospective self-justification, in July 1941 the air corps had proposed establishing several Alaskan dispersal fields, and a September report unabashedly declared that "the defense of Alaska is primarily an AIR DEFENSE." Indeed, the air corps was also considering plac-ing heavy bombers in the Aleutians, a plan advocated initially by Cordell Hull in late 1940 and then by the air corps's first major strategic war plan, AWPD-1, in August 1941.[67]

Good intentions, however, cannot always compete with cold, hard reality. With Roosevelt's administration desperately seeking to re-arm in the face of still considerable domestic isolationism, one can sympathize with Admiral Harold Stark's comment that "it just isn't in the nature of things to get results in peace." Feeling Buckner had the right idea, Marshall referred the Umnak issue to the Joint Board in late August. Rear Admiral Richmond Kelly Turner, the navy's new chief of war plans, was most displeased with Buckner's idea. Possessing a domineering and ambitious ego and convinced that he alone understood the Japanese (based on a very brief 1939 visit to Japan), Turner believed that certain cautious IJN admirals would never risk a war with the United States. He therefore believed that Otter Point and Cold Bay were such bad ideas that he would have preferred having no army air protection whatsoever than having it at Umnak. He eventually succumbed to the pressure and accepted the Umnak proposal, on condition that the army did not "ask us for help."[68] The army then insisted on initiating extended surveys to ascertain cost and proper installation size, to examine meteorological conditions, and to determine the time needed to build runways. It was not until 26 November – after Buckner had dispatched his engineering expert to Washington and Colonel Benjamin Talley impatiently cooled his heels in the American capital for a full week before seeing Marshall – that Umnak and Cold Bay obtained official approval.[69]

Ample reasons existed for acting expeditiously. Japan had applied even greater sustained pressure on Europe's Asian colonies following Germany's conquest of France and Holland in 1940, and Roosevelt responded by imposing trade sanctions against Japan. Still, concerns about Europe relegated the Pacific firmly to the second rank strategically. In June 1940 Embick adamantly opposed Roosevelt's decision to transfer the bulk of the Pacific fleet from California to Hawaii, arguing that America could not both safeguard continental security and intervene in Asian affairs. Then on 12 November 1940, just days after Roosevelt had easily secured an unprecedented third consecutive presidential term, Stark composed one of the war's most influential documents. If Britain fell and America was forced to fight along, Stark worried, "While we might not *lose everywhere,* we might, possibly, not *win anywhere.*" As he firmly believed that America's vital national objectives extended to Britain's survival and the definite diminution of Japanese military power, the admiral doubted ultimate victory could be assured solely by American naval assistance to Britain. Only an overwhelming land offensive could decisively defeat Germany, an option clearly beyond existing British capabilities. Stark therefore offered the president four distinct strategic alternatives: 1) focusing on strict hemispheric defence; 2) concentrating solely on Japan; 3) splitting resources evenly between the Pacific and the Atlantic; and 4) attacking Germany while standing on the defensive in the Pacific. As Stark thought the fourth option – Plan Dog – offered the best hope for victory, he recommended initiating talks with the British, Canadians, and Dutch "to lay down plans for promoting unity of allied effort should the United States find it necessary to enter the war."[70]

Agreeing that Britain could not hope to vanquish Germany on its own, the WPD hotly disputed Stark's rather broad definition of American vital interests and the ability to achieve those goals; it wanted only to aid Britain's naval blockade and bombing campaign against Germany. Marshall, on the other hand, wished solely to extract the promise that if America entered the war, the navy would shift its fleet from the Pacific once offensives against Germany got underway.[71] Roosevelt viewed Stark's conclusions more sympathetically. Having floated the idea of allocating half of America's military production to Britain the day after his election triumph, before finally deciding in December to give Britain the weapons it needed via the "Lend-Lease Act," on 16 January 1941 the president committed America to act defensively in the Pacific while the USN would guarantee that vital supply convoys safely reached embattled Albion.[72]

Less than two weeks later the American-British-Canadian (ABC) staff talks began in Washington. Although Britain pushed hard for an American promise to safeguard Singapore and to intervene militarily if Japan made trouble in southeast Asia, Colonel Joseph McNarney and Admiral Turner affirmed that, as Britain always looked out for its own interests first, America could not "afford, nor do we need, to entrust our national future, to British direction because the United States can safeguard the North American Continent, and probably the Western Hemisphere, whether allied with Britain or not." Equally suspicious of the British, Marshall and Stark refused to make any specific commitments beyond offering technical methods of cooperation.[73] Concerned that pivotal discussions might bog down over Singapore and happy with Stark's Plan Dog, which he viewed as "strategically sound and highly adapted to our interests," British prime minister Winston Churchill pointedly reminded his delegation that "the first thing is to get the Americans into the war," and he felt certain that "we can settle how to fight it afterwards." Once Britain dropped its initial demands, the Americans agreed to support Britain in the southwest Pacific by retaining a substantial naval presence at Hawaii once the war started; the USN would deploy most of its ships in the Atlantic and the Mediterranean, however, so that the Royal Navy could shift to Singapore if need be.[74]

The situation became even more complicated when Germany attacked its erstwhile Soviet ally on 22 June 1941. As Joseph Stalin's stunned and shaken regime tottered on the knife-edge of bloody oblivion before the brutal German onslaught, American planners confronted new concerns. Although Hornbeck doubted whether Japan would overtly aid the German cause for fear that Soviet warplanes would retaliate against Japanese cities, other analysts suspected that Japan would be all-too eager to intervene and permanently destroy the clear threat posed by Siberian bases. If Japan invaded eastern Siberia, American army intelligence postulated that Japan might attack Alaska too, perhaps to cover the Siberian assault or to provide a diversion while Japan moved in the south Pacific. In the worst-case scenario, the MID suggested, Germany and Japan might act in concert to occupy Alaska and vanquish the Soviet Union and America simultaneously. Characterizing the bedevilling situation as far too fluid to permit accurate predictions, on 26 June the MID recommended bringing Alaska's garrison quickly up to wartime strength, immediately initiating Bering Sea aerial patrols, and asking Moscow for permission to use bases in Siberia and the Komandorski Islands. But while the MID noted on 1 July that Alaska was "a great outpost for the only true defense – namely an offensive against Japan," on 27 July Turner admitted that the USN could protect only southern Alaska and the eastern Aleutians. And if the fleet went to the Atlantic, "we might find Alaska full of Russians" or Japanese, although Turner averred that as long as Hawaii remained in American hands, "it would be almost impossible for Japan to bring a direct attack against us."[75]

Turner's disturbing comments about the navy's inability to defend the western Aleutians were confirmed by a July 1941 NWC study. Admitting that controlling the Aleutians would allow Japan to attack American commerce, possibly with a quite deleterious effect on American public morale, the NWC also thought Japan would seek to ensure that the islands could not support an American offensive against the Kuriles or Japan. However, as the chain's capacity to support offensive operations seemed quite limited given its paucity of indigenous resources, the NWC identified Dutch Harbor and Cold Bay as the only bases worth developing (although one officer thought Kiska, Adak, and Amchitka merited major facilities). Matters were not helped much either when the navy jealously complained that Buckner had deliberately usurped its coastal defence role by using air corps planes to patrol Alaska's extensive maritime approaches. Admitting that the USN should be primarily responsible for such activities, an exasperated Marshall told the navy that the need for such army flights had passed. Still, if the situation suddenly changed and the USN could not adequately discharge its aerial responsibilities, then plainly Buckner had the absolute right to safeguard Alaskan security.[76]

Also unhappy with the USN, DeWitt planned to reinforce Dutch Harbor by 10 July and pledged to promptly dispatch even more men once he had corralled the requisite transport shipping. As Alaska possessed just thirty-eight obsolete planes in July 1941, Buckner demanded six squadrons, attesting that one bomber squadron would be far more valuable to his command than an entire infantry division, given that individual ground garrisons might be overwhelmed one by one unless they received adequate air support. With enough planes, Buckner also earnestly asserted, he could annihilate an enemy expedition before it could even alight on Alaskan soil. After Secretary of War Henry Stimson ordered the army to expedite troop deliveries to Alaska, on 15 July it raised the garrison from 18,500 to 24,000 men.[77] But when DeWitt demanded seven squadrons, Brigadier General Carl Spaatz, arguing that underdeveloped Alaskan bases could only support three squadrons, said in late August that he would be able to deliver twenty-five fighters and twenty-six bombers to Buckner by December. Only in mid-November, as war loomed ever more darkly over the boundless Pacific, did Arnold promise that Alaska would eventually have 195 fighters, sixty-eight heavy bombers, and eighty-five medium bombers. Unfortunately, the heavy bombers would not be available until March 1942, while the fighter transfer would depend on the completion of Alaskan airdromes.[78] Once negotiations with Japan had all but collapsed in late November 1941, DeWitt plaintively told Marshall that only thirty-four of Alaska's aircraft could still drag themselves aloft, a number "so small, considering the air task, as to be negligible." DeWitt also proclaimed that if aircraft had to be hurriedly dispatched once a crisis had come, "casualties would be extremely high and ... the units would be ineffective for some time due to the unfamiliarity of the pilots with the elements in which they would have to fly."[79]

DeWitt's pessimism had considerable company as peace slowly ebbed away. Dr. Ruth Gruber, an Arctic expert on special assignment in Alaska for Secretary of the Interior Harold Ickes, noted on 2 December that morale had become an acute problem, as many soldiers considered Alaska to be a prison definitely not worth defending. MID officer C.C. Dusenberg penned an even gloomier outline on 1 December. Despite the fact that Dutch Harbor constituted the most important base in the Alaskan defence system, it could be shelled by an enemy positioned safely out of range, and its many closely packed buildings were highly vulnerable to aerial assaults. Dusenberg thought Japan could easily cut American supply lines in the Gulf of Alaska or steadily advance along the Aleutians using a combination of amphibious assaults, naval and air bombardments, and even parachute landings.[80] Could Alaskan forces oppose such assaults? Colonel Everett Davis, Alaska's air force chief, lacked confidence and on 6 December stated that "the air force is so small, consists of such old equipment, and is in such conditions as to constitute a cadre sent to the territory in advance of the main body for the purpose of gathering information of the geography, developing a technique of cold-weather operation, and principally to develop a plan and facilities for the operations of the main force on its arrival. By no stretch of the imagination can it be accepted as a force able to defend the territory against any attack in force."[81] Davis did not know, of course, that great events the next day would completely alter Alaska's strategic situation and bring much feared invaders to the Aleutians.

Entirely Open to Attack:
Aleutian Defence, December 1941 to June 1942

In mid-1942 General Marshall apprised General McNaughton of some of the many perplexing problems he had to confront as the head of a rapidly burgeoning American army. Morale among the many isolated backwater American garrisons in the Pacific was becoming a perceptible problem, Marshall admitted. Not only were average soldiers adversely affected by ongoing inaction and boredom, local commanders were too often afflicted by what he called "localitis," the tendency to think that their everyday small local problems "vied in importance with those devolving on" their superiors in Washington, DC.[1] No doubt Marshall had Alaska and the Aleutians in mind when he made this comment. Numerous Alaskan commanders had been badgering him ceaselessly for more resources even before the Japanese rudely catapulted the United States into the Second World War by attacking

Pearl Harbor on 7 December 1941. Moreover, those plaintive pleas for assistance – which were not always answered in a satisfactory manner – swelled once the Japanese invaded the western Aleutians in June 1942.

Waves of Japanese carrier-borne aircraft swooped down on an unsuspecting Pearl Harbor on the morning of 7 December. Losing just twenty-nine planes in their murderous assault, the raiders sank or severely damaged eighteen American warships, destroyed 188 aircraft, and inflicted 3,500 casualties on the astonished defenders. A stunning tactical victory and the start of a dazzling campaign that swept Allied forces from the western Pacific and southeast Asia, Pearl Harbor was nonetheless a strategic error of the first magnitude because it initiated a conflict that ended almost four years later with Japan's utter subjugation. With an economy floundering thanks to increasingly stringent economic boycotts, the Japanese had determined that a southward advance to gain vital strategic commodities was necessary, even at the risk of war. Although Japan had opted to negotiate, when those talks stalled, an imperial conference held on 1 December resulted in a decision to fight. Noted American historian Alvin D. Coox likens Japan's resolve to fight the United States and Britain to escaping through a hole by widening it, while John Dower observes that the decision was not easily reached, "nor was it irrational once the decision had been made that Japan could not survive without control of the southern region." British academic H.P. Willmott agrees, as Japan, alone among the major combatants, aspired to a negotiated peace after forcing "her enemies to come to terms with the gains that she intended to make in the opening months of the war."[2]

The decision to fight was not universally welcomed. IJN general staff member Fukudome Shigeru had stated on 6 October that he had no confidence Japan could win a war against America and Britain. IJN commander-in-chief Admiral Yamamoto Isoroku, architect of the Pearl Harbor assault, in October 1940 had advised against war, adding in September 1941 that while he could give America "hell for a year and a half," he could not guarantee what would happen after that.[3] Such objections were brushed aside by other more hard-line leaders who wanted to end decisively the crisis with the United States. Many Japanese officers, especially those in the IJN, preferred to believe that the Americans were a disunited isolationist people, too decadent to properly wage war. Moreover, as Admiral Takagi Sokichi had told a representative of the Imperial Palace on 8 August 1941, if Japan waited while western embargoes inexorably drained its vital strength, "we will be giving

up without a fight. If we make our attack now, the war is militarily calcula-
ble and not hopeless." While Japan's operational intelligence had been very
good, it knew practically nothing about America's economic and military
potential. On 25 December Admiral Ugaki Matome, Yamamoto's chief of
staff, urgently noted the need to study USN tactics and organization thoroughly in order to successfully confront the inevitable retaliation by the
Americans, once they had recovered from their initial losses. The admiral
would have to wait because, as Coox states, Japanese military intelligence collection was generally much better than analysis and estimation.[4]

The devastating onslaught on Pearl Harbor stunned the Americans. In
mid-September 1941 the Joint Board, approving the reinforcement of the
Philippines, had concurred with Marshall's hopeful opinion that bolstering
the distant American possession would be a decisive element in deterring
Japan from undertaking a Pacific war. Moreover, as the diplomatic crisis with
Japan deepened and darkened over the last months of 1941, Churchill had
been willing to consider giving "Hull the latitude that he asks" but the American navy had not been keen to hand control to the State Department. In July
1940 Admiral James O. Richardson, commander-in-chief of the United States
Fleet until the following February, had complained that Stanley Hornbeck
"was exercising a greater influence over the disposition of the fleet than I
was." Admiral Ingersoll had rejected Hull's hard-line attitude towards Japan
and was supported by Stark, who was worried about the USN's ability to find
enough fuel for its future needs. Ingersoll had averred in early November that
the State Department seemed to be operating under the highly dubious and
dangerous assumption that Japan could be defeated militarily in just a few
weeks. Indeed, the Joint Board had advised the president on 3 November not
to send any ultimatum to Tokyo and to put off hostilities with Japan as long
as possible.[5] Ingersoll may not have been too far from the mark, as Stanley
Hornbeck, having firmly concluded that Japan would not risk conflict, had
defied his colleagues to find even "one case in history where a nation went to
war out of desperation.[6] Hornbeck, however, had fallen into the same trap as
the MID; he expected Japan to follow a predictable course of action rather
than plans conforming with Japanese national objectives.[7]

As Roberta Wohlstetter's 1962 study shows, it was not a shortage of intelligence information that had led to the disaster at Pearl Harbor. In fact,
American analysts had been buried "under a plethora of irrelevant" messages,
leaving them unable to discern what information really counted. Matters

did not improve quickly after 7 December. Confronted with multiple serious threats and singularly unable to locate the IJN strike force that had ravaged Pearl Harbor, Americans feared the worst. Lieutenant General DeWitt warned a fearful San Francisco to expect air raids. For Glen Howell, the American

Admiral Yamamoto Isoroku, Commander-in-Chief Imperial Japanese Navy, architect of the attacks on Pearl Harbor and Midway, undated.

liaison officer attached to Canada's Pacific Command, the new and dismal course of events must have been particularly jarring. On 17 November 1941 he had said the Japanese air force could not stand against their American and British counterparts, and asserted that "Japan has no inventive genius." After Pearl Harbor, he saw things quite differently, darkly noting, "If the Japs only knew it, the Pacific coast of the United States and Canada and all of Alaska are entirely open to attack. We have nothing here to defend ourselves." Army intelligence unfortunately agreed. Claiming that Japan seemed to possess "complete information not only of our dispositions but of the habits, customs and traits of the American Army, Navy and people," a 10 December report admitted that the IJN could strike the USN, the west coast, Panama, and Alaska. A WPD assessment produced two days later added that, although Japan might secure an Aleutian base, Alaskan defence ranked below the security of Hawaii, Panama, Brazil, and the continental United States.[8]

The normally ebullient Buckner had been badly shaken by war's sudden onset. A jocular Buckner had told some reporters prior to 7 December that if the Japanese invaded America via the Aleutians and Alaska, "they might make it, but it would be their grandchildren who finally got there; and by then they would all be citizens anyway!" Fuming that he had heard about Pearl Harbor from a junior officer who had telephoned him from Fairbanks after a local radio station had publicly reported the assault, an exasperated Buckner described his command as "a sandlot club." A 10 December warning from the USN, indicating that Japanese forces were approaching the Aleutians, fortunately proved erroneous; still, Buckner feared that the enemy would arrive in force at any moment, given that Alaska was much closer to Japan than Hawaii and it had far less naval protection. The joint army-navy defence plan for Alaska, instituted on 16 December, echoed Buckner's concerns. Although most of Alaska likely faced only minor raids, Unalaska could expect a major assault. As such an assault might be accompanied by raids against other regional facilities, the plan recommended the immediate occupation of potential base sites east and west of Unalaska.[9]

The army was ill equipped to establish any new bases. As of 20 December, it had only 22,000 soldiers in Alaska, and 2,200 of them belonged to air corps units supporting a mere forty-one serviceable aircraft. The navy could muster just four surface vessels, six patrol planes, and two old submarines. Unless the USN allocated more resources to the north Pacific, declared DeWitt, appointed on 11 December to head the newly created Western

Defense Command (WDC), not only would Otter Point remain unfinished but the army would be unable to safeguard key USN facilities in the north Pacific.[10] Just one day into the conflict, Buckner asked for seaplanes for Dutch Harbor, adding hopefully that an aircraft carrier "would add greatly to our strength." Doubtful that the USN would spare one of the three carriers it had in Pacific waters for Alaska, but encouraged by Marshall's promise that two squadrons would soon be winging their way north, on 10 December DeWitt had asked for three air groups for Alaska.[11]

Marshall's promise, given the state of the American military in December 1941, was substantial. The army could field 1.6 million men in forty-seven divisions plus over forty air groups but most of those units were struggling just to train and arm the new recruits. Only seventeen divisions were regarded as combat-ready while the air corps had forty-five modern fighter planes for the entire Pacific coast.[12] Arnold confirmed Marshall's promise and early in the new year the air corps announced it would send four squadrons. Deeming that to be unacceptable, Buckner adamantly maintained that Alaska had escaped a potentially devastating attack in early December only because poor weather in the north Pacific had rendered carrier operations impracticable. Asserting that Japan would soon notice Alaska's continued vulnerability, Buckner demanded eight squadrons immediately and twenty to thirty bomber squadrons flying from Aleutian as well as Siberian airfields by the end of 1942.[13]

Obtaining Soviet cooperation was not a new idea. In June 1941 the United States Naval Institute had suggested attacking Japan from bases in the Aleutians, Siberia, and the Komandorskis. The previous February, seeking to impress the Soviets and to give Japanese leadership something to think about by having USN ships "popping up here and there," Roosevelt had told British ambassador Lord Halifax that he fancied sailing a carrier strike force from Hawaii to Siberia via Attu. This notion appalled the USN. Although Stark dutifully drew up plans to dispatch a carrier, four cruisers, and a destroyer squadron to the Aleutians and possibly Siberian ports, he also managed to kill Roosevelt's plan on that grounds that it was a "childish" ploy probably put forward by an interfering State Department. And when a senior WPD officer had advocated approaching the Soviets on 20 December 1941 about attacking Japan from Siberia, the army had also declined to act.[14] Instead, Arnold rounded up five squadrons. Getting planes to Alaska in the heart of winter, however, proved nightmarish. The rushed operation confirmed

DeWitt's prediction that aircraft would not be shifted easily and safely to Alaska during a crisis. By 25 January, just thirteen of twenty-five fighters had arrived safely in Alaska; six had crashed. Five of thirteen bombers had also been lost, the victims of distance, cold weather, improper winterization, and inexperienced crews.[15]

Then the president directly intervened in Alaskan security affairs. Almost sixty years after his death, Franklin Roosevelt remains an enigmatic commander-in-chief who positively delighted in a chaotic leadership style that often baffled his aides and enabled him to reign supreme. As he told Secretary of the Treasury Henry Morgenthau in May 1942, Roosevelt saw himself as "a juggler, and I never let my right hand know what my left hand does." Roosevelt has been described as both a leader very amenable to military advice,[16] and as a virtual but benign dictator who dominated strategy making and pushed a military leadership lacking in drive and initiative.[17] The latter description would seem to apply here. Roosevelt's sudden renewed interest in the north Pacific was triggered by a 14 January memorandum revealing that existing USN forces could not deal with even minor threats to Alaska, although Admiral Husband E. Kimmel, commander of the Pacific Fleet, and his intelligence officer, Edwin Layton, had discussed the possibility in late 1941 that the Japanese might seek to occupy the Aleutians. Kodiak's submarine facility was only 5 percent complete, nothing had been accomplished at Dutch Harbor, Unalaska's naval station was a quarter done, aerological stations on Attu, Amchitka, Atka, and Umnak were delayed, and only temporary structures were under construction on Kiska and Kanaga. Acutely disappointed, Roosevelt quickly apprised Marshall and Admiral King (commander-in-chief, US Fleet – or CominCH) of his "hunch" that Japan might attack the Aleutians and Alaska in the spring. Marshall thought raids would come "especially at Dutch Harbor where our state of preparations is far from complete," and it was possible Japan would shift assets to occupy Alaskan bases. But Marshall's response exhibited little urgency. Perhaps that was due to the general's renowned unflappable nature and the fact that Alaska, unlike the embattled Philippines, was still inviolate. However, Marshall may also have considered Alaska expendable. In late December, when he and the new Anglo-American Combined Chiefs of Staff (CCS) produced the guiding strategic outline for the Allied war effort, they certified that while Hawaii and Alaska should be retained if possible, their loss would not render any large-scale Japanese invasion of America any less improbable.[18]

In early February Roosevelt publicly announced his desire for an Aleutians-based striking force, to be in put in place by the following summer. Then, at a 17 February press conference he stated that not only was a Japanese attack on Alaska possible but America could not deal with such a threat. Six days later he added that if Japan conquered the Antipodes and the Dutch East Indies, it could then assault North and South America, "including Alaska." Perhaps Roosevelt had aimed to prepare a reeling American public in the event of yet another defeat, perhaps he had sought to justify sending scarce resources to Australia while the American west coast seemed vulnerable. He also may have been signalling to his military advisers that he expected some prompt remedies – a tactic in keeping with what a frustrated Marshall called the "cigarette lighter gesture," the president's flippant "habit of throwing out new operations" and his tendency to be "bored by papers, lengthy discussions, and by anything short of a few pungent sentences." But in one of those pungent sentences, Roosevelt told Churchill in mid-March 1942 that American forces might launch attacks soon against Japan itself from bases in China, Siberia, and even the Aleutians.[19]

Whatever Roosevelt's intent, his intervention heartened Alaskan commanders, who finally managed to find some common ground in their shared sense of crisis. Glenn Howell feared that "we won't get much help until the Japs attack the Aleutians, which I feel sure they will do when the weather favors them in the early summer," while Parker found it impossible to discuss his command's shortcomings without "making my temperature go up." Parker joined Buckner in demanding a northern offensive against Japan, the initiation of immediate discussions with Stalin regarding Siberian bases, the completion of Umnak's airstrip, and the placement of more seaplane stations in the western Aleutians.[20] Hornbeck had also been lobbying Marshall to concentrate substantial offensive forces in the Aleutians to move against the Kuriles and to bolster Soviet confidence. Admiral C.S. Freeman, Parker's superior, eagerly endorsed more Aleutian bases in case the Soviet Union came to blows with Japan. Fervently advocating Soviet-American cooperation, Freeman feared that joint action with the Soviets might be severely limited if Japan occupied Adak Island. As to whether a northern approach to Japan was feasible, Freeman could not say, but he wanted Alaska kept safe just in case. William J. Donovan, the president's coordinator of information since July 1941, and Hanson Baldwin, military columnist for the *New York Times*, agreed. Donovan, like Billy Mitchell, firmly averred that Alaska possessed "unlimited opportunities as a great air base for the employment of long-range bombardment aviation against Japan." It was likely that the Japanese also recognized the danger, and Donovan worried that they would attack Siberia and Alaska once south Pacific operations were concluded. Hanson Baldwin also viewed the Aleutians as a springboard against Japan, but admitted that bad weather and inadequate bases might limit the archipelago's strategic usefulness.[21]

On 5 February Alaska's scattered aerial units were designated the Eleventh Air Force, a somewhat extravagant sobriquet for a formation that fielded just five squadrons and 3,067 personnel. Noting that the Eleventh could not defend existing bases let alone any new Alaskan posts, the Air War Plans Division (AWPD) argued on 15 February that unless more planes were provided immediately, Dutch Harbor would have to be abandoned and the Cold Bay and Otter Point airstrips prepared for emergency demolition. Six days later William O. Butler, the Eleventh's first commander, asked for six more squadrons, which should eventually grow to at least thirty. Cognizant of the enticing allure of an Alaskan aerial offensive, given that urgent needs elsewhere precluded dispatching additional planes, Arnold ordered his commanders to develop "as good a defense for Alaska as its personnel, equipment and facilities would permit."[22]

The navy was even more uncompromising. Admiral Turner categorically rejected claims that the USN could not secure Alaska's sea lanes and labelled as improbable any chance that Japan could gain control of the north Pacific. Admiral King had even less time for Alaskan concerns. Known as a heavy drinker and a womanizer prior to the war and widely feared for his bullying and vicious temper (Marshall thought him "perpetually mean"), King was also praised for his capable administrative style, his keen intelligence, a willingness to take risks, and his absolute commitment to taking the war directly to the enemy. Indeed, his career reflected a desire never to be caught standing still. Beginning with service on a destroyer after leaving the Naval Academy, he had taken on engineering assignments and commands of a refrigeration vessel and then a submarine flotilla, before qualifying as a naval pilot at the age of forty-seven.[23] While he had told the CCS on 11 January that Japan might attempt to seize Alaska, his primary goal – maintaining naval communications to Hawaii and Australia – held top priority. By late February King asserted that Alaska would confront only occasional minor submarine and air raids, as Japanese landings there would probably be unproductive and highly exposed to American counterattacks. Concerned the army was building Alaskan airfields at a hurried pace that far outstripped its ability to stock them with warplanes, King opposed placing any new bases west of Umnak.[24]

A 5 February assessment produced by Admiral Chester W. Nimitz's command at Pearl Harbor (commander-in-chief, Pacific – or CINCPAC) revealed that any hope that Japan had overextended itself "seems to be in vain." With the Japanese rapidly overrunning the Philippines, Malaya, and the Dutch East Indies, the War Department agreed with the CINCPAC assessment. By early March it had 27,000 troops in Alaska (5,500 at Dutch Harbor alone) and over 40,000 before April's end. These were certainly impressive numbers given that the army's chief Pacific theatre planner, Brigadier General Dwight D. Eisenhower, had relegated Alaska to fourth place in his shipping allocations.[25] For Eisenhower, Alaska's needs had to be kept in context. Given the CCS's 31 December ruling that Germany should be beaten first, Eisenhower asserted that America's strategic priorities had to be Britain, the Soviet Union, the Middle East, and India, in that order. Then there were "things that [were] highly desirable and approach[ed] the necessary," Alaska being the most important component of this latter category.[26]

Eisenhower's position was quite unenviable. Japanese forces were running riot in Asia and the Pacific in early 1942, and he had to contend with a very difficult Douglas MacArthur, whose own forces had been bottled up on the Bataan Peninsula in the Philippines since late December. MacArthur remains an extraordinarily controversial figure, revered by many, reviled by others. A recent history of the Second World War, written by two American historians, pulls few punches. When MacArthur "was good, he was very, very good, and when he was bad, he was horrid," plagued as he was by paranoia, a lust for publicity, political ambition, and a "precarious" emotional balance. Just prior to Pearl Harbor MacArthur had told a visiting junior army officer that he did not envision a war with Japan until at least April 1942. But on 4 February, claiming to "see the whole strategy of the Pacific campaign perhaps better than anyone else," a brazen MacArthur argued that the mere threat of a strong naval thrust against Japan's exposed seaward flank would compel a Japanese retreat from the south Pacific. Having served with MacArthur in the Philippines in the 1930s, Eisenhower did not like the man very much. He did not understand why MacArthur had not performed better in December and why he had not safeguarded his vital air forces (destroyed by the

Japanese the day after Pearl Harbor). Eisenhower carped that having now "lost his nerve," MacArthur was putting forward strategies better suited to West Point plebs than to a general fighting a real conflict.[27]

Complaining plaintively about a plethora of amateur strategists and prima donnas seeking to influence strategy making, Eisenhower noted in January 1942 that "the struggle to secure adoption by all concerned of a common concept of strategical objectives is wearing me down." Yet his considered strategic analysis markedly identified army ambivalence towards peripheral strategies "and the beginnings of unified, consistent support of the immediate concentration of American forces preparatory to an assault on German-held territory."[28] It did not explain, however, why Alaska's retention was highly desirable and "approaching the necessary." Roosevelt sought to rectify that on 4 March by ordering the newly created Joint Chiefs of Staff (JCS) to examine the ramifications of a Soviet-Japan conflict, including the option of an American offensive via the Aleutians and Siberia. The army had briefly studied such a possibility, as well as shuttle-bombing runs from the Aleutians, Siberia, China, and the Philippines in late 1941. It had concluded then that the Soviet Union's still considerable Far East forces – 450,000 soldiers, 1,000 aircraft, and 100 ships – might force Japan to concentrate much of its military at home. Nothing had come of those efforts since the army had objected to telling Stalin about the shuttle plan for fear that he might inform Japan. Attempts to learn about Siberian bases had also been unsuccessful, due to Stalin's intense paranoia and keen desire not to provoke Japan while his battered forces were still struggling to rein in powerful German invaders. As a result, when Washington, at MacArthur's prompting, had asked permission in December 1941 to use Siberian bases to raid Japanese cities, the Soviets had declined.[29]

Convinced that Japan and the Soviet Union were on a collision course for war by summer 1942 at the latest, America's military began thinking seriously about supporting Stalin. Three options presented themselves: delivering supplies to the Soviets only; initiating diversionary operations designed to draw Japanese forces away from Siberia; or launching an offensive based on the Aleutians and Siberia's Kamchatka Peninsula. None of the options lacked complications, but the latter was most problematic because it would require more Aleutian bases, an extensive USN fleet presence, and numerous Siberian and Kurile airfields. Army planners thus concluded that they could best assist the Soviets by containing Japan in the south Pacific.[30] Despite this pessimistic conclusion, the Joint Planning Staff (JPS), one of the myriad new agencies reporting to the JCS, suggested talking with Moscow about military cooperation – a recommendation the JCS passed to Roosevelt on 30 March. The president returned the JPS memorandum without comment, although Ambassador William H. Standley strove mightily to extract details of Siberia's military infrastructure from his notoriously tight-lipped Soviet contacts. With the apparent demise of the Siberian option, on 24 March the CCS ruled that Alaska would be subject only to airborne or seaborne raids, and Eisenhower told Alaskan commanders to prepare for Category D assaults in the absence of adequate air protection. The JCS then sealed the matter on 30 March by discontinuing north Pacific operational planning until arrangements could be made with the Soviets.[31]

The abrupt dismissal of an Aleutian-based offensive option left the question of the nature of the Japanese threat in the north Pacific unresolved. The MID thought Japan had three basic strategic alternatives: feint attacks to disperse American forces; raids intended to destroy Alaskan bases and disrupt the steady flow of key Lend-Lease supplies to Siberia; or outright conquest. The latter would give Japan access to Alaska's rich natural resources, provide cover for further offensive action against North America, deal a serious psychological blow to Allied morale, and improve Japan's potential bargaining position in any future peace negotiations. Given the level of force required to conquer Alaska, the MID dismissed that option as improbable. Far more likely were lodgments involving one to three Japanese divisions along Alaska's coast, simultaneous assaults on Siberia and Alaska, or a step-by-step advance along eastern Siberia culminating in an attack on Alaska. Yet even the lodgment alternative, which would require significant naval forces to guard Japan's lines of communication and might prompt a Soviet entry into the war, was deemed to be too risky for Japan. The chance of Soviet intervention might be lessened if Japan captured Unalaska or Kodiak, although the MID believed destructive raids against those bases could achieve roughly equivalent results with far less risk to the Japanese. Simultaneous attacks on Siberia and Alaska could produce local surprise but would compel Japan to disperse its forces, rendering them vulnerable to defeat in detail and reducing enemy elements in the key south Pacific to a bare minimum. Past practice seemed to indicate that the Japanese would favour a more cautious step-by-step approach. Yet even that limited offensive would entail considerable air and naval support, and it would take at least two months to occupy eastern Siberia, thus providing the United States with adequate time to marshal defensive resources. Arguing that bad weather often made regional travel hazardous, the MID maintained that raids were far more likely than lodgments. Until Alaskan defences were improved, the MID cautioned, the only deterrent to attack "would appear to be the Japanese preoccupation elsewhere and perhaps Japanese overestimate of our strength."[32]

Alaska's defensive capabilities improved considerably once engineers completed the vital runways at Cold Bay and Otter Point in early April, except that the air corps had not provided any planes for those bases. Buckner wanted Otter Point to have at least one fighter squadron since it was splendidly placed to defend Dutch Harbor; if left unguarded, however, an enemy could use it to assault the harbour. The AWPD recommended a medium bomber group and a fighter group for Alaska, though Eisenhower doubted allocating any new resources to Alaska was a good idea. It had been a tough few months for the army's chief planner. Flooded by a multitude of messages from MacArthur and compelled to deal at length with suspicious USN officers, the workaholic Eisenhower caustically described MacArthur as a "big baby" who was "losing his nerve" and slammed Admiral King as a "mental bully": if someone were to shoot King, Eisenhower thought, "that might help win this war." Complaining that the navy seemed to want to take over all the islands in the Pacific for its purposes, Eisenhower thought all diversions of effort, including Alaska, should be limited to the absolutely necessary or to those that might be profitable, "since each reduces the rapidity of concentration for the major effort."[33]

Eisenhower's attitude towards Alaskan defence shifted markedly after eighteen B-25 army bombers, led by Colonel James Doolittle, lumbered precariously off the USS *Hornet*'s short deck and bombed Tokyo and a handful of other Japanese cities on 18 April 1942. While Doolittle's raiders inflicted only minimal damage, the daring foray elevated badly battered American spirits by striking directly at the Japanese homeland. Expecting prompt retaliatory assaults against the United States, especially Alaska, the MID feared that Japanese air and submarine attacks could be expected at any time. So when DeWitt asked for five squadrons, Eisenhower, intent on finding a way to scuttle a presidential initiative to send scarce aircraft to Australia, was quite willing to listen. Contending that "the hazard we are accepting in Alaska and the Aleutians with the small aviation forces available in that region" was no longer acceptable, the general wanted the Australian shipment promptly diverted instead to Alaska and Hawaii. Noting that top-of-the-line warplanes remained in critically short supply, Eisenhower counselled Marshall that DeWitt should be told bluntly just what he could count on as reinforcements in an emergency.[34] Unbeknownst to Eisenhower, an emergency of immense magnitude was looming, an emergency that would completely alter Alaska's strategic situation.

Japanese military leaders faced an odd irony that spring. Their nation's stupendous martial triumphs since December 1941 had come so quickly and "with so few losses they had actually outpaced the planning of the Imperial General Headquarters and the staffs of the Army and the Navy."[35] The IJN and the Imperial Japanese Army (IJA) had devised some amorphous notions about capturing Hawaii before moving against the continental United States, Canada, and the Panama Canal until the Americans lost their fighting spirit and the war could be satisfactorily concluded. Turning such vague and extraordinarily ambitious schemes into concrete action, however, proved exceptionally difficult, as Japanese inter-service relations, already badly strained by years of fierce budget wrangling and sometimes even bloody political infighting, had worsened since December 1941. In late January 1942 Admiral Ugaki had fretted about his nation's failure to produce new stratagems, yet senior IJN and IJA commanders did not meet until early March and then again found themselves at loggerheads. Concerned that the Allies might counterattack from India, Australia, and Hawaii, the Japanese navy wanted to strike those points quickly and hard. The more conservative army favoured remaining stolidly on the defensive, consolidating its vast conquests and concentrating its forces against Siberia; it therefore refused to make troops available for any new IJN-led offensives.[36]

Admiral Yamamoto intervened dramatically to break this stalemate. A former naval attaché in Washington in the 1920s and fully cognizant of America's gargantuan industrial and military potential, Yamamoto, a gambler of some renown, sought an immediate decisive naval confrontation while Japan retained the advantage. While his subordinates endorsed invading Australia and seizing the Solomon Islands in the south Pacific, Yamamoto believed that the best chance for entrapping and destroying the USN lay at Midway Island, a tiny speck of land 1,000 miles west-north-west of Pearl Harbor. He reasoned that the USN could not tolerate a Japanese presence so close to its vital Hawaiian base. The IJN's general staff vigorously opposed this scheme for two reasons: Midway's proximity to Hawaii would render

Japanese forces vulnerable to attack from land-based American aviation; further, Midway was slightly too distant from existing Japanese bases for its retention to be assured. Stubbornly refusing to back down, for he felt that a dangerous American riposte would be unlikely once the USN carriers were sunk, Yamamoto carried the day with the IJN by threatening to resign. Unwilling to lose its most esteemed strategist and the architect of its victory at Pearl Harbor, the navy ceded to his wishes. But the recalcitrant IJA, arguing that any attack on Midway would inevitably lead to a much larger invasion of Hawaii, initially rejected Yamamoto's proposed offensive. Whether or not the navy intended to assault Hawaii – and historian John Stephan asserts that it was "safe to assume that every official involved in the planning for Midway knew its big brother, 'Eastern Operation' [Hawaii's capture] was still alive and well" – the IJA soon gave way. Although some Japanese mistakenly believed that Doolittle's planes had flown from the Aleutians or Midway rather than off the deck of the USS *Hornet*, the IJA was embarrassed at being "caught napping just when one was feeling confident and in charge of things" and finally saw a distinct advantage in pushing American forces farther away from Japan. Moreover, once the IJN affirmed it would require relatively few IJA soldiers to supplement its own naval landing forces, the army agreed to invade Midway; Imperial General Headquarters formally approved the Midway plan on 5 May.[37]

The IJA, however, attached a price when it accepted the Midway attack; operations against the Aleutians would be undertaken. Yamamoto chose not to object to this addition, as his subordinates made the point that moving against the Aleutians would safeguard the Midway operation's northern flank and divert American resources away from the main Japanese thrust. Furthermore, after the Doolittle raid, many Japanese officers had convinced themselves that the Aleutians might represent a hitherto largely unrecognized threat to the home islands. In early 1941 IJN aviators had told the press they were confident the American air force would not raid from Alaska. That confidence, however, had faded somewhat by March 1942, when Rear Admiral Tanetsuga Sosa informed reporters that the most likely avenue of attack against Japan would be from the Aleutians, once good weather arrived in the region in May. While a massive IJN armada would entice the USN into a murderous ambush near Midway, the Aleutian task force's goal was "to capture or demolish points of strategical interest in the western Aleutians in order to check the enemy's air and ship maneuvers in the area." Two light aircraft carriers, a seaplane tender, five cruisers, twelve destroyers, and 1,600 soldiers would reduce enemy air strength at Dutch Harbor before seizing Kiska, Attu, and Adak in early June. Only Kiska and Attu would be garrisoned, though those forces likely would be removed before winter's harsh advent.[38]

But Japan's greatest asset – surprise – evaporated thanks to a group of tireless and skilled American crypto-analysts based in Hawaii and led by Joseph Rochefort. Having broken some IJN codes in April, Rochefort's diligent team could soon read substantial portions of their foe's message traffic. The first clue that something big was in the offing came on 26 April, when an Australian-based listening post translated two intercepted IJN messages. The first asked for naval charts for the region stretching from the Gulf of Alaska southwards to British Columbia; the other sought to discover how many planes were stationed at Kodiak and Dutch Harbor. The IJN did not transmit the 5 May authorization, but its communications traffic made numerous references to a location referred to only as "AF." Acting on a simple hunch that AF might be Midway, in mid-May some USN officers cleverly sent out a fake un-encrypted cable stating that Midway's desalination plant had broken down. The ruse worked spectacularly, as the Americans quickly intercepted a Japanese dispatch reporting AF's water shortage. By 20 May Yamamoto's entire operational plan was in American hands, laying bare Japan's intentions.[39] Six Japanese carriers (234 planes), seven battleships, and fifty-seven other vessels were headed to Midway within days.

Rochefort's revelations did not find a unanimously favourable reception. After the USN had fought the IJN to a costly stalemate in the Coral Sea in early May (thus preventing dangerous Japanese amphibious landings in eastern New Guinea that might have then led to assaults on Australia), Admiral King told Marshall on 12 May that Japan would not confront "our task force of two carriers unless they are thoroughly supported and covered by shore-based aircraft." King, though, was far less confident than he seemed. The loss of the USS *Lexington,* King's former flagship, and the serious damage inflicted on the USS *Yorktown* at Coral Sea had led him to consider the drastic option of transferring some of the air groups from his remaining carriers to land-based airfields – a proposal that had appalled some CINCPAC officers. Furthermore, intense rivalry between Rochefort's team and intelligence analysts in Washington proved a hindrance as the latter group, refusing at first to accept that AF really was Midway, asserted that the IJN would not be heading to Midway at all but to the south Pacific once again. Only after several days of agonizing uncertainty did King finally accept that his original assessment of Japanese intentions was probably wrong. Yet when he then asked the Royal Navy to relieve some of the pressure by launching diversionary operations in the Indian Ocean, the British declined, citing their own naval weakness and asserting that there was little evidence of any impending IJN attack against Alaska or Midway.[40] The army air corps and the marines rushed aircraft to Midway, more warships were dispatched to guard Hawaii's maritime approaches, and on 17 May King ordered Nimitz to create Task Force Eight (TF8) to defend Dutch Harbor. Declaring that a state of fleet-opposed invasion existed in the north Pacific, on 21 May King outlined new Alaskan command arrangements: Butler would report to TF8 commander Rear Admiral Robert A. Theobald, and Theobald's relationship with Buckner would be governed by mutual cooperation.[41]

As no aircraft carriers could be spared for Alaska, Theobald had to make due with five cruisers, a seaplane tender, six submarines, and thirteen destroyers. Nimitz had also instructed him to govern his forces "by the principle of calculated risk," meaning that Theobald had to avoid exposing his small force to enemy attack "without good prospect of inflicting, as result of such exposure, at least equal or greater damage to the enemy, or at least frustrating his plans." Then on 20 May, Nimitz went cap in hand to the army to ask for air corps planes for Cold Bay and Umnak since TF8, without any attendant carriers, would be almost completely dependent on the army air corps for defensive and offensive air cover. Meeting Nimitz's request proved difficult. The army had only eighty-one planes in Alaska, and Buckner doubted if he possessed the assets to hold Alaska's vital bases.[42] Although Marshall had deflected three MacArthur missives demanding more resources for the south Pacific with the assertion, "We are accepting great weakness in Alaska-Aleutian Theatre in [the] face of almost a certain heavy attack there,"[43] Arnold dashed the navy's slim hopes of getting many more army planes. Arnold had asked his staff on 18 May whether the Aleutians could support raids against Japan – and had been told that Attu and Agattu might be suitable if fuel-carrying gliders extended bomber ranges – but he did not assign any fighters to Umnak. Displeased that no planes were to be forthcoming, DeWitt decided to dispatch three squadrons from his WDC allocation. But Marshall blocked this transfer once DeWitt informed him that Umnak and Cold Bay could support air operations. As a result Arnold

Admiral Chester W. Nimitz, Commander-in-Chief Pacific Fleet, c. 1942.

brought Alaska's air force strength up to seventy-five fighters and thirty-four bombers.[44] Unable to shift any planes to Alaska without Washington's approval, DeWitt's only remaining alternative was to ask Canada's Pacific Command on 29 May to send two squadrons to Yakutat, east of Anchorage, within twenty-four hours; a delay of even one or two days, he stated, might have serious consequences.[45]

DeWitt had good reason to expect a favourable response because Canadian-American military relations had changed considerably since the 1930s. On 17 August 1940, with France vanquished and Britain tottering uncertainly before German might, Roosevelt had met Prime Minister King to discuss a Permanent Joint Board on Defence (PJBD), a binational agency designed to implement a continental security system. "Perfectly delighted with the whole thing," King had signed Roosevelt's document, according to Stimson, "almost with tears in his eyes." Then in July 1941 the PJBD produced Joint Defence Plan No. Two (ABC-22), with Canada and the United States pledging to jointly defend North America "to their utmost capacity."[46] Under the terms of ABC-22, Canada's navy and air force were obligated to assist Alaska in a crisis. Roosevelt had not allowed Canada to conveniently forget its pledges either. At the Pacific War Council's (PWC) inaugural meeting on 1 April, Roosevelt, commenting that Canada could be doing more in the Pacific, noted that if the Soviets allowed American bombers to use Siberia to attack Japan, the Aleutians could become far more important. If his nation was heavily engaged elsewhere, then Roosevelt might require Canadian assistance to secure Alaska and the Aleutians. State Department official John Hickerson explained to Canadian diplomats that the president had only been playing up Canada's part in the council vis-à-vis Australia and New Zealand, given Canada's recent refusal to assist Australia militarily.[47] Prime Minister King, however, seemed to have taken Roosevelt at his word. At the PWC on 15 April, Roosevelt declared that if Japan invaded the Aleutians, it might subsequently move against mainland Alaska. Agreeing that such a scenario would threaten Canada too, King said he might send some forces to Alaska "later on."[48]

DeWitt did not like the answer he got on 29 May. Claiming that a dearth of information about Japanese plans undermined their ability to make a considered decision, the Canadian Chiefs of Staff allowed the Canadian squadrons to go only as far as Annette Island in the Alaskan Panhandle where they would remain until circumstances dictated a later move to Yakutat. Very upset, DeWitt cabled Pacific Command's air force commander, Air Vice Marshal L.F. Stevenson, on 30 May to ask again for the Canadian planes, and then telephoned Pacific Command chief General R.O. Alexander in Vancouver to drive his demand home. Stevenson, who had been willing to respond affirmatively to DeWitt's initial request, agreed to provide the aircraft as long as Ottawa sent replacements immediately to British Columbia.[49] His Royal Canadian Air Force (RCAF) superiors were far less accommodating. Having agreed on 27 April to send fighters to Annette by 5 May, the RCAF objected when the PJBD asked American and Canadian west coast commanders to redistribute air strength. Maintaining that the PJBD initiative seemed to place the onus on Canada to provide air reinforcements in the event of enemy attack on Alaska, the RCAF asserted that aiding Alaska would be useful only if American forces there were strong. As this was clearly not the case, the air staff advised the Cabinet War Committee (CWC) on 14 May to restrict Canada's role in Alaska. Concurring, the CWC ruled that, since Alaska's defence was to remain America's primary concern, Canadian reinforcements would provide local air support in the Panhandle region only. When Minister of National Defence for Air C.G. Power's air staff met on 31 May, DeWitt's second request was stonewalled. Concurring with CGS Lieutenant General Kenneth Stuart, who thought sending planes to Alaska would expose British Columbia unnecessarily, the air staff announced that the Canadian planes would remain at Annette. That policy, Power said, would remain unaltered until the "situation developed further and [the] purpose of reported enemy concentrations more clearly indicated."[50]

DeWitt then requested Embick's personal intervention. It was a good choice; as a senior PJBD member and a trusted adviser to Roosevelt, Embick was in a position to get his enquiries answered. On 1 June he summoned Major General Maurice Pope, Canada's representative to the Combined Chiefs of Staff, to his office. Telling Pope that Midway Island and Dutch Harbor would be attacked shortly, Embick demanded immediate RCAF assistance. Believing that the Americans had seriously overstated the threat in the Pacific but certain that Embick's concerns were sincere, Pope counselled him to make the case directly to Air Commodore F.V. Heakes in Ottawa. Embick immediately telephoned Heakes to remind him that ABC-22's provisions required Canada to support American efforts to defend North America.[51] Four hours later the RCAF met DeWitt's request. By 3 June the first Canadian bombers had landed at Yakutat, arriving in time to carry out a short patrol over the Gulf of Alaska, "the first operational mission in support of Alaska Defense Command."[52] The fighters reached Anchorage on 8 June but with Japan's subsequent occupations of Attu and Kiska, the Canadian flyers discovered their return home would be significantly delayed.

The RCAF's official history argues that had Canada "been kept fully in the intelligence picture, the complicated and occasionally irascible negotiations" that had led to the Canadian reversal "might have been concluded with far less difficulty than they were." This claim is wrong. Ottawa certainly did not possess all of the raw information flowing within American military circles in May 1942, but the Canadian military had been warned on 18 May about Japan's impending offensive against Midway. Furthermore, three subsequent American dispatches had predicted when the enemy assaults might be expected and had outlined the size of the Japanese fleet approaching Alaska.[53] But while Australia's minister of foreign affairs, H.V. Evatt, cabled his prime minister from Britain on 28 May to say, "There is a fear in some quarters in the United States that Japan will attack Alaska," the Canadians seemed altogether unmoved by such dire apprehensions. That those messages raised few concerns in Ottawa can be explained in part by a strong Canadian military tendency – as exemplified by Pope – to downgrade the general Japanese threat in the Pacific. Further complicating matters, Canada's military and civilian leaders had been engaged in an often antagonistic struggle about the nature and scope of the national war effort from the very start of hostilities in 1939. Despite Skelton's plaintive argument in August 1939 that continental security alone could fully absorb the nation's martial energies, since Canadians could not "in this war ignore the Pacific as we did in the last," Canada's services had devoted nearly all of their resources to the fight against Germany. Even after Pearl Harbor, the Canadian Chiefs of Staff, who admitted that Allied defeats at the hands of the Japanese had adversely affected the Pacific strategic balance in Japan's favour, had declared that it was vitally important not to be "unduly diverted," as Germany remained the greatest threat to Britain. The Canadian army had therefore declined to commit to Alaska's defence in ABC-22 and had played a key role in blocking a PJBD attempt to incorporate British Columbia into an American-dominated unity of command system in 1941-2.[54]

Prime Minister King too had opposed unity of command, but he was conspicuously absent when the RCAF had tried to repel DeWitt's requests. Long concerned about the political threat conscription for overseas service might pose to his government, King had sought to fight a war of limited liability, only to see that wish dashed by France's collapse. Then, after 7 December he had hoped the possibility of Japanese attacks against British Columbia would curtail the growing Canadian military presence in Europe, as the public demanded more home defence. When Canada's military had not responded in the expected manner, King had told two sympathetic Canadian journalists on 27 February that Japan would soon attack Siberia, Alaska, and even British Columbia. By mid-March King had completely won his battle with the military; fearing his job had been at stake, Stuart had created three new home defence divisions.[55] Indeed, King had signalled his intentions on 21 April when he wrote to a supporter: "Not to be able to send planes and ships into American territory, as for example Alaska, and islands that lie beyond, is to risk much in the way of additional co-operation by the United States in the defence of our country, as well as their own, and to convey to American citizens generally a wholly erroneous impression, especially, where, as of present, they are sending troops and ships and men to the United Kingdom, to Australia, New Zealand and India. This is a very serious ground of misunderstanding to permit to continue for any length of time."[56]

While DeWitt was struggling to acquire the coveted Canadian planes, Buckner, Butler, and Theobald were getting acquainted at the USN headquarters on Kodiak on 27 May. The meeting did not go particularly well. As the crucial discussions unfolded, a number of maps repeatedly fell to the floor, prompting an obviously irritated Buckner to demand that Theobald "nail those damned maps on the wall." The admiral then ordered an aide to "batten the charts to the bulkhead," a phrase Brian Garfield alleges may have been deliberately chosen to emphasize Theobald's view that the north Pacific struggle was a naval war.[57] Theobald's relationship with Buckner had thus began badly, and many blamed the dogmatic admiral for the antipathy that developed between them. Lieutenant Commander James Russell, for example, noting that many of his fellow USN officers thought Theobald had sparked the conflict by making clear that Buckner knew nothing about naval combat, praised Buckner as "aggressive, something we appreciated very much"; Theobald, he judged, "was quite the other way." Although Theobald was seen by some as "a caricature of a military officer – rigid, pompous, incompetent and inflated with self-importance"[58] – the brash Buckner had a true talent for alienating even the most easygoing of men. After two years of hard, thankless slogging in an effort to get Alaska's meagre defences in shape, the ever-aggressive and action-oriented Buckner probably, and would naturally have, resented being suddenly "reduced to playing a supporting role to the cautious and cerebral Theobald."[59]

Yet personality conflicts do not fully explain the dismal origins of the Buckner-Theobald contretemps. Command unity also played a major part. After years of endless arguments, in 1935 the American services had reluctantly

Admiral Robert Theobald, 1942.

agreed to appoint theatre commanders to govern joint army-navy military action. But once war came, charging unity of command became a pointless slogan, and Admiral Stark declined Marshall's invitation for the USN to take control of Hawaii and Alaska, affirming that no single officer was qualified to make command decisions for both services. Admiral King's opinion of command unity was no less strident. Roosevelt's stated preference for a single Allied commander to oversee the entire Pacific conflict, and suggestions by some in Washington that MacArthur should fill that role, deeply rankled Ernest King. Most unwilling to allow any army officer to direct his precious fleets, King also protested against a March 1942 army proposal that would have placed the south Pacific firmly under MacArthur's sway. Never one to back down easily, King convinced his fellow Chiefs of Staff to create a separate Pacific Ocean Areas command headed by Nimitz, which in turn was further subdivided into north Pacific, central Pacific, and south Pacific areas. A profoundly disgruntled MacArthur had to content himself with the Southwest Pacific Area (SWPA), encompassing Australia, the Philippines, and the Dutch East Indies and surrounding islands. The JCS would be the final arbiter in Pacific strategy – a decision that went "against all common sense, against the dictates of military doctrine."[60]

In the absence then of command unity in the north Pacific area, as neither the navy nor the army was willing to surrender control of their respective forces, Buckner, Butler, and Theobald had to rely on their own mutual goodwill to get things done. They had agreed on 27 May that if Japan captured Umnak, Dutch Harbor, or Cold Bay, then an invasion of the Alaskan mainland would be declared imminent, clearing the way for regional unity of command. But Theobald had no intention of allowing that exigent eventuality to come to pass. Expecting a Japanese invasion of the Aleutians since February, Theobald pointedly ignored the intercepted Japanese plan that stated an intention to occupy only a handful of the islands in the western Aleutians. He believed instead that the enemy would seek to establish eastern Aleutian bases in order to prevent American bombers from reaching Japan and to take that preliminary step towards further Alaskan operations. Dividing his badly outgunned small fleet into six separate groups, Theobald retained personal command over three cruisers and four destroyers south of Kodiak, in a position to exploit favourable opportunities and deliver attrition attacks upon the enemy forces.[61]

Theobald's refusal to accept the Japanese plan at face value stemmed from his fervent distrust of American intelligence-gathering capabilities and enemy intentions. Theobald had noted acidly that USN intelligence had placed most of the IJN's main aircraft carriers in home waters or the south Pacific on 1 December 1941, when in fact they were secretly steaming towards their fateful rendezvous at Pearl Harbor. Moreover, a series of identical intercepted enemy transmissions in May 1942 had led him to conclude that "the Japanese desire certain information to reach us in the event that we are breaking their codes" in order to draw TF8 away from IJN's true intended objective or to trap his ships "between two strong Japanese forces."[62] In Theobald's defence, General Delos C. Emmons, Hawaii's army commander, told Nimitz on 25 May that CINCPAC was relying too heavily on reports of the enemy's intentions; instead the USN should base its plans on Japan's capabilities and the threat posed by land-based aircraft operating from the Mariana Islands. Neither could Butler accept the Japanese scheme in its entirety, and CINCPAC's Command Summary, noting that the IJN had changed its codes at May's end, pondered whether the enemy was "pulling our leg and using deception on a grand scale" in order to determine American dispositions. Lieutenant Colonel L.V. Castner, Buckner's chief intelligence officer, also believed Japan would attack Cold Bay, Dutch Harbor, or Umnak, although he could not exclude other localities. No one doubted, though, that the Japanese were coming. Three unidentified submarines were spotted in Aleutian waters in late May, one as far west as Umnak. Then on 24 May the USN's Kiska radio station spotted a Japanese seaplane, the first enemy aircraft seen in the region. Just when the first blow might occur was unclear. Bad weather was expected between 3 and 5 June, which would favour the Americans as poor weather usually severely limited carrier flight operations. Even so, Castner warned, Japan often used unsettled weather conditions to attempt covert beach landings.[63]

Dutch Harbor's exposed and anxious garrison was consumed by rampant rumours that 65,000 fanatical Japanese troops were approaching – a most unhappy prospect given that Alaska could boast only 37,690 military personnel on 1 June, and most of them sat rather uselessly at posts far to the east of Dutch Harbor. Just seventy-five army aircraft were serviceable with another seventy-four (excluding the Canadian squadrons) on the way. Otter Point and Cold Bay received their first planes on 1 June: twenty-four planes at Otter Point and twenty-two at Cold Bay. Otter Point was an extremely primitive facility. It lacked traffic control or runway lights, tents and huts had to be lit by candles, ground crews laboured in appalling and sometimes dangerous conditions, and base personnel had to subsist mostly on an unappealing and hardly nutritious diet of white bread and peanut butter.[64]

Japan's Aleutian expedition, commanded by Vice Admiral Hosogaya Moshiro, set out in distinct stages. Rear Admiral Kakuta Kikuji's Second Carrier Task Force, centred around the light carriers *Ryujo* and *Junyo*, left port on 24 May, followed by the slower moving troop ships and their escorts bound for Attu and Kiska. Yet Hosogaya knew rather little about his intended targets. In November 1941 IJN Operational Order No. One had said that the Aleutians should be occupied or devastated at the earliest opportune moment, but Japan's intelligence about the region was limited. In late November 1941 an IJN submarine had explored the archipelago, stopping first at Kiska where the vessel slipped covertly into the harbour. It then proceeded to Adak before heading to Dutch Harbor and then leaving the islands for the long voyage home on 30 November. Its captain had little to report beyond stating that American military preparations in the Aleutians were "very inadequate."[65] Hosogaya erroneously believed that Kiska's harbour froze over during the winter, IJN maps of Unalaska showed only a rough outline of the island's ragged coastline, and Japanese knowledge of Dutch Harbor was limited to just one chart and an unclear photograph dating from the 1920s. One Japanese intelligence estimate placed only light American forces in the Aleutians, another indicated strong garrisons at Dutch Harbor, Kiska, and Attu and suggested one or two USN carriers might be in Alaskan waters.[66] Much of this confusion can be attributed to a Japanese failure to properly appreciate the science of crypto-analysis and the fact the IJA and IJN lacked effective means or even the goodwill to exchange critical intelligence information easily. Some of these broad gaps were filled as Kakuta's force neared Dutch Harbor. Seaplanes had photographed Kiska in mid-May, but inclement weather had interfered with flights to Adak and Attu. Three I-class submarines, equipped with seaplanes, arrived in Aleutian waters in late May. Their patrols ferreted out no American installations on Kiska, Attu, or Adak, and located Theobald's naval force south of Kodiak. Attempts to study Dutch Harbor were frustrated initially when a seaplane crashed, forcing its parent submarine to examine the base at periscope depth on the night of 2 June. Despite the obvious limitations inherent in such an approach, the submersible accurately determined that Dutch Harbor's garrison amounted to 5,000 soldiers, not an entire division as had originally been thought to be the case. Kakuta thus beheld an opportunity to grab Dutch Harbor, but because Yamamoto thought Unalaska could not be retained or supplied easily, he instructed Kakuta to stick to the original raiding scheme.[67]

Kakuta's carriers reached their launch points 180 nautical miles south of Dutch Harbor on 3 June. Despite thick fog and low clouds, the Japanese pilots took off at 4:30 a.m. but when conditions did not markedly improve *Junyo*'s flight leader opted to turn his charges back to the carrier. Seventeen planes from the *Ryujo* soldiered on, arriving at Dutch Harbor just before 6:00 a.m. They met no aerial opposition because Dutch Harbor signallers could not contact the Otter Bay airfield for assistance. Forty minutes later, after losing only one plane to ground fire, the raiders returned to the carriers. As they reported having inflicted little real damage, the mission commanders felt a pressing need to undertake an immediate second assault. But one pilot thought that he had spotted some American ships sheltering in nearby Makushin Bay, so Kakuta instead dispatched planes to attack those vessels. Rapidly deteriorating weather conditions ended the search before the ships could be located, and as the weather was not expected to improve soon, Kakuta opted to turn his carriers towards Adak. Facing high seas to the west and a new forecast of clear skies to the east, Kakuta reversed course on 4 June. The second Japanese strike hit Dutch Harbor at 5:55 a.m. Again facing no American fighters, the raiders destroyed several fuel tanks, badly damaged a hospital, and crippled a transport ship without loss. Ignorant of Otter Bay's existence, the Japanese pilots chose to regroup just five kilometres from that airfield; it was an unlucky decision and the American fighters swooped down on their unsuspecting adversaries. In the ensuing dogfight two American and six Japanese aircraft were lost.[68]

Dutch Harbor would face no more attacks in view of the fact that Midway had ended catastrophically for the IJN. Although preliminary war game exercises had indicated that the IJN might lose two carriers in the anticipated confrontation, umpires unilaterally altered those unfavourable results.[69] Reality proved to be far worse as Yamamoto's armada was bushwhacked by a deadly and lucky USN that eliminated four IJN carriers and killed the finest of Japan's naval air service. Postwar judgments have laid the IJN's stunning defeat squarely on overconfidence, the product of a "victory disease" that had infected Japan's leadership after so many easy triumphs. In Midway's case, as two Japanese veterans of the battle point out, IJN planners seemed to complete their "work entirely on the basis of what the enemy would *probably* do, rather than what he might possibly do or what he was capable of doing." Samuel Eliot Morison argues that if Yamamoto had kept all of his ships together for one decisive blow aimed at Midway instead of scattering them across the central and north Pacific, the admiral would undoubtedly have won. Yamamoto's failure is thus blamed on a penchant for surprise and diversionary tactics. Still, according to historian Ronald H. Spector, most Japanese and American sailors would have found Yamamoto's plan familiar, as it was designed "to engage the American fleet no matter from which direction it came." More important, while the Midway operation was ill conceived and badly executed, "Yamamoto had the right idea: Unless Japan could inflict a shattering defeat on the U.S. early in the war, she would, gradually, be ground down by steadily growing American military power."[70]

Stunned by his severe losses, Yamamoto still controlled a formidable fleet. After briefly contemplating launching a complicated night assault on Midway with his remaining forces, Yamamoto despondently ordered a general withdrawal in the central Pacific and a temporary postponement of

Marines on alert between Japanese attacks on Dutch Harbor, 3 June 1942.

Aleutian operations on 5 June. Disagreeing, Hosogaya argued for the right to continue as planned in the Aleutians, since Kiska's occupation would neutralize Dutch Harbor and forestall any future American advance from the Aleutians. Reluctantly, Yamamoto acceded to his junior's request; Hosogaya could proceed with the landings on Kiska and Attu, but Adak's capture was abandoned due to the island's proximity to Umnak.[71] Just over 500 troops from the IJN's Third Special Landing Force splashed ashore on Kiska on 6 and 7 June, quickly capturing ten of eleven Americans sailors manning the USN weather station (a starving William House cleverly eluded capture until 28 July, when hunger forced him to surrender). Attu's occupation went just as smoothly. At 3:00 a.m. on 7 June, over 1,100 Japanese soldiers captured forty-two Aleuts plus school teacher Charles Foster and his wife Etta Jones. Foster committed suicide under mysterious circumstances, and the remaining captives were removed to Japan, where twenty-four more died in harsh captivity.[72]

In the wake of its Midway defeat, the IJN scrambled to downplay its misfortune while trumpeting its Aleutian successes. First, on 10 June the Japanese navy offered a very incomplete portrayal of what had transpired at Midway, declining to tell even the IJA about the extent of its losses, on the grounds that it was a military secret that could not be entrusted to all of the army members of the Liaison Conference. Only Emperor Hirohito saw the entire report.[73] Second, the IJN played up its minor victories in the Aleutians. American intelligence intercepted Japanese diplomatic messages claiming that the IJN offensive had blocked any sea routes that America might have used to attack Japan itself. Hosogaya seemed to believe such assertions, as he soon had second thoughts about leaving the region once winter had set in. Mistakenly convinced that American air raids against Kiska – which had started on 11 June – meant American air bases existed on Adak and Atka, Hosogaya feared that a precipitate Japanese withdrawal would see the Americans promptly return to the western Aleutians in strength. Agreeing with Hosogaya, on 23 June Imperial General Headquarters ordered the IJN and IJA to secure Kiska and Attu for the time being. Japanese ships also visited Amchitka to determine whether an airstrip could be established there. When no obvious site presented itself, the visitors left Amchitka unoccupied. A modicum of air protection came in late June when eighteen float-plane fighters arrived at Kiska, followed by a convoy in early July that brought 1,200 more soldiers and six midget submarines. Yet as the IJA appeared ready to stay in the Aleutians indefinitely, the IJN left only one destroyer squadron there. Japan's Aleutian operations had enjoyed a fair measure of success. Dutch Harbor had not been hit as hard as Hosogaya would have liked, but his losses had been light and the occupations of Kiska and Attu had gone smoothly. And while Otter Bay's fortuitous airfield had influenced Japan's decision not to occupy Adak, a *Reader's Digest* claim in 1943 that the facility had saved Alaska from invasion is untrue.[74] Japan had no intention of invading mainland Alaska, which was a task beyond its operational capabilities (especially after Midway's losses) even if Japan had possessed a strategic rationale to justify such an assault.

Alaska's defenders, however, could not be certain about Japan's short- or long-term intentions. Although the Australian army had predicted in late 1941 that Japan might attack the Aleutians only because "a force proceeding from Northern Asia against the Hawaiians would leave the Aleutians on its left and rear,"[75] some Americans did not believe Japan's aims were so limited. In the frantic hours immediately following the first Dutch Harbor attack, DeWitt feared that Kakuta might raid as far south as Seattle. Castner thought it far more likely that Dutch Harbor was endangered, given Japan's practice of first bombing and then seizing intended targets. When Japan failed to grab Dutch Harbor, Castner suggested that the enemy, perhaps having incurred heavier losses than anticipated, might be rethinking its strategic options. Castner felt certain that once that re-evaluation was complete, Japan would attempt to wear down American air strength relentlessly before assaulting Umnak, Dutch Harbor, and Cold Bay. Theobald again disagreed. Believing that Japan was deliberately biding its time, waiting for the propitious arrival of better weather and more aircraft, the admiral mused again that the Dutch Harbor raids had been intended to draw an unsuspecting TF8 west into a waiting murderous trap.[76]

Theobald had other problems to consider. The army accused him of withholding news that the Japanese fleet had been detected over 600 kilometres south of Kiska on 2 June, and for failing to mention that the USN had lost contact with its Kiska station until two days had passed. In addition, the army liaison officer at navy headquarters on Kodiak claimed that his USN colleagues had said they were "too busy" to let him read several vital messages.[77] The army's case had considerable merit. The navy had been far too slow in disseminating badly needed information, and inter-service rivalry and ill-defined command procedures had only exacerbated the problem.

However, Theobald's ill-considered judgment to maintain radio silence while at sea had been an unwise choice for an officer charged with the command of a vast region subject to enemy assault. Although Theobald later cited three reasons for his decision – the absence of another flag officer to command the task group, the earlier rebuke of an admiral in the south Pacific who had established his headquarters ashore, and his claim that no one had ever envisaged commanding sea-going units from headquarters ashore – his mediocre performance in early June very nearly cost him his job. Theobald just managed to retain his post, despite an assertion that Alaska's complex strategic circumstances required a naval aviation expert, only when Admiral Freeman personally intervened.[78]

If blame was to be meted out, Theobald doubted any of it rested on his shoulders. On 3 June he had ordered his limited air assets to strike at the IJN task force. The following day, when Kakuta's carriers were spotted south of Unalaska, American planes had failed to hit any enemy vessels, at the high cost of eleven aircraft, despite using positively reckless tactics (including jury-rigging army bombers with torpedoes). Theobald had praised the navy aviators involved while criticizing army air attacks as poorly coordinated and inaccurate, the result of what he saw as the army's psychological overattachment to high-altitude bombing. He had been displeased too with Butler's level of cooperation. The air commander had initially objected to Theobald's suggestion in late May to shift aircraft west of Dutch Harbor. While Butler had backed down shortly thereafter, Theobald was displeased upon returning to Kodiak on 5 June to find a two-day-old telegram from Butler stating that he could not move any bombers to Cold Bay unless directly ordered to do so. Certain that Butler had already agreed to send those planes forward, Theobald had then ordered him to attack, even though the admiral felt very awkward about directing the senior officer of another service and was worried that lukewarm compliance by Butler might produce surface obedience while injuring the creation of a cohesive force capable of defending Alaska.[79]

Thus, in the interest of forming a well-knit force, Theobald registered his complaints only with his navy superiors. Hopes that the matter would be handled in a low-key fashion abruptly vanished when the army asked DeWitt on 6 June to determine whether Butler had been too slow to respond to navy requests. Incensed, Buckner defended any delays as the product of poor communications, a paucity of planes, and the fact that exhausted army air crews had been engaged in stressful round-the-clock operations. Greatly embarrassed that the matter had not been kept private, Theobald and Nimitz had assured Buckner that they were fully satisfied with the army's effort. If such remarks mollified Buckner, the dispute compelled Governor Ernest Gruening to demand a unified command system for Alaska, a demand that again went unfulfilled.[80]

Concerns about command arrangements soon took a back seat when a lumbering PBY-5 amphibious aircraft discovered four Japanese vessels safely anchored in Kiska's harbour on 11 June. As late as 9 June, Rear Admiral C.M. Cooke, King's chief planner, doubted if any Japanese surface vessels remained in Alaskan waters. An unsurprised Theobald directed USN Patrol Wing Four, comprising twenty slow-moving PBYs (patrol boatplanes), to bomb Kiska to prevent the enemy from consolidating its hold. This "Kiska blitz" lasted just three days before Japanese planes chased the seaplane tender USS *Gillis* from Atka. For the loss of two PBYs, the Americans had managed to damage just one Japanese destroyer and had interfered only slightly with

Brigadier General W.O. Butler, Commanding Officer 11th Air Force, and Colonel William O. Eareckson, 11th Air Force, at Fort Glenn, Umnak, 1942.

base construction on Kiska. Army aircraft operating from Umnak continued attacks whenever weather permitted, but little damage was done despite the efforts of Colonel William (Wild Bill) Eareckson.[81] A tactical innovator whose brash attitude, reckless manner (he frequently took on the most dangerous missions), and maverick spirit endeared him to his men and frequently frustrated his superiors, Eareckson became the Aleutian's first larger-than-life hero, often singing to his rookie pilots as they undertook their dangerous raids "to keep their minds on that and they would follow him."[82] They would have ample opportunity to follow Eareckson over the next fifteen months.

All Commanders on Minor Fronts
Regard Their Own Actions As Highly Important:
July 1942 to January 1943

In his seminal and much quoted analysis of politics and military conflict, the renowned nineteenth-century Prussian officer and strategist Carl von Clausewitz noted: "The whole of military activity must ... relate directly or indirectly to the engagement." That is, a soldier was recruited, clothed, armed, and trained "simply that he should fight at the right place and the right time." Further, Clausewitz maintained, "there is no higher and simpler law of strategy than that of keeping one's forces concentrated."[1] But determining just where and when one should fight, of course, is often no easy matter. First, an enemy's intentions are rarely ever known with any certainty, and thus planning to meet a foe's anticipated activities can be a matter of educated guesswork. Second, modern military strategy is usually devised not by one great commander, as in Clausewitz's time (his great exemplar had been Napoleon Bonaparte), but by a committee. And as the truism goes, a horse designed by committee would probably resemble a camel. After Japan's occupation of Attu and Kiska in June 1942, the American military response was badly hampered by a lack of command unity, personality clashes, and the stresses and strains of a global war fought by a multi-nation coalition. The resulting strategic plan for the north Pacific satisfied few.

Admiral Theobald thought that Japan's failure to move east of Kiska after 11 June revealed far more limited enemy goals than he had initially feared. No longer overly concerned that Umnak or Dutch Harbor were in any immediate danger, the admiral believed that the Japanese military would seek simply to retain Attu and Kiska in order to flank Siberia if Japan and the Soviets came to blows. Conversely, Theobald also postulated that Japan might seek to entice American forces to attempt to recapture the lost islands, leaving them vulnerable in turn to attacks from the IJN and land-based aviation. Castner did not share Theobald's assessment. Unless enemy reinforcements were quickly and effectively interdicted, Japan would begin building airstrips on Kiska and Attu to support further advances towards Dutch Harbor. As long as Umnak remained America's westernmost outpost in the Aleutians, Japan's attenuated supply line to Kiska and Attu could be threatened only by USN vessels, an option that would become considerably less effective and far more dangerous once Japanese land-based aviation was operating from Aleutian airstrips. What American forces needed now, Castner argued, were air bases west of Umnak. Amchitka seemed to be the best place but Atka, Kanaga, Adak, and Tanaga might be useful too, and Castner wanted to act speedily as any delays would conspire to favour the enemy.[2]

Castner's keen sense of urgency prompted varying responses. On 12 June DeWitt asked Marshall for four bomber squadrons and an infantry regiment to buttress Alaska. Freeman went even further, advocating an amphibious force backed by carriers to clear the enemy from the Aleutians. Yet this sense of exigency did not exist elsewhere. While he deemed an offensive spirit highly admirable, Captain Parker saw very little logic in establishing any new bases west of Umnak when existing American facilities in the north Pacific region were so weak.[3] The USN's senior leadership agreed. Although King had directed Admiral Nimitz on 6 June to send two carriers, six cruisers, and nine destroyers to Theobald, that plan was soon altered. Believing initially that public opinion would loudly demand a quick riposte in the Aleutians to retake lost American territory, Nimitz ordered Task Force Sixteen to move north from Midway to the Aleutians. Cooler heads then prevailed. Fearing that Yamamoto might be setting an ambush in Aleutian waters (shades of Theobald) and having learned of the possible presence of four Japanese carriers in the north Pacific near Alaska, Nimitz pulled Task Force Sixteen and its scarce flattops back to Hawaii on 11 June. King declined to overrule Nimitz's decision on this matter as he and Cooke, his intellectual alter ego, decided by 14 June that Attu and Kiska could not support Japanese offensive operations. Surmising that Japan's Aleutian invasion was expressly designed to draw American resources away from more vital regions, King and Cooke also concluded that the enemy had grabbed Attu and Kiska in order to attack Siberia or perhaps Alaska's Bering Sea coast. Therefore they recommended negotiating access to Siberian military facilities, fortifying the town of Nome, and putting more planes in the Aleutians to attack Kiska.[4] But the USN intended to do very little in the north Pacific.

Political considerations then intervened. While Governor Gruening feared 10,000 Japanese were "obviously planning to use our Aleutian 'stepping stones' to step our way," Secretary Stimson doubted Japan would push home any Aleutian attacks after its catastrophic Midway defeat. Still, as the secretary noted on 7 June, the president was "troubled of course by the situation in Alaska." The evidence of Roosevelt's interest in the Aleutians, however, is inconclusive and contradictory, as is so much about Roosevelt. On 7 April 1942 Roosevelt had told the Pacific War Council (PWC) that Japan's Aleutian attacks would be significant only because of their potential psychological effect on the American public.[5] Yet in mid-May the president had personally ordered Commander Paul Foster to the Aleutians to investigate rumours of an impending Japanese attack. To Foster's surprise, when his two seaplanes left Kodiak on 18 May for points west, against the express wishes of his own apprehensive Alaskan staff, Buckner had accompanied Foster's party. The group had met a seaplane tender at Kiska a few days later, which had brought numerous desperate messages about Japan's impending attack. Buckner had finally agreed to return to Kodiak on one plane; Foster's craft had followed just a few hours later. Buckner's feckless decision to accompany Foster had been an act of pointless bravado, especially with Japanese forces bearing down on the Aleutians. Foster, too, must have wondered if his Aleutian journey might be hazardous to his career prospects. He realized that his connection to Roosevelt might prove problematic given Admiral King's dogged belief that only he and Leahy should advise the president on naval matters. Further, he feared that he might have stepped into more trouble on returning to Washington in early June by being honest about what he had seen. Asked to meet Roosevelt, Stimson, Secretary of the Navy Frank Knox, and Marshall over the course of two days, Foster delivered such a stinging condemnation of Alaskan communications practices that Marshall decided immediately to shake up the army communications command drastically.[6] A less honourable army commander might have sought Foster's head instead.

The Aleutians debate dominated a cabinet meeting on 5 June. Stimson's bald confession that Alaska lacked sufficient military resources greatly bothered Vice President Henry Wallace. Keenly interested in exploiting an air route to Siberia and concerned that "we have not paid enough attention as we ought to Alaska," Wallace lobbied the president four days later to use Alaska to launch aerial attacks against the Japanese home islands. Roosevelt's typically breezy response was that while Japan might have momentarily taken possession of some distant Aleutian islands, "we could take them back just as easily." When Roosevelt met again with the PWC on 17 June, he described America's north Pacific forces as adequate except for a critical air power shortage. Speaking again to the PWC on 25 June, he noted that while he was somewhat disturbed by the uncertain situation, Japanese forces in the Aleutians were "small, even somewhat infinitesimal as regards ships and men." Looking upon the Pacific conflict as a whole, the president affirmed that Alaska was "definitely in third place insofar as priority of attention on our part is concerned."[7]

Roosevelt did have some concerns, however. On 17 June he warned Stalin about the possibility of Japanese attacks on Siberia and asked the Soviet leader to allow some American aircraft to be based in eastern Siberia. After a slight delay, Stalin agreed to talk and Roosevelt dispatched Major General Follett Bradley to Moscow in late July. Months of frustrating negotiations led to the creation of an Alaska-Siberia air route to deliver Lend-Lease supplies to the Soviets, but utterly failed to gain the Americans access to any Soviet military facilities.[8] Marshall also instructed Buckner to quickly buttress Nome; by early July over 140 plane loads of men and supplies had arrived in that remote outpost, bumping its previously tiny garrison to over 2,000 troops. And when the Joint Chiefs of Staff (JCS) discussed the Aleutians on 15 June, it agreed that Japanese forces should be expelled quickly from Attu and Kiska so they would have no time to dig themselves in. The army also promised to provide eight new squadrons plus replacement aircraft and crews to the Eleventh Air Force.[9]

Such news was tremendously encouraging given that DeWitt had asked Marshall on 14 June about using army and marine units, supported by the bulk of the Pacific fleet, to retake Kiska and draw the IJN into a decisive confrontation in the north Pacific. Not at all inclined to trust the navy's good offices, Buckner suggested occupying Tanaga Island so that land-based army air power could support Kiska operations. DeWitt and Buckner soon had reason to suspect that their needs were not being taken seriously when Brigadier General Lawrence Kuter arrived in Alaska in mid-June. Sent to inspect Butler's command, Kuter promptly alienated Buckner by telling him upon his arrival that the "higher ups who made decisions in Washington" regarded the Aleutians as unimportant. When Buckner testily retorted that it was his job to defend Alaska and to eject the intruding Japanese, Kuter allegedly replied that Buckner's old mission no longer mattered. Announcing his intent to tell DeWitt that Buckner should stop asking for more help, Kuter told Buckner that he was "in the same position as all commanders on minor fronts who regard their own action as highly important, when those higher ups do not take it seriously."[10]

Marshall found himself in a very difficult position. At age thirty-six Kuter was the youngest general in the American army, and had been lauded in the press as an organizing genius blessed with matinee idol looks. Not only did the army chief of staff know Kuter, he had been so impressed by the young officer's ability when they had first met that he had told Arnold to promote Kuter from the rank of major to brigadier general. When Arnold had declined on the grounds that such a dramatic step would alienate the rest of his staff, Marshall had taken the matter into his own hands, promoting Kuter twice in a matter of months.[11] Yet Marshall also had to take Buckner's complaints very seriously, especially when DeWitt warned that Kuter's comments could dangerously undermine Alaskan morale. Maintaining that there must have been some sort of misunderstanding, Marshall gently assured Buckner that his situation was important. No doubt the army chief had a word with Kuter too, for when he subsequently conferred with DeWitt in San Francisco, Kuter claimed that he had not meant to imply that Alaskan operations were not vital. But as Kuter also argued that there was no immediate need to reduce Kiska, an opinion with which DeWitt emphatically disagreed, the Western Defense Command (WDC) chief judged Kuter most insincere.

Then, when DeWitt called on Arnold on 3 July to deplore Kuter's attitude and to press for more aggressive action in the Aleutians, Arnold, counter to DeWitt's expectations, disputed DeWitt's claim that 8,000 Japanese troops were present on Kiska. Concerned that Aleutian air operations could not produce worthwhile results due to poor weather, Arnold decried the "ever increasing tendency to drag more and more airplanes into this theater when in reality it should be the job for ground troops, amphibious troops, and naval vessels, supplemented by a small number of air planes." Arnold therefore wanted to withdraw three Alaskan fighter squadrons in preparation for a major Anglo-American North African offensive planned for late 1942.[12]

Kuter sought to bolster Arnold's position with a press release on 5 July, and it was carried in dozens of American newspapers. Though dismal weather was hindering aerial missions in the Aleutians, Kuter made clear that American pilots were already inflicting severe damage on the Japanese in the region, implying that Butler's command did not require strengthening. On the other hand, Nimitz was willing at least to consider a limited north Pacific offensive. An urbane Texan with a pronounced fondness for classical music, good food, and drink, Nimitz had a reputation as "a realist who possessed an immense capacity for work, a talent for obtaining the best results from others, an almost impeccable judgment of men, and a genius for making prompt decisions."[13] On 29 June he informed King that, since Kakuta's carriers finally appeared to be departing Aleutian waters, the army could take over Attu and Kiska once they had been recovered and then build an airfield on Amchitka, after which Nimitz could provide a marine battalion and some ships. But while his staff recommended keeping two carriers in the north Pacific, King said the marines and ships would be needed in the upcoming Solomon Islands campaign. Until the army found troops for Adak and Atka, King would not move against Kiska and Attu, doubtful that the USN would counter an expected Japanese riposte even if he pulled ships (including carriers) from south Pacific waters. Nor could King determine why holding Kiska would aid either side, "as said possession presented opportunities to [the] other side for profitable attrition tactics." Consequently, when the JCS decided on 2 July to undertake a Pacific offensive in 1942, it chose to fight in the south Pacific rather than in the Aleutians.[14]

Very unhappy with these decisions, Wallace and DeWitt launched their own lobbying offensives. First, the vice president badgered Frank Knox about Alaska. His lobbying was not a good idea for two reasons. The secretary of the navy argued that Japan had moved into the Aleutians simply to track weather coming in from Siberia. Convinced that Japan would move again in the north Pacific by the autumn, Wallace failed to rouse a complacent Knox "because he is resting peacefully in the arms of his admirals." More important, as Samuel Huntington makes all too clear, both Knox and Stimson wielded rather little real power in the Roosevelt administration. As former Republicans recruited by Roosevelt, many other Democratic administration officials regarded them warily. Moreover, they met infrequently with the president and the Joint Chiefs, almost never attended overseas wartime conferences, and had practically no input in the making of military strategy. No doubt realizing his mistake, Wallace again approached Roosevelt, averring that it would be psychologically and tactically sound to remove the Japanese from the Aleutians as soon as possible. Agreeing that ejection made sense psychologically, the president declared that the USN felt very strongly "that it was not a sound thing to do tactically." Unwilling to accept such explanations, on 16 July DeWitt asked permission to occupy Tanaga to forestall Japanese advances and to provide an advanced base for operations against Kiska. DeWitt's request was well timed, for the Military Intelligence Division (MID), cautioning that Japan might move east, sought airfields on Adak, Atka, and Tanaga. Paul Foster, declaring that the need to eject Japan from the archipelago was "so crystal clear as to need no explanation," thought airstrips could be put on Kanaga, Amchitka, and Shemya, the island nearest to Attu. T.H. Robbins, one of Cooke's aides, did not think that a Shemya airstrip was workable since the island was probably in Japanese hands. But because Amchitka showed promise, he backed a step-by-step advance to such islands once army forces became available.[15]

More propitiously, DeWitt's proposal had come when King and Marshall, frustrated by Britain's refusal to countenance Europe's invasion in 1942, were reconsidering American strategy. Although Marshall later intimated to Roosevelt that his support for the "Pacific-First" alternative had been a bluff to compel Britain to accept an early invasion of western Europe, King had been entirely sincere – but the president angrily vetoed the idea on 14 July. Dramatically dressing down a chastened Marshall for even considering an option that Roosevelt likened to "taking up your dishes and going away," the president contended that a Pacific-First strategy had to be rejected because taking the Pacific islands would not affect the world situation before 1944 and because that is "exactly what Germany had hoped the United States would do following Pearl Harbor."[16] Marshall had got off relatively easily given that MacArthur's frequent demands for a Pacific-First policy had led Roosevelt to state that military commanders at Pearl Harbor had very nearly been charged for the same kind of "criminal behavior" MacArthur had exhibited in the Philippines.[17] Notwithstanding presidential opposition, by July 1942 fully 60 percent of the army's overseas ground forces (520,000 troops) and 1,300 of its 2,200 aircraft were stationed in the Pacific theatre.[18] According to historian Mark Stoler, this allocation of resources was far from accidental as the Joint Chiefs, convinced that Roosevelt "was pursuing a militarily and politically disastrous approach as a result of Churchill's baneful influence," had opted for a de facto Pacific-First strategy. Thus, they were receptive to DeWitt's Aleutian scheme. On 23 July the army asked the navy to authorize an occupation of Tanaga and possibly Adak, under Theobald's direction. The navy agreed, provided Tanaga and Adak could be adequately secured against weather and enemy attack.[19]

Theobald had other ideas. He later claimed that he had been bombarded by innumerable nagging dispatches about his plans, dispatches he was certain were knee-jerk reactions to journalists harping on the fact American territory was in enemy hands. Without sufficient forces at hand, Theobald thought little could be done. So after requesting a delay because his ships were scheduled to bombard Kiska on 22 July and because he believed the Tanaga landing would require twice as many ships as he had (including a carrier), the admiral concluded that Tanaga's inadequate anchorage and surrounding high seas rendered it a poor base site. He plumped for Adak, 100 kilometres east of Tanaga, because it possessed an excellent natural harbour. But as Adak lacked flat terrain necessary for an airstrip, Buckner and DeWitt opposed the substitution. The JCS had to break the stalemate. Reconnaissance over-flights had revealed numerous gun emplacements on Kiska and definite signs the Japanese were preparing an airfield. Furthermore, intelligence estimated 8,000 troops were concentrated on Attu and Kiska, although the enemy might have occupied Agattu, Amchitka, and Adak too. Facing such disturbing evidence, the Joint Planning Staff (JPS) supported DeWitt's Tanaga plan, only to see King convince Marshall and Arnold to switch to Adak. The new directive, issued on 22 August, called for diversionary assaults on Atka and Tanaga while the main force attacked Adak.[20] When scouts found Adak unoccupied, Theobald rushed 4,500 soldiers there on 30 August. Atka was occupied on 16 September while Tanaga's landing was cancelled. On

Adak, the Americans discovered a tidal basin that, once drained, would serve as an acceptable runway. Working feverishly, engineers had a rudimentary runway operational in under two weeks. On 14 September Kiska was raided by planes flying from Adak, though the Japanese discovered the American presence only on 1 October, far too late to do anything about it. Adak's bloodless capture was a major coup, but the ongoing Buckner-Theobald feud would overshadow that triumph.

While their personal relationship had not started well at Kodiak in May 1942, the conflict between Buckner and Theobald had remained mostly quiescent in the following weeks, only to worsen considerably once DeWitt issued his Tanaga proposal. Disparaging Theobald's innate cautiousness, Buckner took strong exception to the admiral's opposition to occupying Tanaga, an operation Buckner had suggested to DeWitt. So when the Alaskan commanders sat down on 19 August to thrash out plans for Adak, Buckner made frequent acerbic remarks, which Theobald regarded as "an attack upon me, making it clear that, in his opinion, my recommendations were prompted by my unwillingness to accept necessary and proper wartime risks." Then Buckner regaled the assembly with a colourful doggerel that directly questioned Theobald's personal courage. Understandably incensed, Theobald speedily wired the offending ode to Admiral King and severed all informal contacts with Buckner. Professing profound astonishment at this unexpected turn of events, a defensive Buckner exclaimed that he had intended only to introduce some humour into an otherwise ponderous discussion with the poetic recitation. Adding that he felt no ill will towards Theobald, Buckner thought he and Theobald had thus "mutually smoked each other out" and that the "smoke would blow away with sufficient promptness to give us an unobstructed view of the Japs."[21]

Marshall's biographer claims Buckner either seriously misjudged Theobald's sense of humour or poked fun out of sheer boyish exuberance. Whatever the case, Buckner's misstep nearly cost him his job. Marshall was apparently told that Buckner had contemptuously mocked Theobald, a transgression that "might have been passed over," given Buckner's abilities, were it not for the poem. Despite his own long-standing friendship with Theobald, King considered removing the admiral, and Marshall thought he should respond in kind, though hopefully in a way that would not reflect badly on Buckner. Butler would also be relieved, although Marshall and King agreed to remove no one until Adak was secured, after which "there would be no foundation for comment regarding the change." If that landing failed, Marshall feared "we would have a difficult problem on our hands."[22]

Ironically, Theobald ensured that Buckner and Butler retained their positions. Journeying to Alaska in mid-September, intent on cashiering both Buckner and Butler, DeWitt was startled to hear Theobald praise Butler as a conscientious subordinate who had been demonstrating hitherto unseen leadership qualities. Moreover, though still quite irate, Theobald also opposed relieving Buckner on the grounds that he may not have made his Tanaga objections sufficiently clear for fear of offending DeWitt. Once Theobald's interview with DeWitt ended, Theobald summoned a nervous Buckner to his office and offered his hand in friendship. Buckner eagerly agreed and, greatly pleased, DeWitt immediately asked Marshall to cancel the impending transfers of Buckner, Butler, and Theobald. Marshall was less eager to comply, especially when DeWitt and Theobald immediately engaged in their own small contretemps regarding Pribilof Island garrisons. Sincerely puzzled as to why Alaska seemed to engender so many misunderstandings, Marshall thought Buckner should be transferred quickly, adding that it would be best to shift Butler and Theobald later on. King disagreed. On 7 September he and Nimitz had agreed to support Theobald with the important proviso that if relations between Theobald and Buckner worsened, a move might be in order. Much impressed by DeWitt's sure handling of the sticky situation, King convinced Marshall to reconsider the command shakeup, even though Marshall thought there was no escaping the fact that Buckner had demonstrated a lack of faith in Theobald's willingness to engage the enemy: "However much they may have patched up their differences no man can forget such implications."[23]

DeWitt's skilful handling of this delicate and potentially embarrassing problem did not help him much in a subsequent controversy. As noted previously, the military's initially confused response to Japan's Aleutian offensive in June 1942 had led Gruening to demand a unified command. Foster had also urged the navy in late July to appoint a vice admiral to command an Alaskan theatre of operations. While command unity was no panacea, Foster thought it would be better than the existing system because "experience has taught the futility of attempting control in a theater of actual war operations under a council of co-commanders each with his own inviolate sector." Major General Thomas Handy, of the Office of the Director of Plans and Operations (OPD), doubted whether army and navy officers would accept all the "details involved in the exercise of unity of command unless they, as individuals, are predisposed to agree, even at the sacrifice of their individual prerogatives." It was also unlikely that the services could accede to command unity since naval officers, by virtue of their training and the need to coordinate ship movements, thought about missions in very specific terms. Conversely, army officers tended to adopt a broader interpretation. Despite that, Handy thought there could be no excuse for withholding support from a leader exercising unity of command in a theatre. If the navy and army made that point patently clear, it would do more "to force essential cooperation and reduce much fruitless controversy between the two Services."[24]

Given their past problems with the issue, the services were understandably reluctant to address Alaskan command unity. However, the military found its hand forced by politicians. On 13 July 1942 Robert L. Reynolds, chair of the Senate's Military Affairs Committee, had set up a subcommittee, led by Kentucky Senator Albert E. Chandler, to study the military situation in Alaska and the Aleutians. There was little doubt about the subcommittee's point of view, as Reynolds had already demanded the creation of major Aleutians bases in order to threaten Japan. Moreover, Chandler enjoyed a well-deserved reputation as Congress's most ardent advocate of pre-emptive moves against Japan.[25] As Chandler bluntly explained to the media on 7 August, "People all over the country are more alarmed over the Aleutian situation than about any other phase of the war" – no doubt a reference to public opinion polls finding that, while only 21 percent of Americans could accurately locate Hawaii on a map, 73 percent could identify the Aleutians.[26] Wishing to put the best face forward, Assistant Secretary of the Army John McCloy met with Reynolds and Chandler on 21 July. The army agreed to show the senators anything they might wish to see, while advising the navy about the desirability of presenting the issue of Alaskan defence on "a highly coordinated, team basis." Chandler and associates spent just thirteen days in Alaska, mostly near Anchorage; the committee's visits to Dutch Harbor and Umnak lasted only one-half day. Upon returning home, Chandler exclaimed that although he "felt a whole lot better than when he left for Alaska," he was "alarmed that the military had not given full consideration to Japanese in the Aleutians." His preliminary report, ready on 7 September and arguing the vital need to safeguard the territory's future role as a base for assaulting Japan itself, recommended unified command in Alaska. Moreover, troops and aircraft should be diverted in numbers sufficient "not only adequate to repel any attacks – but to take the offensive at the earliest possible time and dislodge the Japanese troops from the American islands near the Alaskan Mainland."[27]

An outright rejection of Chandler's recommendations was uncertain. In May 1941 the army had flirted briefly with the idea of making the Alaska Defense Command (ADC) a separate theatre command because of its peculiar geography, its isolation, and the special role air power played in safeguarding Alaska. That initiative had stalled despite congressional support for an air force officer to lead the ADC.[28] Still, Marshall told DeWitt on 3 September that although Alaska benefited greatly from WDC resources, it might now be time to make the ADC a separate command led by an air force general. Having vehemently opposed the 1941 initiative, DeWitt viewed the entire North American west coast from Alaska to Mexico as an indivisible geo-strategic whole, labelling any other conception untenable. Arguing that Alaska could "no more be separated from the west coast of the United States in a military sense than it can from a physical or geographical viewpoint," and that tinkering with a workable system could not be justified "by the facts or the practical experience of actual operations," DeWitt demanded that the matter be "dropped indefinitely until when and if a large scale offensive against the Japanese Empire itself is initiated."[29]

DeWitt, however, was facing allegations that he had said too much to Chandler. On 11 September Marshall had asked him to address claims that he had discussed the Adak operation (code-name Fireplace) and the Buckner-Theobald dispute with the senators. The alleged indiscretion had become a hot topic in Congress, thereby "provok[ing] a most serious situation." DeWitt admitted mentioning possible operations against Attu and Kiska and acknowledged telling the senators that Fireplace was pending. But he adamantly denied broaching the Buckner-Theobald clash with Chandler or any of his associates. He resolutely maintained that he had adroitly handled a delicate situation, adding that he had received no guidelines from Washington. Furthermore, he claimed to have warned the senators about the dangers of acquiring secret information "that would, if divulged, lead to great embarrassment" for the military.[30]

DeWitt survived this particular tempest; Chandler's recommendations did not. The JPS dismissed plans to retake Kiska because the USN was in no position to act, given its heavy commitments elsewhere. As to unity of command, the Chiefs carefully weighed all the factors involved, "with the full realization of the necessity for achieving the maximum practicable unity of command, with regard to the realities of the existing situation and the complications produced by geographical, weather and communications considerations," and they agreed that the current system worked. As for giving Alaska more military help, the Chiefs concurred that, while a speedy expansion of Alaskan forces was obviously desirable, their duty was to allocate resources in a manner best calculated to carry out national strategic aims. Given the many competing demands in a vast global conflict, Alaska received the same considerations as any other theatre. Therefore the JCS could "state positively that at any given time the military and naval forces, aircraft and other equipment in the Alaskan area will be the maximum consistent with the over-all strategy of the war."[31]

Adak's consolidation was next on the agenda. Theobald had told Nimitz on 16 September that given Adak's value for further operations, its distance from support facilities, and the chance of Japanese counterattacks, it should be assigned a full division (25,000 men) rather than the planned 5,000-man garrison. Nimitz agreed (as did Buckner), although DeWitt offered only 15,000 soldiers for Adak and 4,000 for Tanaga. Approving those dispositions, Marshall declined DeWitt's request for six air groups for the ADC since there was now "a definite emergency in the South and Southwest Pacific [Guadalcanal], while none is apparent in Hawaii or the Aleutians." Faced with severe manpower and aircraft shortages and forced against his better judgment to accept the impending politically motivated November 1942 invasion of North Africa, Marshall did not think it was feasible to assign any additional combat units to Alaska unless unforeseen developments dictated otherwise.[32]

Marshall had not exaggerated his problems. Although the loftily ambitious 1941 Victory Program had called for the creation of 213 army divisions, subsequent insatiable demands for industrial manpower, the formation of 273 air groups, keen competition with the navy for warm bodies, and various other complications meant only seventy-four divisions would be ready by 1943.[33] In addition, DeWitt was not the only commander crying out plaintively for more aid. Absolutely convinced that his great many enemies would rather see him "lose a battle than America win a war," MacArthur had also been shrilly demanding even more resources for his torturously costly New Guinea campaign. While somewhat sympathetic, on 4 August Marshall informed MacArthur in no uncertain terms "that the pressures to meet the growing dangers of the situation in the Aleutians, to build up again the depleted air force in Hawaii, to meet the debacle in the Middle East, not to mention Russia, China, the losses in ocean tonnage, and the urgent necessity of creating new air squadrons sufficiently trained and equipped to go overseas, make our problem exceedingly difficult and complex."[34] MacArthur may have had something to complain about. From September to December 1942, Alaska fared pretty well in the logistical allocation battle, getting 16,000 new troops and 547,000 tons of cargo; the south Pacific received 36,000 soldiers and 310,000 tons of material, while MacArthur got merely 8,300 men and 157,000 tons.[35]

Concerns about formidable Japanese counterstrokes against Adak proved erroneous. In March and July 1942 Japan's military leadership had estimated that America would not be able to launch a major counter-offensive anywhere in the Pacific until late 1943 at the earliest. Given this highly optimistic (and incorrect) assessment, the Japanese felt assured that they could continue attacks on New Guinea and in the Solomon Islands in relative safety. Indeed, strategic unreality still seemed to be firmly in place in Tokyo, for while tentative plans to occupy Fiji and Samoa were dropped by the IJN in early July, the Japanese fleet advocated a massive assault in the Indian Ocean against Ceylon and the Royal Navy.[36] The Aleutians barely figured in the equation. American army intelligence then opined on 1 October that Japan might still attack in the Aleutians. But because earlier attacks had destroyed most of the enemy's seaplanes in the region, it rightly concluded that Japan would have considerable difficulty launching extensive Aleutian offensives. Despite the fact that they had scouted Amchitka and the Semichi Islands, Japan declined to occupy any islands east of Kiska. Also, most (and perhaps all) of Attu's small garrison was shifted to Kiska on 17 September, while a second reconnaissance of Amchitka, sent on 5 October, compelled the Japanese to conclude that no runway could be built there. So when the Americans occupied Adak, the Japanese were extremely shocked to see them moving so speedily in the Aleutians. Taking Adak back from the Americans, however, was an impossible option, as Kiska's garrison numbered only 3,520 personnel on 30 September.[37]

The Americans had problems too determining their enemy's intentions. The withdrawal of Attu's garrison bewildered ADC intelligence. While some thought it might signal a welcome general Japanese retirement from the entire Aleutian archipelago, the most reasonable explanation centred on a Japanese consolidation on Kiska, perhaps for administrative reasons, perhaps to prepare an attack on Amchitka. Whatever the rationale, Japan's Aleutian forces were to be allowed no time to adapt and prepare. Air raids against Kiska were stepped up; the attacks did considerable damage to buildings and grounded planes but few Japanese personnel died. In August Admiral Ugaki indicated that Kiska and Attu would be safe – unless the enemy used aircraft carriers on a large scale. Nimitz agreed, having concluded reluctantly on 24 September that air power alone could not expel Japan from the Aleutians. Therefore he suggested training troops immediately for future operations to retake Kiska and Attu when the necessary warships and transports would become available.[38]

DeWitt was greatly pleased. Having just hosted an extensive west coast visit from Roosevelt, DeWitt had been most dismayed to learn that the president thought a few old battleships could blast the Japanese from Kiska. Preferring discretion over valour, however, DeWitt had not attempted to contradict Roosevelt to his face, but he confided secretly to Marshall that naval bombardment could accomplish little without amphibious landings. As aerial attacks would not dislodge the Japanese, DeWitt thought "Nimitz's prescription of total destruction is the only answer." While the battleships had seen no action to that point in the war, Nimitz strongly opposed committing any of the vulnerable leviathans to action in the Aleutians. Claiming a need to protect Hawaii, he professed that the risk the ships would face in treacherous northern waters from mines and submarines was sufficient reason not to employ them at Kiska. Admiral King suspected that aerial and naval assaults alone would not recover the Aleutians, and was fully aware that opposed landings were costly endeavours. He therefore decided that more intelligence had to be gathered before he could commit himself to any concrete action. Seeking studies of manpower, landing craft requirements, and suitable Alaskan training sites, King counselled Marshall that vital combat-loaded transports would be unavailable before February 1943.[39]

Hoping to change King's mind – no easy task at the best of times – DeWitt had a plan for Kiska's recapture ready by 12 October. Asserting that the necessary shipping could be found somehow within ninety days, DeWitt admitted that locating trained soldiers would be difficult unless the army immediately ordered the Forty-Fourth Division to undergo intensive amphibious warfare training. Reluctantly, Marshall also concluded that nothing short of an amphibious landing force could eject Japan from the Aleutians. But reminding King that two major amphibious training centres already existed in the continental United States, Marshall attached "no particular significance to the suggestion that troops inured to Alaskan weather are prerequisite" to a successful Kiska operation, practicable in spring 1943 at the earliest. Disinclined to wait, due to fresh intelligence reports of Japan substantially reinforcing Kiska, DeWitt wanted to occupy Tanaga in early November. Alleging that Japan had not sustained heavy Aleutian losses solely for face-saving purposes, and drawing a comparison to the ongoing bitterly fought Solomons campaign, DeWitt believed that the enemy was carefully marshalling forces at Kiska before launching simultaneous assaults throughout the Aleutians. The WDC commander wanted to reinforce nearly every Alaskan outpost, create a separate 15,000-man force to retake Kiska and Attu, and then utilize Alaska to further offensive operations in the Pacific. DeWitt therefore asked again to train the Forty-Fourth Division for a Kiska invasion and lobbied hard for a quick decision.[40]

The navy contested DeWitt's proposal. By choosing to do battle at Midway and then the Solomons, the hard-charging King had deliberately engaged in an opportunistic and very high-risk strategy at a time when another admiral claimed that the USN lacked resources to undertake "more than fifty percent of the desired strategic operations."[41] Having suffered unexpectedly heavy losses in often brutal battles around the Solomons (especially in carriers and cruisers), the USN reduced Task Force Eight (TF8) by three cruisers. Besides, navy planners doubted whether Kiska could be occupied anytime soon given critical shortages of transports, landing craft, and experienced soldiers. Informed on 15 October of the TF8 reductions and of Marshall's decision to abandon the Tanaga operation in favour of Amchitka (the latter offered better potential airfield sites), DeWitt immediately charged that Amchitka could not be easily taken if the navy cuts went ahead as planned. Citing a recent ADC study, which concluded that building a runway on Amchitka would take at least two months, DeWitt argued that it made much better sense to proceed against Tanaga.[42] Marshall worried about material shortages as well. Reiterating the need to take Amchitka because its proximity to Kiska would permit the use of large assault boats and more continuous air support, Marshall demanded that another study be initiated to assess Amchitka's suitability as an air base site. Declaring that he could not make any definite commitments regarding troops for a Kiska operation, except to say a division would be available in 1943, Marshall thought it made more sense to train the Thirty-Eighth Division in Virginia rather than taking the time and effort to convert the Forty-Fourth in Alaska. As for DeWitt's request for reinforcements, Marshall, claiming that "we cannot afford to put an ideal defense on every island," told DeWitt to scrounge the required men in Alaska.[43]

Stubbornly refusing to accept this rebuff as the final word on the subject, DeWitt told Buckner on 29 October to expedite the delivery of more men and equipment to the Aleutians before the USN withdrawals occurred in November, as Adak was draining scarce combat soldiers from Alaska's existing garrisons. As for substituting Amchitka for Tanaga, DeWitt initiated another reconnaissance as ordered. He fretfully thought, however, that an Amchitka airstrip would engender a vigorous response from Kiska (less than 140 kilometres away), as it would not be difficult for Japan to dispatch surface units or heavy bombers to Kiska from the Kuriles. Possessing Amchitka would render Kiska's recapture easier, but DeWitt favoured seizing the former only in tandem with Kiska's invasion or after Kiska had been retaken. Predictably, Buckner backed DeWitt. Having visited Adak in early November, he worried Butler's air units could not stop Japan from bypassing Adak to attack further to the east. Convinced that retaking Kiska would be a difficult and costly business, he desired two divisions staffed mainly by soldiers with Alaskan experience because it was a "fact that troops who have served in Alaska handle themselves about twice as well in the field here as other troops of equal service who have not accustomed themselves to local Alaskan conditions of weather and terrain." Weather would not permit Kiska's invasion before April 1943 but Buckner required formal authorization as soon as possible, plus some reasonably prompt indication about where he could find the required soldiers.[44]

Theobald agreed with Buckner and DeWitt that Kiska would have to be retaken but he lacked their keenness for action. Apprehensive and displeased that the USN had been compelled to fight in the Aleutians without knowing much about Japan's ultimate intentions, Theobald felt certain that undertaking simultaneous operations in the Solomons and the Aleutians violated a fundamental strategic principle advising against split efforts in the same theatre. Certain that Japan would not continue to endure constant air attacks on Kiska much longer without responding, and positive the army had reneged on a promise to put an entire division on Adak, he wanted Adak reinforced before seizing Tanaga. Although Cooke concurred that Adak should be consolidated before a move against Tanaga was initiated, he accepted the army's assessment that Adak's temporary weakness was not serious. Reminding Theobald that the USN had cut TF8 without army concurrence, Cooke said it was up to the army and the JCS to decide how to employ troops in Alaska.[45]

Japan was quite interested in how the Americans intended to utilize their resources. While the IJN had wanted to build airfields on Attu and Kiska, it was surprised by a ferocious and successful USN submarine campaign that sunk two Japanese destroyers and badly damaged three more in Aleutian waters. As a result, by summer's end it decided not to place ground-based aviation on the islands. After Adak's loss, concerned that the Americans might initiate a much more threatening offensive, the Japanese agreed on 31 October to remain in the Aleutians rather than withdraw at the end of 1942 as originally planned. More troops would be sent, Attu re-occupied, and airfields finally begun on Kiska and the Semichis. Plans to occupy Amchitka too were proposed, but as the situation remained murky, those plans would remain in abeyance. Nine-hundred Japanese troops returned to Attu on 29 October, but 1,100 intended for Shemya turned back after their convoy was spotted by American planes; Japan would never occupy Shemya.[46]

Japan's renewed activity in the Aleutians did not go unnoticed. While aerial photographs of Kiska indicated that Japan had nearly 10,000 personnel there, Castner still felt that Japan's Aleutian foothold remained precarious due to the strong American presence on Adak, Japan's inability to replace its Aleutian air losses, and the demonstrated technical superiority of American fighter planes. Japan might be able to stem the steady decline by basing carriers at Kiska, invading Adak, or launching air and naval raids against Adak – although the latter option seemed unlikely, for even the Japanese would not "consider the loss of any of these ships as an equitable price to pay for temporary respite from our attacks." Invading Adak seemed the best alternative, yet Japan would need two full divisions to ensure success. Because American planes could easily strike enemy convoys hard before they neared the island, Castner estimated that Japanese casualties at Adak would approach 50 percent. Raids against Adak would probably be no less costly to the enemy, but as such attacks could inflict serious losses on the Americans too and might also provide cover for assaults on Amchitka or Tanaga, they had to be expected. Only retaking Adak promised long-range security to Japan, and because growing American power might make any future Japanese initiative quite problematic, Japan could grab Adak or build an airstrip on Amchitka to counter the American base on Adak.[47]

The view from London and Washington was different. The British had never worried much about the Aleutians or the north Pacific. In November 1940 Admiral T.S.V. Phillips, the Royal Navy's vice chief (and the commander who died with HMS *Repulse* and *Prince of Wales* under a hail of Japanese bombs and torpedoes in December 1941), had considered the possibility of a Japanese advance on the Aleutians. Though such an attack was conceivable, any chance the Japanese might have to exploit a victory in the Aleutians would be lost once the element of surprise had evaporated and the USN had mustered sufficient strength in the region to counter the enemy offensive. Once the Japanese had landed in the western Aleutians in June 1942, Britain's Foreign Office assumed that the occupation was intended only to support future Japanese operations against Siberia, not North America. On 9 September 1942 the British Joint Intelligence Committee played down the enemy's offensive capabilities. Arguing that Japan would consolidate its existing sphere of influence in order to sustain prolonged hostilities, it concluded that Japan would not attack Australia, India, and Hawaii, or push eastward in the Aleutians. The Combined Intelligence Committee (CIC) concurred on 8 November. It described Japan's seizure of the western Aleutians as a defensive measure to block attacks on Japan itself, and ruled that this "occupation is likely to be consolidated but probably not extended, Kiska being considered a sufficient counter to Dutch Harbor as an air and submarine base." These assessments were spot on. While Ugaki had pushed hard for additional offensive Aleutian operations, his superiors had no intention nor even the capability to move against Adak in strength. When the IJN and IJA convened on 7 November to consider their strategic options, the talk was not of imminent offensives but of destroying counterattacking enemy forces to crush Allied fighting will.[48]

For DeWitt the detection of Japanese transports at Attu and Kiska in mid-November, coupled with increased Japanese activity on Kiska, strongly portended a reinforcement of Kiska, the re-occupation of Attu, or preparations for offensive action somewhere along the Aleutian chain to the east anywhere from Adak to Kodiak, possibly before or coincident with an attack in the southwest Pacific. Claiming that ongoing poor weather was making Adak's reinforcement difficult and complaining that Alaska's security needs were still going largely unaddressed, DeWitt wanted another regimental combat team. Buckner, absolutely convinced that the enemy was rebuilding its resources for a surprise assault on Adak, thought Japan could sneak substantial forces past American naval screens to reinforce Attu and Kiska, raid coastal Alaska, or invade Amchitka or Adak. If he were Japan's Kiska commander and had guarantees of strong support, Buckner felt sure he "could think of many enterprises highly annoying to Alaska Defense Command."[49]

Marshall remained quite unmoved. The army was reorganizing its divisions into more flexible regimental combat teams, and Marshall wanted to keep those units in the continental United States until the cumbersome changeover was complete. He also fervently believed that DeWitt could find additional troops for Aleutian operations from the units already in Alaska. Furthermore, navy and army intelligence thought recent north Pacific developments had not discredited the CIC's analysis. On 18 November the Office of Naval Intelligence, noting that recent American raids had destroyed nearly all of Attu's float planes, thought such successes had greatly reduced the probability of enemy assaults on Adak or Amchitka, although a new force might be assembled under a cover of anti-aircraft protection. Three days later the War Department's strategic forecast mentioned only that Japan might send weak reinforcements to the Aleutians as it was likely to focus on the more critical southwest Pacific.[50]

The navy then rescued DeWitt. Having been instructed by King to study a possible invasion of Kiska, by November's end CINCPAC averred that Japanese attacks on Alaska appeared remote. They believed that the "material advantage to be gained is negligible" and that such assaults probably exceeded enemy capabilities. Nimitz's staff believed Japan had occupied Kiska either because it made a good submarine base or because it could threaten Siberian communications if Japan and the Soviet Union came to blows. Certainly Japan's hold on Kiska would be more secure if it also possessed Amchitka or Umnak, but CINCPAC planners doubted whether Japan could do much more than launch occasional raids in the archipelago. As for American options, blockading Kiska seemed to be the least costly way to retake the Aleutians. Unfortunately, frequent fogs and heavy cloud cover made systematic air patrols difficult, while a truly effective seaborne barrier would require too many valuable ships. As bombing probably would not dislodge the firmly dug-in enemy, the navy proposed occupying Amchitka and then Kiska.[51]

Deciding that the earliest date any invasion of Kiska or Attu could be mounted was 15 May 1943, King ordered Theobald to submit "as early as practicable a plan for the expulsion of Japs from [the] Aleutians." King's suggestion far exceeded what Marshall wanted, but the army commander was willing at least to consider attacking Kiska.[52] Political pressure had changed Marshall's mind. A displeased Marshall had told Vice President Wallace on 21 October that "too much emphasis had been placed on the Aleutian Islands and that the army had been forced by political pressure to send too much strength up there" – a direct reference to congressional charges that the military had to be pushed to begin the task of ousting Japan from the Aleutians. Even the White House was feeling the heat. Frustrated by public opinion – and some newspapers had dug up Mitchell's 1935 comment that "he who holds Alaska will hold the world" after the Japanese had occupied the Aleutians – during his 12 October Fireside chat the president railed against "typewriter strategists who expound their views in the press or on the radio." When a newspaper editorial characterized Japan's Aleutian presence as a threat to America, Roosevelt peevishly complained that the journalist in question had got it all wrong; Japan's occupation of Kiska was giving American forces the opportunity to sink even more IJN ships.[53]

On 22 November Theobald reported that some Japanese had been spotted on Amchitka, a disturbing portent given that radio intercepts had indicated the enemy was set to occupy the Semichis and Amchitka. Intent on beating Japan to the punch, Nimitz suggested grabbing Amchitka as soon as possible. Buckner very much wanted to comply with CINCPAC wishes but the second survey of Amchitka ordered by Marshall some weeks earlier had not taken place, a problem Buckner was only too happy to blame on Theobald's refusal to provide a PBY aircraft to transport a small reconnaissance party to Amchitka. When the admiral reversed that decision a few days later, the expedition's commander, Colonel Benjamin Talley, was meeting with Marshall in Washington. Once Talley returned to Kodiak in late November, Theobald informed him that no planes could be spared as the enemy was contemplating seizing Amchitka. Buckner told DeWitt on 25 November that he intended to press for the Amchitka survey once he arrived in Kodiak, adding most pointedly that "Admiral Theobald is aware of your desire and that of General Marshall to have the reconnaissance finished quickly."[54]

This crossing of swords was the proverbial last straw. After failing to convince a stubborn Theobald that his personal and professional relations with Buckner had not been well handled, King and Nimitz removed Theobald on 8 December. Rear Admiral Thomas C. Kinkaid, an aggressive veteran of the Solomons campaign, replaced him. Slated to take over officially in early January, Kinkaid's first job was to convince the army to move against Amchitka. Buckner certainly needed no persuading but Embick cautioned Marshall on 26 November that he saw little wisdom in developing Amchitka "until we can more definitely envisage our assumption of the offensive in that region." DeWitt too was unenthusiastic, especially if taking Amchitka meant postponing the Tanaga operation or delaying Kiska's invasion. Further, DeWitt had supported Theobald's refusal to give Talley the requisite planes, since Theobald had a duty to "conserve his ships and seaplanes to be ready to counter enemy action with his entire force." Still, when Kinkaid visited DeWitt in San Francisco on 12 December, he quickly convinced DeWitt to drop Tanaga in favour of Amchitka's seizure, an alteration that promptly gained the approval of Nimitz and King.[55]

For Nimitz, Amchitka seemed an adequate replacement for Kiska. Although he had hoped that Japan's withdrawal from Attu in September signalled an impending general evacuation from the Aleutians, the return of the Japanese to Attu and Kiska's subsequent reinforcement seemed to indicate that Japan might move against the Semichis and Amchitka. Assuming Amchitka could provide airstrip sites, Nimitz wanted Kiska operations delayed until more amphibious troops were available. Having been warned too by his staff on 14 December that Japan might grab Amchitka or the Semichis, King asked Marshall to approve Amchitka's occupation. Believing also that Japan might attack Amchitka and Adak, the army realized that undertaking a full-fledged invasion of Kiska before May 1943 was unlikely given TF8 weakness and a shortage of trained troops. Therefore, by 17 December the two services had agreed to take Amchitka "to render Kiska untenable as an operating base for the enemy" and to provide an advanced base for a possible operation against Kiska.[56]

Talley's reconnaissance party finally arrived at Amchitka on 17 December. While aircraft raided nearby Kiska to distract the enemy, thirteen specially selected scouts and intelligence officers paddled ashore from the PBYs. As the scouts expertly fanned out to check for recent Japanese activity on the bleak island, Talley found a suitable airfield site in a dry lagoon. Poor weather the next day, however, prevented the PBYs from returning to extract Talley's exposed team. Salvaging some canned food from a wrecked American submarine "like children on Christmas morning, full of anticipation," the Americans had to hide from two Japanese float planes that overflew the island before the PBYs finally arrived on 19 December to remove them. Once they had read Talley's report stating that a landing strip could be built, on 21 December the Joint Chiefs ordered an immediate seizure of Amchitka.[57]

The planning effort quickly ran into problems. Ever the wet blanket, Theobald protested against DeWitt's assertion that just 5,560 troops, including 3,000 men for the initial landing, would suffice to take Amchitka. While DeWitt was certain the USN could fulfill its promise to prevent any Japanese intervention, Theobald and Buckner were concerned Japanese forces would be able to infiltrate at will despite the best efforts of the navy and the air force, and wanted the entire occupation force involved in the initial assault. DeWitt denied ever saying that the lower figure would suffice, claiming instead that he wanted a minimum of 6,000 soldiers. He further contradicted Theobald's version of events by saying that when he and Kinkaid had discussed possible enemy retaliation, "no one at any time expressed confidence that [the] movement would be unopposed or that [the] navy could prevent anything coming to either Formula [Amchitka] or Longview [Adak]."[58] How this misunderstanding arose is unclear. Certainly, because his poor relations with the army and Buckner had led directly to Theobald's removal from command, the admiral had no reason to make DeWitt's life any easier. Perhaps Theobald had heard DeWitt's alleged comments second-hand, or had simply misunderstood them. It is possible too that DeWitt had made the comments attributed to him and then altered his position after the fact to safeguard his position. Theobald's own plan for the Aleutians, ready on 29 November, recommended taking Kiska in a surprise attack rather than grabbing Amchitka first. Once a crestfallen and bitter Theobald finally left Kodiak on 7 January 1943, even Kinkaid, complaining that he was "continually arguing or reciting his woes in a contentious fashion," thought it "a relief to have him go." After the war, official USN historian Samuel Eliot Morison opined that Theobald "deserved a better fate than to have his reputation smothered in northern mist."[59] Perhaps so, but in 1942 few held that view.

As the army and navy gathered forces for Amchitka, inclement weather greatly hindered aerial raids, but on 5 January army planes sank two Kiska-bound Japanese transports laden with reinforcements and badly needed heavy equipment for a planned airfield. The American force splashed ashore on Amchitka on 11 January though one destroyer and two vital transports ran aground in very rough seas. Over 2,000 troops managed to drag themselves damply ashore, including several teams of engineers who feverishly began building the vital airstrip. All expected a determined Japanese response once their presence was discovered, and as Amchitka was visible from Kiska on a clear day, that presence would undoubtedly be noticed sooner rather than later. Although Buckner cautioned them that Japanese responses could range from the covert insertion of troops to a full-scale amphibious assault involving carriers and other major surface ships, Castner doubted whether Japan would risk any valuable carriers given the desperate battles occurring near the Solomons. Castner warned them, however, about the high probability of some sort of Japanese counterattack at Amchitka, an opinion shared by the navy's Future Plans Division. Noting that Amchitka's occupation would render the enemy's position in Kiska precarious, the navy feared a violent reaction. On 15 February, one day before the engineers completed the airstrip, some Kiska-based Japanese aircraft struck Amchitka. The raids inflicted only minor damage to the runways and killed a handful of American soldiers. And even this limited Japanese reaction was curtailed after Amchitka-based fighters tumbled two Japanese bombers from the skies on 18 February.[60] Once again American arms had achieved a significant Aleutian victory with insignificant losses in men and material. That lucky streak unfortunately would not last.

5

Total Destruction Is the Only Answer:
Westward to Attu

Perhaps one of Clausewitz's most famous discussions concerns the frustratingly elusive concept of "friction." As a soldier for almost forty years, Clausewitz had marvelled at an interesting and maddeningly common phenomenon: despite good planning and strategy making, once battle was joined, "countless minor incidents – the kind you can never really foresee – combine to lower the general level of performance, so that one always falls short of the intended goal." Thus emerged the very quotable aphorism that "everything in war is very simple, but the simplest thing is difficult."[1] The bloodless occupation of Amchitka in January 1943, like the previous operation against Adak, should have made matters much clearer and simpler for the Alaskan commanders. Yet the return of Amchitka to American control only intensified the already muddled strategic debate about what now needed to be done in the north Pacific – an involved debate that would lead to a major operational compromise and a hideous battle for Attu in May 1943.

The Western Defense Command's (WDC) December 1942 assessment admitted that Japan could probably no longer mount any major offensive actions in the north Pacific. DeWitt's chief intelligence officer, Colonel John Weckerling, demurred. Thinking Kiska and Attu represented potential springboards from which Japan could move in any direction, Weckerling doubted if Japan's current inability to construct Aleutian airfields guaranteed permanent enemy inactivity. Agreeing, DeWitt wanted 25,000 soldiers assembled quickly to assault Kiska. Major General Handy ordered the Seventh Motorized Division, originally intended for operations in North Africa's searing deserts, to get ready for the frigid Aleutians. Marshall had played an important part in this decision. Facing an overabundance of motorized formations, the army chief agreed to provide one division but warned DeWitt that no final decision to act against Kiska had been made.[2] The navy found this decision very confusing. Having been advised by Theobald in November 1942 that it would take a reinforced corps (40,000 troops) to defeat the 10,000 Japanese soldiers on Kiska, the army's offer of just one division for Kiska seemed to indicate that the Office of the Director of Plans and Operations (OPD) and DeWitt were talking about completely different operations. The navy desired two divisions even though its Future Plans Section questioned whether ejecting the Japanese was currently feasible, citing enemy strength, a shortage of trained American forces, a lack of sufficient transports, and the necessary employment of naval forces elsewhere, without which an operation of that magnitude would not be possible.[3]

The naval forces required to support a landing on Kiska would be substantial. Theobald had estimated that two carriers and thirty-three other ships would be essential to counter any Japanese surface riposte. He had also hoped to employ seven full marine regiments so that Kiska and Attu could be made into staging fields for an invasion of the Kurile Islands, "if this should later be selected as the best overwater route for attacks upon Japan." Declaring that marines were simply unavailable, Nimitz believed six army regiments (30,800 men), two to four battleships, five or six cruisers, five or six flattops, and thirty-one destroyers were needed, asserting that the forces sent against Kiska should be in sufficient strength to clean the place out quickly, "without such delays as we are experiencing at Guadalcanal." Once Amchitkan airfields were operational, Nimitz hoped vigorous aerial assaults might eliminate the need to hit Kiska with an amphibious assault. If Japan reinforced the Aleutians, Nimitz worried that Kiska's invasion, "a very difficult operation which will probably incur heavy losses of personnel even if the place has been well 'softened up,'" would become inevitable. Having long acquiesced to the inevitable, DeWitt had his own plan ready on 31 December. DeWitt asked for four regimental teams, five carriers (244 aircraft), thirty-nine other warships, and 345 army warplanes. Ultimate command would rest with Kinkaid and Nimitz, while DeWitt and Kinkaid would formulate the operational plans. Approving this scheme on 9 January, Nimitz selected Admiral Francis W. Rockwell to head the assault, and then created a joint army-navy planning team – Task Force Fifty-One (TF51) – at San Diego so that the Seventh Division might gain valuable amphibious warfare expertise from the marines.[4]

Altogether unconvinced that any of this was necessary, one of King's aides warned him that an assault on Kiska would result in heavy American losses. Furthermore, achieving victory would depend largely on the capacity of air power to eliminate enemy defences, and then on the ability of troops to close with and destroy forces in rough terrain. Nimitz's force proposals seemed eminently reasonable, yet army plans to put substantial bases on Kiska and Amchitka were disconcerting, since Alaska's garrison could then exceed 135,000 soldiers, a level of strength far "beyond future needs as visualized at this time." Admiral R.S. Edwards, King's chief of staff, concurred. Advising "careful consideration of probable losses in connection with other commitments," and believing that events were leading to an unavoidable transfer of a considerable part of the Pacific fleet to the Atlantic, Edwards suggested stopping the westward advance at Amchitka to ensure the availability of sufficient naval resources for the Solomons after meeting other demands.[5]

Support for strong offensive action in the Aleutians, however, was growing. Sent to inspect the Eleventh Air Force in late 1942, Colonel Charles G. Williamson worried that continual Alaskan operations and the harsh climate were rapidly eroding aircrew morale and diminishing military effectiveness. He also calculated that it made little sense to fight in the south Pacific at the end of a 10,000-mile supply line when Japan itself was the key target. Likening current American strategy to punching a puffy feather pillow, Williamson averred that like a pillow, Japan could not be crushed by striking at every point along its defensive perimeter. He therefore wanted to attack the Kuriles as "the first step toward attainment of the primary objective, complete annihilation of Japanese power. Subsequent steps would be obvious and would keep Japan so thoroughly occupied that most resistance elsewhere would cease very quickly."[6]

Williamson had very limited influence on the planning process, but Ernest King had much more. Increasingly frustrated by the inability to nail down a date for the invasion of western Europe, which he blamed on British intransigence, King slowly became more interested in action in the Pacific, including operations in the north Pacific. He argued after the war that the Joint Chiefs had rarely paid much attention to staff studies,[7] but in September 1942 he had asked the JCS to study the advantages of attacking Japan via Alaska and Siberia. And while the admiral had acknowledged that America did "not *now* have the 'tools' for such a campaign," given heavy commitments elsewhere, "next summer may see us not only in such case as to enable us to strike at Japan but in such case that is the most *useful*, perhaps vital, thing we can do." King had read an 1942 army study that conceded that little was known about the Kuriles. Instructed to pursue the study findings, the Joint Planning Staff (JPS) presented its tentative findings on 1 January 1943. The JPS predicated its report on two vital assumptions: that Japan would retain Kiska and a belligerent Soviet Union could hold Siberia. Aiding the Soviets would therefore entail a massive and expensive expansion of numerous Alaskan and Siberian ports, the capture of key Kurile points to safeguard communications, and the provision of at least twelve American divisions. As such an operation would have a huge impact on current and future Pacific initiatives and would definitely be impossible without active Soviet belligerence, the JPS deemed it beyond its mandate. Also set aside was an extraordinarily ambitious plan to insert fifteen to eighteen American divisions onto the Asian mainland. Providing air and naval support to the Soviets seemed workable, but only if ample American forces were added to an already substantial Soviet military effort. Given that it knew so little about Soviet capabilities, the JPS lacked sufficient information on which to base reasonably supported conclusions "as to ways and means which would be appropriate and practicable for a campaign by American forces against Japan via a northern route, for the purpose of aiding Russia and exploiting the availability of Russian territory to strike by air at Japan proper." A daunted JPS therefore recommended several more cautious avenues: preparing an army division for the special rigours of arctic warfare; developing a series of supply bases in

Alaska and Siberia; studying the use of Soviet bases to bomb Japan; taking Kiska as soon as possible; and planning to reinforce Kamchatka for an eventual invasion of the Kuriles.[8]

The Joint Chiefs dealt with the JPS submission on 5 January. As King stated that the study was the first of its kind, not surprisingly a circumspect JCS requested that more research be done on the subject before it made any decision. Moving to the Kuriles in strength, however, held very little attraction for Marshall. As he was deeply engaged in the difficult and politically dangerous process of cutting the army's anticipated roster from 213 to 120 divisions, Marshall patently opposed any scheme that might absorb twenty of those valuable formations in Asia when American forces had not yet invaded Europe. Marshall also had the challenging task of dealing with British members of the Combined Chiefs of Staff (CCS) who vigorously opposed any operational plans that might seriously interfere with the progress of the war against Germany. In March 1942 the notoriously Anglophile Canadian high commissioner to Britain, Vincent Massey, had commented that although "the great majority of Americans realise that despite the spread of the war into the Pacific they cannot win the war without Great Britain," the recognition did not "necessarily mean that all will be well in the garden of Anglo-American relations." Massey was correct. There were problems from the very start. In March 1942 Field Marshal Sir John Dill, selected by Churchill the previous December to head Britain's new Joint Staff Mission in Washington, DC, delivered a fairly cutting assessment of American officials. Roosevelt lacked "a tidy mind" and did not like to face "ugly" facts. Arnold was "approachable" but was a "big" talker, propounding "heresies with gusto": fortunately Arnold could be controlled by Marshall's "wise hand." Admiral King was "able, but a little too conscious of that fact," afraid that others were always trying to get at him, and was at "his worst" in a formal conference. Only Marshall was deemed "outstanding" as he was direct, clear headed, and "without suspicion." Not surprisingly then, combined CCS meetings since December 1941 had often been fractious affairs. The British frequently complained that the Americans were "completely dumb and appallingly slow"; the Americans often found their British colleagues patronizing and maddeningly elusive. Such discord had prompted Marshall to endorse King's demand for a Pacific-First approach, but after the onset of serious logistical problems, Marshall re-emphasized Europe again, a policy reversal that, according to Admiral Leahy, had to be considered less than final.[9]

This American strategic split was on display for all to see when the CCS convened at Casablanca in January 1943 for a conference that produced a grand Allied strategy blending American and British concepts.[10] In late December 1941, Prime Minister Churchill had assured his more aggressive advisers that the Pacific conflict, after the initial shock had subsided, would not absorb an unduly large proportion of American forces. He had therefore recommended letting the Americans "regain their naval power in the Pacific and not discourage them from the precise secondary overseas operations which they may perhaps contemplate." By January 1943 though, the British Chiefs of Staff had become most impatient with dual American demands for a too speedy return to the European continent and strong action against Japan. Thus they attempted to decisively set the proper tone prior to the conference by maintaining that as Germany remained the primary threat, any contemplated Pacific offensives should block only obvious Japanese threats to key Allied bases and communications.[11] Marshall did his best to deflect King's increasingly strident demands for a greater Pacific effort and to compel the reluctant British to accept a timely invasion of France. He proposed allocating 70 percent of Allied resources to Europe. But when King addressed the CCS on 14 January, his advocacy for some rather extensive Pacific campaigns elicited little British sympathy. Inclined to view King as exceedingly narrow-minded, "blunt and stand-offish, almost to the point of rudeness," and "intolerant and suspicious of all things British," the British Chiefs haughtily dismissed his Pacific plans.

Having opposed Churchill's attempts to bind America to Britain via the CCS as akin to selling one's "birthright for a plate of porridge,"[12] the icily formidable chief of the imperial general staff, General Alan Brooke, thought that Marshall's 70-30 split was a most unscientific way to formulate global strategy. He feared that extended Pacific operations "would inevitably lead to an all-out war with Japan and it was certain that we had not sufficient resources to undertake this at the same time as a major effort against Germany." Air Chief Marshall Sir Charles Portal recommended standing on the defensive and inflicting losses when Japan attacked. Most unimpressed, convinced that indefinitely deferring Pacific offensives would allow Japan to dictate the war's course, King coldly insisted that it was essential to maintain the initiative against the Japanese and not wait for them to make the first move.[13]

A JPS plan presented on 17 January utterly failed to improve matters. While the document acknowledged that Germany's defeat was the coalition's primary goal, it recommended subjecting the Japanese to continual pressure, sufficient in power and extent to absorb the disposable Japanese military effort. That meant five separate offensives in 1943 ranging from Burma's steaming jungles to Kiska's icy tundra – attacks that would absorb at least 250,000 troops, thousands of aircraft, plus the majority of the USN's new ships. The British immediately voiced strong objections, and subsequent and stormy discussions on 17 January failed to bridge the Anglo-American gap despite King's assurance that he was hoping only to "put us in a position of readiness from which we can operate against Japan after Germany ha[s] been defeated." Exceedingly frustrated by this unpleasant turn of events, Marshall asserted that the United States must retain the initiative against Japan, as it was bearing numerous hazards and vulnerabilities in a number of theatres, including the Aleutians. Picking up on Marshall's implication that this intolerable strategic stalemate could not be allowed to continue much longer, the British reluctantly agreed to pressure Japan militarily as long as Germany's

The Anglo-American Combined Chiefs of Staff, assorted other military officers, and President Franklin Roosevelt and Prime Minister Winston Churchill at the Casablanca Conference, January 1943.

final defeat was not prejudiced. That concession came with a heavy price however; the anticipated five Pacific offensives were cut to two – one in New Guinea, the other in Burma. Planning for other assaults, including Kiska's invasion, could proceed but any decision about undertaking further operations would have to be made at some unspecified later date by the Combined Chiefs, not the Joint Chiefs alone.[14]

This type of concession greatly unsettled the Americans and made for extremely intense arguments when the Combined Chiefs reconvened on 18 January. Marshall bitterly alleged that the British military desired to keep strong forces dormant in Britain, waiting to exploit future German weakness rather than undertaking an active offensive in the Pacific. Brooke, who espoused the view that Marshall possessed "practically no strategic vision" and that an exceedingly shrewd but "swollen-headed" King positively lacked a global operational point of view,[15] complained that seeking Japan's defeat first would cause the Allies to lose the war. Marshall pointedly responded that the global conflict could not be won quickly if the Americans neglected the Pacific theatre and left the Japanese to consolidate their gains and unnecessarily strengthen their position. Intense bickering thus ensued as the British relentlessly sought to wear the Americans down. An exasperated King, described by Warren Kimball as "crankily anti-British," acidly complained that Britain's argument really meant doing nothing to beat Japan. Confronted by King's assertion that Britain had little or no right to frame the Pacific war's direction, given America's ultimate responsibility for that campaign, and unwilling to see Roosevelt and Churchill drawn in, as no one knew where that might lead, the British opted to find an acceptable compromise. In return for a JCS promise that "operations in the European Theater will be conducted with the object of defeating Germany in 1943 with the maximum forces that can be brought to bear upon her by the United Nations," the British affirmed on 19 January that offensives against Japan could go ahead as long as they were "kept in such limits as will not, in the opinion of the Combined Chiefs of Staff, jeopardize the capacity of the United Nations to take advantage of any favorable opportunity that may present itself for the decisive defeat of Germany in 1943."[16]

Quite cognizant that this concordance was tenuous at best, Marshall set out to guarantee that the British would find no further grounds to question the final Pacific planning document. Alaska became the sacrificial lamb. Although the OPD justified Kiska's invasion as a precursor to further north

Pacific operations, it also questioned whether Japan could reinforce its Aleutian garrisons or substantially interfere with American activities in the region. Retaking Kiska and Attu would certainly permanently remove any threat to Alaska, but American losses would be heavy, leading to another increase in the Alaskan garrison. Swayed by OPD logic, Marshall told the JCS on 22 January that he questioned the desirability of declaring an intention to clear the Aleutians because the British would use the scale of any proposed Kiska invasion as a "yardstick by which they might attempt to judge the magnitude of other operations in the Pacific Theater." Marshall was most unwilling to risk further divisive strategic quarrels that could threaten an early Allied invasion of western Europe. He believed it was essential for the British to "understand that we will not commit ourselves to any large-scale operation in Alaska." So when the Pacific planning document was finalized, the passage referring to the capture of the western Aleutians was modified to read to "make the Aleutians as secure as may be."[17]

Brooke had complained in 1942 that, while he accepted the need for a policy of give and take with America, he could not "help feeling it is we who are doing all the giving and our friends who are doing all the taking." Some Americans disagreed. Despite the fact that American resources assigned to the Pacific matched the effort made against Germany well into 1944, General A.C. Wedemeyer concluded, "We came, we listened, and we were conquered." To use his phrase, the American services had lost their shirts at Casablanca.[18] The president also made clear that he disliked the USN's complicated and confusing island-hopping strategy and that he desired some new decisive plan to strike back at Japan. But the navy's guiding central Pacific strategy did not deviate from its original course. As Stimson noted in his diary, the navy, which was "dead anxious to fight in the Pacific," had "been barely loyal in regards to following the plans." But on 4 February King told Nimitz the Kiska plans would have to be revised given critical shortages of transports and landing craft. In turn, Nimitz told Kinkaid that while he was studying the option of attacking the Kuriles, he wished to know if Kiska could be subjected to an air siege, an option that could potentially be far more economical than a direct amphibious assault. Then offering the hope that things might be changed for the better, Nimitz asked Kinkaid to move his naval headquarters from Kodiak to the Aleutians, as "this would tend to emphasize the offensive objective we have in mind, as against the 'defense' of Alaska."[19]

The OPD had a different idea. Having decided in 1942 that its staff officers needed first-hand experience of Pacific conditions, it had sent some observers to accompany the Amchitka task force. Building on that experience, in February 1943 the highly influential Colonel Ray T. Maddocks outlined three courses of action that could lead to the substantial reduction of Alaska's garrison: using air and naval forces to wage an implacable war of attrition in the Aleutians; occupying Attu with 15,000 troops followed by an attritional campaign against Kiska; or using 30,000 soldiers in a full-scale assault upon Kiska. None of these options was seen as particularly attractive. The first might neutralize Japan's bases and sap enemy strength without appreciably debilitating American resources, but it offered too few obvious advantages to warrant the potentially heavy drain on American resources badly needed elsewhere. Retaking Kiska would severely reduce Japan's ability to mount future regional operations yet it too would be costly in time, manpower, equipment, and shipping, and would probably engender a major military confrontation requiring even more reinforcements. Therefore, as timely action against Japan itself was improbable, assaulting Attu and Kiska could not be justified, which left the attritional campaign as the best option. If the military truly desired an Aleutian offensive, Maddocks asserted, it would have to hit a less heavily defended Attu; once Attu was in American hands, Kiska's reduction would be much easier.[20]

Such caution found a receptive audience. When DeWitt asked for more aircraft, Handy declined the request because the army could not promise to undertake any offensive Aleutian operations quickly, given heavy commitments elsewhere. If and when the services had committed themselves to Aleutian action, then "every effort will be made to assign proportionate means to the task directed." The navy's Strategic Plans Division (SPD) was not at all keen to expand the north Pacific war. Facing strong American bases at Adak and Amchitka, Japan could reinforce Kiska, build an airstrip on Attu, or withdraw completely from the Aleutians because "anything less than a 3/4 Midway Force will only result in the restoration of our position no matter what the immediate advantages might be." Evacuation seemed unlikely and the SPD ruled that Japan would seek, as it had tried and failed at Guadalcanal, to hang on desperately with clearly insufficient means. This interservice consensus was confirmed by the Joint Intelligence Committee (JIC) on 5 March. Dismissing the chance of any Japanese attacks in the Aleutians for the remainder of 1943, the JIC thought Japan would require at least one new division and 150,000 tons of additional shipping just to hold its own at Kiska and Attu. As poor weather, persistent American attacks, and an elongated and very vulnerable supply line made Japan's Aleutian position quite precarious, the JIC expected Japanese forces would venture out only occasionally to try to forestall Allied penetration of their weakening Pacific defensive barrier.[21]

The JIC's prediction was prescient. Although many historians argue that the IJN's catastrophic defeat at Midway was the turning point in the Pacific conflict, others maintain with considerably more credibility that Japan's excessively costly loss in the lengthy Guadalcanal campaign represented the actual shift in strategic postures in America's favour.[22] This was not clear, though, in early 1943. Averring that Japan continued to possess large fleet units, almost untouched manpower, and an efficient air force, DeWitt believed that Japan would attempt to further the impression that it was "impotent, or too busily occupied elsewhere, in order to induce overconfidence and a relaxation of vigilance."[23] Agreeing, Kinkaid told Nimitz on 20 February that he wanted to step up air attacks on Kiska once Amchitka's air base was functional. Concurring with Nimitz's opinion that Kiska would be an exceptionally tough nut to crack, Kinkaid thought increased air raids might indicate whether Kiska could be shattered without excessive cost. Then the United States could go on to the Kuriles if Soviet forces and bases were available. Unfortunately, given the Soviet Union's titanic death struggle with Adolf Hitler's Germany, Kinkaid doubted if Stalin would volunteer to fight Japan. Still, a Soviet entry into the Pacific conflict might be advanced considerably "if we show that we are going after the Kuriles in a big way." But realizing that he could not buck the heavy tide of senior command opinion, Kinkaid cleverly altered his approach. Noting that he lacked sufficient shipping to attack Kiska, on 7 March the admiral, taking a page from Maddocks, suggested grabbing Attu instead, after the advent of better weather in mid-April. As Attu's garrison appeared to number only 500 men, Kinkaid thought one reinforced army regiment, two or three battleships, three or four cruisers, and two destroyer squadrons would do the job. After the fall of Attu, the invading force could build an airstrip or move against Shemya.[24]

Belying his well-earned stubborn reputation, Buckner also speedily adapted. On 12 February he told DeWitt that the retention of Attu in Japanese hands would negate American control of Kiska. Ever aggressive, Buckner was "firmly convinced that the only way to solve the Japanese problem is to

Christianize the Japs and the only way of Christianizing them is to give them a Christian burial." But by 9 March, concerned that a speedy decision about Kiska was unlikely and wishing to take full advantage of the approaching mild weather, Buckner said he would support Kinkaid's Attu plan if the JCS quickly decided the matter. Buckner's wish was granted, although it took some considerable doing on DeWitt's part. King told Nimitz and DeWitt on 10 March that the JCS favoured attacking Attu with the forces already assigned to the stalled Kiska operation and any resources Nimitz could spare. The Alaskan commanders could only tentatively begin to organize the relevant units, however, as final approval was expected to be granted only on 12 March at the Pacific Military Conference in Washington, DC. When that eminent gathering singularly failed to authorize any Aleutian operations – Cooke explained that poor weather and force shortages were delaying attacks – on 17 March a frustrated DeWitt issued his own directive for Attu's recapture at the earliest practicable moment.[25] Five days passed before DeWitt received a response. Having learned that Japan had finally begun constructing an airfield on Attu, King told Marshall that if the enemy built airstrips on Shemya and Agattu, "our eventual recapture of those areas will be rendered very much more difficult." So when Marshall and his aides met on 22 March to consider King's recommendation that the Attu attack should proceed as soon as possible, they did not object as long as DeWitt found the required transports from existing allocations. On 22 March the JCS authorized Operation Landcrab, Attu's invasion.[26]

Displeased with army intimations that his three-regiment force allotment for an Attu operation seemed excessive, DeWitt telephoned General John E. Hull in Washington on 23 March to assert that retaking Attu and Shemya would require two regiments for the initial landings plus a third in reserve. DeWitt won this battle. As long as he had the support of the north Pacific service commanders (and he did) and did not ask for any more ships, the army would not oppose his Aleutian plans. The Seventh Division's Seventeenth Regiment would grab Attu, the Fourth Composite Regiment would occupy Shemya, and the Thirty-Second Regiment would act as a floating reserve. Once the operations were ended, the Fourth would be speedily removed, leaving the other units behind to act as semi-permanent garrisons.[27]

The Americans, though, were not alone in seeking to strengthen their position in the Aleutians. Japan had been rudely jolted from its strategic paralysis after Amchitka's loss. Fearful that a precipitous withdrawal from Attu and Kiska would expose the Kuriles to an American attack, the Japanese decided on 4 February to hold the western Aleutians at all costs and to improve defences in the Kuriles. They aimed to have air bases ready on Kiska and Attu by March's end, with other fields put in the Semichis at some later unspecified time. The IJA had sent some 1,500 troops to the Aleutians since November 1942 but several supply ships, some carrying vital heavy construction equipment needed to build the projected airstrips on Kiska and Attu, had been sunk by American planes and submarines. The IJA had also lost fifty-nine transports in October and November 1942 around Guadalcanal alone, compared with just twelve such vessels in the entire Pacific from December 1941 to September 1942.[28] Unwilling to place any additional scarce transports at risk, Vice Admiral Hosogaya Moshiro ruled that submarines alone would now shuttle supplies to the distant Aleutians. Concerned that the slender lifeline to its isolated Aleutian garrisons could not be adequately maintained in this fashion, the IJA forced Hosogaya to mount a supply convoy on 3 March. When that strongly guarded contingent sailed safely to Attu six days later, the army dispatched an officer from the Aleutians on 15 March to lobby for additional men and supplies. His efforts met with success; another convoy carrying 550 soldiers and supplies, accompanied by eight warships and commanded personally by Hosogaya, left the Kuriles on 23 March.[29]

The USN was waiting. Having intercepted Japanese messages regarding the second supply mission, it assigned Task Group 16.6, led by Rear Admiral Charles H. McMorris, to foil Hosogaya's plan. With only two cruisers – the *Salt Lake City* and the *Richmond* – and four destroyers, McMorris sallied out confidently, as American intelligence sources believed that the IJN could muster just two cruisers and four destroyers for the entire north Pacific.[30] Horrified to encounter Hosogaya's considerably superior Japanese armada near the Komandorski Islands, McMorris commented with some understatement that "the situation had now been clarified, but it had also radically and unpleasantly changed." He had no choice but to fight when Hosogaya's ships rapidly moved to block his eastward retreat. Five hours of very confused fighting ensued, after which the *Salt Lake City*, having sustained considerable damage, was left dead in the water. Temporarily abandoning the powerless vessel, a desperate McMorris ordered his destroyers to launch a near suicidal torpedo attack to cover his retreat. But moments later the Japanese ships turned away at high speed to the west, much to the relief of the USS *Monaghan* crewmen, who had begun to say their final goodbyes as the warship began its desperate attack run. The IJN vessels had incurred rather little damage in the intense fight. However, having intercepted numerous American radio signals demanding the provision of immediate air support, the Japanese vessels mistook the odd splashes created by American high explosive shells for aerial bombs (the USN ships had very nearly exhausted their armour piercing ordnance). With his own stocks of ammunition and fuel running dangerously low, Hosogaya opted to withdraw back to the Kuriles rather than risk the run to the Aleutians. For this caution, his IJN superiors retired Hosogaya in July. As for McMorris, despite charges that he had unnecessarily abandoned the *Salt Lake City* to a dismal fate (the ship miraculously survived with relatively few casualties), he became Nimitz's chief of staff in May.[31]

McMorris's nearly disastrous encounter prompted two initiatives. Worried that a much stronger IJN armada would soon return to the Aleutians, Kinkaid asked for three battleships, two heavy cruisers, and four destroyers to bolster the existing Attu blockade. Although the admiral did not demand an aircraft carrier, he determined that dive bombers and torpedo planes for Amchitka as well as a full reserve for the Eleventh Air Force would be quite helpful. Admitting that his wish list was extensive, Kinkaid reminded Nimitz that additional naval and aerial forces would be required once the Aleutians were retaken and amphibious operations begun in the distant Kuriles. Having already assigned thirty vessels to cover Attu's invasion, Nimitz doubted if he could detach any additional ships for blockade duty.[32] The second initiative concerned the Komandorskis. DeWitt argued that the archipelago's proximity to Attu made it a fortress and sentinel guarding the Bering Sea, which, if taken by Japan, could threaten the Aleutians. Further noting Japan's treacherous "proclivity for attacking nations with whom she is on peaceful relations," he was certain Japan would grab the Komandorskis when convenience outweighed its neutrality treaty with the Soviets. But as in 1941, DeWitt failed to make his case stick. Although "alive to the dangers inherent in the seizure of the Komandorski Islands by Japan," Marshall doubted whether anything could be done, as Stalin's ongoing failure to acknowledge American appeals for Siberian bases showed his determination not to upset northeast Asia's delicately balanced strategic status quo.[33]

Indefatigable as ever, DeWitt wrote Marshall on 1 April to argue for the commencement of even more intensive air assaults to soften up Kiska. He hoped the island could be retaken in September 1943 by a task force similar in strength and composition to that which he intended to send against Attu. Planning to be in Alaska until late May, DeWitt promised to have further recommendations for Kiska ready for the army chief upon his subsequent return to his California headquarters. Hearing rumours that Buckner might soon be transferred out of Alaska, DeWitt wanted to delay any move until after Kiska's recapture. Then, as Buckner suggested that Major General Charles H. Corlett (Kodiak's garrison commander) should lead the Kiska attack given his extensive Alaskan experience, DeWitt wanted Corlett transferred to Fort Ord in June to supervise the Kiska force's training. Responding to DeWitt on 8 April, Marshall stated only that he would await DeWitt's promised recommendations before coming to any definite conclusions. Also thinking a brief pause might be in order, Kinkaid wisely cautioned DeWitt to delay sending any new Kiska proposals to Nimitz until after Attu had been occupied. Kinkaid remained eager to move west, but if Attu could be captured and an airfield quickly built on Shemya, then Kiska could be pounded "unmercifully." If they could first expel the Japanese from the Aleutians, B-24 bombers could launch nuisance diversion raids against the Kuriles while more important operations could be undertaken elsewhere.[34]

Unfortunately, planning for Attu's recapture was somewhat problematic. While DeWitt described his relations with Admiral Rockwell as "fine, pleasant and profitable," Kinkaid complained to Nimitz on 14 April that Rockwell had neglected to send him any information about the San Diego-based planning sessions, beyond a so-called "master plan" that Kinkaid disdainfully regarded as hardly more than an outline. Most important, Rockwell had given Kinkaid the definite impression that he intended "to deposit the assault force on Attu and pull out for San Diego the next day, lock, stock, and barrel, taking with him all the ships which he considers belong to him." Two days later, after seeing Rockwell's operational plan for the Attu attack – which omitted Shemya – Kinkaid accused Rockwell of seeking to depart Attu without any thought that a major enemy force might sally forth from the Kuriles soon after the first landings. If Rockwell's TF51 did leave, Kinkaid thought the remaining ships would be unable to both cover Attu and Shemya and protect American supply lines. Certainly Kinkaid did not object to some vessels departing once the landings had begun, but he wished to retain at least two battleships and as many of the destroyers as possible. Concerned that Rockwell's understanding of command arrangements was quite unsound, Kinkaid asked Nimitz to direct Rockwell to report directly to him. Nimitz failed to assuage Kinkaid's concerns. Certain that Rockwell clearly understood his responsibilities and would offer the army "all possible cooperation in carrying out his scheme of maneuver," Nimitz blamed the problem between Kinkaid and Rockwell on the inherent difficulties involved in formulating a complex plan when the principal players were thousands of miles apart. Confident that Rockwell and Kinkaid could easily mend fences once they had finally met face to face, Nimitz declined to write formally to Rockwell as three separate documents had named Kinkaid as Landcrab's supreme commander.[35]

Admiral Thomas Kinkaid on Adak Island, May 1943.

Personality clashes and command arrangements were not the only problems afflicting Attu's planning process. Not one American government agency had ever completely surveyed Attu's rugged interior; only the island's lengthy ragged shoreline had been accurately mapped.[36] Furthermore, aerial reconnaissance flights in March had revealed the existence of 500 new foxholes near the unfinished runway plus numerous well-considered gun positions. By mid-April American intelligence believed Japan had 1,700 troops, supported by artillery and engineers, on Attu. The Japanese actually had over 2,500 men on the island but even the lower assessment prompted the delivery of another combat team to TF51, bringing the total number of soldiers assigned to Landcrab to 11,000. Rockwell's staff devised five different operational plans by the time TF51 set sail from California on 24 April. Upon arriving in Alaska, Rockwell adopted Plan E. The main American ground elements would land at Massacre Bay on Attu's southern coast before linking up with a smaller force coming from Holtz Bay in the north. The battle, excepting mopping up operations, was expected to take just three days.[37]

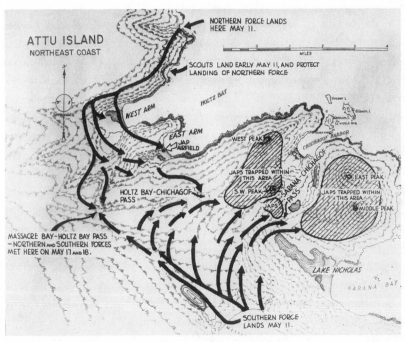

American Army Air Force map of American landings and subsequent operations on Attu Island, May 1943.

Indications that all was far from well soon emerged. First, on 5 May four Japanese ships ferrying supplies to Kiska were detected. That convoy turned back once the battle for Attu got underway but uncertainty about its size and mission would haunt the USN throughout the bitter struggle for Attu.[38] As for planning, while Kinkaid thought that a meeting between the various army and navy staffs on 25 April had cleared up "many minor points of great importance in the minds of individuals," others were not so certain. Although the marines attached to the training teams in California generally lauded the Seventh Division's cooperative attitude and eagerness to learn, they later claimed that the landing plan was overly complex, especially for troops with no previous amphibious warfare experience and far too little general combat training.[39] Poor weather and stormy high seas then postponed the assault until 11 May. When TF51 finally approached Attu that morning, unremitting dense fog prevented most air strikes from being launched. As the first soggy American soldiers splashed ashore on Attu's less than sun-dappled beaches, they met no welcoming blast of enemy fire. That was fortunate, as a scouting force sent to screen the Holtz Bay landing had lost its boats to strafing American warplanes minutes after disembarking. At the Massacre Bay beach, three landing craft were lost and twelve men drowned thanks to rough seas and rocks.[40] Attu's Japanese commander, Colonel Yamasaki Yasuyo, having been warned that an attack was imminent, had ordered his men to take up hilltop battle stations rather than try to stop the far more numerous invaders on the lengthy shoreline. Just how the Japanese learned of the assault remains a matter of debate, but only forty-four Americans had been killed by sundown on 12 May, seemingly demonstrating that it had not been "unreasonable to suppose that within a few days Attu would be taken."[41]

Units trying to seize vital mountain passes on 13 May, however, soon encountered extremely fierce resistance from mostly unseen Japanese defenders who poured relentless and accurate heavy fire down on them from well-fortified ridge lines. The American soldiers were confronted by persistent fog that severely limited air and naval fire support, and suffered terribly from cold weather compounded by unsuitable clothing and boots that kept their bodies neither warm nor dry. The troops tried desperately to close with a ghostly enemy they rarely glimpsed amidst a bleak snowy environment mostly devoid of cover. Attacks frequently bogged down when the inexperienced American soldiers, confronting "a defense based on daring, deception and excellent use of terrain," went to ground at the first sign of resistance; once on the ground, their frustrated officers often had great trouble getting the disheartened and freezing men up and moving again. By the night of the 13th some American units were clearly exhibiting signs of physical and mental exhaustion. When no discernible headway against the Japanese positions had been achieved by nightfall on the 14th, ground force commander Major General Albert E. Brown reluctantly reported to his good friend Rockwell that any "progress through [the] passes will, unless we are extremely lucky, be slow and costly, and will require troops in excess to those available in my command."[42]

The excruciatingly slow advance had not come as a surprise to officers with Alaskan experience. As Major J.L. Black, a Canadian officer attached to ADC, noted after the battle, one could not expect poorly conditioned troops to walk more than one mile over the hilly wet terrain so common in the Aleutians without becoming completely exhausted. Colonel Verbeck, Buckner's intelligence officer, had landed on Attu on 11 May and very nearly been

American forces unloading supplies on an Attu beach, 13 May 1943.

killed by trigger-happy American troops when he and his two Japanese-American interpreters had been mistaken for enemy soldiers.[43] Noting that assigning only three days to take Attu had been far too optimistic a forecast given the harsh local conditions and the size of the enemy force, Verbeck warned on 13 May that the Japanese were quite well trained for the climate and terrain in which they were operating. He also correctly predicted that in the face of greater American numbers and far superior firepower, the Japanese would cleave closely to the rugged passes and ridges while launching well-timed hit-and-run attacks to delay Brown's push forward. Indeed, on 14 May in a daring move, the Japanese launched their own amphibious assault, landing 150 troops behind American front lines near Holtz Bay.[44] Their American adversaries faced daunting and severe conditions. Artillery pieces often sank in the boggy terrain, and unremitting cloud cover and fog greatly limited aerial support. Wounded and injured troops had to be carried by upwards of six or eight stretcher bearers up and down steep icy terrain when infrequent lulls in the bitter fighting allowed them to be moved, robbing weakening front-line formations of badly needed combat personnel. Lieutenant Donald E. Dwinnell of the Thirty-Second Regiment, having taken two long days to finally take a key Japanese position blocking the advance, described the effort as "rugged, like attacking a pillbox by way of a tightrope." Charles K. Paulson, a platoon commander in the Seventeenth Infantry, had landed at Massacre Bay on 11 May only to find that his command had become separated from the main American force. Surrounded by the enemy, Paulson's men suffered terribly from sleep deprivation, exposure, and lack of food that brought on bouts of severe vomiting, before they were finally reunited with their unit on 15 May. Paulson's commander, Colonel E.P. Earle, died on 12 May, killed by a sniper as he and an Alaskan Scout surveyed enemy positions in a dangerous no-man's land.[45]

A greatly concerned Kinkaid did not think he had time to allow Brown to adjust to existing conditions. Reports sent on 15 May indicated that the Japanese were bringing mortars forward. Once those accurate and deadly weapons were in place, American formations, already suffering higher losses than the Japanese in small unit firefights, would sustain even greater casualties. Even more dangerous, American intelligence suspected that Japan was dispatching as many as four separate fleets to the north Pacific. Rockwell's keen concerns about his exposed ships only heightened when a Japanese submarine barely missed his flagship, the *Pennsylvania*, with four torpedoes on

15 May. Less than five hours later, claiming that Attu could not be taken with the forces currently available to him, Brown boarded the *Pennsylvania* to demand reinforcements.[46] Initially Rockwell thought that Attu's very narrow beaches were far too congested to allow more troops to come ashore, but he soon sent a battalion, which arrived from Adak on 17 May. Brown, however, was not present to greet or command the new unit. Kinkaid became disgruntled by the lack of progress and extremely worried that a superior IJN force would soon compel TF51's withdrawal from Attu. He decided on 16 May, after first obtaining approval from Buckner and DeWitt, to replace Brown despite Rockwell's apparently incensed request that Kinkaid meet with Brown before taking any precipitate action. Despondent, Brown wearily made his way to Adak on 17 May to meet DeWitt and Kinkaid. The meeting went badly. DeWitt apparently told Brown that he should never have been selected to command at Attu, while Brown accused DeWitt of forcing the three-day operational schedule on him. He then requested another regiment and some engineers to build a road network. Although Kinkaid viewed Brown as "a very nice chap, very well put together," he regarded the general's demands – and his concern that it might take sixty days to prevail against the Japanese – as a sign that Brown's confidence had evaporated. The general had to go.[47]

Brown's removal came just as American troops finally commandeered the critical high ground above Holtz Bay and impelled the tiring Japanese to withdraw reluctantly towards Chichagof Harbor. After three days of costly unproductive attacks against Japanese positions in Jarmin Pass, on 17 May Colonel Wayne Zimmerman, Earle's replacement, operating on an intuition, sent a patrol into the pass. It found that the battered enemy had pulled back, leaving only three dead troops behind.[48] Once the bedraggled northern and southern American contingents linked in the middle of the island on 18 May, the Japanese garrison's fate was sealed, although its doomed men died hard. Heavy combat persisted for almost two more weeks amidst abominable conditions on both sides. Supplying the American troops remained arduous, as spare parts shortages, accidents, and rugged conditions had worn down the USN's small vessels to such an extent that the army urgently had to request replacements. On 26 May the Thirty-Second Infantry, instructed to seize a pass, met heavy opposition until Private First Class Joe Martinez took it upon himself to clear enemy trenches with blasts of close range automatic weapons fire. But he too was soon cut down; Martinez won the Medal of Honor posthumously.[49] The anticipated Japanese riposte from the Kuriles, however, proved considerably less daunting than had been feared. Fifteen Japanese bombers flying from Paramushiro Island attacked USN vessels with torpedoes on 22 May. Not one ship suffered a hit, while the raiders lost one plane to naval gunfire. Sixteen more bombers appeared the next day, only to be bushwhacked by army warplanes operating from Amchitka. This time five Japanese bombers fell burning from the sky. No further air raids came and no IJN force ventured close to the Aleutians.[50]

By nightfall on 28 May the Japanese garrison's situation was most dire. Less than 1,000 fit soldiers and 600 wounded remained, penned up in harrowing conditions at Chichagof Harbor. With absolutely no hope of evacuation and surrender an impossible option – even on the dubious assumption that the Americans would be willing to take any prisoners[51] – Yamasaki ordered his remaining able men to assault American positions and capture enemy artillery so that they could continue the fight. After killing their wounded with morphine injections and grenades, the Japanese troops

American army soldier, suffering from frostbitten feet, being evacuated from Attu Island, May 1943.

assailed the American lines at 3:30 on the morning of 29 May. Smashing blindly through the American defences, the initial frenzied attack swiftly overran a medical clearing centre. Many of the prostrate American wounded were viciously bayonetted as they lay helplessly in their sick beds, although twelve men managed to survive by playing dead in their tents as confused Japanese troops milled about. The crazed and shrieking attackers very nearly reached the coveted American gun batteries before a hastily cobbled group of combat engineers conclusively shattered their assault with concentrated murderous automatic weapons fire and desperate hand-to-hand combat. Hundreds of Japanese were slain and many others ended their lives rather than surrender. This failed attack ended organized Japanese resistance on Attu, although some Japanese stragglers were discovered and killed even months later. A deserted Shemya was occupied by American forces on 30 May, leaving only Kiska in enemy hands.[52]

Reasserting American control over Attu had not come cheaply. Only twenty-three Japanese, almost all of them wounded and helpless, had been taken prisoner; 2,351 were buried the by Americans while a few hundred more had been interred by their own side. Of the more than 15,000 American soldiers who had landed on the island, 549 had been killed, 1,148 had been wounded, and more than 2,100 had fallen victim to trench foot, exposure, and frostbite brought on by harsh weather and inadequate clothing. Attu ranked behind only Iwo Jima in 1945 as the second most costly American battle in the Pacific in terms of losses in proportion to the number of troops involved.[53] Indeed, the conflict on Attu, portrayed much later as "a study in the ultimate folly of man and his weaknesses,"[54] had not even subsided before the post-mortems had begun. Naval officer James Bush praised the army troops as willing to fight but described them as poorly prepared, badly equipped, and "just pitiful." Other naval and army officers made much of the fact that the Seventh Division, composed mostly of California-trained troops, had performed poorly compared with soldiers possessing Alaskan experience. If Kiska were to be attacked, critics held that the men selected would have to be in top physical shape, well versed in amphibious warfare and small units tactics, properly equipped, and present in the Aleutians for at least a month before the landings began.[55]

Command arrangements also fell under the microscope. While assessing problems with training, combat loading, and shipping shortages in particular, Rockwell felt that the ultimate victory at Attu had "completely justified" his organization and command systems. While another naval officer praised Rockwell's drive, intelligence, and skill in handling various personalities, others held quite divergent views. Marine Corps General Holland Smith had been asked by Rockwell months earlier to draw up Attu's tactical plan. Citing insufficient information, he had declined to do so but then Nimitz had given him the job of training the Seventh Division in amphibious warfare techniques. Smith deplored the lack of a joint planning headquarters and the fact that Rockwell had remained aboard the *Pennsylvania* in Holtz Bay during the operation while Brown had resided on a transport in Massacre Bay. Finally, on 2 June Nimitz apologized to Kinkaid for failing to compel Rockwell to report to Kinkaid from Landcrab's inception.[56]

But it was Brown's performance that attracted the most attention. Rockwell's chief of staff, Robert Dennison, avowed that Brown had wasted valuable shipping space by bringing his personal sedan to Attu despite the island's utter lack of roads. Brigadier General William E. Lynd of the Inspector General's Office relayed that Brown, having judged himself "competent to prepare the plans and operate without advice as to local conditions in Alaska," had failed to adapt to local conditions. Thus he had launched unimaginative and costly conventional assaults despite advice from Verbeck and others that employing infiltration tactics might be more fruitful.[57] After the war, asserting that DeWitt had set a three-day deadline to assuage USN concerns about leaving its warships too long in a vulnerable spot, Brown declared that he had told Rockwell, DeWitt, and Buckner on 1 April that Attu's fight would probably be far more protracted. But James Bush stated that while in transit to Attu, Brown had said that the island could be taken in just three days, dismissing Bush's assertion that it took American forces that long to occupy undefended Adak and Amchitka. Perhaps Brown's comments to Bush reflected his need to follow the party line. After all, his April declaration had prompted DeWitt to seek Brown's removal even before TF51 had departed California.[58]

Citing numerous problems beyond his control – unreliable maps, unexpectedly heavy opposition, Earle's unfortunate death, poor weather, bad radios, a shoddy supply system, and inexperienced troops – Brown protested his removal even though DeWitt and Kinkaid claimed that Brown had told them on 17 May that he would have fired himself under the circumstances. Brown's second in command at Attu, Major General Archibald V. Arnold, defended Brown's performance and blamed poor army-navy cooperation and Kinkaid's inability to understand the effects of terrain and weather on infantry combat, which left the admiral unable to "evaluate the prospects of the outcome." Most important, Lieutenant General L.J. McNair, commander of army ground forces, thought that although a pessimistic Brown may not have "fought with sufficient vigor or sound tactics," had Brown's situation been better appreciated by Kinkaid, DeWitt, and Buckner on 16 May, he might not have been removed from command. According to historian D. Colt Denfeld, Brown's claim that an additional sixty days would be needed to subdue Attu was the product of a misunderstanding following Colonel Talley's request for engineering supplies and equipment for the final battle and post-battle construction – an anticipated period of sixty days. Brown's removal did not prevent him from heading another division in Europe (indeed, DeWitt thought that Attu had given Brown much needed experience that would stand him in good stead in another divisional command), although he was not officially cleared of any wrong-doing until 1949.[59] With Attu now firmly back in American hands, planning for Kiska could begin in earnest.

6

A Strong Alaska Means a Foot-Loose Fleet:
Kiska's Capture

In *On War* Carl von Clausewitz recognizes that even when determination does "not suffice to bring about a great decision, one may still want to mount a strategic attack against a minor objective." If the attack succeeds, the "situation reverts to a state of rest and balance"; if serious difficulties are encountered, then the advance can be halted and "replaced either by offensives of opportunity or by mere strategic maneuvers."[1] Attu's bloody recapture definitely qualified as a serious difficulty. It should have brought an end to further Aleutian operations, with the Americans leaving the Japanese garrison on Kiska to wither painfully and die on the vine. Indeed, some American strategists, appalled by the butcher's bill for Attu, attempted to make that case. The more adamant advocates of further attacks, however, succeeded in putting their plans into action at Kiska, and were helped considerably by less

136

ardent officers who simply wanted to end the Aleutian campaign finally and decisively so that key military resources could be used elsewhere. The result was a peculiar, unopposed invasion that did little to burnish American military reputations.

The War Department told an impatient DeWitt on 19 April that he could begin assembling two infantry regiments at Fort Ord in California for possible employment in the Aleutians after the recapture of Attu. Knowing all too well that such a notification did not formally authorize Kiska's invasion, Kinkaid hoped Nimitz and DeWitt would nudge the Joint Chiefs of Staff (JCS) to sanction an attack quickly for September 1943.[2] It was not only the JCS that needed prodding though. In mid-May Britain's political and military leadership again descended on Washington for the Trident Conference, intending to argue the impossibility of concentrating Allied efforts against Japan while holding Germany at bay. The British commanders wanted to push the notion that defeating Germany first "would hasten the ultimate defeat of Japan, since it would release substantial aid for war in the Pacific, particularly naval and air forces and in addition might well bring in Russia against Japan."[3] The Joint Chiefs, as at Casablanca, did not object to retaining Germany's defeat as the coalition's primary strategic goal. Still, they contended that a major European offensive could be mounted simultaneously with unremitting pressure expressly designed to force Japan's final and unconditional surrender. Once Germany was utterly smashed, the full weight of Allied power could be directed against Japan, unless "conditions develop which indicate that the war as a whole can be brought more quickly to a successful conclusion by the earlier mounting of a major offensive Japan, [at which point] the strategical concept set forth herein may be reversed."[4]

The British found this qualification quite unnerving. Further, King's intent to attack Formosa and the Marianas and to acquire vital bases astride Japanese communications deepened their never quiescent qualms. As for the north Pacific, King commented pointedly that the United States had bided its time before retaking Attu. But he airily dismissed the threat of a Japanese Aleutian counterattack as remote and described any American drive towards the Kuriles as likely to be beset with difficulties. Nevertheless he wanted to grab Kiska soon to avoid retaining considerable forces in the Aleutians.[5] Unlike the meeting at Casablanca, this time the British did not put up much of a fight. First, as Australia's foreign minister, H.V. Evatt, revealed, a radiantly confident Churchill was "far keener on Pacific activities than during last year, when our position was much worse." In addition, Marshall had agreed to a British proposal to attack Italy that summer and sufficient shipping was apparently available for both Pacific and European operations. Therefore on 25 May the Combined Chiefs of Staff (CCS) approved several Pacific offensives, including the "ejection of the Japanese from the Aleutians."[6]

But the base brutality of the battle for Attu and the too lengthy American casualty list gave some American officers pause as they contemplated what might come at Kiska. Over 15,000 soldiers had been needed to eliminate 2,500 Japanese on Attu; Kiska's garrison was thought to number 9,500 men, a force more than strong enough to mount a robust mobile defence. Although the Military Intelligence Division (MID) believed Attu's recapture would probably prevent Japan from reinforcing Kiska, the latter's formidable fortifications meant the enemy would in all likelihood refuse to abandon the island without a fight.[7] Thus DeWitt faced the problem of finding sufficient forces to retake Kiska. The Seventh Division's harrowing ordeal on Attu had left it in very poor shape, and the army wanted to shift that unit out of Alaska anyway. In March the JCS had authorized a 110,000-man troop ceiling for Alaska, a deceptively large figure that included thousands of aircrew, construction engineers, and sundry support personnel not attached to combat units. While the ceiling could be exceeded for another Aleutian operation,[8] the order to assemble just two regiments in California did not bode well. Certainly more soldiers would be needed to conquer Kiska. Where could they be found?

One option involved the Special Service Force (SSF), established in mid-1942 to operate in rugged northern Scandinavia. The formation had been considered for Aleutian operations later that year but Handy had opposed sending it to Alaska for fear that it would languish there unused.[9] Despite various proposals to dispatch it to the Soviet Union, New Guinea, and Sicily, the elite joint Canadian-American unit had idled restively, prompting its commander in February 1943 to beg for an assignment in Alaska. Convinced that the SSF's special arctic warfare skills were tailor-made for Aleutian conditions, Colonel Robert T. Frederick wanted to fight on Attu or Kiska. Sensitive to the SSF's embarrassing plight and noting with some considerable regret that the unit should have been used on Attu, Marshall suggested at Trident that it be deployed on any future operations in the Aleutians.[10]

Visiting Vancouver on 19 April, DeWitt told the head of Canada's Pacific Command that the invasion of Attu by the United States was imminent and that a subsequent move against Kiska was likely. Catching the obvious hint, an overeager Major General George Pearkes (recently removed from a Canadian division in Britain very much against his will) enthusiastically suggested that Canada might participate in any attack on Kiska and asked to send a small team of observers to Attu. Pleased to see his initiative fall on such fertile ground, DeWitt approved the observer request and promised full cooperation in any future shared action with Pacific Command.[11] DeWitt also received key support from John Hickerson. As secretary of the American section of the Permanent Joint Board on Defence (PJBD) and one of the few "Canadianists" in the State Department, on 8 May Hickerson broached possible Canadian participation in Aleutian operations with Major General Pope. Hickerson, a tough Texan not known for mincing words, bluntly told Pope Canada had done little to date in the war with Japan. Rising to the bait, Pope promptly retorted that not only had there been rather little scope for action, but Canadian air and naval elements had been present in Alaska since mid-1942. Most important, Pope did not see the sense in sending any Canadian soldiers to Alaska since the American army currently had several unemployed divisions at its ready disposal. Confiding it was just a matter of time before Aleutian operations got under way, Hickerson again suggested involving Canadian troops. The threat posed by Japan in the north Pacific was admittedly slight but, as the Aleutians were part of North America, Hickerson pledged that the United States would formally invite Canada to send troops to Alaska. He thought a token Canadian role would be appropriate and later informed Embick that he had approached Pope because Canada had "not thus far had occasion to do much fighting ... my guess is that such an invitation would be gratefully accepted." While military considerations had to remain paramount, Hickerson felt certain this was an occasion when public policy and military considerations might well coincide. He believed "it would really help a lot in Canada, especially in the western provinces" if Canadians fought in the Aleutians, given that the Canadian army's ongoing inactivity had engendered considerable and often pointed political controversy both at home and abroad.[12]

Senior USN officers took a decidedly different view. Cooke vigorously opposed using Canadian troops, as "we are not in need of assistance and, except as an aid to their morale, I see no reason for bringing them in at this late date in the operations. No great political benefits are apparent." Declaring that Alaska's troop ceiling had been set for logical and practical reasons,

Cooke asserted that adding Canadian troops to the mix would assuredly complicate matters. Admiral King agreed that the Canadians would be an unwanted complication, especially as they were not needed. Still, while he advised against Canadian army participation in Aleutian operations, King added that if the War Department really desired Canadian assistance, he would not object.[13]

The War Department warmly welcomed King's compromising attitude, as both the Office of the Director of Plans and Operations (OPD) and Buckner very much desired Canadian troops even if they only relieved American soldiers from static garrison duty. Asked on 21 May whether he wanted Canadian units, DeWitt responded that while he did, their use at Attu other than as garrison troops after mopping up simply was not feasible given obvious time constraints. Eager to determine if Canada would provide men for Kiska or other Aleutian duties, DeWitt asked Marshall for permission to meet with Pearkes again on 24 May.[14] A two-pronged recommendation emerged from this second chat with Pearkes: Canada would provide an infantry battalion and an anti-aircraft battery for garrison duty on Amchitka by mid-June; and a brigade would be made available by 1 August for Kiska's invasion. Happy to accept the garrison supplement, the War Department held the brigade proposal in abeyance until the JCS had ratified Kiska's invasion. It also quickly reminded DeWitt that the Canadians would have to be included within Alaska's established troop ceiling.[15]

American commanders, however, continued to debate how to gainfully employ Canadian soldiers. Though he wanted to use the Canadians, Colonel McNarney worried that the limited time available to train those troops would restrict their use to a floating reserve, an opinion shared by Admiral Edwards. Even DeWitt thought the Canadians could function only to reinforce American units once the initial landings had taken place. DeWitt's primary concern was Canadian reluctance to give them a definite answer about the brigade. If Canada declined to participate, he told General Hull, the manpower shortfall could possibly be made up with troops already in Alaska but only if the army immediately offered another regiment from the continental United States. DeWitt, however, needed a speedy resolution so that preparations could get firmly under way.[16]

Kenneth Stuart was partly responsible for the Canadian delay. Pearkes had cabled the Canadian Chief of the General Staff (CGS) on 20 April to describe his meeting with DeWitt. He told Stuart only that DeWitt had mentioned a projected operation in the Aleutians commencing early in May.[17] As a result, Stuart took no action at all until Pope's wire describing the meeting with Hickerson crossed his cluttered desk on 10 May. Hickerson had chosen well, for Pope, the "best informed of Canadian generals and the one with the most enquiring mind,"[18] thought Canadians should "be desirous of associating ... in such a project rather than sit quietly awaiting an invitation to do so." Quite interested in the Aleutians at this point, Stuart advised Pope not to approach Marshall but then he changed his mind, possibly because allowing Pearkes and DeWitt to settle the matter on the west coast risked alienating the powerful American army commander. Stuart's instructions to Pope were simple; since it would be helpful to participate even in the latter stages of an Aleutian operation, Stuart could offer an infantry battalion and some anti-aircraft guns.[19]

Meeting Marshall on 13 May, Pope was troubled by Stuart's admission that Minister of Defence J.L. Ralston had not been consulted. Although he contemplated advising Stuart to bring Ralston into the picture, remembering that Stuart had boasted about his ability to handle Ralston, Pope "hesitated for a moment and was lost." Marshall offered few details and, declining any firm commitments, promised to confer with DeWitt before getting back to Pope.[20] DeWitt and Pearkes, however, were surely setting a quick pace. Convinced that accepting DeWitt's proposals would raise sagging morale and give his men much-needed combat experience, on 25 May Pearkes recommended taking up both invitations promptly. Stuart delightedly agreed but he required formal political approval before he could proceed any further. On the morning of 26 May he thus presented a detailed memorandum to the Cabinet War Committee (CWC). Repeating Pearkes's reasons, Stuart added that moving soldiers to an active theatre would raise army prestige, diminish Canadian public hostility towards home defence "zombie" conscripts, improve relations with the United States, and demonstrate Canada's ongoing interest in the Pacific conflict. Furthermore, the move would be in accordance with PJBD plans approved by both national governments.[21] Surprised, the CWC delayed its decision for another day to study the issue, and Prime Minister King left the meeting greatly disturbed. Just days before, unhappy with previous communication lapses, the CWC had warned its military advisers to ensure the prompt delivery "of all important secret reports and information which had come to the attention of the Chiefs of Staff." As the 26 May meeting unfolded, the ever-wily King realized that Ralston had no prior knowledge of Stuart's proposals. Convinced that Stuart had covertly initiated discussions with DeWitt without Ralston's knowledge or approval, the prime minister petulantly commented that Ralston, not Stuart, should have brought the matter to the CWC's attention.[22]

King's ire rapidly dissipated, thanks to the efforts of Under-Secretary of State for External Affairs (USSEA) Norman Robertson, who had replaced Skelton after his sudden death in January 1941. Robertson represented a new breed of younger and more aggressive Canadian officials intent on ensuring that the great powers, while entitled to lead in international affairs, should share control in particular areas of expertise or interest "with such other powers as are able and willing to make a definite contribution." This notion of "functionalism"[23] dovetailed into Robertson's views about the north Pacific. A native British Columbian, in early 1942 Robertson had advised that, although a Japanese invasion of Canada was a fairly remote possibility, not every Allied nation had to make its primary martial contribution in Europe. Concerned then that the Canadian army's plans for Europe were both excessive and politically dangerous, Robertson had endorsed organizing special commando units for action in the north Pacific. Robertson's views had not altered with the passage of time. Recalling a 1942 crisis in Australian-Canadian relations brought on by a Canadian high commissioner's rash and unfulfilled promise of military aid to the antipodes, the USSEA postulated on 27 May 1943 that dispatching Canadian forces to Alaska might deflect any new Australian demands for Canadian help and remind Canberra that "the United States was not the only American country helping in the Pacific war."[24] More important, Robertson viewed Aleutian participation as a useful means to better relations with Washington and to counter a growing American military presence in Canada. He had remarked in December 1941 that the United States, possessing a new conscious sense of its manifest destiny and a corresponding disposition to take decisions and accept responsibilities, had "not too tactfully handled" Canadian issues since the United States had entered into the war. As a result, he hoped that Canadian soldiers fighting in the Aleutians would reinforce the good impression made by the dispatch of aircraft and ships to Alaska in 1942. In addition, the presence of thousands of Americans on defence-related projects throughout northwest Canada led British High Commissioner Malcolm Macdonald to conclude in April 1943 that the sheer scope of that activity – a so-called "army of occupation" – was becoming a serious political problem. Sharing Macdonald's concerns,

Robertson stated that "the active participation of our troops in plans for recovering Northwest America would to a certain extent balance the impression created here and in the United States by the predominant part played by the Americans in defence activities in Northwest Canada."[25]

The prime minister's comments to the CWC on 27 May clearly reflected Robertson's influence. King repeated the USSEA's justifications almost verbatim but still fretted that Canada's small contribution would inevitably pale in comparison to American effort. Moreover, Canada would probably accrue little credit from any victory, while a military failure would undoubtedly reflect disproportionately on his government. Having thus obliquely referred to the disastrous loss of nearly 2,000 Canadian soldiers at Hong Kong in December 1941, King chose not to sign on to any Aleutian venture until the CWC was officially approached by Washington. When C.G. Power weighed in to say he favoured attacking Kiska but opposed the static garrison option because it reminded him of Hong Kong (Power's son had been captured at Hong Kong), Stuart emphasized that Canadian west coast security would not be impaired if DeWitt's proposals were accepted. King then asked if Aleutian operations would hinder the development of the Canadian army in Britain, at which point Stuart realized that he was on the carpet. He promptly explained that he had made absolutely no commitments to the Americans and thereby pacified the CWC. In turn, the CWC agreed to entertain Aleutian operations if an invitation came directly from Roosevelt or Stimson. King indicated that he, however, did not eagerly await any such overture; it could prompt demands in parliament and by the press to explain the rationale for Canadian participation and the place of Aleutian operations in global Allied strategy. Since Roosevelt had not mentioned any Aleutian activity and there was no indication that the notion of retaking Kiska had grown out of the Casablanca conference, King feared such questions could prove most embarrassing politically.[26]

King had been far from truthful. On 20 May Roosevelt had briefed him and other Pacific War Council (PWC) officials in Washington about Attu and Kiska. Indeed, when Roosevelt stated that Attu's recapture would neutralize Kiska, King responded that Japan's occupation of the Aleutians "had been a matter of grave concern to Canada and that Canada welcomes and applauds every measure to evict the Japanese from the Aleutian area."[27] Perhaps King's renowned memory had failed him, but that is doubtful. Upon learning that Hickerson had contacted Pope, an irked King had been certain that the PJBD, as an advisory body only, had no right at all to intrude upon operational planning. He also believed that Stuart and Pearkes had seriously overstepped their authority by discussing Aleutian operations with the Americans without gaining prior political approval. Not opposed in principle to dispatching troops to Alaska, King thought the military's procedure had been incorrect.[28] In this context then, King's claim of ignorance regarding the Aleutians was probably his attempt to rein in an overeager and incautious Canadian military.

Reining in the military assumed even greater importance when a livid Ralston stormed into King's office on 28 May purporting that reporters had just told him Canadian troops were already on Attu Island. King averred that Stuart would certainly have to answer to him for this disturbing new development, and noted worriedly: "It was indeed an alarming moment in that it indicated that the army are going ahead with operations without the Cabinet having even sanctioned them." When Ralston dragged an utterly chastened Stuart that evening to King's beloved country estate north of Ottawa, the CGS confided that the soldiers in question amounted to only eight observers sent by Pearkes. Admitting that he should have sought Ralston's approval before letting Pearkes proceed, Stuart promised that no commitments had been made, and he blamed Pearkes for moving too quickly. No additional troops would go to Alaska until the entire Cabinet had met to mull over the issue. In the meantime King instructed Ralston to announce that the Attu observers were part of a joint Canadian-American effort to safeguard the Pacific coast. Yet the next morning, after reading some dismal accounts of Attu's bloody fighting, an appalled King nearly blocked Canadian army involvement in the Aleutians. He let the process continue, however, fearing that a negative answer would damage relations with the United States (and his valued friendship with Roosevelt) and might prompt Stuart's resignation. Unwilling to lose Stuart – a rare general who both opposed dispatching conscripts to Europe and had some sympathy for French Canadians – King consoled himself that by fighting in the Aleutians, Canada would prevent America from taking all the credit for protecting the west coast.[29]

Canada's marked delay in responding to DeWitt's proposals was noticed in Washington. On 27 May McNarney asked Pope if Canada would send units to Kiska. Pope responded that although Ottawa would no doubt agree, he had to await the arrival of formal instructions.[30] When those instructions arrived later that day, a dismayed Pope discovered that Ottawa wanted Stimson to issue a formal invitation. He pointed out that it would be "more consonant with our self-interest to let the Americans know we wished to play our part in the expedition than to seek lamely the 'cover' of an invitation from them." Having been told by Hickerson that the War Department preferred to do business with the dominions through Britain's Joint Staff Mission, Pope warned Stuart that Marshall might refuse the Canadian demand.[31] As Marshall was unavailable, Pope met instead with McNarney on 28 May. Reluctant initially to accept Canada's request, McNarney abandoned his opposition when his staff found no inherent objection to meeting Ottawa's demand. Stimson's letter came to Pope the next day. It stated that "participation by the Canadian army alongside United States troops in the common cause, either as garrison forces or in offensive operations in the area in question, would be highly gratifying to the United States War Department." Stimson also indicated that all arrangements would "be made by the U.S. Joint Chiefs of Staff, or their representatives with Canadian military officials."[32]

Stuart sent Stimson's letter to Ralston on 31 May. Citing administrative difficulties and explaining that he believed such duties duplicated the army's unpopular home defence role, Stuart dropped the garrison alternative and sought permission only to assemble a brigade to attack Kiska. The CWC quickly granted its assent on 31 May, although Ralston delayed his rejoinder to Stimson until 3 June. The reason for this delay is unclear. Ralston had a well-earned reputation for paying excessive attention to detail but he resented Stuart's handling of the Aleutian discussions. He may have been deliberately tardy to remind the CGS who really grasped the reins of power. Moreover, Ralston's acceptance was conditional. While operational details should be left to the militaries, Canada's defence minister insisted that the actual dispatch of the Canadian brigade, code-named Greenlight Force, would be subject to the satisfactory completion of these operational arrangements. This condition plagued the formation of the Canadian brigade group until its dispatch to Kiska in August, as politicians and generals quibbled endlessly over control and even over the eligibility of soldiers to serve in the unit.[33]

This tiresome "constant hunting for cover," as Pope described it, could potentially "produce an adverse reaction on the part of the U.S. Army, to say the least." But DeWitt was unaware of the Ottawa contortions and urged the War Department to put a burr under the Canadians to set things moving. Washington's response was not reassuring; while Pope clearly understood the urgency of the matter, Ottawa obviously did not.[34] Canada had added much-needed soldiers to Amphibious Task Force Nine (ATF9) but DeWitt faced another urgent problem: his unexpected and imminent transfer to Washington to assume command of a joint amphibious warfare college. He was concerned that the switch had been prompted by his all-too-prominent role in the controversial evacuation of Japanese-Americans from west coast communities in early 1942, and worried that the transfer might injure his career. Citing his north Pacific experience, the ongoing negotiations with Pearkes, and his concern that his potential successor would "receive credit for the successful culmination of a series of developments and operations that had been accomplished by another," DeWitt begged to be left in place on the west coast until 15 October 1943.[35]

DeWitt had good reason to be concerned; not everyone thought he had performed well since Pearl Harbor. On the night of 8-9 December 1941, confronting a nervous and frightened crowd at the office of San Francisco's mayor, DeWitt had excoriated the impromptu gathering for showing panic. Japanese planes might bomb the city, he admitted, but he showed little sympathy, advising the people to "learn to take it. You've got to take it, and if you

Canadian soldiers belonging to Le Régiment de Hull boarding a troopship in the Aleutians, August 1943.

can't take it, get the hell out of San Francisco before it comes." Such comments had not impressed the notoriously acerbic General Joseph Stilwell. Stationed briefly in California prior to being shifted to a controversial post advising the Chinese in mid-1942, Stilwell had found DeWitt's command "jittery" and amateurish in the days following America's entry into the war. General McNair had also said to Stilwell in late January 1942 that DeWitt had "gone crazy and needed ten refusals before he realizes that it is 'No.'" Furthermore, DeWitt and Marshall had a history. When Marshall had taken command of the army in 1939, Roosevelt had passed over the more senior DeWitt for that position, possibly because as a career logistics officer, DeWitt was not seen as suitable command material. And while they had enjoyed friendly relations for decades, Marshall often found DeWitt "obdurate." Marshall's response to DeWitt's plea was not encouraging. Denying that the Japanese evacuation had prompted DeWitt's relocation, the army head asserted that the transfer had been initiated because DeWitt possessed crucial knowledge of combined operations and because he had previously headed the Army War College. Concluding that the course was clear in his mind, Marshall asked DeWitt to come to Washington.[36]

Although Marshall later relented, allowing DeWitt to stay on until after Kiska's recapture, the impending transfer spurred DeWitt to even greater efforts. On 30 May he and Nimitz submitted their joint plan for the Kiska operation. Code-named "Cottage," the scheme anticipated using two full USN task forces, TF51 and TF16, plus five regimental combat teams. Kinkaid would command the invasion, scheduled for 15 August. Chosen to lead the ground forces despite an inexperienced staff, Corlett sought to produce a flexible preliminary operational design. Since so many ATF9 troops lacked combat experience and exposure to harsh Aleutian conditions, Corlett wanted to carry out a full practice landing on Kodiak before the force embarked for Kiska.[37]

Some officers continued to question the need to attack Kiska. Wedemeyer, chief of the OPD's Strategy and Policy Group (SPG), counselled that any invasion would have to be preceded by a lengthy softening-up process to weaken the defenders. And although the USN claimed that Kiska's recapture would confer more north Pacific operational opportunities, such claims could not be taken seriously; there was little to fight "against in that area which is not conducive to extensive military commitments by either the Japanese or ourselves." Wedemeyer therefore advised resisting any "precipitate action which is suggested by the navy." He thought the navy had to "be made to realize that Kiska has no strong offensive possibilities from the enemy viewpoint now that we are established on Attu, Adak and Amchitka. We are therefore justified in a meticulous approach to the problem of eliminating the Japanese from that area." Major General Muir S. Fairchild of the Joint Strategic Survey Committee (JSSC) exhibited even less ardour, as "it would be well to leave Kiska as a bait to attract Japanese shipping within range of our air and naval forces, thus enabling us to increase our attrition on this vital and vulnerable possession."[38]

JSSC opinions could not be easily ignored. Formed in November 1942, its three members, drawn equally from the army, navy, and army air corps, were charged explicitly with advising the Joint Chiefs on all matters of combined, grand, and global strategy. Indeed JSSC power, in the opinion of historian Brian Villa, was at times equal in influence to the Joint Chiefs themselves.[39] A JCS meeting on 8 June did little to illuminate the Aleutian issue. Marshall thought any decision about moving towards Kiska should be left up to the USN, with the proviso that the navy be mindful of the fact that the operation could entail severe army losses. As King was unwilling to make any decision at that time, the Joint Chiefs dumped the matter on the JPS. It had much to consider, for the SPG firmly opposed invading Kiska. Although ATF9's roster had reached 29,000 soldiers, Kiska's garrison was thought to exceed 10,000 men. Attu's task force had suffered heavy losses despite outnumbering the Japanese five to one. Consequently the SPG, noting that the threat to Alaska emanated from Japan proper and not Kiska, thought it better to let the Japanese stay on Kiska, "thus inflicting attrition on enemy shipping and naval forces, than to seize it, especially in view of the relatively large forces required for the operation." The JPS acknowledged that Kiska's recapture could produce heavy losses and might lead only to limited reductions in Alaska's huge garrison. It nonetheless recognized significant advantages: boosting American civilian morale once Japan was driven from American soil (recognized by the SPG); lowering enemy morale; diverting Japanese resources to the north Pacific; acquiring valuable battle experience; and putting air and submarine bases on Kiska. As to letting Kiska wither on the vine, the JPS asserted that just four Japanese transports a month could sustain Kiska's garrison indefinitely. It thus recommended allowing DeWitt and Nimitz to set an operational target date. Therefore, on 11 June JCS authorized Kiska's invasion for August or September.[40]

Operation Cottage's final approval spurred a frenzy of activity. On 16 June the army ordered troops at Fort Ord to begin their arduous transformation into battalion landing groups (BLGs). By 21 June the navy had initiated intense exercises at San Diego to prepare the transport and landing craft crews for the very difficult task ahead.[41] Kinkaid ordered aircraft to bomb Kiska at every conceivable opportunity, sent more ships to aggressively patrol Kiska's maritime approaches, and requested a minimum addition of three battleships, eight cruisers, and three squadrons of destroyers to his existing fleet. Buckner had his own wish list. He noted that Alaska's 110,000-man ceiling was not excessive, as those troops were defending an area "covering an east-west distance approximately equal to that between Charleston, South Carolina, and Los Angeles, California, and a north-south distance about equal to that between Iceland and London." That being the case, he feared Japan might send a division against his Aleutian bases, "possibly by-passing some of the most westerly, just as we did in the case of Kiska." Never shy, Buckner boldly argued that "a strong Alaska means a foot-loose fleet" and that it was far more economical to bolster army detachments in the territory than to hold large fleet units for their protection.[42]

Two new appraisals belittled Buckner's concerns about Japanese leap-frogging in the Aleutians. Doubting if Japan would risk major naval action anywhere in the Pacific, the Joint Intelligence Committee (JIC) felt that Kiska's garrison would doggedly resist any invasion even if outside Japanese intervention were limited to submarine attacks, bombing missions from the Kuriles, seaborne supply runs, and naval demonstrations. The Combined Intelligence Committee (CIC) echoed this judgment. As Japan's overall Pacific strategy seemed defensive, the CIC expected that the enemy would only seek to buttress its security perimeter. Japanese forces would probably fight to the death to retain their individual strong-points, but the CIC thought Japan had resigned itself to losing the Aleutians while greatly strengthening the Kuriles. If the Japanese on Kiska did opt to fight to the last man, a 5 July Western Defence Command (WDC) study by Weckerling painted a grisly future for many Cottage participants. The Japanese garrison was liberally supplied with artillery and sitting on high ground overlooking all the suitable landing sites. It had also enjoyed a full year to prepare formidable fortifications. Weckerling had some potentially good news to offer. Sustained Allied bombing, diet-related illnesses, and other wastage factors had probably inflicted considerable losses on the Japanese – but even then the fighting was expected to be severe. Although Weckerling declined to estimate losses, Pearkes was told to expect thirty casualties and six fatalities for every 100 soldiers.[43]

As the soldiers prepared for their Kiska rendezvous, the Eleventh Air Force dramatically stepped up its bombing runs over the island. Having dropped just over 3,000 tons of explosives on Attu and Kiska by June 1943, army aircraft hailed almost 900,000 pounds of bombs onto Kiska in July alone. Such attacks were far from simple cakewalks, as the American and Canadian raiders faced the "most concentrated [anti-aircraft fire] in the world ... except for Malta." On numerous occasions in July and August, American ships also blasted Kiska with thousands of high-explosive rounds. Although Japanese facilities suffered considerable damage from these assaults, the garrison's well-dug-in soldiers were left largely untouched – except for some frazzled nerves. As Private Takahashi noted in his diary, USN "marksmanship is really a sad case."[44]

The ATF9 tactical schemes had also been set in place. Drawn up again in San Diego, the plans received Kinkaid's immediate approval. Nearly 35,000 soldiers – supported by five battleships, forty other ships, and 262 land-based aircraft – would start landing on Kiska on 15 August. Sixty minutes prior to the H-hour, naval vessels would approach Gertrude Cove on Kiska's southern edge in a diversionary manoeuvre designed to draw Japanese attention while the real assault began on the northwest shore. Two SSF regiments would spearhead the attack by moving rapidly inland to knock the defenders off balance, with the remaining troops coming ashore over the following two days. Absolutely determined not to repeat Attu's many errors, Kiska's planners relentlessly emphasized that soldiers had to speedily seize ridges and passes while maintaining continual contact with the foe via aggressive patrolling and fire and movement tactics. Another bitter lesson, the need to acclimatize troops, did not go unheeded. Most ATF9 soldiers arrived in the Aleutians a full month before D-Day for intense training and the doling out of specialized clothing and footwear designed to prevent a repeat of Attu's unfortunate weather-related losses. Almost all of the units participated in a highly successful full-scale dress rehearsal landing carried out on 3 August. The absence of the specialized Eighty-Seventh Mountain Infantry Regiment, however, threatened to delay the attack's start. Slated to arrive in the Aleutians on 4 August, the Eighty-Seventh, in Kinkaid's opinion, would require two weeks of training before it could go into action. Kinkaid therefore conferred with the other force commanders on 30 July and then asked Nimitz to push D-Day back to 24 August. But when Marshall made it clear on 7 August that he did not think this was the time to be ultra-conservative, Nimitz, asserting that a postponement would delay other Pacific operations, retained the 15 August target date.[45]

Six hundred heavily armed SSF members silently paddled ashore on Kiska before daylight broke on 15 August. After securing their beachhead, the SSF troopers moved inland rapidly as the main force's first wave landed at 6:20 a.m. The seas were remarkably and uncharacteristically calm, yet very thick and persistent fog rendered movement extremely difficult and tension spiked as apprehensive men quizzically pondered the total absence of enemy opposition. By nightfall 7,000 Allied soldiers were settling in for an uncomfortably cold and nervous night. Not one Japanese combatant had been spotted although one American patrol had reported finding hot coffee and enemy grenades in an abandoned trench. The next day, plagued again by heavy and unrelenting fog, the troops reached most of their objectives well ahead of schedule; there was no resistance except for "a few Jap riflemen" who had to be driven by fire from one position. As the initial Attu landings had

American and Canadian forces landing on Kiska Island, 15 August 1943.

been undisputed, Alaska Defense Command (ADC) intelligence thought the absence of resistance indicated that "the enemy ha[d] established a position of such merit that any action forward of that position would not be justified by the costs involved or the advantages to be gained." But as the Allied forces had still not met resistance by 18 August, it became quite clear that a hasty evacuation of the Japanese garrison had been accomplished in late July or early August.[46]

The Japanese had indeed covertly withdrawn their Kiska troops on 29 July. Emperor Hirohito had paid rather little attention to the north Pacific but the loss of Attu caught his attention. In a rare moment of imperial pique, on 6 and 7 June he lambasted representatives from the IJA and IJN for this latest defeat. He lamented the lack of army-navy cooperation, a frequent imperial complaint since the Japanese had evacuated the tattered remnants of their starving Guadalcanal garrison in early February 1943. The emperor further criticized their inability to hold Attu or to reinforce its embattled garrison after the Americans attacked, and wondered why Japanese forces were not striking back at the Allies, adding plaintively, "Isn't there some way, some place, where we can win a real victory over the Americans?"[47]

But the chastened Japanese military had already reluctantly decided on 19 May to pull its forces from Kiska after concluding that nothing could be done to save Attu or to seriously interfere with general American operations in the Aleutians. Given overwhelming American air and naval superiority in the north Pacific, using surface vessels to remove Kiska's garrison seemed suicidal. The Japanese therefore employed submarines. Despite possessing many large submersibles capable of ferrying a large number of soldiers, removing more than 6,000 personnel from Kiska would take months, even if the IJN used all of its available craft and American opposition proved slight. In actuality, that opposition proved to be quite significant, for the USN had once again cracked the IJN's codes. By 23 June, when the IJN cancelled the evacuation effort, only 820 Japanese troops had been removed from Kiska yet three submarines were lost and many more vessels damaged.[48] Japan had no choice then but to employ surface craft. Since many of its ships lacked radar, the IJN had to hope for the onset of poor weather and fog to shield a dangerous high-speed run towards Kiska. The first attempt came on 7 July when twelve ships commanded by Rear Admiral Kimura Masatomi left the Kuriles bound for Kiska. But when inclement weather and fog failed to materialize on cue, Kimura had to return home. A second attempt begun on 21 July was more successful. The fog finally arrived in a thick blanket that lasted for days, although it proved to be a mixed blessing when one destroyer returned home after sustaining heavy damage in a collision. Kimura's force arrived at Kiska at 1:40 p.m. on 29 July without further incident. Within an hour the ships had speedily loaded 5,100 men and begun the risky voyage home. Not one member of the garrison remained although most weapons were left behind or dumped in the harbour. Before leaving, Japanese engineers had set timed explosives to give the impression that work on the island's defensive positions was continuing.[49]

Kimura had been very lucky indeed, for a sizeable USN task force had been seeking to annihilate his small flotilla. American intelligence had surmised that Japan would try to sneak supplies to Kiska on 26 July, a prediction that acquired considerable credibility when a PBY spotted seven unidentified ships 320 kilometres southwest of Attu and American decoders intercepted a message from Kiska's commander stating that the night of 25-6 July would be "favorable or unfavorable for something."[50] At 12:45 a.m. on the morning of 26 July the radar screen on one USN ship patrolling 130 kilometres south of Kiska showed a surface bogey (an unidentified radar target) bearing 060 degrees and at a distance of fifteen nautical miles. When other American ships also reported up to six target pips on their radar screens, the two battleships present opened fire at 1:13 a.m. at a distance of nearly seventeen kilometres. For thirty minutes the American guns blazed away as the pips appeared intermittently until the task force commander ordered a cease fire. Several hours of intense searching failed to determine whether any targets had been struck, if indeed there had been any targets to hit. In fact, Kimura's ships had been nowhere near the battle scene. Subsequent USN investigations into the "Battle of the Pips" failed to offer any concrete answers for the radar contacts. Some thought the pips had signalled surfaced Japanese submarines or pods of whales. Others argued that they were radar reflections from distant mountain peaks, while Brian Garfield offers a unique explanation for the mysterious radar contacts – immense seabird flocks whirling and landing on the sea.[51]

Some Americans had considered that Japan might withdraw its Kiska garrison; after all, it had evacuated the tattered remnants of its Guadalcanal force just months earlier. But after the bitter struggle for Attu, many American officers firmly bought into the stereotype of the trapped Japanese choosing to fight to the death; they therefore rejected the possibility of a withdrawal, especially one without a prior fight. Nimitz had told Kinkaid on 29 July that the Japanese had written off Kiska as a loss except for sporadic and weak attempts to run in supplies. But the assumption that Japan would not or could not withdraw its Kiska garrison blinded American commanders to mounting evidence that the Japanese had already departed. Radio transmissions from Kiska suddenly ceased on 29 July, but commenting that there had been frequent communications silences in the past (including one ten-day gap), army signallers drew no special inference from the latest enemy silence.[52] Moreover, pilots raiding Kiska claimed to have encountered light flak between 3 and 13 August, while aerial photographs taken after 29 July seemed to indicate that the Japanese had constructed new buildings and defensive emplacements. One fighter pilot even reported having strafed fleeing Japanese soldiers on 11 August. Much of this apparent evidence was discussed by ATF9 officers on Adak at a special intelligence briefing on 7 August. Three options were offered as plausible: a mutiny in the Japanese garrison that had prompted the removal of the mutineers; the evacuation of most senior officers and technical personnel, leaving behind a smaller force; and the most likely alternative, the dispersal of the entire Kiska garrison into well-concealed small battle groups that hoped to reduce the effectiveness of American ground and air firepower. A complete withdrawal was not deemed possible, for as one SSF officer concluded on 12 August, even if the Japanese wanted to leave Kiska, that option was improbable given the superior American naval presence in the region.[53]

Despite these claims, by 11 August the JIC had decided that the Japanese might have partially evacuated Kiska's garrison, a conclusion Holland Smith thought should have been tested. But Smith and his marines lacked credibility among army commanders even though they had played a considerable role in preparing ATF9 for its task. It had been Smith who had convinced Corlett to undertake the practice landings. Over 150 marine instructors had gone to Canada and Alaska to put ATF9 through its amphibious paces, and Smith and his staff had accompanied the force to Kiska. Marine colonel Graves B. Erskine, however, claiming that many army officers "took a rather dim view of a bunch of Marines coming up there to tell them what to do," stated that they had declined to let him see the operational plan.[54] As evidence mounted in early August that Kiska had been abandoned, some marines pushed for an armed reconnaissance, with one unidentified officer volunteering to undertake the mission himself. His marine boss, Colonel

John McQueen, had not been so certain, even after Major J.N.M. Davis concluded on 12 August that the Japanese had evacuated the area.[55]

In his postwar memoirs Smith declared that after having failed to convince an army pilot to take him on a low-level overflight of Kiska, he had requested the dispatch of an immediate armed reconnaissance team. His request was denied. Not only did higher command not believe that the Japanese had fled, it worried that a captured scout might reveal the impending attack to the defenders. When Smith contended that the mysterious disappearance of some buildings on Kiska could be explained if the wood had been used to build rafts to transport troops to an evacuation fleet, he became "the object of ridicule." Although Kinkaid believed that some of Kiska's garrison might have left, he assumed the main enemy force simply "had gone into the hills and were holding strong positions." Major France Q. Wilson, the army air force's North American theatre intelligence officer, had a different opinion. Noting both the shortage of enemy barges and Kiska's dismantled buildings, Wilson reasoned that the Japanese had dispersed into numerous small units scattered throughout the western Aleutians and perhaps even the Komandorskis. Believing such a strategy to be consistent with Japanese practice in the south Pacific, Wilson feared that "the fall of Kiska would be an anti-climax with the discovery that another island had been fortified in the meantime, a thought greatly appreciated by the oriental mind." Unable to determine the truth amidst the competing contentions, the JCS decided Cottage should proceed as planned "on the supposition that the original scale of defense still existed."[56]

One must wonder if Smith's biting criticisms of the army and navy played at least some role in this intelligence debacle. Smith had never had any qualms about expressing his contempt for "Generals who were Admirals and Admirals who wanted to be Generals." Further, according to a Rockwell aide, Smith had been quite frustrated because he had been denied the post of landing force commander at Kiska, something William Mack thought was only right given that no marine units were attached to ATF9.[57] Had Holland's scouting idea been heeded numerous lives would have been saved. Despite lacking an enemy to confront, the invaders suffered over 300 casualties. Landing on an island supposedly inhabited by 10,000 fanatical Japanese troops had made the soldiers very jittery, especially after a Tokyo Rose radio broadcast, heard as the men were boarding landing craft, promised they would be massacred on the beaches.[58] Wading through bone-chilling surf had also left many SSF troopers temporarily incapacitated on Kiska's black sand beaches. The extraordinary fog that smothered Kiska on 15 and 16 August made matters worse as nervous soldiers often fired before confirming their target's identity; even when hails had been correctly made and answered, some troops had fired anyway just in case the respondents were enemy soldiers posing as Americans. By nightfall on 16 August, twenty-eight Americans had died and another fifty had been wounded. Only four fatalities and a handful of the injured had come to a bad end thanks to Japanese mines and booby-traps; the rest had been struck by "friendly fire." The toll could have been far worse for, as one American lieutenant noted, his troops were shooting at anything that moved.[59] Seventy sailors aboard the destroyer *Abner Read* also perished when a Japanese mine tore off its bow on 18 August.

Had the Japanese stayed to contest the invasion, casualty lists would certainly have been very much longer. Although Captain Norman F. Fontes of ATF9 headquarters thought most units had performed well, some had arrived in Alaska seriously under-strength. While those units had been topped up with troops taken from ADC, many replacements, taken from static garrison duties, "were not up to average in their states of training or physical condition for an amphibious operation." That unfortunate fact had led to "constant bickering to obtain ample reinforcements to cover shortages existing in personnel." Kenneth A. Ward, ATF9's acting assistant chief of staff of operations, put matters even more bluntly. Painting a disturbing portrait of inter-service rivalry, Ward claimed that at one crucial moment in the landing navy crews had refused direct army requests to shift the supply runs from congested beaches to Kiska's harbour. Had the enemy been there to contest the assault, Ward felt certain the first wave of attackers "would have been wiped out, not due to the enemy contact, but primarily due to the fact that additional troops could not have been landed in sufficient quantities with proper supplies to reinforce the beachhead."[60]

Once Kiska was secure, an ADC survey team inventoried Japanese defences. Although bombing had badly damaged or destroyed every building on Kiska, it had inflicted surprisingly little harm to the numerous artillery pieces, machine guns, and other fortified positions littering the island. High ground or steep impassable cliffs – liberally peppered with interlocking Japanese machine guns and firing pits – overlooked nearly every landing beach. With few valleys offering suitable exit routes from the shoreline, the invaders might have found it difficult, if not impossible, to develop or retain beachheads in the face of determined Japanese opposition. According to the ADC study, had the enemy stayed to fight, retaking Kiska could have resulted in at least 7,000 Allied casualties. DeWitt was "certain that we would have suffered 5,000 killed."[61] Fortunately the Japanese had not been present on Kiska, and for the first time in fifteen months no Japanese lingered anywhere in the bleak Aleutian archipelago. The stepping-stone bridge from Asia to North America had been sealed after a great and costly effort. It remained to be seen whether that traffic flow would be reversed, and whether the promise of the northern route to Japan, offered by Mahan and Mitchell, Bywater and Buckner, would be realized. DeWitt, Buckner, and Kinkaid certainly hoped to see that promise fulfilled but they would find their strategic foes numerous and strong.

We Have Opened the Door to Tokyo:
Plans to Take the Kurile Islands, 1943-5

Kiska's recapture had been the felicitous culmination of an arduous campaign, a test of endurance against a determined foe, harsh weather, and vast distances. Yet that hollow victory did not end the debate about what might come next in the north Pacific. Clausewitz would not have been surprised. He had commented that an attack should normally have well-defined limits leading ultimately to the re-assumption of a defensive tactical posture. In practice, however, a general might seek to push on "further than he expected; after a more or less brief period of rest he often acquires new strength; but this should not be considered as a second, wholly separate action."[1] For DeWitt, Buckner, and Kinkaid, an attempt to push on across the Pacific towards the Japanese-held Kurile Islands, and perhaps even Japan itself, was inseparable from the recapture of the western Aleutians. Indeed, for these indefatigable men, securing the Kuriles was seen as the absolutely logical cul-mination of the march to Kiska and Attu. That opinion, though, was not unanimously shared by key planning agencies in Washington or by General Marshall. As an Australian intelligence report noted in late August 1943, while retaking Kiska meant the "Allied threat had moved a step nearer to things," that victory probably did not mark an immediate threat to Japan itself.[2] The Australians were correct; there would be no drive across the north Pacific.

Most soldiers, especially those unfortunate enough to have been based in the Aleutians since 1941, were very keen to leave the archipelago after Kiska fell back under American control. Troop morale was fast crumbling in the desolate islands, with manifold cases of severe clinical depression, suicide attempts, and numerous assorted disciplinary problems. One physician, Benjamin Davis, noted that he could easily pick out men who had been present in the region for more than six months: "They had a peculiar stare, you couldn't mistake it. We called it the Aleutian stare. Once I was in a plane with six GIs in straitjackets, and they all had it, the Aleutian stare. They'd been on those islands too long."[3] General DeWitt, however, was not as eager to put the Aleutians behind him. In August 1943, claiming time was of the essence, he wanted to assemble troops, create a major staging facility on Adak, and confirm Buckner as the commander of any future Kuriles expedi-tion. DeWitt also went to Marshall and begged to be kept in place at the Western Defense Command (WDC), arguing that he could be of greater service to Marshall, the war effort in general, the Pacific theatre effort in particular, and especially ongoing north Pacific operations if he retained his present assignment.[4]

Marshall did not repeal DeWitt's transfer, and an American attack on the Kuriles never materialized despite considerable efforts. In January 1943 the Joint Planning Staff (JPS) had ruled that operations against the Kuriles were beyond its scope because they would require considerable resources and Soviet assistance to succeed. That opinion had not altered by May 1943 when the JPS's new blueprint to defeat Japan emphasized offensives in the south Pacific and in China. Altering this plan was possible only if a belligerent Soviet Union allowed American forces to operate in Siberia. If that occurred, there might be a need for "major amphibious operations against the Kuriles and possibly Sakhalin to establish bases from which air cover and naval sup-port could be effected." Enthusiasm for this option was scarce, however, as a lack of suitable bases and poor weather "would prevent a bombing effort from the Kuriles from contributing in an appreciable degree to an extensive bombardment."[5]

The difficulty entailed in carrying out aerial operations across the vast north Pacific had not been exaggerated. The first trial came on 10 July 1943 when eighteen bombers flying from Amchitka and Attu raided Paramushiro. Some of the planes peeled off to attack nearby Japanese transports while the remainder dropped their payloads blindly through thick clouds – that was the first time land-based bombers had struck Japan. Inclement weather and persistent cloud cover foiled two additional attacks on 10 and 11 July, but six planes sent to Shimushu Island on 18 July found clear skies and only slight enemy opposition. The bombers hit rather few of their intended targets but managed to take some invaluable photographs revealing that the enemy was substantially strengthening the Kuriles. Two additional raids – on 11 August and then on 11 September – fared poorly. Nine B-24 bombers struck Shimushu in the August attack; one American plane was shot down while a second badly damaged craft had to seek sanctuary on Soviet territory. The 11 September mission ended disastrously. Ten of the eighteen craft failed to return; three had been shot down while seven others had to accept internment in Siberia after sustaining heavy damage that prevented their safe return to the distant home base. With fully half of its striking force now gone, the Eleventh Air Force suspended Kurile missions until February 1944. When the flights resumed, most aircraft carried cameras rather than bombs.[6]

Such inconclusive results, not surprisingly, failed to discourage an unflagging DeWitt. On 30 July he beseeched Marshall again to order a move against the Kuriles once Kiska was retaken. DeWitt argued that this new step would retain the offensive initiative, force Japan to divert resources from other more vital areas, stretch the Japanese military's already straining logistical system, and provide bases from which American bombers could strike Japan itself. Consequently, he thought, the 54,000 personnel assigned to Operation Cottage could handle the estimated 13,500 Japanese troops present in the Kuriles provided more bombers were made available. DeWitt was quick to attest that Kurile operations would reduce Alaska's garrison without addressing the unhappy possibility that even more American soldiers would be required to hold the conquered Kuriles. He asked the Joint Chiefs of Staff (JCS) to occupy the Kuriles by May 1944 in order to destroy hostile forces in that area, deny the enemy Paramushiro and Shimushu, and establish bases for future operations against the enemy on Hokkaido.[7]

Admiral Kinkaid's plans were only slightly less ambitious. As the USN's Pacific fleet would field seventeen fleet carriers and twelve battleships by October 1943, Kinkaid hoped to use some of that awesome maritime power even though Nimitz had told him in July that the navy was still spread far too thinly for his comfort. Current Aleutian-based forces could launch nuisance air and sea raids against the Kuriles, but if the army air force (AAF) agreed to provide new long-range B-29 Superfortress bombers for Alaska, then even northern Japanese targets would be reachable. Very keen to employ Soviet bases but sceptical that the Soviets could adequately protect eastern Siberia from Japanese predation, Kinkaid was very certain multiple amphibious landings against the Kuriles could succeed if the Soviets entered the war. However, as he informed Assistant Secretary McCloy when the latter visited Kiska in late August, the United States could attack either in the central Pacific or in the Kuriles; it did not have the resources to do both.[8]

Kinkaid's suggestions may have had some impact. Concerned that anticipated heavy losses at Kiska might delay further operations, the Strategic

Admiral Thomas Kinkaid, General John DeWitt, Assistant Secretary of War John McCloy, General Simon Buckner, General Landrum, and General Whittiker, at Adak Island, August 1943.

Plans Division (SPD) had considered cancelling Cottage in early August in favour of a quick dash to Paramushiro before Japan could properly fortify the Kuriles. Beyond throwing the enemy off balance and inflicting serious losses, a Kuriles thrust might finally convince Stalin to abandon his neutrality pact with Japan. Still, the SPD opted not to roll the strategic dice for two reasons. First, it thought that extra ships required for the Kuriles would force the cancellation or postponement of south and central Pacific operations. Second, occupying Paramushiro would place American forces in the same position suffered by Japan's bypassed Kiska garrison; they would be isolated at the end of a long and tenuous line of communications and vulnerable to a foe operating along much shorter interior lines. Kinkaid's proposal had been given a rough ride by the JPS too on 6 August. Although invading the Kuriles would pin down enemy forces at home, especially if the landings were augmented by occasional surface force feints, the planners maintained that active north Pacific operations should cease with Kiska's capture. The Combined Staff Planners (CSP) disagreed. Taking the Kuriles could open key sea routes to Siberia, divert Japanese attention from more vital theatres, provide bases to assail Japanese communications, or lead ultimately to an invasion of Hokkaido. They recommended drawing up plans for an unspecified date when more resources could be found or if the Soviet Union and Japan came to blows. Apparently agreeing, the Joint Chiefs told the Combined Chiefs of Staff (CCS) on 9 August that an assault on Paramushiro was under consideration as such an attack could aid other operations by pinning Japanese forces close to home.[9]

When the CCS convened at the stately Château Frontenac hotel in scenic Quebec City on 14 August, American strategic disunity was once again on display. Demanding considerably more resources for the widening Pacific conflict, King suggested that the two primary American advances via New Guinea and the Marianas might be supplemented by one advance via Paramushiro. Marshall was already concerned that ambitious USN central Pacific plans might siphon badly needed resources from MacArthur's command. He preferred to believe that Chinese manpower and bases might offer a far less costly alternative to "fighting our way through the [Pacific] Islands." Despite the fact that neither the JCS nor the CCS had formally ratified the JPS's recommendation to place the Kurile operations on the strategic backburner, Marshall told DeWitt on 14 August that the present Allied strategy did not include attacking the Kuriles, although such operations might be a valuable diversion later on. Furthermore, until policy regarding the final campaign against Japan was finally clarified, Adak's support facility was "disapproved." If conditions changed, Kurile operations would be reconsidered.[10]

Marshall's battle to limit operations in the north Pacific was not yet finished. The CPS's 18 August strategic appreciation made a good case for occupying the northern Kuriles in anticipation of a Soviet entry into the conflict, a recommendation that received considerable JCS attention. King thought the USN could find the necessary vessels to take the Kuriles in 1944 but he also admitted after the war that he was "*always* against going into Japan." For him, the primary consideration had to be what would follow Paramushiro's capture. Disconcerted by the formidable logistical demands entailed in moving substantial forces to the Kuriles, Marshall again recommended deferring any talk about attacking the Kuriles until central Pacific operations were wrapped up. When King then suggested that some Aleutian troops should be transferred to other theatres, Admiral Cooke advocated retaining a large Aleutian garrison just in case troops might be needed to intervene in the Kuriles or Siberia. Surprisingly, Marshall averred that, excepting the Special Service Force (SSF) and the Seventh Division, most Aleutian troops should stay put for the moment.[11]

The Office of the Director of Plans and Operations (OPD) rightly pointed out that shifting the Seventh would exclude any continued westward advance from Alaska until a new force was collected, trained, equipped, and transported to the Aleutians. Concerns that north Pacific operations might be scuttled grew when the army decided in late August to reduce Alaska's garrison to 80,000 soldiers. Despite General Hull's claim that an offensive task force would not be included under this revised manpower ceiling,[12] this ruling did not bode well given scheduled air force reductions. The AAF plan for Japan's defeat, presented on 20 August, citing various political and military difficulties, advised against initiating a bombing offensive launched from Siberia. While two B-29 groups could be in the Aleutians by May 1945, Arnold decided "now that the show was over in Alaska and the Aleutians, immediate steps should be taken to reduce our forces in that theater." Four bomber squadrons were promptly removed from Alaska.[13]

The JPS also resisted DeWitt's 30 August proposal, ruling that the scheme made no attempt to solve the problem of garrisoning the northern Kuriles and that it did not clearly indicate how this operation would play a vital part in Japan's ultimate defeat. Should an attack be launched against northern Japan – and the army was considering striking Hokkaido directly – then invading the Kuriles might jeopardize that operation. Thus the JPS advised against attacking the Kuriles in 1944 but approved a western Aleutians base to support future timely operations against northern Japan. These questions were far from settled when the JCS discussed Alaska at length on 7 September. For Marshall, who had been buttonholed by a congressional committee about removing troops from the Aleutians only days after Kiska's recapture, the matter had some importance. In late August he had instructed the army to send some transports to Alaska in order to extract soldiers, an order that "took off the heat." So on 7 September, given that maintaining a large numbers of idle soldiers in the bleak Aleutians was a rather expensive proposition, Marshall pondered whether these sizeable garrisons could still be justified. King was also considering placing limits on contemplated naval installations in the western Aleutians, yet he and Cooke were quite reluctant to decide on the matter until the Kurile situation was clarified. The JCS therefore referred the problem to the JPS and followed up Marshall's suggestion to bring Buckner and Admiral John W. Reeves, the USN's Alaskan sector commander, to Washington for consultations.[14]

Buckner and Reeves met with the JPS on 15 September. Having confidently declared after Attu's recapture that "we have opened the door to Tokyo," Buckner wanted to storm that gaping portal by hitting the Kuriles in May 1944 with nine divisions plus 18,000 corps troops. He also desired the use of three carrier task force groups because, in his view, Soviets would be convinced to abandon their neutrality pact with Japan only if the Americans went "full blast." The ever-aggressive Buckner favoured "a showdown action" with Japan immediately after the northern Kuriles were secured. One must wonder if Buckner really believed his extremely ambitious scheme could pass muster with his suspicious superiors in Washington. Still, Buckner knew he had the support of Reeves and Kinkaid. In fact, Kinkaid wanted the Joint Chiefs to set 15 May 1944 as the firm date for the first landings in the Kuriles. Cooke was also on side. If the JCS approved a Kurile offensive, then, Cooke thought, "we should set our sights beyond Paramushiru and keep pressing forward, refusing to accept a stabilized situation." When the JPS and the Alaskan representatives reconvened on 20 September, Buckner, knowing that garrison reductions directly threatened his complex scheme, maintained that if American forces in the north Pacific declined substantially, Japan would simply shift units to other theatres. Siding with Buckner, Cooke wanted the

100,000-man ceiling reinstated in case Kurile operations were approved. When army colonel F.N. Roberts demanded that the garrison be reduced immediately to 80,000, a deadlocked JPS referred the issue and Buckner's proposal to the Joint War Plans Committee (JWPC) for further study. In the interim, Nimitz ordered Kinkaid to prepare plans for a May 1944 attack on the Kuriles.[15]

Concerned that Buckner's aggressiveness had scared off support for north Pacific offensives, Reeves asserted that gaining some limited Kurile footholds did not necessarily mean large-scale operations against northern Japan had to follow automatically. Instead, Reeves believed that once Paramushiro fell and central Japan was within bombing range, Japanese air and naval forces, seeking to expel superior American forces, would exert "an immediate and important effect on the outcome of the war with Japan."[16] Still, the JWPC was the body to settle such matters, at least in theory. The Joint Chiefs had created the JWPC in 1943 after the Casablanca conference to ensure that they would never again lack key information to guide their strategic decisions.[17] Bombarded with options, the JWPC realized there would be serious long-term consequences for any decision, which would reach

deep into a region of the world in which not only our enemy, Japan, but also our ally, Russia, is keenly interested. No one can forecast the pattern of our future relationships with either of these great powers. Come what may during or after this war – the justification or not for large or small garrisons, the requirement or not to furnish support to Russia on short notice should she go to war with Japan, whether or not operations are conducted against Paramushiru, whether or not Russia or Japan or both are strong or weak, friendly or unfriendly in the post war period etc. – common sense demands that we properly organize this area for defense and for offense, and at the earliest practicable date.[18]

The JWPC therefore urged prompt decisions concerning Alaska's garrison, Adak's planned staging base, and the future of north Pacific operations. The JPS had no trouble recommending Adak's base and constructing airfields to handle B-29s. Determining the size of Alaska's garrison proved problematic, however. Its naval members wanted 100,000 soldiers kept in the region just in case Paramushiro had to be grabbed quickly. The army thought that contingency was so unlikely that retaining 100,000 troops to meet it could not be justified, particularly given the pressing need elsewhere for service troops and the overall manpower problem confronting the army. A compromise was struck. The JPS agreed to retain the 100,000-man ceiling provided Kurile operations were mounted in spring 1944. If operations did not materialize or were delayed until 1945, then Alaska's garrison would be cut to 80,000 by July 1944.[19]

The ink on this deal was barely dry before the Joint Strategic Survey Committee (JSSC), doubting an attack on Paramushiro was even possible before 1945, downgraded the threat to Alaska to Category A (probably free from attack). As such, the JSSC judged that Alaska would not need more than 80,000 men after July 1944. And while the JSSC countenanced the creation of Aleutian facilities with the capacity to support B-29 raids against Japan, it rejected constructing a substantial base complex on Adak. When these questions came before the Joint Chiefs in late September, General Handy took issue with the Adak recommendation because the facility might be needed to block a Japanese invasion of Kamchatka. As for the garrison question, the JCS decided on 28 September – in the absence of King and Marshall – to reduce troops in Alaska to 80,000 by July 1944 or sooner if circumstances permitted. Once back in Washington on 5 October, King argued that Japan retained the capability to return to the Aleutians "in force," and therefore objected strenuously to the Alaskan defence category reductions. Marshall's counterattack against King was equally vigorous. Insisting that "the retention of the Aleutian Islands in Category 'D' was a concession of superhuman powers to the Japanese," he declared that Japan would not risk increasingly scarce warships against the archipelago's land-based aircraft. Marshall's viewpoint prevailed; the JCS approved the category reductions, with the 80,000-man ceiling, and authorized only those facilities receiving a stamp of approval from the JSSC.[20]

Although the garrison reduction seemed to support "the premise that operations against Paramushiru and the Kuriles would not be feasible until the spring of 1945,"[21] the JCS had not explicitly rejected that option despite an exhaustive JWPC study objecting to Kurile operations. The JWPC viewed simultaneous assaults on all Japanese strong points in the Kuriles as beyond American capabilities, and dismissed seizing only Paramushiro and Shimushu because that would waste assets in a costly defensive struggle. A third choice was somewhat more acceptable: a three-phase scheme starting with the seizure of the northern Kuriles and followed by continuing assaults southward through the following spring. Taking the Kuriles could injure Japanese morale, raise American spirits, provide bases within easy flying distance of Japan's industrial heartland, and force the enemy to weaken its defences elsewhere to buttress its position at home. Yet even this more limited plan would require eight infantry divisions, four armoured battalions, two ranger regiments, 684 AAF aircraft, fourteen battleships, forty carriers, 140 other warships, hundreds of transports and landing craft, and nearly 1,700 naval planes. The JWPC thus could not recommend any Kurile operation in 1944 prior to Germany's defeat, as it would definitely bring to a halt offensive operations in other Pacific areas dependent on naval support. Furthermore, it unreservedly declared that north Pacific operations should be limited to air strikes, naval sweeps against Japanese shipping, and submarine and carrier raids against the Kuriles and Hokkaido.[22]

The JWPC's recommendations never made it to the Joint Chiefs for their considered perusal. The JCS's official historian for the Pacific conflict states only that the JPS's AAF representative demanded the Kuriles be occupied, regardless of whether Japan would subsequently be invaded, so that B-29s might be based in the islands. Consequently, a JPS plan presented four days later allocated two complete B-29 groups to the Aleutians and stated that Kurile bases would materially enhance the value of strategic bombing.[23] Nevertheless, it is difficult to accept that one officer's reservations blocked the transmittal of the JWPC's recommendations to the JCS, especially since Arnold's strong doubts about the Kuriles were on the record. Given that Marshall, at King's suggestion, had instructed Buckner on 8 November to plan for a spring 1944 attack on the Kuriles in order to take advantage of any unforeseen events,[24] a more plausible explanation is that King and Cooke had blocked the circulation of the JWPC report.

The most unanticipated event was the Soviet Union's entry into the war. JPS's analyses in this period never failed to mention Soviet collaboration as an absolutely necessary precursor to any American entry into the Kuriles, while the Combined Staff Planners noted expectantly that if the Soviets entered the war, north Pacific operations could assume a far greater importance and might require a major redeployment of forces. Predictably, the JWPC held a more pessimistic view. Accurately calculating on 20 November 1943 that the Soviet Union "will not of her own choice enter the war against Japan until 2 or 3 months after the defeat of Germany," it believed that Stalin would not desire American forces based on Soviet territory even if major American ground elements were available. That possibility was unlikely as long as Germany remained unbowed, so the JWPC concluded that the United

States could best support the Soviets in northeast Asia by invading Japan itself. Moreover, if Japan managed to shut Siberia's sea approaches completely, the JWPC warned, it might be impossible for American forces to reopen those routes completely without first seizing Hokkaido. If the war in Europe ended by December 1944, then adequate resources for such a monumental effort might become available because planned operations in the Philippines and the central Pacific would "make extremely difficult, if not impracticable, the release of forces from the Pacific Ocean and Southwest Pacific Areas in time to enable them to be moved to the North Pacific, acclimated, and equipped for an operation in the Kuriles in May-June 1945."[25]

The JWPC had cause to be pessimistic. When a devastated Germany finally capitulated in May 1945, only 1.2 million American army personnel and twenty-one divisions were in the Pacific theatre, as opposed to 5.2 million soldiers and sixty-eight divisions in Europe. In order to meet future combat needs against Japan, no less than fifteen divisions and sixty-three air groups would have to be transferred from Europe. Moreover, as 72 percent of the American public expected at least a partial and quick demobilization involving perhaps 2 million men, the army opted to release those men who had served longest, robbing many units of their best and most experienced men. As Richard Frank rightly points out, this was a recipe for chaos, as the planned invasions of the Japanese home islands in late 1945 and early 1946 loomed ever closer.[26]

Such pessimism was not ameliorated by the JCS's inability to agree to a long-term plan for Japan before Churchill and Roosevelt's meeting with China's Chiang Kai-Shek in Cairo in late November 1943. The United States intended to field forty divisions in the Pacific; it wanted a USN-led thrust into the central Pacific, plus a second advance by MacArthur's forces along the New Guinea-Dutch East Indies-Philippines axis. Agreeing at least to consider Kurile operations, the CCS wanted to discern whether the Soviets would fight Japan or provide assistance to American forces in the Kuriles. Both the American army and the USN came away from the Cairo talks pleased. King had told Nimitz in July 1943, "We must be so committed to the central Pacific that the British cannot hedge on the recall of ships from the Atlantic." Handy crowed that the Pacific plan's great strength was its flexibility; not only could the Joint Chiefs switch the emphasis to either offensive axis, British acceptance meant that the United States had "almost complete liberty in the Pacific without reference to the British Chiefs of Staff."[27]

The Combined Chiefs also convinced Roosevelt to seek Stalin's unequiv-ocal promise to join the Pacific war and to aid an invasion of the Kuriles. Stalin had offered a tantalizing hint of possible cooperation in a meeting with General Patrick Hurley in November 1942. Sent to Moscow by Roosevelt to draw Stalin out on the subject of Japan, Hurley, as he told a British diplo-mat, had been stunned to hear the Soviet dictator tell him that the United States should attack Japan in a pincer movement from the north and south. When Hurley hurriedly asked if that meant the Soviets would be willing to allow American forces access to Siberian bases, Stalin said yes, only to have Soviet foreign minister V. Molotov protest strongly against his leader's state-ment. Stalin promptly backtracked, but asserted that once his hands were not full, "the day would come when he would be able to offer the co-operation the General referred to." When Roosevelt met Churchill and Stalin in Iran in November 1943, he therefore again raised the issue of Soviet cooperation against Japan. Stalin assented only to study further American proposals, adding that islands near Japan "should remain under strong control to pre-vent Japan's embarking on a course of aggression."[28] Stripping Japan of its various outlying possessions had already been discussed by Roosevelt and British foreign secretary Anthony Eden the previous March. Although the Kuriles had not specifically come up at their meeting, both Roosevelt and Eden had wanted to form a special United Nations board to consider the "future defense and maintenance of peace and establishment of strong points," with the president adding that "the northern latitudes China, Russia, and the United States were concerned in establishing a system that would prevent future Japanese aggression."[29]

One reason why the Kuriles had not been explicitly mentioned derived from some American confusion about the status of the archipelago, confu-sion rooted in the Soviet-Japanese non-aggression pact. The preliminary Soviet price for that deal had been the return of Sakhalin Island, lost after the Russo-Japanese War of 1904-5, and the reacquisition of the northern Kuriles, peacefully purchased by Japan in 1875. While the Soviets dropped those demands when the actual pact was signed,[30] Sumner Welles claimed that Roosevelt had told him in September 1943: "The Russians should, of course, get back the Kurile Islands and southern Sakhalin, ceded under the Treaty of Portsmouth [of 1905]." Welles's assertion was corroborated by State Department official Charles Bohlen, who served as Roosevelt's interpreter at the 1945 Yalta Conference. Historian Marc Gallicchio, however, attests that

Roosevelt was not operating under any such misperception. Addressing the Pacific War Council (PWC) in January 1944, the president stated that Stalin wished "all of Sakhalin to be *returned* to Russia and to have the Kurile Islands *turned over* to Russia."[31]

It appears that Roosevelt might have intended to hand over the Kuriles; the Australian minutes of the PWC meeting indicate that he "had mentioned to Stalin that the Russians should have the Kuriles so as to make the trade going in and out [of Siberia] secure from a military point of view." The JWPC had probably already weighed in, however, with a coolly realistic assessment based on considerations of pure power politics. The committee remarked that the Kuriles commanded Siberia's outlets to the Pacific and argued that without their active participation against Japan the Soviets would be unable to negotiate the final disposition of the Kuriles, which might be to the United States's long-term strategic advantage. Recalling its comments about the north Pacific's import in the still nebulous postwar world, the JWPC stated that an American occupation of the Kuriles would make the United States less dependent on Soviet assistance in the Pacific war while "continued U.S. possession of the northern Kuriles upon the close of hostilities, and their military development would close the North Pacific against any invasion mounted in the Far East with a destination in the Western Hemisphere."[32]

This very early expression of the controversial "containment" strategy that dominated American policies towards Communism in the postwar world did not gain unanimous acceptance in Washington's halls of power. The president's Post-War Advisory Committee (PWAC) had much to say about the Kuriles. Formed in early 1942, the PWAC was designed to draft a "preparatory" peace plan so that all the president would "have to do is to reach into a basket and fish out solutions that are sound."[33] In August 1942 the subcommittee agreed that Japan should not retain any territories obtained by aggression. It had been inclined, however, to let Japan keep Okinawa and the Kuriles but probably not Sakhalin, a conclusion its Political Problems Subcommittee had approved in March 1943.[34] The PWAC's Territorial Subcommittee, headed by George Blakeslee, had disagreed. De facto leader of the State Department's Far Eastern Area Committee, the influential Blakeslee believed that Japan should be rapidly reintegrated politically and economically into the postwar world, a Wilsonian position clearly favoured by an increasingly ill and marginalized Cordell Hull.[35] In July 1943 the Territorial Subcommittee had split over the Kuriles. Some members thought that the Soviets might desire Paramushiro and Shimushu, others suggested internationalizing the islands, while still others thought the United States should use the Kuriles to form an Asian flyway that would not require obtaining Soviet or Canadian transit rights. In December 1944 Blakeslee accepted that the Soviet Union had a substantial claim to "Shimushu, Paramushiro and Araito, on the grounds of propinquity and the consequent desirability of controlling those islands to prevent them from becoming a military menace if in the possession of a hostile power." Most important, although Japan had a good legal case to allow it to retain most of the Kuriles after the war, Blakeslee feared that Stalin might demand all of the islands as a quid pro quo for fighting Japan. Placing the entire archipelago under the aegis of an international organization might solve the problem, especially as Blakeslee worried that occupying the Kuriles would place the Americans "in a distant and dangerous position in case of future difficulties with the Soviet Union." The result was yet another compromise; Blakeslee advised letting Japan keep a demilitarized southern Kuriles while the rest would fall under the sway of a Soviet-led international organization.[36]

Japan's increasingly desperate and marginalized foreign ministry had a similar solution in mind. Even as the garrison in Attu was still fighting its doomed battle in May 1943, the foreign ministry began to consider the possibility that the Americans might use the Aleutians to attack the Kuriles or even the Japanese home islands. Thus it asked Stalin whether he intended to uphold the neutrality treaty. But while the Soviets responded on 21 May 1943 that they would adhere to the neutrality pact, severe German defeats in Africa and on the Soviet front, combined with the rapid collapse of Benito Mussolini's Italian regime in September 1943, compelled the Japanese to give the Soviets some added incentives to keep the peace. Throughout 1943 and early 1944 Tokyo sent out tentative feelers to Moscow regarding possible territorial and political concessions in northeast Asia. Finally on 6 September 1944 the foreign ministry suggested paying a dear price to maintain Soviet neutrality, including recognizing Soviet spheres of influence in Manchuria and Inner Mongolia, renouncing the anti-Comintern Pact and the Axis alliance, and returning southern Sakhalin and the northern Kuriles to Moscow. Moreover, the Japanese also wanted to discuss the possibility of a Russo-German peace treaty and a potential joint alliance with Stalin directed against Britain and the United States. But a special Japanese emissary discovered that Stalin had no interest in altering his current relationship with Japan. Rebuffed, Japan's Supreme War Council agreed on 28 September to continue efforts to forge a new understanding with Moscow.[37]

The Japanese were not naïve; an intelligence report issued by the Imperial Headquarters in February 1945 rightly predicted that the Soviets would undoubtedly abrogate the neutrality pact and attack Japan whenever it suited their purposes.[38] Despite little interaction with an increasingly irrelevant State Department,[39] the American military began showing some interest in the Kuriles in late 1944. On 23 October 1944, citing critical officer shortages and a lack of strategic consensus, Marshall declined King's request to select a corps staff to study operations in the Kuriles. Nimitz, who had responded to Kinkaid's late 1943 request for guidance regarding north Pacific strategy by dispatching him a cribbage board, had a change of heart in November 1944. With an end to the European conflict in sight, with most of Japan's Mandate Islands in American hands, with MacArthur's return to the Philippines set for December, and with the JCS's July 1944 authorization of an invasion of Japan scheduled for 1945-6,[40] Nimitz asked for "the best estimate as to the necessity for an operation in the Spring of 1945" in order to establish secure communications to Siberia. The resulting JPS report indicated a still meagre appetite for Kurile operations. Opening secure sea routes to Siberia would entail seizing Hokkaido and controlling the Sea of Japan, an impossibility until substantial forces arrived from Europe. Even if the Soviets joined the war, their forces would confront a large and formidable Japanese army possessing considerably shorter interior lines of communication and supply. The Joint Intelligence Committee (JIC) also doubted if the Soviets could overcome the estimated 100,000 Japanese soldiers that would be in the Kuriles by spring 1945.[41]

Arnold was utterly fixated on crushing Japan with strategic bombing and in dire need of useable air bases that could bring his cherished bombers within range of Japan's vulnerable industrial heartland. By December 1944 he was avidly eyeing airfields in Siberia and the Kuriles. Cooke and King had been waiting for just such an opportunity. Having noted in July 1944 that America did not require Soviet assistance since it could deploy as many divisions in northeast Asia as could the Soviets, on 10 December Cooke urged King to press hard for attacks on the Kuriles by May 1945 – if the European war ended by mid-February. King had convinced the JCS the previous July to begin plans to open a sea route through the Kuriles in order to support

Siberian airfields. But he lost a bitter struggle with MacArthur over the question of retaking the Philippines, wishing to seize Formosa instead.[42] He was insistent on spreading the enemy's diminishing air and naval assets as widely as possible, and wanted Kurile operations to begin by May 1945.[43]

For Maurice Pope, intent on obtaining a prominent and visible place for Canada in the American-led invasion of Japan rather than some subsidiary role in the Kuriles, King's effort to alter American strategy made it exceedingly difficult to elicit accurate forecasts of prospective operations. On the day that King asked the JCS to consider Kurile operations, Nimitz and other service representatives were discussing operational possibilities at CINCPAC headquarters. Their considered conclusion was that any attempt to take the Kuriles prior to a Soviet entry would be very costly and would undoubtedly precipitate Japanese offensive operations against Siberia. Consequently, only after gaining prior Soviet approval should the United States send two divisions to Kamchatka. Quoting directly from Nimitz's report, the JPS savaged King's proposal. It rejected the notion that attacking the Kuriles would draw substantial enemy forces away from the central Pacific. It was also unconvinced that Kuriles bases would substantially increase the tonnage the AAF could drop on Japanese targets or even safeguard sea lanes to Siberia. If the USN desired sea communications to Siberia, then American forces on Kamchatka might be able to neutralize Japanese forces at Paramushiro and Shimushu. Given the need to equip forces for north Pacific conditions, the JPS doubted if sufficient men and material could be ready within six months of the war's end in Europe. It therefore recommended withholding any decision about moving ahead with Kurile operations.[44]

Twelve days later the JPS contradicted itself by declaring that if Kamchatka's possession could not guarantee safe passage to Siberia, it might be necessary to seize the northern Kuriles. That option held no appeal for the Joint Chiefs. On 22 January 1945, as an obviously ailing Roosevelt prepared to make the trying journey to Yalta in the Soviet Crimea to see Stalin and Churchill, the Joint Chiefs thought that insufficient resources in the Pacific precluded an attack on the Kuriles. They wanted the president to sound out Stalin about what he might be willing to contribute to north Pacific campaigns without making any formal commitments to undertake operations in that region.[45] In mid-December Ambassador W. Averell Harriman had already spoken to Stalin in Moscow about the Kuriles. As Harriman told Roosevelt at Yalta on 4 February, Stalin had argued that he was entitled to the entire Kuriles chain and to Sakhalin after Japan's defeat. Harriman expected the tough-minded Soviet leader to raise the matter quickly with the president at Yalta but Stalin waited until 8 February – two days after the JCS had stated that the US would not invade the Kuriles – to bring up the issue obliquely. Asserting his intent to declare war on Japan within three months of Germany's defeat, the Soviet leader simply mentioned his earlier discussions with Harriman. Roosevelt admitted hearing about that conversation and stated that "there would be no difficulty whatsoever in regard to the southern half of Sakhalin and the Kurile Islands going to Russia at the end of the war." Obviously surprised that Roosevelt had been so accommodating, Stalin speedily presented an accord assigning to the Soviet Union the Kuriles, Sakhalin, and certain economic and political rights that had formerly been exercised in northern China by czarist Russia, most particularly control of railways in Manchuria and access to warm-water ports. Stalin, Roosevelt, and Churchill inked a formal agreement on 11 February.[46]

Notorious among his aides for his "almost invariable unwillingness to dictate any memoranda of his conversations with foreign statesmen,"[47] Roosevelt took his reasons for the 11 February agreement to his grave two months later, when he died from a massive stroke. Ernest King attested in 1951 that he had advised Roosevelt to give Stalin only the southern half of Sakhalin as a "sop." Forced by the press in January 1946 to explain Roosevelt's seemingly bewildering actions at Yalta, Acting Secretary of State Dean Acheson admitted that the Soviet occupation of the Kuriles had never been intended to be permanent. But Roosevelt may well have known exactly what he was doing. In July 1945 Churchill informed the Australian government that Roosevelt and he had agreed at Yalta "to see that the Soviet claims were fulfilled without question after the defeat of Japan." Historian John Lewis Gaddis notes that the PWAC's Kurile plan had been unaccountably left out of the briefing book prepared for the president's use at Yalta. But even if Roosevelt had seen that document, Russell D. Buhite argues, he probably would not have resisted "Soviet entreaties over those territories since no one in February of 1945 was much inclined to preserve Japanese possessions." Exhausted by relentless meetings and eager to secure Soviet aid in order to limit American casualties if Japan had to be invaded, an ailing Roosevelt was willing to give Stalin pretty much what he wanted. For Marc Gallicchio, Roosevelt's decision to grant a Soviet sphere of influence in northeast Asia was made because the president, faced with growing Soviet power and concerned about the possibility of a postwar American relapse of isolationism, sought to ensure that his relationship with Stalin would survive into the uncertain postwar era. John J. Stephan offers a more heroic explanation: Convinced that Stalin had even grander expansionist Asian designs than he had revealed at Yalta, Roosevelt quickly assented to forestall additional and possibly more extensive Soviet demands.[48]

The American military split over the president's decision to allow the Soviet Union to occupy the Kuriles or other parts of northeast Asia. For Buckner, commanding the invasion of Okinawa, Roosevelt had erred. Thus he told Nimitz on 23 April 1945 that Okinawa should be retained by the United States in order to check further Japanese aggression and block the Soviet Union from expanding into the Pacific from the Chinese ports it might acquire at the war's end. Whereas the Joint Chiefs had stated in November 1943 that Kurile bases might complement a postwar American defensive chain stretching from Siam north to Korea, Secretary of War Stimson had no problem ceding the Kuriles to Stalin as long as America retained "permanent landing rights therein, as the islands are located in a great circle route to Japan from the United States, and would substantially shorten our mileage on air voyages following this route." Some officers in the Strategy and Policy Group (SPG) also agreed that the Soviet Union's long-range strategic intentions were rather benign. These officers doubted that the Soviets could threaten the United States since they demonstrably lacked strong naval and strategic air forces. It was difficult to imagine that possessing the distant Kuriles could bestow any significant advantage upon Stalin's military. The SPG gave its recommendation to President Harry S. Truman as he prepared to meet Stalin and Churchill in occupied Germany in July 1945. While it was undesirable for the United States to occupy the Kuriles, they thought Truman should retain an airfield there to facilitate movement from the Aleutians to Asia.[49]

Some still opposed letting the Soviets have the Kuriles. In February 1944 the British COS had suggested that an American advance into the Kuriles might "become of great importance to encourage and exploit an early Russian entry into the war." But a year later as worries about Stalin's postwar policies grew, Britain's Post Hostilities Planning Staff (PHPS) warned that allowing the Soviets to occupy the Kuriles could threaten the Aleutians; its solution was to let Japan retain the islands, albeit in a demilitarized condition. And when Churchill signed the Yalta deal, the PHPS tried again, drafting a letter for the British COS in which it reiterated its belief that a Soviet presence in the Kuriles would threaten American and Canadian strategic issues. On the other side of the Atlantic, in 1943 an official in the Far Eastern Unit of the Bureau of Foreign and Domestic Commerce described the Kuriles as the place of origin for north Pacific weather. According to him, "He who controls the weather observation points of the islands appears to be in a position to have advance information on the strength and movements of winds, and is thus likely to have some strategic advantage in the air routes between North America and eastern Siberia." Colonel Charles Bonesteel broke with his SPG colleagues about the Kuriles in 1945, bluntly pointing out that "unless we kid ourselves we know damn well the only Asiatic enemy we are guarding against is Russia. Therefore why spend all the men and fortune we have to get security in the Pacific and then not make the effort to hold a base near the obvious springboard of the most possible route of attack against us?"[50] Bonesteel's superior, Brigadier General G.A. Lincoln told his staff to determine which Kurile island would best suit the interests of the United States, although he was somewhat worried about the "tangled" security problems, including "the enigma of Russia," that would face the next generation of Americans. Yet when Truman talked with Stalin in mid-July, the Kuriles found no place on the official agenda except as a very small part of an agreement setting out American and Soviet operational boundaries in northeast Asia. While the Soviets conceded that all but the archipelago's northernmost islands would fall within America's operational zone, the Americans, indicating they had no plans to take the islands, did not dispute Soviet control of the Kuriles once hostilities had ceased.[51]

Once the Soviets launched a stunningly successful blitzkrieg against Manchuria on 8 August and quickly destroyed Japan's surprisingly brittle Kwangtung Army there (three months to the day after the final German surrender, as Stalin had promised), the American military took another look at Kurile operations. It was concerned that a rapid and total Japanese collapse might permit the Soviets to occupy part of Japan itself. The JWPC recommended grabbing Paramushiro or Matsuwa Island "in order to assist any negotiation for post-war airfield rights therein." Bonesteel did his best to help. Instructed to draw up General Order Number One, the document framing Allied occupation zones in the Pacific, Bonesteel failed to place the Kuriles in any of those zones, making it appear as though they were still available. Lincoln described the omission as a simple oversight but Gallicchio claims that Bonesteel had deliberately expunged the Kuriles in order to encourage aggressive American commanders to occupy the islands, in the absence of concrete orders to the contrary, so that the Soviets would not get them first. MacArthur's command, preparing to occupy Japan and describing the Kuriles as outlying islands properly under USN jurisdiction, did nothing.[52] When Assistant Secretary of War McCloy lobbied his political superiors on 11 August to occupy the Kuriles, Secretary of State James Byrnes replied: "We had agreed to give the Kuriles to the Russians and we couldn't go back on that." But under some USN pressure, on 12 August Byrnes authorized the navy to grab the southern portion of the archipelago.[53] Having noticed the omission of the Kuriles from General Order Number One, a displeased Stalin contacted Truman on 17 August to demand that the Kuriles and northern Hokkaido be placed immediately within a Soviet occupation zone. Truman was unwilling to allow Stalin any access to Japan itself. He confirmed that the Kuriles would fall under Soviet control, although Byrnes insisted Moscow be told that Washington desired air-base rights on some of the Kurile Islands for military and commercial purposes. The insulted Soviet leader saw his Hokkaido hopes dashed and asserted that "demands of such nature are usually laid before a conquered state or such an allied state which is in no position to defend with its own means parts of its territory." He did "not believe that the Soviet Union could be included among such states." Setting aside the landing rights issue, Truman reminded Stalin that transferring the Kuriles to Soviet control would not become final until a Japanese peace treaty had been signed.[54]

Truman's warning to Stalin proved to be irrelevant. Conversely, Stimson's May 1945 warning was prescient: "The concessions to Russia on Far Eastern Matters made at Yalta are generally matters which are within the military power of Russia to obtain regardless of U.S. military action short of war."[55] What Truman would not offer, the powerful Red Army would simply take. On 18 August, three days after a battered Japan had finally agreed to surrender to the Allies to avoid further destruction and possibly the removal of the emperor, Soviet amphibious forces assaulted Shimushu. Employing landing craft and specialized training acquired from American forces in Alaska, the invaders suffered 2,000 casualties in the initial assault. But recovering from this early reverse, by 4 September the Soviets had taken the entire archipelago after considerable hard fighting. In February 1947 the Supreme Soviet amended the national constitution, incorporating the Kurile Islands formally into the Soviet Union. The end of the Cold War and the Soviet Union's sudden and unexpected collapse in the early 1990s have so far not altered the status of the Kuriles. Japan, backed by the United States, has urged the new Russian state to return the "Northern Territories," that is, the four Kurile islands lying closest to Japan. But the absence of a formal peace treaty between Russia and Japan as well as the vagaries of Russian nationalist politics have prevented any settlement of the Kurile problem to this very day, and the two countries are therefore technically still at war.[56]

Stepping Stones to Nowhere

The choice of the Joint Chiefs of Staff (JCS) not to employ Buckner's open door to Tokyo rendered the Aleutians a strategic backwater again. Some enemy patrol planes and submarines had been spotted near Attu in September 1943 but intelligence had judged them as attempts "to alert the enemy's defenses in the Kuriles against impending attack or to obtain intelligence that will facilitate raids or attacks on our bases." Nine Japanese aircraft struck Attu on 13 October, their bombs falling harmlessly into the frigid waters of Massacre Bay. This assault, however ineffectual, prompted a quick re-examination of the enemy's intent and capabilities in the region. Alaska Defense Command (ADC) intelligence, while admitting that enemy air and naval attacks on the Aleutians were not impossible, believed that Japan could not risk attacking the Aleutians; any such operation would develop into a major confrontation, in which American forces would hold all the advantages.[1]

The fact that the Japanese would not be coming back to the Aleutians allowed for some changes. On 1 November 1943 President Roosevelt, at the army's request, finally created a separate Alaskan Department over which Buckner presided until the general departed his beloved Alaska in June 1944. The new command status did not save Alaska's garrison from significant reductions. In December 1944 Alaskan bases east of Adak – excepting only Anchorage's Fort Richardson and Elmendorf Airfield – were put on housekeeping status. From a peak of 152,000 personnel in 1943, Alaska's military contingent plummeted to 60,000 in 1945 and then to just 19,000 in 1946. Butler left for Europe, while the Eleventh Air Force and Fleet Air Wing Four soldiered on, flying over 1,500 sorties against the Kuriles by the end of the war. Kinkaid departed in October 1943 to head up MacArthur's naval contingent in the southwest Pacific. A much reduced North Pacific Force, composed mainly of obsolete cruisers and destroyers, bombarded the Kuriles on fifteen separate occasions. In one particularly successful sweep in the war's final weeks, the fleet sunk eleven small Japanese vessels near the Kuriles.[2]

Sharp military power reductions did not mean that the strategic usefulness of the Aleutians had ended. Kiska had not been back in American hands long before the Joint Planning Staff (JPS) began pondering whether the Aleutians could assist with deception campaigns mounted against Japan. The British had been pushing America since 1942 to formulate such complex campaigns, and Theobald had suggested using fraudulent radio traffic as early as March 1942 to create the impression that American forces were steaming towards the Kuriles. The JPS waited until May 1943 to recommend deception schemes, although Cooke insisted on an overarching Pacific stratagem rather than allowing the various theatre commanders to cobble together their own disparate plans. The JPS's vague deception guidance plan emerged on 13 September 1943. Its north Pacific portion suggested only that air attacks against the Kuriles might form part of a disinformation campaign to compel Japan to bring forces to the Kuriles "except at the time of an operation there." Arnold slammed this report, considering it so general as to be almost meaningless, and wondered "whether the sequence of events in the Pacific was so far along and so firm" that it would not be feasible to create overall deception measures. The JCS subsequently decided that the three Pacific commanders should formulate their own schemes.[3]

As historian Katherine L. Herbig notes, the "reaction from the field to the new policy was a resounding silence."[4] Nimitz, MacArthur, and Admiral William F. Halsey (commander of the South Pacific Area) declined to submit any plans. Frustrated, the Joint Chiefs asked Buckner on 3 November to produce his own north Pacific deception blueprint. By 12 January 1944 Buckner's plan was ready: he proposed creating a fictional build-up for a bogus Kurile operation in August 1944. But there were two major problems with his strategy. Besides exaggerating force strength in the Aleutians, it failed to explain just what scenario he intended to put across to the Japanese. Moreover, it assigned strategic control to the army – a condition Nimitz found difficult to accept. When he finally agreed to allow the army to control the deception scheme, Nimitz convinced the JCS in February 1944 to tie a fake Kurile assault to a very real attack on Saipan Island, scheduled for June. Titled Operation Wedlock, the deception plan was intended to produce enough fraudulent radio traffic to convince Japan that five American and two Canadian divisions were preparing to seize Paramushiro and Shimushu. Thus American troops passing through Seattle were issued arctic clothing, while the army built dummy facilities and landing craft at Attu.[5]

Buckner's plan seemed to work. In addition to the six Japanese army battalions present in the Kuriles before 1943, three of the ten battalions withdrawn from Kiska in 1943 were also sent to the Kuriles. Japan had reinforced the islands, wrongly estimating that the United States had 400,000 soldiers, 700 aircraft, and a powerful naval flotilla based in Alaska. (There were in fact only 64,000 men, 350 planes, and six ships in place.) By late 1943 over 27,000 Japanese troops resided in the islands, a figure that climbed to over 80,000 by autumn 1944. Even more had been dispatched, but a deadly USN submarine campaign had killed 10 percent of the Japanese soldiers sent to the Kuriles.[6] Yet the numbers were deceptive. On 30 September 1943 the Japanese military, with Emperor Hirohito's full knowledge, identified the Kuriles as one of the key points to be retained in a strategic perimeter stretching southwards to eastern New Guinea and Burma. But in late July 1944 Japan's military pointedly excluded the Kuriles from the list of places – including the home islands (but not Hokkaido), Taiwan, the Philippines, and the Ryukyu Islands – that it would defend to the death. Therefore, despite incorrectly detecting an American task force leaving Hawaii in mid-May bound for the Kuriles, the Japanese took no special precautions to meet the fraudulent June 1944 invasion, as they had been unconvinced that "this menace was immediate or of primary importance."[7]

Despite criticism that Wedlock had not satisfactorily produced the multi-sourced message traffic normally created by a real invasion force, Nimitz and the JPS decided in August 1944 to continue the deception under a new moniker. Operation Husband was designed to convince the enemy that seven divisions and over 1,000 aircraft were in the Aleutians. The Japanese were not fooled. By the end of September, putting the number of divisions in Alaska at three, they withdrew assets from the Kuriles. Although Husband's replacement – Operation Bambino – managed to keep most of the 80,000 Japanese troops in the Kuriles a little while longer, by August 1945 only 25,000 Japanese soldiers remained. Given that Japan had begun reinforcing the Kuriles before the American deception plans got under way, and that those plans failed to keep Japanese air and naval assets from leaving the archipelago, it seems unlikely that Wedlock, Husband, and Bambino hindered Japan's war effort by much. Japan's Aleutian experience had taught the Americans that the north Pacific "could only be a secondary theater, useful for feints or diversions, not a primary route" to Japan.[8] Even in victory the northern route to Japan did not deliver on its promises.

In a six-hour visit to Juneau in August 1944, Roosevelt observed that Alaska would be a key point in defending the Pacific and the region stretching to Siberia along the line of the Aleutian Islands. Yet the war's end left Alaska's strategic role rather uncertain. While the Joint Chiefs had ruled in November 1943 that Alaska and the Aleutians would anchor a Pacific defensive line, by 1945 part of that defensive perimeter – namely the Kuriles – was in Soviet hands. Nevertheless the Aleutians could still fulfill a useful military role, in light of increasing tensions between the United States and the Soviet Union. By the end of 1945 the American military established a listening post on Adak, its sensitive antennae pointed west towards the Soviet Union. Indeed, on 3 September 1945 the last American aerial mission over the Kuriles sought intelligence about Soviet forces based there. Two B-24 bombers attempted to take some high-altitude photographs of the Kuriles but were sent back by Soviet fighters before they could accomplish their covert mission. Just over a month later, Shemya's Twenty-Eighth Bomber Group was deactivated, although the 404th Bomber Squadron was kept in the Aleutians until January 1947 to complete a mapping project of the Aleutians and mainland Alaska.[9]

Initially, the American military did not believe that the Soviet Union posed a serious and immediate threat to the United States or its Alaskan outposts. The JCS thought Stalin would seek primarily to dominate eastern Europe in order to guard against a resurgent Germany. It doubted whether the Soviet Union could carry out any further territorial expansion until it had fully recovered economically, possibly in 1952 at the earliest. The Joint Intelligence Staff's October 1945 assessment was even more optimistic; the Soviets would need fifteen years to restore their manpower and industrial losses, ten years to modernize their crippled transportation systems, five to ten years to manufacture atomic bombs and an effective strategic air force, and perhaps twenty years to assemble a proper deep water navy.[10] On 21 December 1945 the JCS thought it unnecessary to post air and ground forces in Alaska, "except for training, acclimatization, experimental purposes, limited reconnaissance and surveillance, and for limited local defense of selected bases." It determined that "the probability of trouble developing in the Alaskan Area as a result of conflict between U.S. and USSR policies is fairly remote. The Soviet capability to launch a major operation against the Alaskan Area in the next five years is estimated to be almost nil." But the JCS also recommended strengthening facilities so that Alaska could support any necessary future offensives, "bearing in mind that the strategic importance of this region with respect to trans-polar attack by and defense against aircraft and special weapons vis-à-vis the United States and the strategic heart of the USSR or any other European power will increase with the development of these weapons."[11]

By 1946 American military attitudes had hardened, as the West and the Soviets quarrelled endlessly and fruitlessly about Germany's future and Stalin's refusal to allow truly free elections in occupied eastern European states. In August of that year, the Joint War Plans Committee (JWPC) and the JPS agreed that the Soviets were probably quite capable of launching limited air and commando attacks on Greenland, northern Canada, Alaska, and even the continental United States. They assumed that by 1950 the Soviets would be able to hit America with guided missiles and long-range planes carrying atomic weapons; they might even be able to seize some territory in Canada and Alaska. As the JWPC recommended creating air warning and air defence systems to counter the Soviet threat, in 1947 the air force began building Eielson Air Force Base, the world's largest airfield, south of Fairbanks, and upgraded existing facilities at Kodiak, Shemya, and Adak.[12]

As in the 1930s, a debate soon emerged about the role Alaska might play in American security. In August and September 1946 General Eisenhower expressed his wish to split command responsibilities in the Pacific between the army and the USN, for he was concerned that the Soviet Union might be able to threaten Alaska. But as in 1942 Eisenhower had to contend with his old boss from the Philippines, Douglas MacArthur. Eisenhower wanted MacArthur, the virtual ruler of Japan since that nation's surrender in August 1945, to take responsibility for defending northeast Asia. He expected Mac-Arthur to provide support for possible American operations in China and the Philippines. Meanwhile, the navy would back MacArthur's command and also concentrate on the security of the maritime approaches to the United States and Alaska. Having apparently undergone a considerable change of heart since 1942, Eisenhower seemed to think that Alaska and the Aleutians now constituted the most important portion of the Pacific theatre. MacArthur, though, was quite unimpressed with any plan that might render his a supporting role buttressing the eastern Pacific – especially a scheme offering to give the navy complete control of the central Pacific if it promised to secure Alaska. If the Soviets were foolish enough to attack Alaska, MacArthur opined, echoing his demands to Eisenhower in early 1942, his forces in Japan and Korea could launch a devastating strike at the vulnerable underbelly of the Soviet offensive.[13]

MacArthur did not win this fight but neither did Eisenhower – at least where Alaska was concerned. The new Department of Defense decided in 1947 to create Alaskan Command (ALCOM), the first unified tri-service command in the nation. But as John Whitehead asserts, ALCOM's first job was to demobilize much of Alaska's military assets. The Strategy and Policy Group (SPG) began studying Alaska's situation in early 1946 and suggested that a garrison of just 13,000 soldiers was needed – a figure General Lincoln admitted had been chosen without any official army or air force input. That number had not changed much by the following July, with Lincoln explaining that he wanted a small army garrison and a large air force for the territory.[14] The USN too was trying to assign priorities with little or no input from the other services. In April 1946 it toyed with the idea of abandoning Dutch Harbor and Attu, but it was concerned that such a step might alienate the army. Consequently, it decided that the Coast Guard might be persuaded to maintain those facilities. But in September 1946, probably after learning of the army's own limited plans, Admiral J.H. Towers identified only Adak as one of three bases in the Pacific (along with Pearl Harbor and Guam) that should be maintained over the long term.[15]

The JWPC reaffirmed in August 1947 that Alaska might experience harassing Soviet raids and the Joint Strategic Plans Committee (JSPC) recommended two divisions to protect the new air force bases in December. The view at the top was quite different, however. In November 1948 the air force asked for only two fighter groups for Alaska, with perhaps just one-third of a group to be placed in the Aleutians. Then in April 1949, shortly after a retired General Eisenhower told Congress that Alaska's defences were "in no shape to meet the potentialities of war," the JCS ordered a return to Kilbourne's pre-war heartland concept of defence, which promised to safeguard only Fairbanks, Anchorage, and Kodiak; the rest of Alaska was deemed expendable. All Aleutian bases, with the exception of Adak's naval station and Shemya's air base, were closed. This step engendered a brief flurry of press attention. In August 1947 *Collier's* ran an article that argued that an undefended Aleutian chain was a "gaping" undefended back door to "the American continent." Using language eerily reminiscent of Hector Bywater and Billy Mitchell, its author predicted that America was not only squandering an ideal base for offensive operations against the Soviets, it risked losing the Aleutians to an enemy who might find a very dangerous military use for them. By 1949 a journalist writing for the *New York Journal-American* averred that the newly abandoned Alaskan airfields could invite a Soviet assault. These warnings had little effect. In 1949 Congress opted to defer action on planned defence spending in Alaska ($138 million), leaving Governor Gruening to fume that Alaska was now defenceless and "could be taken tomorrow by a minor-scale airborne invasion."[16]

The coming of war in Korea in June 1950 brought some attention to the north Pacific when the Alaskan Task Force, formed by the Preparedness Subcommittee of the Senate's Committee on Armed Services, studied the territory's security needs. As in 1946 Eisenhower plumped for stronger defensive measures in Alaska. Indeed the general believed that Alaska's defence was so important that it should rank above all other aspects of national defence. But while its determined and ambitious chair, Lyndon Johnson, stated that "the security of every American home begins in the snows of Alaska," the task force's 1951 recommendations for more troops and planes fell by the wayside. The navy expanded its Adak and Kodiak bases in the 1950s to counteract a growing Soviet submarine threat; the air force returned to Shemya, but the major bases remained at Anchorage and Fairbanks. As the Department of Defense noted in 1952, the means for an air defence of Alaska were "meagre" and the land, air, and sea protection available to Alaska (and much of the rest of North America) was "in general inadequate."[17] Still, the notion that the Aleutians might somehow constitute a military bridge between Asia and North America remained. Two officers studying at the Naval War College in 1983 also warned of the threat of a Soviet pre-emptive strike against Alaska, making specific reference to Japan's 1942 offensive. The officers praised the Aleutians as potentially valuable forward deployment bases in the event of hostilities with the Soviets, or if American facilities in Japan were lost. They therefore wanted substantial ground forces in place in Alaska and possibly the Aleutians to guard against such a strike and to safeguard Alaska's substantial oil reserves. But the last word belongs to the commander of the navy's Adak installation in 1972. Interviewed in 1972 by the *Washington Post*, Captain G.F. Thummel described his command as "an excellent stepping stone" in the event of a war with the Soviets.[18] When the Soviet Union ceased to exist in 1991, the Aleutians once again became stepping stones to nowhere.

The fiercely contested struggle for the Aleutians during the Second World War should have been avoided. It is difficult, though, to determine just how the combatants could have taken another path once Japan occupied the western Aleutians in June 1942. The Japanese were concerned that American bombers might employ Aleutian bases to bomb Japan's vulnerable cities, and this fear seems to have been justified in retrospect, given the horrendous damage bombing inflicted on Japanese cities by American aircraft in just a few months in 1945. Japan's military therefore opted to render any potential American advance via the north Pacific – the shortest path to Japan – much more difficult. Once in the Aleutians, as former IJN officer Masatake Chiyaya admits, Japan's high command formed preconceptions and misconceptions about the region and about American military capabilities. Certain that the barren and mountainous Aleutians could not support large-scale land-based aviation, the Japanese military failed to begin building airstrips on Kiska and Attu until it was far too late; none of the planned airstrips were complete when the Americans returned to Attu and Kiska in 1943. Japan had also clearly underestimated the magnitude and speed of the American counterattack that soon rendered the reinforcement of its distant Aleutian outposts virtually impossible.[19]

Recent historical studies paint a rather dismal picture of Japanese strategy making. Edward Drea blames the failure of the Imperial Japanese Navy to develop a coherent grand scheme for the entire conflict on inter-service rivalry, ineffective command and control, a tendency to think solely in tactical and operational rather than strategic terms, and a pre-war preoccupation with the threat posed by the Soviet Union. David Evans and Mark Peattie argue that Japan possessed "a set of perceived threats, nebulous ambitions, and a keen ability to exploit a strategic opening." They maintain that the USN's inability to launch a major cross-Pacific offensive until 1943 had more to do with time constraints and the inability to organize America's vast industrial potential than with the losses the American fleet sustained at Pearl Harbor. Thus Admiral Yamamoto might have been much better advised to abandon the Pearl Harbor attack in favour of maintaining the IJN's traditional "wait-and-react" strategy in the western Pacific. The Japanese navy consistently undercut its own chances for strategic success in two important ways: first, it failed singularly to concentrate its strength at key moments in Midway or Guadalcanal;[20] and second, it neglected to address adequately its own logistical needs because it placed too much confidence in its ability to win a decisive initial confrontation.[21] Yet having blundered into an Aleutian campaign for all the wrong reasons, the sacrifice of just over 5,300 Japanese servicemen, fifty ships (mostly cargo vessels and landing craft), and seventy aircraft was perhaps not a terribly high price to pay to secure Japan's northern flank for over fifteen months.

Certainly Governor Gruening thought so. In his opinion, had the USN properly developed Kiska prior to the war rather than concentrating on Sitka and Dutch Harbor, "the entire history of North Pacific warfare would have been substantially different." A frustrated Gruening, embittered by wartime inter-service rivalry, alleged that Japan immobilized American forces about fifty times more numerous, thereby forcing the United States to use up enormous amounts of vital shipping and other material. Thus, he noted unhappily, while "the battle of Alaska has ended ... it may be reasonably concluded that the Japs won it."[22]

Whereas Gruening's damning assessment may be extreme, judging the American side of the Aleutian equation is a complex undertaking. Not only did Americans have to contend with a highly dangerous and unpredictable adversary, they were doubly burdened by the long-running debate about the value of the northern route to Japan and a confusing command system that encouraged strategic arguments. In the first instance, Alaska and the Aleutians attracted more than their share of strategic prophets. Mahan, Bywater, and Mitchell – none of whom had ever visited the islands – allowed a simple reading of geography to buttress their opinions that the Aleutians would be absolutely key in prosecuting any war with Japan. They were not easily discouraged by the dismal climate and the lack of adequate resources needed to support a major military effort. American audacity and American technology could overcome any and all obstacles.

In the interwar period, none of the military services had much time for Aleutian prophets. Naval planners may have adopted Mahan's blue water prescription – that the USN must always seek the destruction of an enemy's main fleet – but they opposed the admiral's advocacy for a northern route to Japan. Instead, they stuck stubbornly by their own Plan Orange scripture and undertook a relentless attritional campaign in the central Pacific. Similarly, the army demonstrated little interest in Alaska. Such indifference can be blamed partly on years of political and financial neglect that transformed the army into a "tight-knit, hard-drinking, hard-bitten long-service" force that was "almost as far from the army of atomic bombs, proximity fuses, electronic counter-measures, and radar as it was from the Continentals who fought at Yorktown 175 years earlier."[23] Was the army uninterested in Japan as well? Although Brian McAllister Linn argues that the American army viewed Japan as a primary opponent from 1907 onwards, Russell Weigley disagrees. He asserts that prior to the Second World War the army's indifference to Japan arose from the latter's geographical remoteness, condescension regarding the perceived marked inferiority of Japanese military and technological prowess, a fear of Asian entanglements, the fact that the USN's domination of Pacific strategic planning left it little room to act, and a concern that the army would be left "'to hold the bag' for the nation's venture into imperialism and seapower."[24]

Given that neither Mahan, Bywater, nor Mitchell had ever set foot on the windswept Aleutians, one might see how a simple geographical analysis convinced them that the Aleutians rendered Japan vulnerable to an American assault. Buckner, DeWitt, and Kinkaid, however, spent considerable time in the stormy north Pacific and the barren Aleutians, and yet they too were seduced by the enticing siren song of the Aleutian offensive. An avid hunter, Buckner so loved Alaska that he intended to retire there after the war. In fact, his frequent requests to Washington regarding the provision of hunting licenses for his men led McCloy to wonder: "Why don't generals stick to their knitting?"[25] More important, Buckner, DeWitt, and Kinkaid succumbed to

Marshall's "localitis" affliction. Certainly it is a commander's duty to take his responsibilities seriously, and conscientious leaders eager to act are the stuff that make good militaries. Still, excessive eagerness can breed recklessness and it is far too easy to lose one's perspective and to be overcome by what seem to be pressing parochial priorities. The Aleutian campaign is a prime exemplar of these problems. Even if the Alaskan commanders thought they possessed good reasons to undertake hard-hitting north Pacific offensives, Japanese garrisons on Attu and Kiska could have been left to wither painfully on the vine without risking anything Americans held dear. Precedents had been set by MacArthur's leapfrogging tactics in the southwest Pacific, where well-defended targets of some considerable magnitude – Rabaul and Truk for example – had been safely bypassed. Rabaul and Truk, however, had never been American territory, and as Roosevelt indicated in June 1942, losing the western Aleutians could have a psychological impact on the American public. Robert Dennison, Admiral Rockwell's chief aide at Kiska, hit it squarely on the head when he told a postwar interviewer that the American counter-offensive in 1943 had not been motivated by a perceived Japanese threat but by the fact that "it was United States territory. That's something you don't do. You don't come over and grab some of our land. So we had to take it back regardless of strategy. We couldn't just let them sit there."[26]

Japan's invasion of the western Aleutians was also a stroke of good luck for Buckner. After months of neglect and access to rather few resources in Alaska, he finally had a chance to employ an exceedingly powerful, versatile, and lavishly equipped arsenal, which he firmly intended to use to good effect against a much hated foe. There seemed to be no restraints in sight (the federal government spent more than a billion dollars in Alaska between 1941 and 1945[27]) and the American military was fielding dozens of divisions, scores of aircraft, and hundreds of warships. Add to that Buckner's training in an American way of war – born of massive industrial potential and a need for overwhelming victory – that sought a strategy of annihilation.[28] Can one blame him for believing that the resources existed to create another Pacific axis that would strike directly at the enemy's vital heartland? It is a rare manager, civilian or military, who would not jump at the chance to become an empire-builder, and Buckner was not a man to resist his impulses.

Appearances were deceiving though. American military potential, while certainly immense, was not limitless. The army's 1941 Victory Plan envisaged 213 divisions (premised on a concern that the Soviet Union might not survive) but by 1943 that figure had fallen to ninety as industry, the air corps, and the navy took their share. In addition, the army's overly lavish use of service personnel and a tendency, as Marshall displeasingly noted, to discharge men who still "could render further useful service," did not help matters much. By the end of the war all ninety divisions were on active service overseas. Had the Axis Powers managed to mount an offensive on the scale of Germany's massive 1944 Battle of the Bulge assault, the American army's "divisional cupboard would have been bare," concludes one American historian.[29] Furthermore, senior officials worried that the American public might not have the stomach for a long and bloody war. That concern troubled those who framed Plan Orange prior to 1941, and in December 1943 Roosevelt warned the electorate against a tendency "to assume a quick end to the war." Frank Knox put matters even more bluntly. He doubted whether the American public would "have the guts to stay with it to the finish."[30] He admitted in 1943 that his nation was quite unprepared for a butcher's bill – nothing of the sort had been seen since the ghastly Civil War. In this context then, it is not surprising that both Marshall and the JPS opposed attacking the Kuriles. Marshall was genuinely concerned that no democracy could afford to "fight a Seven Years' War."[31] In addition, attacks on the Kuriles threatened to absorb twelve to twenty American divisions in a potentially brutal fight at the distant end of a tenuous supply line.

Enthusiasm for further north Pacific operations were tempered by other considerations as well. No discussion of the Aleutian campaign would be complete without noting the climate's impact on operations. Brian Garfield asserts that "no general or admiral was as powerful as the weather" in the Aleutians,[32] and there can be no doubt that weather often made Aleutian operations exceedingly difficult, especially for aviators. Of the 225 Allied planes lost in the Aleutians, only forty-one were downed by Japanese aircraft or anti-aircraft fire; the remainder fell victim to accidents, most of which were weather-related.[33] Weather, though, was not a decisive strategic or tactical factor in the ultimate American victory on the Aleutians. It certainly complicated matters and made living conditions in the field deplorable and, as at Attu, often deadly for the men forced to fight on the ground. But North Africa's barren deserts or New Guinea's pestilent jungles and steep mountains offered their own climatic complications. For example, during the 1942-3 battle for New Guinea – a campaign that cost more than 3,100 American and Australian lives – over 24,000 American and Australian troops from a total of just 35,000 men suffered from debilitating tropical ailments like malaria or dengue fever.[34] Because Japan did not make the archipelago's retention a life-or-death issue (as it did for many island groups in the south and central Pacific), the United States was able to mass overwhelming combat strength and to expel the enemy from the Aleutians. The climate and the lack of indigenous resources in the Aleutians may have prolonged the struggle and rendered it more expensive but it did not alter the ultimate outcome.[35]

The sheer size of the Aleutian logistical effort caused concerns too. As one British general has so aptly put it, "It takes little skill or imagination to see *where* you would like your army to be and *when;* it takes much more knowledge and hard work to know where you can place your forces and whether you can maintain them."[36] Although Buckner and DeWitt complained constantly that Alaska was not receiving its proper share of resources, from December 1941 to January 1943 Alaska obtained 14 percent of all cargoes (3.38 million tons) shipped by army transport vessels, ranking it third behind only North Africa (over 6 million tons) and Europe (3.72 million tons) but ahead of the south Pacific and southwest Pacific theatres (1.45 million and 2.27 million tons respectively).[37] Given that Alaska's defence effort peaked in 1943 at just over 150,000 personnel, one can understand why many American planners believed additional north Pacific operations might not offer a good return on investment. Supplying Alaska's needs had been quite difficult, given the general shortage of transports, the competing needs of other theatres, and the peculiar geography and nature of the north Pacific war, which demanded numerous isolated garrisons and airstrips strung along a lengthy line of communications. The prospect of lengthening an already elongated supply line across the stormy north Pacific into the enemy's strategic backyard without a firm promise of Soviet assistance would have been foolhardy. The American services had learned their lesson at Guadalcanal and in New Guinea in 1942, when resource shortages very nearly proved disastrous for them.[38] Matters were far worse for the Japanese. In the war's dismal last two years, every Japanese combatant had to get by on a mere two pounds of supplies per day; their American foes were backed by a mind-boggling four tons per man.[39]

Soviet aid in the Kuriles was the chimera that bedevilled American strategy making. Given the paucity of developed facilities west of the Aleutians, any American task force headed to the Kuriles would have found it very difficult to operate effectively without active Soviet support or at least untrammelled access to Siberian bases. Neither DeWitt nor Buckner seemed to really comprehend just how vital Soviet assistance was for the success of their proposed Kurile venture, nor did they understand how difficult it would be to get a paranoid Stalin to provide that help. Stalin had signed a non-aggression pact with Japan in 1940, which Japan had honoured despite considerable pressure to join Germany's attack on the Soviet Union in 1941. His hands were more than full with the brutal death struggle with Germany. He was unwilling to add to his nation's onerous burdens while the brutal Nazi invaders remained unvanquished, even when Germany's eventual defeat became obvious. If Soviet diplomat Ivan Maisky is to be believed, the ever-suspicious Stalin might have deliberately dragged his feet on any promise to fight Japan as "revenge for their [Anglo-Americans'] dragging their feet on the second front" in France.[40] When Stalin agreed to attack Japan three months after Germany's defeat, the Soviets happily accepted American aid for their own invasion of the Kuriles. They permitted the Americans to establish a handful of weather stations in eastern Siberia,[41] but refused to allow American forces to operate from within their territory.

The Soviet Union, of course, was not the only recalcitrant ally known to the United States. Billy Mitchell may have regarded Canada as America's natural ally in the north Pacific, but until the advent of the Second World War most Canadian civilian and military officials worried far more about American encroachments on Canadian sovereignty than they did about Japanese aggression. Even after Pearl Harbor, Canadians remained reluctant to act in the Aleutians because of their nation's heavy commitment to the war with Germany. Only in 1943 did Canada finally opt for a much larger north Pacific obligation. This decision was based on a desperate need to find a useful combat role for the mostly inactive Canadian army and, equally important, a victory after disastrous losses at Hong Kong in December 1941 and then Dieppe in August 1942. The dispatch of the Canadian soldiers to Kiska marked the first – but not the last – time that Canadian troops would operate under American command. Despite DeWitt's complaint that the Canadians had initially been "sort of helpless" after the creation of Greenlight Force,[42] the Canadians had performed pretty well at Kiska.

That able performance, however, did not help Pearkes and Stuart in their odd attempt to attach a division to an American force bound for the Kuriles. Despite the dressing-down he received from King and Ralston in late May 1943, Stuart initiated a secret study just days later concerning the possible use of Canadian troops in the Aleutians, northwest Asia, and the southwest Pacific. This project was so secret that the officers involved were ordered to shun official communication channels and filing systems. Pearkes showed even less good judgment after discussing Kurile operations with DeWitt on 5 July 1943. He told some of his officers that Kiska was the "first step to Tokyo" and that Greenlight Force would be the forerunner of larger expeditions from Pacific Command. With Pearkes intent on providing at least three brigade groups for an invasion of the Kuriles, on 30 August Stuart presented the Cabinet War Committee (CWC) with a complex scheme that streamlined home defence formations in order to provide troops for Europe and the Pacific.[43] This time Stuart's heavy-handed attempt to suggest that Canada might be embarrassed if it could not meet any additional American requests for help ran headlong into an unbending prime ministerial roadblock. King had already risked ample political capital by using home defence conscripts at Kiska for little or no return; he had little time for any additional ventures. While he could accept the need to keep forces in reserve just in case, King pointedly rebuked Stuart for seeking additional manpower commitments just in case America came calling. No Canadian troops would be headed to the Kuriles.[44]

Canada's involvement in the Aleutians made it easier for the Canadian army and the government to accept a place in the scheduled invasions of Japan at America's side. The alternative of aiding Britain in southeast Asia was a far more politically dangerous option given King's reliance on French Canadian electors. King nonetheless showed little enthusiasm when agreeing to participate in the campaign against Japan. The prime minister was certain Canada would not get much credit for anything it might do in the Pacific, but thought that he had "an obligation to share" in Japan's final defeat. But when Churchill recommended in September 1944 that Canada might have a place in a campaign along the Aleutians and the Kuriles, King angrily retorted that he "did not wish to have our men assigned to any second Kiska role"; it would be Japan itself or nothing. As in 1943, however, the American services – and especially Admiral King – were not terribly eager to accept Canadian or British aid for the final assault on Japan. Only after President Roosevelt intervened did the Canadians and British obtain permission to attach forces to that prospective final campaign against Japan.[45] With the war's end, Canadian interest in the north Pacific faded. Prime Minister King was intent on reducing both taxes and the size of the military. With Roosevelt dead King felt little obligation to the United States and thus rejected Major General Guy V. Henry's proposal for talks to determine the future of Canadian-American military cooperation. As Pope told the Americans, since Canada's north faced no invasion threat "over the next one or two decades" and there was no possibility of major operations on or near Canadian territory in that time frame, Canada saw no need for "complete uniformity of equipment, organization and training of the Forces of our two countries." Of course, the door was left open for further meetings "for the purpose of making a broad survey of the requirements of North American joint defence."[46] Only in the late 1950s with the rise of a serious Soviet aerial and missile threat to North America did Canada agree to wed its security more tightly to the United States. The Aleutian connection may not have cemented the Canadian-American security connection but it helped matters along.

Britain too had opposed operations in the Aleutians on the grounds that any effort in such an unimportant theatre, and the wider Pacific war generally, wasted precious resources given that Germany was the primary and more dangerous foe. The Joint Chiefs had found it difficult enough to convince their British counterparts to support two axes of advance in the central and southwest Pacific; only at Casablanca, and after much argument, did the British reluctantly accept the rationale for clearing the Japanese from the Aleutians. Obtaining that British acquiescence had been bitter and divisive, not just for Anglo-American relations but within the JCS as well. Had the Americans pushed hard for an advance on the Kuriles, which might have evolved into a massive invasion of Japan, the British probably would not have cooperated unless Germany had already been smashed. Such an operation would have meant a complete reformulation, not just of the Pacific campaign, but of the entire Allied war effort. Having been forcibly reminded by Roosevelt in 1942 that a Pacific-First alternative was unacceptable, Marshall had made certain that Britain would have no good reason to complain about American intentions. Admiral King's central Pacific offensive and MacArthur's island-hopping campaign in the southwest Pacific would continue unabated, but the march to the Kuriles was placed firmly on a strategic backburner.

DeWitt's and Buckner's attempts to remake Allied strategy would surely have been quashed far earlier had separate Pacific theatres not existed. Warren F. Kimball puts the matter quite forcefully, claiming the American military's

Pacific "parochialism later caused delays and cost lives." Even the official army history notes that the Pacific command arrangements "led to duplication of effort, and keen competition for the limited supplies of ships, landing craft and airplanes; and it placed on the Joint Chiefs the heavy burden of decision in many matters that could well have been resolved by lesser officials."[47] Yet it is difficult to envision just how that flawed arrangement could have been avoided. King's antipathy to army control over his ships and the need to give MacArthur, who had Republican support for an appointment as supreme commander over the entire army and navy, a "task commensurate with his supposed greatness," led to the split in the Pacific command system in 1942.[48] The two services could have established a system of unified command for the north Pacific. Under the terms of their 1935 joint action pact, the army and navy consented to appoint a theatre commander to oversee all military activities, with the important proviso that the officer selected could neither "infringe upon the administrative and disciplinary functions of component services" nor direct "how a competent commander was to carry out his mission."[49] But when Marshall had suggested that option to the USN in December 1941, it had forcefully declined responsibility for Alaska and Hawaii on the grounds that no single commander could direct both services adequately. The navy agreed finally on 17 December 1941 to assume control over Hawaii, but Alaska was another matter altogether. Thus Nimitz and DeWitt had to blend their respective command systems without a set of clearly understood or accepted rules. As one analyst so masterfully puts it, "Even professional, intelligent men such as Nimitz, King, Marshall, and DeWitt who surely understood joint relationships as spelled out in 1935, failed to keep personal biases from diluting the chain of command, ... a glaring deficiency [that] would manifest itself in persistent interservice bickering, poor command and control and a lack of unity in effort as major operations were conducted."[50]

The situation might have improved somewhat if the JCS had agreed on a common approach to the Aleutians. Their failure to appoint a joint commander for the entire Pacific had made the Joint Chiefs the de facto theatre commanders in the war against Japan. Yet their impossibly heavy workload made any sustained examination of the north Pacific campaign by those four men virtually impossible. Moreover, without an intervening theatre chief to buffer them, the Joint Chiefs had to deal directly with the numerous schemes dispatched by Buckner, DeWitt, Kinkaid, and Theobald. Therefore the Joint Chiefs grew to rely heavily on the plethora of agencies that sprang up after December 1941 to guide the American and Allied war effort, including the JPS, the JWPC, the JSSC, the Combined Chiefs organization, as well as the existing service units such as the army's Office of the Director of Plans and Operations (OPD) and the navy's Strategic Plans Division (SPD). The various Aleutian proposals were frequently referred to these groups, especially to the JPS and the JWPC, and if those bodies had managed to agree and accept a particular proposal, the Joint Chiefs would probably have given it their stamp of approval. However, the various agencies reporting to the JCS, the CCS, and the respective national military services were not required to coordinate their affairs or even to keep each other informed of their activities. Sometimes they did but many times they failed to cooperate. For example, the JWPC, which was designed to cut through some of the bureaucratic red tape plaguing the American high command, failed in 1943-4 to clarify Kurile plans. This was not the body's only such failure, and in early 1945 General Lincoln lambasted JWPC members for sitting in an "ivory tower," producing "little themselves and that very slowly." And when the JWPC did complete studies, they were "often so discoordinated [sic] that we have to work on them again."[51]

Even when this process worked, it was most cumbersome and agreement below the JCS was not always achieved, forcing the Joint Chiefs to sort matters out. Personal differences and clashing personalities within the JCS did not help either. According to his biographer, Admiral King preferred to closely monitor and control the USN's Pacific activities because he distrusted Nimitz, viewing him as an inconsistent "fixer" inclined to be overly lenient towards his subordinates and prone to accepting bad army advice.[52] Furthermore, King and Arnold disliked each other and frequently "engaged in acid dialogue that reflected old and poisonous differences between the army and the navy over military policy." Fortunately for the American war effort, although King and Marshall initially did not like each other very much, "as the war progressed, King, the greater strategist, often gave way to Marshall, the greater man."[53] A reading of JCS decisions about the north Pacific Alaska bears this out. King frequently pushed for a wider American effort in that region when he could envision definite advantages; but when Marshall stood opposed, those initiatives usually failed.

On those occasions when the services either could not or would not act in the north Pacific, it was sometimes left to Roosevelt to force the issue. That was hardly accidental given that the Joint Chiefs, as Roosevelt's informal creation, lacked a true charter or statutory protection and really served at presidential whim. When they could not agree, they had little choice but to seek Roosevelt's mediation.[54] On 3 August 1944, while visiting Adak, Roosevelt claimed that his service advisers had laughed when he told them "back in 1940, or early in 1941" that "our next war is going to be in the Aleutians and down in the Southwest Pacific." In early 1942 Roosevelt had played a key role in forcing the military to safeguard Alaska. Once the war effort kicked into overdrive, the president, with notable exceptions such as the quashing of the Pacific-First alternative, let his service advisers run the war, a marked departure for a leader who "normally skilfully played subordinates off against each other in order to maximize his authority." This approach may have reflected Roosevelt's "self-confidence, confidence in his Chiefs, and the presence in the President's mind of the prevailing American ideas as to the nature of the war and the manner in which it should be conducted."[55] On the other hand, it may have stemmed from some form of political or personal weakness. In September 1944, while attending the second Quebec conference, a defensive Roosevelt, harried at a press conference, justified the lack of a unified commander for the Pacific conflict on the grounds that "human nature was not so constituted for one man to be able to grasp the bewildering variety of difficulties involved" in the Pacific's vast distances. And while Roosevelt never completely lost his interest in Alaskan affairs, after 1942 he never forced his opinion about the Pacific on the military, even if he complained in early 1943 that at the current snail's pace of advance, American military forces would not occupy Japan until the year 2000.[56] Perhaps if he had made his views known from the start, much of the confusion regarding the Aleutian campaign would have been avoided.

Samuel Eliot Morison correctly notes that the Aleutian campaign had no appreciable effect on the wider outcome of the war. Had the United States invaded the Kuriles in 1944, the north Pacific conflict might have contributed much to Japan's defeat, and it is abundantly obvious that only war between the Soviet Union and Japan would have "made the North Pacific a major theatre of operations."[57] If the Aleutian campaign had little impact upon the war's outcome, it accelerated Alaska's development. A sleepy and isolated territory containing just 75,000 inhabitants prior to 1941 (including 1,000 service people), by 1950 Alaska boasted 112,000 civilians and 26,000 military personnel.[58] With the increased population and new infrastructure came renewed demands for statehood, a status that Alaska achieved in 1959. Nine years later the massive Prudhoe Bay oil discovery was made on Alaska's distant North Slope, bringing new prosperity and new challenges to the northern pioneers of the United States.

Notes

Introduction

1   C.P. Stacey, *Official History of the Canadian Army in the Second World War*, vol. 1, *Six Years of War: The Army in Canada, Britain and the Pacific* (Ottawa: Department of National Defence, 1955), 500-5; Walter A. McDougall, *Let the Sea Make a Noise: A History of the North Pacific from Magellan to MacArthur* (New York: Basic Books, 1993), 635; Jonathan M. Nielson, *Armed Forces on the Northern Frontier: The Military in Alaska's History, 1867-1987* (Westport, CT: Greenwood Press, 1988), 164; and Gerhard L. Weinberg, *A World at Arms: A Global History of World War II* (Cambridge: Cambridge University Press, 1994), 633.

2   Samuel Eliot Morison, *Strategy and Compromise* (Boston: Little, Brown and Company, 1958), 90; and B.H. Liddell Hart, *History of the Second World War* (London: Cassell, 1970), 500-1.

3   Hisashi Takahashi, "The Japanese Campaign in Alaska As Seen from the Historical Perspective," in *Alaska at War, 1941-1945: The Forgotten War Remembered*, ed. Fern Chandonnet (Anchorage: Alaska at War Committee, 1995), 38; and Takijiro Onishi quoted in Alvin Coox, "Aleutian Islands," in *The Historical Encyclopedia of World War II* (New York: Facts on File, 1980), 11.

4   John Haile Cloe, *The Aleutian Warriors: A History of the 11th Air Force and Fleet Wing 4* (Missoula, MT: Pictorial Histories, 1990); and Brian Garfield, *The Thousand-Mile War: World War II in Alaska and the Aleutians* (New York: Bantam Books, 1969).

5   Mark S. Watson, *Chief of Staff: Prewar Plans and Preparations* (Washington, DC: Department of the Army, 1950), 454-8.

6   Brian McAllister Linn, *Guardians of Empire: The U.S. Army and the Pacific, 1902-1940* (Chapel Hill: University of North Carolina Press, 1997), xi-xii.

7   Edward S. Miller, *War Plan Orange: The U.S. Strategy to Defeat Japan, 1897-1945* (Annapolis, MD: Naval Institute Press, 1991), 334-5.

8   McDougall, *Let the Sea Make a Noise*, 633.

9   Editorial, *The Times of London*, 14 October 1856.

Chapter 1: One of Our Great Strategic Points

1   Brigadier Lovell H. Rousseau to Secretary of State William H. Seward, 5 December 1867, in *Alaskan Historical Documents since 1867*, ed. Ronald Lautaret (Jefferson: McFarland and Company, 1989), 7-9. See also John Haswell, "Transfer of Alaska to the United States," 6 May 1879, University of Rochester Library, William H. Seward Papers, file 6707, reel 184.

2   Seward quoted in Walter LaFeber, *The Clash: U.S.-Japanese Relations Throughout History* (New York: W.W. Norton and Company, 1997), 27; John M. Taylor, *William Henry Seward: The Definitive Biography of Abraham Lincoln's Controversial Secretary of State* (New York: HarperCollins, 1991), 275; and Jonathan M. Nielson, *Armed Forces on the Northern Frontier: The Military in Alaska's History, 1867-1987* (Westport, CT: Greenwood Press, 1988), 7.

3   Nielson, *Armed Forces on a Northern Frontier*, 6; James R. Gibson, "The Sale of Russian America to the United States," in *Russia's American Colony*, ed. S. Frederick Starr (Durham: Duke University Press, 1987), 285; Albert A. Woldman, *Lincoln and the Russians* (New York: Collier Books, 1961), 19; Walter LaFeber, *The Cambridge History of American Foreign Relations*, vol. 2 of *The American Search for Opportunity, 1865-1913*, ed. Warren I. Cohen (Cambridge: Cambridge University Press, 1995), 12; and "Treaty of Cession," 20 June 1867, in *Alaskan Historical Documents since 1867*, ed. Ronald Lautaret, 1-4.

4   Taylor, *William Henry Seward*, 281; Frederick W. Seward, *Reminiscences of a War Time Statesman and Diplomat, 1870-1913* (New York: J.P. Putnam, 1916), 360; Nielson, *Armed Forces on a Northern Frontier*, 5; Banks speech, *Congressional Globe*, 40th Congress, 2d session, 30 June 1868, appendix, 338; Butler

quoted in Woldman, *Lincoln and the Russians,* 260; and Gibson, "The Sale of Russian America to the United States," 271-2.

5 Claus-M. Naske, *A History of Alaska Statehood* (Lanham, MD: University Press of America, 1985), 3; Claus-M. Naske and Herman E. Slotnick, *Alaska: A History of the 49th State* (Grand Rapids: William B. Eerdmans Publishing, 1987), 61; Nielson, *Armed Forces on a Northern Frontier,* 17-23; and Russell F. Weigley, *History of the United States Army* (New York: Macmillan, 1967), 267.

6 Vincent Ponko Jr., "The Navy and the Aleutians before World War II: The Story of a Flirtation," *The Alaska Journal* (Spring 1983): 128-9; Morgan Sherwood, *Explorations in Alaska, 1856-1900* (New Haven: Yale University Press, 1965), 76; and Nielson, *Armed Forces on a Northern Frontier,* 51 and 59-60.

7 Nielson, *Armed Forces on a Northern Frontier,* 67-8.

8 Major-General J.C. Ardagh, "Memorandum Respecting the Clayton-Bulwer Treaty," 9 December 1898, in *British Documents on Foreign Affairs: Reports and Papers from the Foreign Office Confidential Print,* series C, *North America, 1837-1914,* ed. Kenneth Bourne, vol. 10, *Expansion and Rapprochement 1889-1898* (Frederick, MD: University Publications of America, 1987), 468; and Akira Iriye, *Pacific Estrangement: Japanese and American Expansion, 1897-1911* (Cambridge: Harvard University Press, 1972), 54.

9 Iriye, *Pacific Estrangement,* 74-5.

10 Ronald Spector, "The Triumph of Professional Ideology: The U.S. Navy in the 1890s," in *In Peace and War: Interpretations of American Naval History, 1775-1978,* ed. Kenneth J. Hagen (Westport, CT: Greenwood Press, 1978), 179; Roosevelt to Cecil Arthur Spring Rice, 19 March 1904, in *The Letters of Theodore Roosevelt,* ed. Elting E. Morison, vol. 4 (Cambridge: Harvard University Press, 1951), 760; Roosevelt to Theodore Roosevelt Jr., 10 February 1904, in *The Letters of Theodore Roosevelt,* ed. Morison, vol. 4, 72; and Roosevelt to Henry Cabot Lodge, 16 June 1905, in *The Letters of Theodore Roosevelt,* ed. Morison, vol. 4, 1230.

11 Ponko, "The Navy and the Aleutians before World War II," 129; Joint Board memorandum, 10 June 1904, National Archives and Records Administration (hereinafter NARA), Records of the Joint Board, RG225, series 16, M1421, reel 9; Roosevelt to Elihu Root, 26 July 1907, in *The Letters of Theodore Roosevelt,* ed. Elting Morison, vol. 5 (Cambridge: Harvard University Press, 1952), 730; and Consul-General C.W. Bennett to Sir Edward Grey, 5 December 1907, in *British Documents on Foreign Affairs: Reports and Papers from the Foreign Office Confidential Print,* series C, *North America, 1837-1914,* ed. Bourne, vol. 12, *North American Affairs, 1906-1907* (Frederick, MD: University Publications of America, 1987), 276.

12 Root and Sperry quoted in Richard D. Challener, *Admirals, Generals, & American Foreign Policy 1898-1914* (Princeton, NJ: Princeton University Press, 1973), 244 and 225. As early as 1902 some Japanese naval officers viewed America as the greatest potential threat to Japanese ambitions in Asia; David C. Evans and Mark R. Peattie, *Kaigun: Strategy, Tactics, and Technology in the Imperial Japanese Navy, 1887-1941* (Annapolis, MD: Naval Institute Press, 1997), 138-9, 142-4, and 187-9; and Ronald Spector, *Professors at War: The Naval War College and the Development of the Naval Profession* (Newport, CT: Naval War College Press, 1977), 96.

13 Count Gleichen to Sir M. Durand, 12 November 1906, in *British Documents on Foreign Affairs,* ed. Bourne, vol. 12, *North American Affairs, 1906-1907,* 146-7; Robert Seager II, *Alfred Thayer Mahan: The Man and His Letters* (Annapolis, MD: Naval Institute Press, 1977), 483-7; and Edward S. Miller, *War Plan Orange: The U.S. Strategy to Defeat Japan, 1897-1945* (Annapolis, MD: Naval Institute Press, 1991), 93.

14 Samuel P. Huntington, *The Soldier and the State: The Theory and Politics of Civil-Military Relations* (Cambridge: Belknap Press of Harvard University Press, 1957), 277-9; and Nielson, *Armed Forces on a Northern Frontier,* 83.

15 William Reynolds Braisted, *The United States Navy in the Pacific, 1909-1922* (Austin: University of Texas Press, 1971), 128; Lieutenant Colonel Joseph P. O'Neal, "The Military Geography of the Puget Sound Area," Army War College Records, 1914-15, Session, NARA, United States Army Continental Defenses, 1914-1940, RG394, box 1; Captain Hood, "Report Respecting the Naval Situation in the

Pacific," 19 February 1908, in *British Documents on Foreign Affairs: Reports and Papers from the Foreign Office Confidential Print*, series C, *North America, 1837-1914*, ed. Bourne, vol. 13, *North American Affairs, 1908-1909* (Frederick, MD: University Publications of America, 1987), 96; Russell F. Weigley, *Towards an American Army: Military Thought from Washington to Marshall* (New York: Columbia University Press, 1962), 179 and 191-2; and R.M. Johnston, *Arms and the Race: The Foundations of Army Reform* (New York: The Century Company, 1915), 120-44, 176-86, and 192-215.

16 Spring-Rice to Grey, plus "Memorandum by Captain Grant on the Relative Conditions of the American Navy and That of Japan," and "Memorandum by the Military Attaché to the British Embassy at Washington on the Military Considerations of America and Japan in January 1914," all 27 January 1914, in *British Documents on Foreign Affairs: Reports and Papers from the Foreign Office Confidential Print*, series E, *Asia, 1860-1914*, ed. Ian Nish, vol. 10, *North-East Asia after the Russo-Japanese War, 1905-1914* (Frederick, MD: University Publications of America, 1989), 368-72; Senior Member Joint Board to the Secretary of the Navy, "Strategy of the Pacific," 18 December 1919, NARA, RG225, JB325, series 28-d, reel 9; Joint Planning Committee to the Joint Board, "Extent and Development of Pacific Bases Required for Campaign in the Pacific," 27 April 1920, NARA, RG225, JB304, series 90, reel 5; W.C. Cole, Glen E. Edgerton, and H.G. Hamlet to Chairman of the Inter-Departmental Alaska Board, "Coaling Stations for Commercial and Naval Uses in the Aleutian Islands," 25 February 1921, NARA, General Correspondence of the Alaska Territorial Governor, RG348, M939, file 23-20, reel 82; and Nielson, *Armed Forces on a Northern Frontier*, 83-4.

17 John Braeman, "Power and Diplomacy: The 1920's Reappraised," *Review of Politics* 44 (July 1982): 347.

18 E.W.B. Morrison, "Report of the 9th Corps Area, USA," August 1921, National Archives of Canada (hereinafter NAC), E.W.B. Morrison Papers, vol. 4, file US Army.

19 Morinosuke Kajima, *The Diplomacy of Japan 1894-1922*, vol. 3, *First World War, Paris Peace Conference, Washington Conference* (Tokyo: Kajima Institute of International Peace, 1980), 488-95; Roger Dingman, *Power in the Pacific: The Origins of Naval Arms Limitation, 1914-1922* (Chicago: University of Chicago Press, 1976), 209-10; Braisted, *The United States Navy in the Pacific*, 646; Sir C. Eliot to Marquess Curzon, 21 September 1921, in *British Documents on Foreign Affairs: Reports and Papers from the Foreign Office Confidential Print*, series C, *North America, 1919-1939*, ed. D.K. Adams, vol. 8, *Treaties and International Negotiations, 1919-1921* (Frederick, MD: University Publications of America, 1991), 204; and David Alvarez, *Secret Messages: Codebreaking and American Diplomacy, 1930-1945* (Lawrence: University Press of Kansas, 2000), 11. A copy of the Washington Naval Treaty is in NARA, International Conference Records, Conference on the Limitations of Armaments, US Delegation, Records of A.H. Miles, 1921-22, RG43, entry 100, box 4, file F60. USN opposition is summarized in Rear Admiral Harry S. Knapp, "The Limitation of Armament at the Conference of Washington," *Proceedings of the American Society of International Law* (1922): 16-19.

20 Greg Kennedy, "Depression and Security: Aspects Influencing the United States during the Hoover Administration," *Diplomacy & Statecraft* 6 (July 1995): 352 and 368; Gerald E. Wheeler, *Prelude to Pearl Harbor: The United States Navy and the Far East, 1921-1931* (Columbia, MO: University of Missouri Press, 1968), 57; Pratt quoted in Craig L. Symonds, "William Veazie Pratt," in *The Chief of Naval Operations*, ed. Robert William Love Jr. (Annapolis, MD: Naval Institute Press, 1980), 72; Eliot to Curzon, plus extracts from Captain Marriott dispatch, 25 May 1921, in *British Documents on Foreign Affairs*, ed. Adams, vol. 8, *Treaties and International Negotiations, 1919-1921*, 136-8; Carl Boyd, "Japanese Military Effectiveness: The Interwar Period," in *Military Effectiveness*, ed. Allan R. Millett and Williamson Murray, vol. 2, *The Interwar Period* (Boston: Allen and Unwin, 1988), 142; Evans and Peattie, *Kaigun*, 197-8; and Edward J. Drea, *In the Service of the Emperor: Essays on the Imperial Japanese Army* (Lincoln: University of Nebraska Press, 1998), 28.

21 Sadao Asada, "From Washington to London: The Imperial Japanese Navy and the Politics of Naval Limitation, 1921-30," in *The Washington Conference, 1921-22: Naval Rivalry, East Asian Stability and the Road to Pearl Harbor*, ed. Erik Goldstein and John Maurer (Ilford, UK: Frank Cass, 1994), 147-91.

22 Ponko, "The Navy and the Aleutians before World War II," 123-30; and Hilary P. Jones to the Secretary of the Navy, "Report of Commander Fleet Base Force on Alaskan Reconnaissance," 26 March 1924, Naval Historical Center (hereinafter NHC), Strategic Plans Division (hereinafter SPD), series III, box 35.

23 Hector C. Bywater, *Sea-Power in the Pacific: A Study of the American-Japanese Naval Problem* (Boston: Houghton Mifflin, 1921), 269; and Bywater, *The Great Pacific War: A History of the American-Japanese Campaign of 1931-33* (Boston: Houghton Mifflin, 1925), 194-6. William H. Honan argues that Yamamoto, while stationed at Japan's American embassy in the 1920s, read *The Great Pacific War's* account of a Japanese assault on Pearl Harbor; William H. Honan, *Visions of Infamy: The Untold Story of How Journalist Hector C. Bywater Devised the Plans That Led to Pearl Harbor* (New York: St. Martin's Press, 1991).

24 See Joseph J. Corn, *The Winged Gospel: America's Romance with Aviation, 1900-1950* (New York: Oxford University Press, 1983).

25 Major General T. Monoher to the Chief of Staff, "Authorization for the Alaska Flying Expedition," 8 April 1920, Library of Congress (hereinafter LC), William Mitchell Papers, box 8; Mitchell to General Charleton, 18 October 1919, LC, Mitchell Papers, box 7; and H.H. Arnold, *Global Mission* (New York: Harper and Harper Brothers, 1949), 97-8.

26 Nancy Fogelson, *Arctic Exploration & International Relations 1900-1932* (Fairbanks: University of Alaska Press, 1992), 81.

27 Trenchard quoted in Eugene M. Emme, "The American Dimension," in *Air Power and Warfare: The Proceedings of the 8th Military History Symposium United States Air Force Academy 18-20 October 1978*, ed. Alfred F. Hurley and Robert C. Ehrhrat (Washington, DC: Government Printing Office, 1979), 64; and Jerold E. Brown, *Where Eagles Land: Planning and Development of U.S. Army Airfields, 1910-1941* (New York: Greenwood Press, 1990), 53-4.

28 Alfred F. Hurley, *Billy Mitchell: Crusader for Air Power* (Bloomington: Indiana University Press, 1975), 13-14; and Mitchell quoted in Norman Edward Rourke, *War Comes to Alaska: The Dutch Harbor Attack, June 3-4, 1942.* (Shippensburg: Burd Street Press, 1997), xiv. Mitchell's 1912 report had warned that Japan could occupy much of western America unless 500,000 soldiers were based on the west coast; Iriye, *Pacific Estrangement,* 220-2.

29 Mitchell, "Preliminary Report of Inspection of Air Service Activities in the Hawaiian Department," 10 December 1923, United States Air Force Academy Library (hereinafter USAFA), Mitchell Papers; and "Report of Inspection of Air Service Activities by B.G. William Mitchell," October 1924, USAFA, Mitchell Papers. In 1932 Japanese officials worried that Tokyo could be destroyed by ten tons of incendiary munitions; Kenneth P. Werrell, *Blankets of Fire: U.S. Bombers over Japan during World War II* (Washington, DC: Smithsonian Institution Press, 1996), 39.

30 Loring C. Christie, "The Anglo-Japanese Alliance," 1 June 1921, reprinted in *External Affairs* 18 (September 1966): 402-13; and "Report of Inspection of Brig. General Wm. Mitchell, Assistant Chief of Air Service During Winter – 1923," USAFA, Mitchell Papers.

31 Mitchell quoted in Hurley, *Billy Mitchell,* 79; Air Service document, "The Round the World Flight," 1923, USAFA, Leigh Wade Papers, file U-672-AS; Bissell quoted in "HMCS 'Thiepval' Naval Questionnaire," attached to Commander Cosmo Hastings to District Intelligence Officer, Esquimalt, 27 September 1924, NAC, Department of National Defence Records, RG24, vol. 11924, file 1091-7-1; and Arnold quoted in United States Air Force Museum, *World Flight Chronicle,* 1999, <www.wpafb.af.mil/museum>, (30 August 2002).

32 Mitchell quoted in James J. Cooke, *Billy Mitchell* (Boulder, CO: Lynne Rienner, 2002), 161; Hurley, *Billy Mitchell,* 100; William Mitchell, *Winged Defense: The Development and Possibilities of Modern Air Power – Economic and Military* (New York: G.P. Putnam's Sons, 1925), vii-viii and 219; "Col. William Mitchell's Opening Statement before the President's Board of Aeronautic Inquiry on Conditions Governing Our National Defense and the Place of Air Power Beside Sea Power and Land Power," October 1925, LC, William Mitchell Papers, box 20.

33 Lieutenant Colonel G.T. Perkins, "Canadian Trip," June 1926, NARA, War Department Records, RG165, Military Intelligence Division Correspondence (hereinafter MID), 1917-41, file 2694-36; and C.F. Hamilton memorandum, March 1921, NAC, C.F. Hamilton Papers, vol. 3, file 12.

34 Russell F. Weigley, *The American Way of War: A History of American Military Strategy and Policy* (New York: Macmillan, 1973), 231; Coolidge quoted in Carl H. Builder, *The Icarus Syndrome: The Role of Air Power Theory in the Evolution and Rise of the U.S. Air Force* (New Brunswick: Transaction Publishers, 1994), 53. H.H. Arnold, the future commander of the army air corps in the Second World War, warned Mitchell not to insult army and navy commanders publicly at the hearings. But Mitchell had shrugged him off, averring he was serving the good of the service and the nation. Thomas M. Coffey, *Hap, Military Aviator: The Story of the U.S. Air Force and the Man Who Built It, General Henry H. "Hap" Arnold* (New York: Viking Press, 1982), 123; and Cooke, *Billy Mitchell,* 170.

35 Burke Davis, *The Billy Mitchell Affair* (New York: Random House, 1967), 185; Brigadier General Harry A. Smith to Chief of Staff, "Report of Brigadier General William Mitchell, Air Service on Trip to Pacific Ocean," 18 November 1925, NARA, War Plans Division (hereinafter WPD), RG165, file WPD 2050; and Weigley, *The American Way of War,* 233. See also James P. Tate, *The Army and Its Air Corps: Army Policy toward Aviation, 1919-1941* (Maxwell Air Force Base: Air University Press, 1998), 2-3. Pre-Second World War planning is discussed in Richard A. Preston, *The Defence of the Undefended Border: Planning for War in North America, 1867-1939* (Montreal: McGill-Queen's University Press, 1977). Even if the army assaulted Canada, Major General W.D. Connor expected a public clamour against it and could not "conceive of the President agreeing to any such move"; Connor to Assistant Commandant, 10 March 1928, Military History Institute Archives, Army War College Curriculum Records, file 111-12.

36 Michael S. Sherry, *The Rise of American Air Power: The Creation of Armageddon* (New Haven: Yale University Press, 1987), 21.

37 Miller, *War Plan Orange,* 3-5.

38 Louis Morton, "Interservice Co-operation and Political-Military Collaboration," in *Total War and Cold War: Problems in Civilian Control of the Military,* ed. Harry L. Coles (Columbus: Ohio State University Press, 1962), 141-2.

39 Admiral C.F. Hughes to the Secretary of the Navy, "Joint Army and Navy Basic War Plan – Orange," 14 June 1928, NARA, RG225, series 280, M1421, reel 9; United States, Joint Board, *Joint Action of the Army and Navy 1927* (Washington, DC: Government Printing Office, 1927), chap. 5, 30; and Hughes to the Secretary of the Navy, "Joint Army and Navy Basic War Plan – Orange. Estimate of the Situation," 11 January 1929, NARA, RG225, series 280, reel 9.

40 Kennedy, "Depression and Security," 349 and 363; Captain Allan Buchanan to Herbert Hoover, 28 February 1930, Herbert Hoover Presidential Library, Herbert Hoover Presidential Papers, box 35, file Cabinet Navy Aeronautics Bureau; Captain Macnamara to Sir Ronald Lindsay, 18 May 1932, in *British Documents on Foreign Affairs: Reports and Papers from the Foreign Office Confidential Trust,* series C, *North America, 1919-1939,* ed. D.K. Adams, vol. 19, *International Competition and Naval Rivalry, 1929-1934* (Frederick, MD: University Publications of America, 1995), 213; Thomas G. Cranford Jr. memorandum, attached to Joseph C. Grew to the Secretary of State, no. 131, 21 September 1932, in *Foreign Relations of the United States: Diplomatic Papers, 1932,* by Department of State, vol. 4, *The Far East* (Washington, DC: Government Printing Office, 1948), 706-15; John W. Troy, *Annual Report of the Governor of Alaska to the Secretary Interior for the Fiscal Year Ended June 30, 1933* (Washington, DC: Government Printing Office, 1933), 56; and Major General B.D. Foulois to the Adjutant General, 23 May 1933, NARA, Army Air Forces (hereinafter AAF) Central Decimal Files 1917-38, RG18, Project Files – Airfields, Alaska, file 300 Misc. Alaska. In May 1933 Japan had asked that the *Hakuyu Maru* be allowed to stop in the Aleutians. Concerned about setting a precedent for future Japanese voyages, the USN had insisted the ship stop only at Dutch Harbor. But the vessel claimed that poor weather, a need for water, and engine difficulties had forced it to put in three times at Attu in June. By mid-June 1933

the United States agreed to allow Japanese ships only if they were escorted by Coast Guard cutters; Stanley Hornbeck to Grew, 20 May 1933, NARA, Department of State Diplomatic Post Files, Japan 1930-41, Tokyo Embassy, RG84, file 862.8, reel 13; State Department to Tokyo Embassy, telegram 57, 10 June 1933, NARA, Department of State Diplomatic Post Files, Japan 1930-41, Tokyo Embassy, RG84, file 862.8, reel 13; State Department to Grew, telegram 322, 31 July 1933, plus memorandum of conversation between Mr. Salisbury, State Department, and Mr. Miura, Second Secretary of the Japanese Embassy, 25 July 1933, NARA, Department of State Diplomatic Post Files, Japan 1930-41, Tokyo Embassy, RG84, file 862.8, reel 13; and Hornbeck to Grew, 16 June 1933, Hoover Institution on War, Revolution, and Peace (hereinafter HI), Stanley K. Hornbeck Papers, vol. 184, file Grew, Joseph C. Correspondence 1933.

41 Brian McAllister Linn, *Guardians of Empire: The U.S. Army and the Pacific, 1902-1940* (Chapel Hill: University of North Carolina Press, 1997), 169, xii.

42 Brown, *Where Eagles Land,* 97-8; "Report of Special Committee, General Council, on Employment of Army Air Corps under Certain Strategic Plans," 11 October 1933, NARA, WPD General Correspondence 1920-1942, RG165, entry 281, file WPD 888; and Lieutenant Colonel C.H. Mason, "Defense of Alaska," 18 January 1934, NARA, MID 1922-44, RG165, file Alaska 6800.

43 Woodring quoted in William O. Odom, *After the Trenches: The Transformation of U.S. Army Doctrine, 1918-1939* (College Station: Texas A&M University Press, 1999), 106; Lieutenant Colonel F.S. Clark to General C.E. Kilbourne, "Policy of the United States As a Neutral, in a Russo-Japanese War," 1 March 1934, NARA, RG165, file WPD 3834; and Kilbourne to Deputy Chief of Staff, "Revision of War Plans – Orange," 28 February 1934, NARA, RG165, file WPD 2720-54.

44 WPD, "The Military Situation in Alaska," March 1934, NARA, RG165, file WPD 3512-1; Brigadier General Andrew Jones to Kilbourne, 20 March 1934, NARA, RG165, file WPD 3512-1; and Kilbourne to General Douglas MacArthur, "Army Garrison for Alaska – Peace and War," 10 April 1934, NARA, RG165, file WPD 3512-1.

45 Mary Childers Mangusso, "Anthony J. Dimond: A Political Biography," PhD diss., Texas Tech University, 1978, 315; Anthony J. Dimond speech, 30 March 1933, *Congressional Record – House,* 73rd Congress, 1st session, vol. 77, 1056; Dimond speech, 5 March 1934, *Congressional Record – House,* 73rd Congress, 2nd session, vol. 78, 3754-5; and United States Congress, House, *A Bill to Provide More Effectively for the National Defense by Augmenting the Military Garrison and Establishing Military Utilities in Alaska,* HR 9524, 73rd Congress, 2nd session.

46 Ernest Gruening, *The State of Alaska* (New York: Random House, 1954), 315; Mangusso, "Anthony J. Dimond," 324 and 326; and Kilbourne to MacArthur, "Report on HR 9524," 10 July 1934, NARA, RG165, file WPD 3512-2.

47 Edward T. Layton, with Roger Pineau and John Costello, *And I Was There: Pearl Harbor and Midway – Breaking the Secrets* (Old Saybrook: Konecky and Konecky, 1985), 51.

48 Jeffrey M. Dorwart, *Conflict of Duty: The U.S. Navy's Intelligence Dilemma, 1919-1945* (Annapolis, MD: Naval Institute Press, 1983), 55; Lieutenant Commander G.T. Owen, "Final Report of the Operations of VJ Squadron One-F Aircraft, Base Force As a Unit of the 1934 Aleutian Survey Expedition," Appendix H of the 1934 Aleutian Islands Survey Expedition Final Report, 30 October 1934, NHC, SPD, series III, box 56; and Ponko, "The Navy and The Aleutians," 131.

49 Dern to Secretary of State Cordell Hull, June 1934, NARA, Department of State Decimal File 1930-39, RG59, file 811.2342/421.

50 Roosevelt quoted in Kennedy, "Depression and Security," 362; Keith D. McFarland, *Harry H. Woodring: A Political Biography of FDR's Controversial Secretary of War* (Lawrence: University Press of Kansas, 1975), 84 and 120; and Robert Dallek, *Franklin D. Roosevelt and American Foreign Policy, 1932-1945* (New York: Oxford University Press, 1979), 36. MacArthur told Roosevelt that if America lost its next war and "an American boy, lying in the mud with an enemy bayonet through his belly and an enemy boot on his dying throat, spat out his last curse, I wanted the name not to be MacArthur but

Roosevelt." When Roosevelt demanded an apology, MacArthur offered his resignation only to be told not to be ridiculous. MacArthur claims to have vomited on the White House steps on his way out. Geoffrey Perret, *Old Soldiers Never Die: The Life of Douglas MacArthur* (New York: Random House, 1996), 173; and Michael Schaller, *Douglas MacArthur: The Far Eastern General* (New York: Oxford University Press, 1989), 17-18.

51 Foulois and Mitchell quoted in Timothy Moy, *War Machines: Transforming Technologies in the U.S. Military, 1920-1940* (College Station: Texas A&M University Press, 2001), 58. See also John F. Shiner, "General Benjamin Foulois and the 1934 Air Mail Disaster," *Aerospace Historian* 25 (December 1978): 221-30.

52 The coastal defence battle is discussed in John F. Shiner, "The Air Corps, the Navy, and Coast Defense, 1919-1941," *Military Affairs* 45 (October 1981): 113-20; and John F. Shiner, *Foulois and the U.S. Army Air Corps 1931-1935* (Washington, DC: Office of Air Force History, 1983).

53 Adjutant General to the Chief of the Air Corps, "Alaskan Flight," 15 May 1934, NARA, RG18, box 706, file 373.

54 For more on the agreements, see O.D. Skelton to Warren D. Robbins, no. 54, 2 June 1934, NARA, RG59, Decimal File 1930-39, file 811.2342/422.

55 "Impressions of Canadian Defence Policy – December 1934, by Sir Maurice Hankey," 1 January 1935, Public Record Office (hereinafter PRO), Maurice Hankey Official Papers, CAB63/8; Sub-Committee of the Joint Service Committee (JSC), "The Maintenance of Canadian Neutrality on event of war between Japan and the U.S.A.," 10 March 1933, NAC, Department of National Defence (hereinafter DND) Records, RG24, vol. 2692, file HQS 5199-A; and A.G.L. McNaughton to R.B. Bennett, "Sino-Japanese Dispute. Possible Commitments in Respect to the Maintenance of Neutrality," 24 February 1933, in *Documents on Canadian External Relations*, vol. 5, *1931-35*, ed. Alex I. Inglis (Ottawa: Department of External Affairs, 1973), 336-9.

56 Deputy Minister of National Defence L.R. LaFleche to Skelton, 9 June 1934, NAC, Department of External Affairs Records (hereinafter DEA), RG25, vol. 1684, file 53-AB; and McNaughton memorandum, 15 June 1934, NAC, DEA, RG25, vol. 1684, file 53-AB.

57 Brigadier General J. Sutherland Brown to Colonel W.W. Foster, 31 December 1932, Queen's University Archives, Kingston, ON, J. Sutherland Brown Papers, box 1, file 11.

58 Pierre de la Boal to John Hickerson, 23 June 1934, NARA, RG59, Decimal File 1930-39, file 811.2342/460; and Norman Hillmer, "The Anglo-Canadian Neurosis: The Case of O.D. Skelton," in *Britain and Canada: Survey of a Changing Relationship*, ed. Peter Lyons (London: Frank Cass, 1976), 76. King thought Skelton was Canada's ablest public servant and Bennett, who had intended to fire him after his election in 1930, found he could not do without Skelton; diary entry, 7 August 1930, NAC, W.L.M. King Papers, Diaries; and John Hilliker, *Canada's Department of External Affairs*, vol. 1, *The Early Years, 1909-1946* (Montreal: McGill-Queen's University Press, 1990), 137.

59 Skelton to LaFleche, 12 and 13 June 1934, NAC, RG25, vol. 1684, file 53-AB; and Skelton to Robbins, no. 59, 14 June 1934, NARA, RG59, Decimal File 1930-39, file 811.2342/425.

60 LaFleche to Skelton, 13 June 1934, NAC, RG25, vol. 1684, file 53-AB.

61 Robbins to Hull, no. 648, "Discussion in Canadian Senate of Canada's Neutrality," 18 June 1934, NARA, RG59, Decimal File 1930-39, file 811.2342/431; Boal to Hull, no. 644, "Projected good will flight from the United States to Alaska," 15 June 1934, NARA, RG59, Decimal File 1930-39, file 811.2342/426; Skelton to Bennett, "United States' Request re Flight to Alaska," 15 June 1934, NAC, RG25, vol. 1684, file 53-AB; and Skelton to Robbins, no. 62, 18 June 1934, NAC, RG25, vol. 1684, file 53-AB.

62 Frank Waldrop, "Army to Make Mass Flight to Alaska," 21 June 1934, *Washington Herald*; Robbins to Hull, no. 659, "Projected Washington-Alaska Flight," 22 June 1934, NARA, RG59, Decimal File 1930-39, file 811.2342/431.

63 Colonel H.H. Arnold, "Report on the Alaskan Flight," October 1934, NARA, RG18, box 705, file 373; Harold M. Collins, "Visit of United States Army Bombing Squadron," 28 July 1934, NARA, RG18, box

705, file 373; and Benjamin D. Foulois, with C.V. Glines, *From the Wright Brothers to the Astronauts: The Memoirs of Major General Benjamin D. Foulois* (New York: McGraw Hill, 1968), 230 and 271.

64 Murray Green, "Hugh J. Knerr: The Pen and the Sword," in *Makers of the United States Air Force*, ed. John L. Frisbee (Washington, DC: Office of Air Force History, 1987), 106; and Perret, *Old Soldiers Never Die*, 184-5. Arnold received the Distinguished Flying Cross for the mission only after Mac-Arthur had left the army.

65 McNaughton to General A.A. Montgomery-Massingberg, 31 July 1934, NAC, Ian Mackenzie Papers, vol. 30, file X-28; H.H. Wrong to Bennett, 27 September 1934, NAC, R.B. Bennett Papers, vol. 281, file U-110, reel M-1028; and army general staff, "Unguarded Alaska?" 5 February 1935, Directorate of History and Heritage, DND, Kardex File 74/256.

Chapter 2: He Who Holds Alaska Will Hold the World

1 Japanese Foreign Office statement, 29 December 1934, Hoover Institution on War, Revolution, and Peace (hereinafter HI), Stanley K. Hornbeck Papers, vol. 307, file Naval Conference 1934; Lindsay to Sir John Simon, 15 February 1934, in *British Documents on Foreign Affairs: Reports and Papers from the Foreign Office Confidential Print*, series E, *Asia, 1914-1939*, ed. Ann Trotter, vol. 13, *Japan, January 1934 – December 1934* (Bethesda, MD: University Publications of America, 1992), 104-5; and Herbert P. Bix, *Hirohito and the Making of Modern Japan* (New York: Perennial, 2001), 149-50.

2 "Statement of Secretary of State, Mr. Cordell Hull, Relative to the Japanese Government's Notice of Intention to Terminate the Washington Naval Treaty," 29 December 1934, National Archives of Canada (hereinafter NAC), Governor General's Records, RG7, G21, vol. 641, file 34804; *New York Times* quoted in Lindsay to Simon, 31 December 1934, in *British Documents on Foreign Affairs: Reports and Papers from the Foreign Office Confidential Print*, series C, *North America, 1919-1939*, ed. D.K. Adams, vol. 19, *International Competition and Naval Rivalry, 1929-1939* (Frederick, MD: University Publications of America, 1995), 264-5; Hornbeck, "Naval Disarmament," 7 August 1934, HI, Hornbeck Papers, vol. 307, file Naval Conference 1935; Hornbeck, "Naval Limitation and Contemporary Diplomatic Effectiveness," 31 December 1936, HI, Hornbeck Papers, vol. 15, file Armaments; Kilbourne to the Chief of Staff, "Denunciation of the Washington Treaty of 1922 by Japan," 26 December 1934, National Archives and Records Administration (hereinafter NARA), RG165, file WPD 3804; and Dern to Roosevelt, 27 December 1934, NARA, RG165, file WPD 3804.

3 J.J. McSwain to Roosevelt, 28 May 1934, Franklin Delano Roosevelt Library (hereinafter FDRL), Roosevelt Official Files (hereinafter OF), file OF25u; Robert W. Krauskopf, "The Army and the Strategic Bomber, 1930-1939," *Military Affairs* 22 (Summer 1958): 88; and Shiner, *Foulois and the U.S. Army Air Corps*, 215.

4 Wilcox testimony, 11 February 1935, *Hearings before the Committee on Military Affairs House of Representatives Seventy-Fourth Congress, First Session, on H.R. 6621 and H.R. 4130, February 11-13, 1935* (Washington, DC: Government Printing Office, 1935), 7-8; Kilbourne to Wilcox, 28 January 1935, NARA, RG165, file WPD 3798-5; and Kilbourne testimony, 11 February 1935, *Hearing before the Committee on Military Affairs*, 16-17. HR 4130 is in the *Congressional Record*, vol. 78, 1331-3.

5 See Dimond and Mitchell testimony, 11 and 13 February 1935, *Hearings before the Committee on Military Affairs*, 29-32 and 113-21.

6 Norman A. Graebner, "Hoover, Roosevelt and the Japanese," in *Pearl Harbor As History: Japanese-American Relations 1931-1941*, ed. Dorothy Borg and Shumpei Okamoto (New York: Columbia University Press, 1973), 35; and Eliot A. Cohen, "The Strategy of Innocence? The United States, 1920-1945," in *The Making of Strategy: Rulers, States, and War*, ed. Williamson Murray, MacGregor Knox, and Alvin Bernstein (Cambridge: Cambridge University Press, 1994), 445.

7 John Haile Cloe and Michael F. Monoghan, *Top Cover for America: The Air Force in Alaska 1920-1983* (Missoula: Pictorial Histories, 1984), 21; and Brigadier General O. Westover to the Adjutant General, 9 May 1935, NARA, RG18, file 686 Alaska Training Fields.

8 Carl Spaatz quoted in Stuart Symington Oral History Interview, 29 May 1981, Harry S. Truman Presidential Library, Oral History Collection.

9 Russell F. Weigley, *History of the United States Army* (New York: Macmillan, 1967), 415; and Brian McAllister Linn, *Guardians of Empire: The U.S. Army and the Pacific, 1902-1940* (Chapel Hill: University of North Carolina Press, 1997), 178.

10 Ronald Schaffer, "General Stanley D. Embick: Military Dissenter," *Military Affairs* 37 (October 1973): 90.

11 Brigadier Stanley D. Embick to Commanding General, Philippine Department, "Military Policy of U.S. in Philippine Islands," 19 April 1933, NARA, RG225, file WPD 3251-15; Linn, *Guardians of Empire*, 178-9; and Embick, "Military Aspects of the Situation That Would Result from the Retention by the United States of a Military (Including Naval) Commitment in the Philippine Islands," 2 December 1935, NARA, Records of the Office of the Secretary of War, RG107, box 3.

12 Henry L. Stimson and McGeorge Bundy, *On Active Service in Peace and War* (New York: Harper Brothers, 1947), 506; Colonel Walter Krueger, "Memo: Our Policy in the Philippines," 28 October 1935, NARA, RG165, entry 284, box 17, file 573; Roosevelt to the Secretary of the Navy, 9 December 1935, NARA, RG225, JB305, series 573, JPC Development File; and Schaffer, "General Stanley D. Embick," 91.

13 Jonathan G. Utley, "Franklin Roosevelt and Naval Strategy, 1933-1941," in *FDR and the U.S. Navy*, ed. Edward J. Marolda (New York: St. Martin's Press, 1998), 48; Commander A.S. Carpender memorandum, 17 December 1935, NARA, RG165, entry 284, box 17, file 573; and Linn, *Guardians of Empire*, 180.

14 Krueger to Craig, "Joint Army and Navy Basic War Plan - Orange," 28 October 1937, NARA, RG165, file WPD 2720-104; Craig to Chief of Naval Operations (CNO), "Joint Army and Navy Basic War Plan – Orange," 3 November 1937, NARA, RG165, file WPD 2720-104; Krueger, "Some Basic Thoughts on the Joint Basic War Plan Orange," 22 November 1937, NARA, RG165, file WPD 2720-104; and Craig to Joint Army and Navy Planning Committee (JANPC), "Joint Army and Navy Basic War Plan – Orange," 10 November 1937, NARA, RG165, file WPD 2720-104.

15 "Joint Army and Navy Basic War Plan – Orange," 21 February 1938, NARA, RG225 JB325, series 618, M1421, reel 10; Mark W. Lowenthal, "Roosevelt and the Coming of the War: The Search for United States Policy 1937-42," in *The Second World War: Essays in Military and Political History*, ed. Walter Laqueur (London: Sage, 1982), 53; and Louis Morton, "Germany First: The Basic Concept of Allied Strategy in World War II," in *Command Decisions*, ed. Kent Roberts Greenfield (Washington, DC: Department of the Army, 1960), 9-11.

16 L.T. Gerow memorandum, early 1937, NARA, RG165, file WPD 3512-21; Admiral W.D. Leahy to Roosevelt, 23 August 1937, in *Franklin D. Roosevelt and Foreign Affairs, Second Series January 1937-August 1939*, ed. Donald B. Schewe, vol. 6, *July-September 1937* (Cambridge: Harvard University Press, 1969), 363; and Bruce W. Bidwell, *History of the Military Intelligence Division, Department of the Army General Staff: 1775-1941* (Frederick, MD: University Publications of America, 1986), 317. The USN's Alaskan intelligence apparatus in the mid-1930s comprised four junior officers, two customs agents, and a railway mail clerk; D. Adams Frost, Thirteenth Naval District, to the Director of Naval Intelligence (hereinafter DNI), 18 May 1936, NARA, Records of the Office of the Chief of Naval Operations, Office of Naval Intelligence Planning Branch, RG38, box 7.

17 Claude Swanson to Roosevelt, 1 May 1935, FDRL, Franklin Roosevelt Papers, President's Secretary's File (hereinafter PSF), box 64; Dimond to Swanson, 20 April 1936, Rasmussen Library (hereinafter RL), University of Alaska-Fairbanks, Anthony J. Dimond Papers, box 16, folder 16; Strategic Plans Division (hereinafter SPD) to WPD, "Naval Requirements – Alaska," Autumn 1936, Naval Historical Center (hereinafter NHC), SPD series III, box 35; and Rear Admiral Ernest J. King to Fleet Admiral A.J. Hepburn, "Naval Air Bases in Alaska," 1 September 1936, NHC, SPD series III, box 35.

18 Commander Hutchins, "Strategic Areas Alaska and the Aleutian Islands," 1936, NHC, SPD, series III, reel 22, Scholarly Resources Inc.

19 Hepburn to CNO, "Naval Air Bases in Alaska," 6 October 1936, NHC, SPD, series III, reel 22,

Scholarly Resources Inc.; Admiral W.H. Standley to Dimond, 9 November 1936, RL, Dimond Papers, box 16, folder 226; and Mangusso, "Anthony J. Dimond," 332.

20 Dorothy Borg, *The United States and the Far Eastern Crisis of 1933-1938: From the Manchurian Incident through the Initial Stage of the Undeclared Sino-Japanese War* (Cambridge: Harvard University Press, 1964), 239. Leahy thought that "the United States even with its present naval strength and military resources should be able to remain neutral if our foreign relations are skilfully handled which judging from antecedent probability is much to expect from the Department of State"; diary, 14 September 1936, Library of Congress (hereinafter LC), William Leahy Papers, box 1. In December 1921 Japan agreed that "no military or naval bases shall be established in" the island groups it had taken from Germany in the First World War; "Agreement between the United States of America and Japan," 12 December 1921, in *British Documents on Foreign Affairs: Reports and Papers from the Foreign Office Confidential Print*, series C, *North America, 1919-1939*, ed. D.K. Adams, vol. 10, *Cables and Mandates, 1920-1925* (Frederick, MD: University Publications of America, 1991), 110-12.

21 Arnold quoted in Cloe and Monoghan, *Top Cover for America*, 19; Michael S. Sherry, *The Rise of American Air Power: The Creation of Armageddon* (New Haven: Yale University Press, 1987), 59; diary entry, 20 November 1936, in *The Secret Diary of Harold L. Ickes*, ed. Harold L. Ickes, vol. 2, *The Inside Struggle 1936-1939* (New York: Simon and Schuster, 1954), 7.

22 Lieutenant Colonel R.P. Hartle and Captain R.E. Ingersoll, "Preliminary Statement Prepared by the Subcommittee on 'National Defense,'" November 1937, NARA, RG165, file WPD 3512-24.

23 Roosevelt to Norman H. Davis, 27 November 1934, in *Franklin D. Roosevelt and Foreign Affairs*, ed. Edgar B. Nixon, vol. 2, *March 1934-August 1935* (Cambridge: Belknap Press of Harvard University Press, 1969), 263; Galen Roger Perras, *Franklin Roosevelt and the Origins of the Canadian-American Security Alliance, 1933-1945: Necessary But Not Necessary Enough* (Westport, CT: Greenwood Press, 1998), 33-4; Sumner Welles to Norman Armour, 24 February 1935, FDRL, Sumner Welles Papers, box 25, file 7; and diary entry, 31 July 1936, NAC, W.L.M. King Papers.

24 Roosevelt speech, 14 August 1936, FDRL, Roosevelt Papers, President's Personal Files, series 1820, file 1st Carbon.

25 DND, "Alaskan Air Defences," 30 September 1936, NAC, H.D.G. Crerar Papers, vol. 13, file 958C.009 (D226); Colonel H.D.G. Crerar, "An Appreciation of the Defence Problems Confronting Canada with Recommendations for the Development of the Armed Forces," 5 September 1936, Directorate of History and Heritage (hereinafter DHH), Kardex File 74/256; Christie, "Memorandum on Defence Policy," 1 September 1936, NAC, Loring Christie Papers, vol. 27, file 9; diary entry, 9-10 September 1936, NAC, W.L.M. King Papers; Minister of National Defence Ian Mackenzie to King, plus attached Joint Service Committee (JSC) memorandum, "An Appreciation of the Defence Problems Confronting Canada with Recommendations for Development of the Armed Forces," 16 November 1936, NAC, W.L.M. King Papers, Correspondence, vol. 221, file Mackenzie-1936; and C.P. Stacey, *Official History of the Canadian Army in the Second World War*, vol. 1, *Six Years of War: The Army in Canada, Britain and the Pacific* (Ottawa: Department of National Defence, 1955), 11-13.

26 Christie, "Re Monroe Doctrine," 16 February 1937, in *Documents on Canadian External Relations*, vol. 6, *1936-1939*, ed. John A. Munroe (Ottawa: Department of External Affairs, 1977), 177, and Skelton memorandum, February 1937, NAC, O.D. Skelton Papers, vol. 27, file 9. The American army shared Skelton's assessment of Canada's security; see Military Intelligence Division (hereinafter MID) report, "Canada: Political Estimate," 1 June 1937, NARA, RG59, Decimal File 1930-39, file 842.00/504.

27 Diary entry, 5 March 1937 and 1 December 1936, NAC, W.L.M. King Papers.

28 Skelton quoted in Helen Howard Moorhead to Raymond L. Buell, 22 March 1937, LC, Raymond L. Buell Papers, box 10; Roosevelt to Hull, 4 August 1937, and Hull to Roosevelt, August 1937, FDRL, Roosevelt Papers, PSF, file Hull, Cordell: 1933-37.

29 Armour to J. Pierrepont Moffat, 2 September 1937, NARA, Department of State Post Records, Canada, entry 2195A, RG84, file 800.1 1937 Chief Executive.

30 John Lamberton Harper, *American Visions of Europe: Franklin D. Roosevelt, George F. Kennan, and Dean G. Acheson* (Cambridge: Cambridge University Press, 1994), 60.

31 Moffat to Armour, 14 September 1937, NARA, RG84, entry 2195A, file 800.1 1937 Chief Executive.

32 Armour to Secretary of State for External Affairs (SSEA), no. 564, 14 September 1937, NAC, RG25, vol. 1739, file 221; Skelton to Christie, 16 September 1937, NAC, RG25, vol. 1739, file 221; and Christie memorandum, 12 November 1937, NAC, RG25, vol. 1739, file 221.

33 Armour memorandum, 9 November 1937, NARA, RG84, entry 2195A, file 800 1937 Political Affairs Defense and Foreign Policy.

34 Roosevelt "Quarantine" address, 5 October 1937, in *An American Primer*, ed. Daniel J. Boorstin (Chicago: University of Chicago Press, 1966), 847-52; John E. Wiltz, *From Isolation to War, 1931-1941* (New York: Thomas Y. Crowell, 1968), 63; Neville Chamberlain to Lord Tweedsmuir, 19 November 1937, Queen's University Archives, John Buchan Papers, box 9; and Mark M. Lowenthal, *Leadership and Indecision: American War Planning and Policy Process 1937-1942* (New York: Garland Publishing, 1988), 20-5. According to Norman Davis, the "Quarantine" speech was intended to impress upon Americans that their national interests were threatened by "international anarchy." Davis argued that "it would be a mistake to read into it anything more specific"; Hornbeck, "Memorandum of Conversation, Brussels," 2 November 1937, HI, Hornbeck Papers, vol. 129, file Conversations. Davis had written much of Roosevelt's speech but the president had added the quarantine portion; Adolf Berle memorandum, 13 October 1937, FDRL, Adolf Berle Papers, box 210, Diary 1937.

35 Armour memorandum, 9 November 1937, NARA, RG84, entry 2195A, file 800 1937, Political Affairs Defense and Foreign Policy; Welles to Roosevelt, 20 December 1937, FDRL, Roosevelt Papers, PSF, file State: 1937; Roosevelt to Welles, 22 December 1937, FDRL, Roosevelt Papers, PSF, file State: 1937; Roosevelt to King, 21 December 1937, NAC, King Correspondence, reel C3729, p. 207146; King to Roosevelt, 30 December 1937, NAC, King Correspondence, reel C3729, pp. 207148-207149; Armour to Welles, 8 January 1938, NARA, RG59, Decimal File 1930-39, file 842.20/68; Skelton, "Conversations on West Coast Defence," 10 January 1938, NAC, RG25, vol. 2959, file B-80. Assistant Secretary of State Adolf Berle thought only Welles could keep America out of a war, for "he is the only one who apparently keeps his head working aside from his emotions"; Berle memorandum, 13 October 1937, FDRL, Berle Papers, box 210, Diary 1937.

36 Hugh L. Keenleyside to Escott Reid, 14 May 1937, NAC, Escott Reid Papers, vol. 34; Crerar to Colonel W.W.T. Torr, 13 January 1938, DHH, Kardex File 000.8 (D3); Major General E.C. Ashton to Mackenzie, "Observations on Canada's Defence Policy," 14 October 1937, DHH, Kardex file 112.3M2009 (D27); and Ashton to Crerar, 29 November 1937, NAC, RG24, vol. 2448, file HQC631-52-1.

37 Ashton to Mackenzie, "Conversations held in Washington, D.C., on the 19th and 20th January, 1938," 26 January 1938, DHH, Kardex File 112.3M2009 (D22).

38 John Major, "William Daniel Leahy," in *The Chiefs of Naval Operations*, ed. Robert William Love Jr. (Annapolis, MD: Naval Institute Press, 1980), 102. When Roosevelt won the 1932 election, Leahy rejoiced, as the country and the USN "will now be directed by a man whose point of view is wholly American"; diary entry, 12 November 1932, LC, William Leahy Papers, box 1.

39 Commander Percy W. Nelles, "Conversations held in Washington, D.C. on the 19th and 20th January, 1938," January 1938, NAC, W.L.M. King Memoranda and Notes, vol. 157, file F1411. According to Leahy's diary, he had "an interesting talk" at the Canadian Legation; diary, 19 January 1938, LC, William Leahy Papers, box 2.

40 JSC to Mackenzie, 14 April 1938, DHH, Kardex File 181.006 (D276); and JSC, "A Review of Canada's Position with Respect to Defence, July 1938," 22 July 1938, NAC, Ian Mackenzie Papers, vol. 30, file X-50.

41 Christie to Skelton, "Canadian Defence Policy," 24 June 1938, NAC, Skelton Papers, vol. 27, file 8; Sub-Committee No. 2, "A Survey of Canada from the Theater Point of View," 28 January 1938, NARA, RG165, MID, file 1000-Canada; Lowenthal, *Leadership and Indecision*, 27-32; and Herbert Marler to SSEA, 9 February 1938, NAC, King Correspondence, reel C3736, pp. 216622-216629.

42 Colonel Sherman Miles to War Plans Division (hereinafter WPD), "Plans for Alaska in an Orange War," 16 March 1938, NARA, RG165, file WPD 3512-29; Krueger to Major General A.J. Bowley, Fourth Army, "Concentration Plan, The Army Strategical Plan – Orange, 1938," 15 April 1938, NARA, RG165, file WPD 2720-107; Major Chas. C. Quigley to WPD, "'Secret' Letter No. 2720-111, WPD, 23 February 1938," 27 April 1938, NARA, RG165, file WPD 2720-107; Bowley to WPD, "Defense of Alaska under the Army Strategical Plan – Orange," 17 November 1938, NARA, RG165, file WPD 2720-107; and WPD, "Transfer of Chilkoot Barracks, Alaska, to the Department of the Interior and the reestablishment of this garrison at some other location in Alaska," 7 October 1938, NARA, RG165, file WPD 3512-30.

43 Weigley, *History of the United States Army,* 417; United States Resource Commission, *Alaska, Its Resources and Development* (Washington, DC: Government Printing Office, 1938), 205-6; and CNO, "Floating Dry Docks," 2 February 1937, NHC, series III, box 67.

44 House of Representatives, *Report on Need of Additional Naval Bases to Defend the Coast of the United States, its Territories, and Possessions* (Washington, DC: Government Printing Office, 27 December 1938), 20-2 and 31.

45 Edward S. Miller, *War Plan Orange: The U.S. Strategy to Defeat Japan, 1897-1945* (Annapolis, MD: Naval Institute Press, 1991), 241 and 251; Borg, *The United States and the Far Eastern Crisis,* 249-50; Major, "The Navy Plans for War, 1937-1941," 244; Samuel Eliot Morison, *History of the United States Naval Operations in World War II,* vol. 3, *The Rising Sun in the Pacific 1931-April 1942* (Boston: Little, Brown and Company, 1948), 33-4; Hans Schmidt, *Maverick Marine: General Smedley D. Butler and the Contradictions of American Military History* (Lexington: University Press of Kentucky, 1987), 242; and Major A. Franklin Kibler memorandum, 2 May 1939, NARA, RG165, file WPD 2720-135.

46 Arnold notes taken at the White House, 14 November 1938, FDRL, Roosevelt Papers, OF, file OF25t; and Joint Board minutes, 9 November 1938, NARA, RG225, JB301.

47 JANPC, "Study of Joint Action in Event of Violation of Monroe Doctrine by Fascist Powers," 21 April 1939, NARA, RG225, JB325, series 634; and Mark S. Watson, *Chief of Staff: Prewar Plans and Preparations* (Washington, DC: Department of the Army, 1950), 98-9.

48 Joint Board minutes, 6 May 1939, NARA, RG225, JB301; "Joint Army and Navy Basic War Plan – Rainbow No. 1," 14 August 1939, NARA, Adjutant General's Office, Operations Branch Special Projects – War Plans "Color" 1920-1948, RG407, box 98. Rainbow 2 dealt with a Pacific defensive effort with allied assistance, Rainbow 3 a Pacific war without aid; Rainbow 4 envisioned offensives in South America or the eastern Atlantic, while Rainbow 5 outlined African and European operations to defeat Germany and Italy; Ray S. Cline, *Washington Command Post: The Operations Division* (Washington, DC: Center for Military History, 1985), 56; and Maurice Matloff and Edwin M. Snell *Strategic Planning for Coalition Warfare 1941-1942* (Washington, DC: Department of the Army, 1953), 7-8.

49 R.S. Crenshaw, USN War Plans Division, to CNO, "Defense of Kodiak and Sitka," 29 November 1939, NHC, SPD, series V, box 96; Brigadier General George V. Strong to Bowley, 10 October 1939, NARA, RG165, file WPD 3512-47.

50 Roosevelt quoted in Robert Dallek, *Franklin D. Roosevelt and American Foreign Policy, 1932-1945* (New York: Oxford University Press, 1979), 197-9; Weigley, *History of the United States Army,* 422; David M. Kennedy, *Freedom from Fear: The American People in Depression and War, 1929-1945* (New York: Oxford University Press, 1999), 430; and Marshall quoted in Michael S. Sherry, *Preparing for the Next War: American Plans for Postwar Defense, 1941-45* (New Haven: Yale University Press, 1977), 3.

51 Marshall quoted in Michael S. Sherry, *In the Shadow of War: The United States since the 1930s* (New Haven: Yale University Press, 1995), 35; Marshall to Harry Woodring, 7 September 1939, and Marshall, "Subject: Increases in the Army," 8 September 1939, in *The Papers of George Catlett Marshall,* ed. Larry I. Bland, vol. 2, *"We Cannot Delay," July 1, 1939-December 6, 1941* (Baltimore: Johns Hopkins University Press, 1986), 52-4; and Keith D. McFarland, *Harry H. Woodring: A Political Biography of FDR's Controversial Secretary of War* (Lawrence: University Press of Kansas, 1975), 115.

52 Claus-M. Naske and Herman E. Slotnick, *Alaska: A History of the 49th State* (Grand Rapids: William

B. Eerdmans Publishing, 1987), 109-10; "Report of Board of Officers on Survey of Airfields with Recommendations for the Alaska Base, June 7 to August 8 1939," August 1939, NARA, RG165, file WPD 3512-38; and Stetson Conn, Rose C. Engelman, and Byron Fairchild, *The Western Hemisphere: Guarding the United States and Its Outposts* (Washington, DC: Department of the Army, 1964), 228.

53 Marshall to Roosevelt, 22 November 1939, NARA, RG165, file WPD 3512-50.

54 Diary entry, 23-4 April 1940, NAC, W.L.M. King Papers; Dimond quoted in Cloe and Monoghan, *Top Cover for America*, 23; Watson, *Chief of Staff*, 164-5; War Department, "Outline of War Department Program for National Defense," 13 April 1940, NARA, RG165, file WPD 3674-16; diary entry for 13 May 1940, FDRL, Henry Morgenthau Jr. Presidential Diaries, fiche 5; Marshall to Bernard Baruch, 14 May 1940, in *The Papers of George Catlett Marshall*, ed. Bland, vol. 2, *"We Cannot Delay,"* 212; Forrest C. Pogue, *George C. Marshall: Ordeal and Hope, 1939-1942* (New York: Viking Press), 16-32; and Stetson Conn, "Between World Wars," in *American Military History*, ed. Maurice Matloff, vol. 2: *1902-1996* (Conshohocken: Combined Books, 1996), 77. Senator Schwellenbach of Washington had claimed on 8 April that Siberian base construction served no purpose "unless [the Soviet Union] believed at some time that in the future that Alaskan territory might be available to her alone or through action with Japs"; Cloe and Monoghan, *Top Cover for America*, 24.

55 Admiral H.R. Stark to JANPC, 21 February 1940, NARA, RG225, JB312, series 650, reel 7; Crenshaw to CNO, "Defense of Alaska," 8 April 1940, NHC, SPD, series V, box 96; Strong to Marshall, "Alaska," 20 April 1940, NARA, RG165, file WPD 3512-59; and Strong to Marshall, "Dispatch of Forces to Alaska," 10 May 1940, NARA, RG165, file WPD 4297.

56 Cloe and Monoghan, *Top Cover for America*, 22; and Arnold to Marshall, "Report on Inspection Flight to Alaska," 22 July 1940, NARA, RG18, file 686 Alaska Landing Fields.

57 Joint Board to the Secretary of War, "Defense of the Naval Bases at Sitka and Kodiak," 14 August 1940, NARA, RG225, JB312, series 650, reel 7.

58 Brian Garfield, *The Thousand-Mile War: World War II in Alaska and the Aleutians* (New York: Bantam Books, 1969), 52-3.

59 David G. Wittels, "Lieutenant General Simon Bolivar Buckner," in *These Are the Generals*, ed. Walter Millis (New York: Alfred A. Knopf, 1943), 72-3; Nicholas Evans Sarantakes, *Keystone: The American Occupation of Okinawa and U.S.-Japan Relations* (College Station: Texas A&M University Press, 2000), 4; Charles Hendricks, "Race Relations and the Contributions of African-American Troops in Alaska," in *The U.S. Army and World War II*, ed. Judith L. Bellafaire (Washington, DC: Center for Military History, 1998), 171; and Cloe and Monoghan, *Top Cover for America*, 32.

60 Garfield, *The Thousand-Mile War*, 312.

61 Brigadier General Simon Bolivar Buckner to Lieutenant General John L. DeWitt, "Defense of Naval Establishments in Alaska," 9 October 1940, NARA, United States Army Commands (hereinafter USAC), Alaskan Department Records, RG338, file 660-2; Buckner to DeWitt, 24 October 1940, NARA, RG18, file 600.12 Alaska Construction; Buckner to Arnold, 25 October 1940, NARA, RG18, file 600.12 Alaska Construction; and Conn et al., *Guarding the United States and Its Outposts*, 227-8.

62 DeWitt to Adjutant General, 9 November 1940, NARA, RG338, Alaskan Department, file 660.2.

63 Buckner to DeWitt, 12 October 1940, NARA, RG338, Alaskan Department, file Lt. Gen. Buckner's Miscellaneous Correspondence.

64 Miles to WPD, "G-2 Estimate of the Situation – Alaska," 27 January 1941, NARA, RG165, file WPD 4297-2; CNO to Marshall, "Alaskan Bases – Development of," 7 February 1941, NHC, SPD, series V, box 96; Lieutenant Colonel R.W. Crawford to Gerow, 3 February 1941, NARA, RG165, file WPD 4297-2; and Colonel J.W. Anderson to Marshall, "Reinforcements for Alaska in Event of Emergency," 15 March 1941, NARA, RG165, file WPD 4239-21.

65 Anderson to Marshall, "Airfields at Chignik and Unalaska," 19 April 1941, NARA, RG165, file WPD 4239-21; John Haile Cloe, *The Aleutian Warriors: A History of the 11th Air Force and Fleet Wing 4* (Missoula, MT: Pictorial Histories, 1990) 15, 29, and 53; DeWitt to Marshall, 2 June 1941, NARA, RG338,

Alaskan Department, file 381; DeWitt to Marshall, 4 June 1941, NARA, RG338, file 201; Alaska Defense Command (ADC), "Extract from Report of Reconnaissance of Otter Point, Cold Bay, Port Heiden," 5 July 1941 NARA, RG18, file 300 Misc. Alaska.

66 Captain R.C. Parker to Lieutenant Colonel Tourtellot, 8 September 1941, NARA, RG165, file WPD 4239-21; Parker to Admiral R.K. Turner, 8 September 1941, NARA, RG165, file WPD 4239-21; Lieutenant Colonel Clayton Bissell to WPD, 6 August 1941, NARA, RG18, file 300 Misc. Alaska; and Cloe, *The Aleutian Warriors*, 53-4.

67 H.H. Arnold, *Global Mission* (New York: Harper and Harper Brothers, 1949), 211; Chief of the Air Corps Major General Geo. H. Brett to WPD, "Dispersion Fields, Alaska," 2 July 1941, NARA, RG165, file WPD 4503; Colonel Frank M. Kennedy and Lieutenant Colonel Harold L. Clark to Arnold, "Report on Alaska," 3 September 1941, NARA, RG18, file 333.1 Alaska Inspection; and Kenneth P. Werrell, *Blankets of Fire: U.S. Bombers over Japan during World War II* (Washington, DC: Smithsonian Institution Press, 1996), 45. Hull had said that flying 500 bombers from the Aleutians to Japan would "teach them [sic] a lesson." Hull's notion is mentioned in John Morton Blum, *The Morgenthau Diaries: Years of Urgency 1938-1941* (Boston: Houghton Mifflin, 1965), 366. AWPD-1 proposed using the Aleutians and the Philippines to shuttle bombers to bases in Siberia; Robert Frank Futrell, *Ideas, Concepts, Doctrine: A History of Basic Thinking in the United States Air Force 1907-1964* (Maxwell Air Force Base: Air University, 1971), 60.

68 Stark quoted in Michael. D. Pearlman, *Warmaking and American Diplomacy: The Struggle over Military Strategy, 1700 to the Present* (Lawrence: University Press of Kansas, 1999), 226; Marshall to CNO, "Construction of Airdromes in the Aleutian Islands and the Alaskan Peninsula," 19 August 1941, LC, H.H. Arnold Papers, box 151, file 686 Alaska; JANPC to Joint Board, "Construction of Airdromes in the Aleutian Islands and the Alaskan Peninsula," 3 September 1941, NARA, RG225, JB 312, M1421, reel 7; Gordon W. Prange, with Donald M. Goldstein and Katherine V. Dillon, *At Dawn We Slept: The Untold Story of Pearl Harbor* (New York: Penguin Books, 1991), 40; Waldo Heinrichs, *Threshold of War: Franklin D. Roosevelt & the American Entry into World War II* (New York: Oxford University Press, 1988), 122; and Turner to Parker, 20 September 1941, NARA, RG165, file WPD 4239-21.

69 Crawford to the Adjutant General, "Construction of Airdrome and Port Facilities on Umnak Island, Alaska," 23 September 1941, NARA, RG225, JB312, series 718, M1421, reel 7; JANPC to the Joint Board, "Construction of Airdromes in the Aleutian Islands and the Alaskan Peninsula," 24 November 1941, NARA, RG225, JB312, series 718, M1421, reel 7; Joint Board to Stimson, "Construction of Airdromes in the Aleutian Islands and the Alaskan Peninsula," 27 November 1941, NARA, RG225, JB312, series 718, M1421, reel 7; and B.B. Talley and Virginia M. Talley, "Building Alaska's Defenses in World War II," in *Alaska at War, 1941-1945: The Forgotten War Remembered*, ed. Fern Chandonnet (Anchorage: Alaska at War Committee, 1995), 61.

70 Matloff and Snell, *Strategic Planning for Coalition Warfare 1941-1942*, 16; and Stark to Secretary of the Navy Frank Knox, 12 November 1940, FDRL, Roosevelt Papers, PSF, file Navy Department: Plan Dog.

71 Matloff and Snell, *Strategic Planning for Coalition Warfare 1941-1942*, 27; Colonel Jonathan W. Anderson to Marshall, "National Policy of the United States," 13 November 1940, NARA, RG165, file WPD 4175-15; Marshall to Stark, "Tentative Draft, Navy Basic War Plan – Rainbow No. 3," 29 November 1940, in *The Papers of George Catlett Marshall*, ed. Larry I. Bland, vol. 2, *"We Cannot Delay,"* 360-1; and Marshall to Stark, "Joint Basic War Plans, Rainbow Nos. 3 and 5," 2 December 1940, in *The Papers of George Catlett Marshall*, ed. Bland, vol. 2, *"We Cannot Delay,"* 362.

72 Dallek, *Franklin D. Roosevelt and American Foreign Policy*, 252-8; and Marshall to Gerow, "White House Conference of Thursday, January 16, 1941," 17 January 1941, NARA, RG165, file WPD 4175-18.

73 Colonel Joseph McNarney and Rear Admiral R.K. Turner, "Joint Instructions for Army and Navy Representatives for Holding Staff Conversations with the British, Including an Agenda for the Conversations," 21 January 1941, RG225, JB325, series 674; Marshall and Stark, "Statement by the Chief of Naval Operations and the Chief of Staff," 27 January 1941, NARA, RG165, file WPD 4202-1; Embick et al. to

Marshall, "Dispatch of United States Forces to Singapore," 12 February 1941, NARA, RG165, file WPD 4202-1; and Lord Halifax to the Four Dominion High Commissioners, 14 February 1941, Public Record Office (hereinafter PRO), Foreign Office Records, United States Correspondence 1941-1945, FO371/27887.

74 Churchill, "Prime Minister's Minute," 22 November 1940, PRO, Premier's Office Records, PREM3/61/6; Winston Churchill to A.V. Alexander and Admiral Dudley Pound, 17 February 1941, in *The Churchill War Papers*, ed. Martin Gilbert, vol. 3, *The Ever-Widening War 1941* (New York: W.W. Norton, 2000), 234-6; and ABC-1 report, "United States-British Staff Conversations," 27 March 1941, PRO, Cabinet Office Records, CAB122/1582.

75 Hornbeck to Hull, 24 June 1941, HI, Hornbeck Papers, vol. 376, file Secretary of State 1941; MID to WPD, "Estimate of the Situation Concerning the Security of Alaska," 26 June 1941, NARA, War Department, Office of the Director of Plans and Operations, RG165, Exec. File 8 book A; Miles to WPD, "Alaskan Security re the German-Russian War," 1 July 1941, NARA, RG165, file WPD 4297-3; and General Board minutes, 27 June 1941, NARA, Department of the Navy, Proceedings of the General Board of the US Navy 1900-1950, RG80, reel 25.

76 Naval War College (NWC), "The Strategic Area Alaska, the Aleutians and Kurile Islands," 19 July 1941, NHC, SPD, series II-B, box 32; and Gordon Rowe to Rear Admiral J.S. McCain, 4 August 1941, HI, John Sydney McCain Papers, box 2; and Watson, *Chief of Staff*, 458.

77 DeWitt to Adjutant General, 4 July 1941, LC, Arnold Papers, box 125, file 452.1 Alaska; Buckner to DeWitt, 16 July 1941, NARA, RG338, Alaskan Department, file 201; Buckner to Marshall, 24 July 1941, NARA, RG338, Alaskan Department, file 201; and Karl C. Dod, *The Corps of Engineers: The War against Japan* (Washington, DC: Office of the Chief of Military History, 1966), 35.

78 DeWitt to Adjutant General, "Defense of Alaska, Air Combat Units," 18 July 1941, LC, Arnold Papers, box 84, file 320.2 Alaska; Brigadier General Carl Spaatz to Crawford, 20 August 1941, NARA, RG165, file WPD 4464-7; and Arnold to Buckner, 19 November 1941, NARA, RG18, file 320 Misc Alaska.

79 DeWitt to Marshall, 26 November 1941, NARA, RG338, Alaskan Department, file 201.

80 Ruth Gruber to Ickes, 2 December 1941, LC, Harold L. Ickes Papers, box 93, file Alaska (1); and Lieutenant Colonel C.C. Dusenberg to Assistant Chief of Staff G-2, "Visit to Alaska," 1 December 1941, NARA, RG165, MID, file Alaska 1100.

81 Quoted in Cloe, *The Aleutian Warriors*, 63.

Chapter 3: Entirely Open to Attack

1 Marshall quoted in Maurice A. Pope, *Soldiers and Politicians: The Memoirs of Lt.-Gen. Maurice A. Pope* (Toronto: University of Toronto Press, 1962), 170.

2 Alvin D. Coox, "Japanese Military Education and Planning before Pearl Harbor," in *Military Planning in the Twentieth Century: Proceedings of the Eleventh Military History Symposium*, ed. Harry R. Borowski (Washington, DC: Office of Air Force History, 1986), 70; John W. Dower, *War without Mercy: Race and Power in the Pacific War* (New York: Pantheon Books, 1986), 259; and H.P. Willmott, *The Barrier and the Javelin: Japanese and Allied Pacific Strategies February to June 1942* (Annapolis, MD: Naval Institute Press, 1983), 3.

3 Saburo Ienaga, *The Pacific War 1931-1945* (New York: Pantheon Books, 1978), 134; Frederick D. Parker, *A Priceless Advantage: U.S. Navy Communications Intelligence and the Battles of Coral Sea, Midway, and the Aleutians* (Washington, DC: Center for Cryptologic History, 1993), 1; and Hiroyuki Agawa, *The Reluctant Admiral: Yamamoto and the Imperial Navy* (New York: Kodansha International, 1982), 232.

4 Alvin Coox, "The Pacific War," in *The Cambridge History of Japan*, vol. 6, *The Twentieth Century*, ed. Peter Duus (Cambridge: Cambridge University Press, 1998), 325; Takagi quoted in Herbert P. Bix, *Hirohito and the Making of Modern Japan* (New York: Perennial, 2001), 406-7; Akira Iriye, *Power and Culture: The Japanese-American War, 1941-1945* (Cambridge: Harvard University Press, 1981), 1; and diary entry, 25 December 1941, in *Fading Victory: The Diary of Admiral Matome Ugaki 1941-1945*, ed.

Donald M. Goldstein and Katherine V. Dillon (Pittsburgh: University of Pittsburgh Press, 1991), 61-2; and Coox, "Japanese Military Education and Planning before Pearl Harbor," 75. See also Michael A. Barnhart, "Japanese Intelligence before the Second World War: 'Best Case' Analysis," in *Knowing One's Enemies: Intelligence Assessment before the Two World Wars*, ed. Ernest R. May (Princeton: Princeton University Press, 1984), 424-55.

5 Churchill to Anthony Eden, 23 November 1941, in *The Churchill War Papers*, ed. Martin Gilbert, vol. 3, *The Ever-Widening War 1941* (New York: W.W. Norton, 2000), 1499; Richardson quoted in Gordon W. Prange, with Donald M. Goldstein and Katherine V. Dillon, *At Dawn We Slept: The Untold Story of Pearl Harbor* (New York: Penguin Books, 1991), 38; Joint Board minutes, 19 September and 3 November 1941, National Archives and Records Administration (hereinafter NARA), RG225, JB301; and Edward T. Layton, with Roger Pineau and John Costello, *And I Was There: Pearl Harbor and Midway – Breaking the Secrets* (Old Saybrook: Konecky and Konecky, 1985), 176-7.

6 Hornbeck quoted in Warren F. Kimball, *Forged in War: Roosevelt, Churchill, and the Second World War* (New York: William Morrow and Company, 1997), 105. Hornbeck argued that Japan's rational leadership would back down; Hornbeck, "Situation: Far East: Japanese Intentions," 16 July 1941, Hoover Institution on War, Revolution, and Peace (hereinafter HI), Stanley K. Hornbeck Papers, vol. 253, file Japan: US General; Hornbeck, "On Running Amuck," 16 August 1941, HI, Stanley K. Hornbeck Papers, vol. 219, file Japan: Running Amuck 1941; Hornbeck memorandum, 15 October 1941, HI, Stanley K. Hornbeck Papers, vol. 376, file Secretary of State 1941; and Hornbeck memorandum, 1 December 1941, HI, Stanley K. Hornbeck Papers, vol. 26, file Berle, Adolf A. 1938-41.

7 Bruce W. Bidwell, *History of the Military Intelligence Division, Department of the Army General Staff: 1775-1941* (Frederick, MD: University Publications of America, 1986), 475.

8 Roberta Wohlstetter, *Pearl Harbor: Warning and Decision* (Stanford: Stanford University Press, 1962), 387; "Army Warns West Coast to Prepare for Bombing," *New York Herald Tribune*, 10 December 1941; Howell quoted in Timothy Wilford, *Pearl Harbor Redefined: USN Radio Intelligence in 1941* (Lanham, MD: University Press of America, 2001), 114; diary entry, 31 December 1941, Naval Historical Center (hereinafter NHC), Glenn Howell Papers, box 25; Lieutenant Colonel P.M. Robinett to Commanding General Field Forces, "Brief Estimate of the Situation in the Pacific," 10 December 1941, NARA, RG165, file WPD 4544-28; Gerow to Marshall, "Brief Current Strategic Estimate," 12 December 1941, NARA, RG165, file WPD 4622-37. The USN told British officers in Washington, DC, that Japanese reconnaissance planes had overflown San Francisco on 11 December 1941, and that a raid on that city had been avoided thanks to heavy mists in the region. Admiral Little to the First Sea Lord, no. 425, 12 December 1941, National Archives of Canada (NAC), RG24, vol. 11979, file NM 501-5.

9 Buckner quoted in Samuel Eliot Morison, *History of the United States Naval Operations in World War II*, vol. 4, *Coral Sea, Midway and Submarine Actions May 1942-August 1942* (Boston: Little, Brown and Company, 1950), 162-3; "Oral History of Colonel James Bush," 24 May 1982, Albert F. Simpson Historical Research Center, Maxwell Air Force Base (hereinafter AFS), 3; Buckner quoted in Brian Garfield, *The Thousand-Mile War: World War II in Alaska and the Aleutians* (New York: Bantam Books, 1969), 12; OPNAV to Naval Services Headquarters Ottawa and Commanding Officer Pacific Coast Esquimalt, 10 December 1941, Franklin Delano Roosevelt Library (hereinafter FDRL), Roosevelt Papers, Map Room Files (hereinafter MRF), box 36; Buckner to Arnold, 8 December 1941, Library of Congress (hereinafter LC), H.H. Arnold Papers, box 125, file 452.1 Alaska; and "Joint Alaskan Sector Defense Plan Rainbow No. 5, Commander, Alaskan Sector Thirteenth Naval District and the Commanding General, Alaskan Defense Command Fort Richardson, Anchorage, Alaska December 1941," 16 December 1941, NARA, RG338, Alaskan Department, box 403.

10 Office of the Director of Plans and Operations (hereinafter OPD), "United States Forces in the World Outside of Continental United States as of December 20, 1941," 20 December 1941, NARA, RG165, OPD, Exec. File 4, book 3; Marshall to Deputy Chief of Staff, "Activation of Western Defense Command and Its Designation As a Theater of Operations," 11 December 1941, in *The Papers of George*

Catlett Marshall, ed. Larry I. Bland, vol. 3, *"The Right Man for the Job," December 7, 1941-May 31, 1943* (Baltimore: Johns Hopkins University Press, 1991), 13-14; and DeWitt to Marshall, 22 December 1941, LC, Arnold Papers, box 151, file 686 Alaska.

11 Adjutant General to DeWitt, "Supplementary Directions for Western Defense Command," 11 December 1941, NARA, RG165, file WPD 4612-1; Buckner to DeWitt, 8 December 1941, NARA, RG338, file 201; and DeWitt to Adjutant General, 10 December 1941, NARA, RG165, file WPD 4464-7.

12 Maurice Matloff, "World War II: The Defensive Phase," in *American Military History*, ed. Matloff, vol. 2, *1902-1996* (Coshohoneck: Combined Books, 1996), 93.

13 Captain Hugh T. Fullerton to DeWitt, 11 December 1941, LC, Arnold Papers, box 84, file 320.2 Alaska; Major J.W. Ramsey to Arnold, "Air Defense of Alaska," 3 January 1942, LC, Arnold Papers, box 84, file 320.2 Alaska; Buckner to DeWitt, "Aggressive Air Operations from Alaska," 3 January 1942, LC, Arnold Papers, box 84, file 320.2 Alaska; and Buckner to DeWitt, "Temporary Shelter and Stockages of Army Air Fields, Alaska," 14 January 1942, NARA, RG165, file OPD 320.2 Alaska Defense Command. Commander J.R. Tate of the USN's Sitka station said Japan could have taken Dutch Harbor in December 1941 "if the weather had permitted"; diary entry, 8 January 1942, Rasmussen Library (hereinafter RL), Ernest Gruening Papers, Diaries, box 4.

14 W.L. Goldsborough, "The Aleutians – Their Strategic Importance," *United States Naval Institute Proceedings* 67 (June 1941): 830-4; A.S. Watt, First Secretary of the Australian Legation Washington, DC, to the Australian Department of External Affairs, 12 February 1941, National Archives of Australia (hereinafter NAA), Correspondence Files of the Department of External Affairs, series A981, item Far East 26A; George Carroll Dyer, *The Amphibians Came to Conquer: The Story of Admiral Richmond Kelly Turner* (Washington, DC: Department of the Navy, 1969), 174; Waldo Heinrichs, *Threshold of War: Franklin D. Roosevelt & the American Entry into World War II* (New York: Oxford University Press, 1988), 74; Morison, *History of the United States Naval Operations in World War II*, vol. 4, *Coral Sea, Midway and Submarine Operations*, 56; and General Albert C. Wedemeyer, "Far East," 20 December 1941, HI, Albert C. Wedemeyer Papers, vol. 74, file 74.1.

15 Cloe and Monoghan, *Top Cover for America*, 19; Michael S. Sherry, *The Rise of American Air Power: The Creation of Armageddon* (New Haven: Yale University Press, 1987), 47-8; and William A. Goss, "Air Defense of the Western Hemisphere," in *The Army Air Forces in World War II*, ed. Wesley Frank Craven and James Lea Cate, vol. 1, *Plans and Early Operations January 1939 to August 1942* (Chicago: University of Chicago Press, 1948), 304.

16 Roosevelt quoted in Warren F. Kimball, *The Juggler: Franklin Roosevelt As Wartime Statesman* (Princeton: Princeton University Press, 1991), 7; and Samuel Eliot Morison, *Strategy and Compromise* (Boston: Little, Brown and Company, 1958), 14-15.

17 Russell F. Weigley, *History of the United States Army* (New York: Macmillan, 1967), 453; Eliot A. Cohen, "The Strategy of Innocence? The United States, 1920-1945," in *The Making of Strategy: Rulers, States, and War,* ed. Williamson Murray, MacGregor Knox, and Alvin Bernstein (Cambridge: Cambridge University Press, 1994), 435; and Kent Roberts Greenfield, *American Strategy in World War II: A Reconsideration* (Baltimore: Johns Hopkins University Press, 1963), 52. Greenfield cites over twenty instances when Roosevelt overruled his military advisers and twelve other occasions when he initiated military policy.

18 Layton testimony, United States Congress, *Hearings before the Joint Committee on the Investigation of the Pearl Harbor Attack: Part 26, Hart Inquiry* (Washington, DC: Government Printing Office, 1946), 234; Director of Naval Districts Division to Naval Aide to the President, "Material and Operational Readiness, Alaskan Area," 14 January 1942, FDRL, Roosevelt Papers, President's Secretary's File (hereinafter PSF), box 1; Roosevelt to Captain McRae, 20 January 1942, FDRL, Roosevelt Papers, PSF, box 1; Roosevelt to Marshall and King, 20 January 1942, FDRL, Roosevelt Papers, Official Files (hereinafter OF), box 2; Marshall to Roosevelt, "Possibility of Attack on the Aleutian Islands and Kodiak and the Alaskan Mainland," 21 January 1942, FDRL, Roosevelt Papers, OF, box 2; and CCS, "American-British

Grand Strategy," ABC-4/CS-1 WW-1 (Final), 31 December 1941, NARA, RG165, OPD, file ABC384 No. America (29 Nov 1942).

19 Stetson Conn, Rose C. Engelman, and Byron Fairchild, *The Western Hemisphere: Guarding the United States and Its Outposts* (Washington, DC: Department of the Army, 1964), 253; Roosevelt press conference 806, in Franklin D. Roosevelt, *Complete Presidential Press Conferences of Franklin D. Roosevelt*, ed. Jonathan Daniels, vol. 19, *1942* (New York: Da Capo Press, 1972), 151; Roosevelt Fireside Chat, 23 February 1942, FDRL, Roosevelt Papers, President's Personal Files, series 1820, file 1st Carbon; and Marshall quoted in Michael D. Pearlman, *Warmaking and American Diplomacy: The Struggle over Military Strategy, 1700 to the Present* (Lawrence: University Press of Kansas, 1999), 230; and Winston S. Churchill, *The Second World War*, vol. 4, *The Hinge of Fate* (Boston: Houghton Mifflin, 1985), 175.

20 Diary entry, 25 January 1942, NHC, Howell Papers, box 26; Parker to Admiral C.S. Freeman, 21 January 1942, LC, Ernest J. King Papers, box 11; and Buckner and Parker, "Joint Army-Navy Plans for Alaska," 31 January 1942, NARA, RG165, file WPD 4503-14.

21 Hornbeck memorandum, 23 January 1942, HI, Hornbeck Papers, vol. 425, file US Policy 1942; Hornbeck to Marshall, 27 February 1942, HI, Hornbeck Papers, vol. 293, file Marshall, General George Catlett; Freeman to Chief of Naval Operations (CNO), "Joint Army-Navy Plans for Alaska," NARA, RG338, Alaskan Department, box 100, file 370.26; William J. Donovan to Roosevelt, 18 February 1942, FDRL, Roosevelt Papers, PSF, box 148; and Hanson W. Baldwin, "Strategy in Pacific," *New York Times*, 20 February 1942.

22 John Haile Cloe, *The Aleutian Warriors: A History of the 11th Air Force and Fleet Wing 4* (Missoula, MT: Pictorial Histories, 1990), 75; Air War Plans Division (AWPD) to Director Air Defense, 15 February 1942, LC, Arnold Papers, box 84, file 320.2 Alaska; Colonel William O. Butler to Arnold, "Alaska Air Force," 21 February 1942, LC, Arnold Papers, box 84, file 320.2 Alaska; and Arnold to the Adjutant General, "Aggressive Air Operations from Alaska," 16 February 1942, LC, Arnold Papers, box 84, file 320.2 Alaska.

23 Marshall quoted in Mark A. Stoler, *Allies and Adversaries: The Joint Chiefs of Staff, the Grand Alliance, and U.S. Strategy in World War II* (Chapel Hill: University of North Carolina Press, 2000), 69. King's qualities are explored in Thomas B. Buell, *Master of Sea Power: A Biography of Fleet Admiral Ernest J. King* (Boston: Little, Brown and Company, 1980); Robert William Love Jr., "Ernest Joseph King," in *The Chiefs of Naval Operations*, ed. Love Jr. (Annapolis, MD: Naval Institute Press, 1980), 137-79; and Williamson Murray and Allan R. Millett, *A War to Be Won: Fighting the Second World War* (Cambridge: Belknap Press of Harvard University Press, 2000), 336. Eisenhower described King as "an arbitrary, stubborn type, with too much brains and a tendency toward bullying his juniors," while Stimson despised him, claiming that "he is firm and brave outside the White House, but as soon as he gets in the presence of the President he crumbles up." John Ray Skates asserts that King was "perhaps the most disliked allied leader of World War II": Eisenhower quoted in Robert William Love Jr., "Ernest Joseph King," in *The Chiefs of Naval Operations*, ed. Love Jr. (Annapolis, MD: Naval Institute Press, 1980), 402-3, n.41; Stimson quoted in Buell, *Master of Sea Power*, 189; and John Ray Skates, *The Invasion of Japan: Alternative to the Bomb* (Columbia, SC: University of South Carolina Press, 1994), 18.

24 Turner to King, 5 February 1942, LC, Ernest J. King Papers, box 13; King to Major General Merrit A. Edson, 29 September 1949, LC, Ernest J. King Papers, box 17; CCS minutes, 11 January 1942, reel 1, Wartime Conferences of the Combined Chiefs of Staff: Arcadia, Casablanca, Trident, vols. 1 and 2, Scholarly Resources Inc.; and King to CNO, 21 February 1942, NHC, Strategic Plans Division (hereinafter SPD), series V, box 103.

25 "Briefed Estimate of the Situation," 5 February 1942, CINCPAC Command Summary, NHC; Howell to Freeman, "U.S. Army Forces and Bases in Alaska," 7 March 1942, Directorate of History and Heritage (hereinafter DHH), Kardex File 169.009 (D138); Conn et al., *Guarding the United States and Its Outposts*, 255; and Matloff and Snell, *Strategic Planning for Coalition Warfare 1941-1942*, 156.

26 CCS, ABC-4/CS-1, WW-1 (Final), "American-British Grand Strategy," 31 December 1941," NARA, RG165, OPD, file ABC 384 No. America (29 Nov 1942); and Brigadier Dwight D. Eisenhower to Marshall, "Strategic Conceptions and their application to Southwest Pacific," 28 February 1942, in *The Papers of Dwight David Eisenhower,* vol. 1, *The War Years,* ed. Alfred D. Chandler (Baltimore: The Johns Hopkins University Press, 1970), 149-55.

27 Murray and Millett, *A War to Be Won,* 185 and 205; MacArthur quoted in Karl R. Bendetsen Oral History Interview, 24 October 1972, Harry S. Truman Presidential Library; MacArthur to Marshall, 4 February 1942, Records from General Headquarters United States Army Forces Pacific, General Douglas MacArthur Foundation (hereinafter GDMF), RG4, reel 593; diary entry, 13 January 1942, *The Eisenhower Diaries,* ed. Robert H. Ferrell (New York: W.W. Norton, 1981), 43; and Michael Schaller, "General Douglas MacArthur and the Politics of the Pacific War," in *The Pacific War Revisited,* ed. Gunter Bischoff and Robert L. Dupont (Baton Rouge: Louisiana State University Press, 1997), 22.

28 Eisenhower notes, 4 and 22 January 1942, Chandler, *The Papers of Dwight David Eisenhower,* 39 and 66; and Richard W. Steele, *The First Offensive 1942: Roosevelt, Marshall and the Making of American Strategy* (Bloomington: Indiana University Press, 1973), 102.

29 Roosevelt to Marshall and Stark, 4 March 1942, NARA, RG165, file OPD 380.3 Russia; Gerow to Marshall and Roosevelt, 17 December 1941, NARA, RG165, Exec. file 8, book 1; Miles to Marshall, "Russian Offensive against Japan," 15 December 1941, NARA, RG165; Grace Person Hayes, *The History of the Joint Chiefs of Staff in World War II: The War against Japan* (Annapolis, MD: Naval Institute Press, 1982), 131-2; and John J. Stephan, *The Russian Far East : A History* (Stanford: Stanford University Press, 1994), 240. Sherry describes the shuttle scheme in *The Rise of American Air Power,* 110-12 and 116.

30 "The O.N.I. Weekly," 11 March 1942, DHH, Kardex File 112.3M1013 (D6); and OPD, "An Analysis of the Lines of Action Open to the United States for the Rendition of Assistance to Russia in the Event of Hostilities Between Russia and Japan in the Spring of 1942," 8 March 1942, NARA, RG165, OPD, file ABC 381 (1-23-42).

31 Hayes, *The History of the Joint Chiefs of Staff,* 132; Richard M. Leighton and Robert W. Coakley, *Global Logistics and Strategy 1940-1943* (Washington, DC: Department of the Army, 1955), 273; Eisenhower to Adjutant General, "Temporary Shelter and Stockages at Army Air Fields, Alaska," 25 March 1942, NARA, RG165, file OPD 320.2 Alaska Defense Command; and Louis Morton, *Strategy and Command: The First Two Years* (Washington, DC: Center for Military History, 1989), 420.

32 Colonel T.J. Betts to War Plans Division (hereinafter WPD), "Japanese Threat to Alaska," 1 April 1942, NARA, RG165, Military Intelligence Division Correspondence (hereinafter MID), file Alaska 6800. See also Brigadier General Raymond E. Lee to Assistant Chief of Staff WPD, "Lines of Action Open to Japan," 14 March 1942, HI, Wedemeyer Papers, vol. 72, file 72.7; and Geographic Division, Coordinator of Information, "The Weather Element As Related to Invasion Possibilities in the Aleutian Islands Region, Alaska," 30 March 1942, FDRL, Roosevelt Papers, PSF, box 128.

33 Buckner to DeWitt, 31 March 1942, NARA, RG338, Alaskan Department, file 201; Colonel H.A. Craig to Arnold, "Alaskan Air Force," 3 April 1942, LC, Arnold Papers, box 84, file 320.2 Alaska; Eisenhower quoted in Love, "Ernest Joseph King," 148-9; Eisenhower quoted in Carlo D'Este, *Eisenhower: A Soldier's Life* (New York: Henry Holt, 2002), 293 and 297; and Eisenhower to Stimson, "Review of Current Situation," 12 April 1942, in Chandler, *The Papers of Dwight David Eisenhower,* 241-3.

34 MID, "Estimate of Enemy Capabilities in Alaska for Months of May to July," 5 July 1942, NARA, RG165, MID, file Alaska 6800; DeWitt to Marshall, 3 May 1942, NARA, RG338, Alaskan Department, file 201; DeWitt to Marshall, 5 May 1942, NARA, RG165, OPD, file 452.1, ADC; Marshall to Roosevelt (written by Eisenhower), 4 May 1942, in Chandler, *The Papers of Dwight David Eisenhower,* 280-1; and Eisenhower to Brigadier General St. Clair Street, "Measures to meet current threat in Pacific," 20 May 1942, NARA, RG165, OPD, file OPD 381 PTO.

35 Paul S. Dull, *A Battle History of the Imperial Japanese Navy (1941-1945)* (Annapolis, MD: Naval Institute Press, 1978), 133. From 8 December 1941 until 30 April 1942 the IJN lost just thirty-two warships,

totalling less than 62,000 tons, and thirty-eight auxiliary and merchant vessels, totalling less than 200,000 tons. H.P. Willmott, *The Second World War in the Far East* (London: Cassell, 2002), 78 and 81.

36 Layton et al., *And I Was There*, 383-4; John J. Stephan, *Hawaii Under the Rising Sun: Japan's Plans for Conquest after Pearl Harbor* (Honolulu: University of Hawaii Press, 1984), 85; Kiyoshi Ikeda, "Japanese Strategy and the Pacific War, 1941-5," in *Anglo-Japanese Alienation 1919-1952: Papers of the Anglo-Japanese Conference on the History of the Second World War,* ed. Ian Nish (Cambridge: Cambridge University Press, 1982), 134; diary entry, 25 January 1942, in Goldstein and Dillon, *Fading Victory,* 78; Mitsuo Fuchida and Masatake Okumiya, *Midway. The Battle That Doomed Japan: The Japanese Navy's Story* (Annapolis, MD: Naval Institute Press, 1955), 48-53; and Edward J. Drea, *In the Service of the Emperor: Essays on the Imperial Japanese Army* (Lincoln: University of Nebraska Press, 1998), 34.

37 Masanori Ito and Roger Pineau, *The End of the Imperial Japanese Navy* (New York: Norton, 1962), 57-60; Agawa, *The Reluctant Admiral,* 303; Gordon M. Prange, with Donald M. Goldstein and Katherine V. Dillon, *Miracle at Midway* (New York: McGraw-Hill, 1982), 23-4; Morton, *Strategy and Command,* 109; Stephan, *Hawaii Under the Rising Son,* 108, and 114-15; and Hisashi Takahashi, "The Japanese Campaign in Alaska As Seen from the Historical Perspective," in *Alaska at War, 1941-1945: The Forgotten War Remembered,* ed. Fern Chandonnet (Anchorage: Alaska at War Committee, 1995), 36. Some of the captured Doolittle fliers claimed they had flown from the Aleutians; diary entry, 19 April 1942, in Goldstein and Dillon, *Fading Victory,* 113.

38 Naval Attaché report No. 42, 12 March 1941, NARA, Office of the Chief of Naval Operations, Selected Naval Attaché Reports Relating to the World Crisis 1937-1943, RG38, series M975; Tanetsuga quoted in Edwin P. Hoyt, *Japan's War: The Great Conflict* (New York: McGraw-Hill, 1986), 264; and Jakuo Mikami, "Aleutian Naval Operations: March 1942-February 1943," in *The Naval Armament Program and Naval Operations (Part II),* vol. 5, *War in Asia and the Pacific* (New York: Garland Publishers, 1980), 8-10.

39 Parker, *A Priceless Advantage,* 43; entries for 26 April and 1 May 1942, NHC, CINCPAC Command Summary; W.J. Holmes, *Double-Edged Secrets: U.S. Naval Intelligence Operations in the Pacific During World War Two* (Annapolis, MD: Naval Institute Press, 1979), 88-9; and Ronald Lewin, *The American Magic: Codes, Ciphers and the Defeat of Japan* (New York: Farrar, Strauss and Giroux, 1982), 81-111.

40 King to Marshall, "Situation in South Pacific and Southwest Pacific Areas as of the end of May, 1942," 12 May 1942, NARA, RG165, OPD, Exec. file 8, book 5; Layton et al., *And I Was There,* 408-17; Admiralty to King, 20 May 1942, GDMF, RG4, reel 589; and Stephen W. Roskill, *The War at Sea 1939-1945,* vol. 2, *The Period of Balance* (London: Her Majesty's Stationery Office, 1956), 37.

41 King to Nimitz, no. 172220, 17 May 1942, HI, Robert A. Theobald Papers, box 9, file Dispatches AIDAC; King to Commanders Western Sea Frontier and Northwest Sea Frontier (NWSF), 17 May 1942, NHC, SPD, series XII, box 136; entry for 18 May 1942, NHC, CINCPAC Command Summary; and King to Nimitz, no. 211700, 21 May 1942, NARA, RG165, OPD, Exec. file 8, book 5.

42 Nimitz to Theobald, "Operation Plan No. 28-42," 21 May 1942, HI, Theobald Papers, box 10, file Cincpac No. 28-42 May 21; "Estimate of the Situation. Attack on Hawaiian and Alaska bases Part I – Mission," 26 May 1942, NHC, CINCPAC Command Summary; Nimitz to Theobald, 21 May 1942, NHC, SPD, series XII, box 175; Nimitz to King, no. 200143, 20 May 1942, HI, Theobald Papers, box 9, file Dispatches AIDAC; and Commander NWSF to Nimitz, no. 190244, 19 May 1942, HI, Theobald Papers, box 9, file Dispatches AIDAC.

43 Marshall to MacArthur, 22 May 1942, GDMF, RG4, reel 593; and MacArthur to Marshall, 24 April, 25 April, and 8 May 1942, GDMF, RG4, reel 593.

44 Arnold to Colonels C.P. Cabell and L. Norstad, 18 May 1942, LC, Arnold Papers, box 39, file Japan; and Cabell and Norstad to Arnold, 21 May 1942, LC, Arnold Papers, box 39, file Japan; Butler to Arnold, "Immediate needs of 11th Air Force," 15 May 1942, LC, Arnold Papers, box 84, file 320.2 Alaska; DeWitt to Buckner, 19 May 1942, NARA, RG338, Alaskan Department, file 201; Marshall to DeWitt, no. 1072, 20 May 1942, in Chandler, *The Papers of Dwight David Eisenhower,* 312-13; McNarney to King, "U.S.

Air Reinforcements of U.S. forces in Alaska," 26 May 1942, and McNarney to Marshall, 28 May 1942, NARA, Records of the Office of the Chief of Staff (hereinafter OCS), RG165, box 107, file Alaska.

45 Howell to General R.O. Alexander, 29 May 1942, NAC, RG24, vol. 18823, War Diary Pacific Command Headquarters, 1-30 May 1942.

46 Diary entry, 17 August 1940, Yale University Library, Henry L. Stimson Papers; and "Joint Canadian-United States Basic Defense Plan No. 2," 28 July 1942, in *Documents on Canadian External Relations*, vol. 8, *1939-1941*, part 2, ed. David R. Murray (Ottawa: Department of External Relations, 1976), 249-61.

47 Murray, ed. *Documents on Canadian External Relations*, vol. 8, *1939-1941*; PWC minutes, 1 April 1942, FDRL, Roosevelt Papers, MRF, box 168, folder 3; and diary entry, 2 April 1942, NAC, Maurice Pope Papers, vol. 1. The crisis in Canadian-Australian relations, prompted by a rash unauthorized promise of aid by Canada's High Commissioner in Australia, is explored in R.G. Haycock, "The 'Myth' of Imperial Defence: Australian-Canadian Bilateral Military Cooperation, 1942," *War and Society*, 21 (May 1984): 65-84; and Galen Roger Perras, "'She should have thought of herself first': Canada and Military Aid to Australia, 1939-1945," in *Parties Long Estranged: Canada and Australia in the Twentieth Century*, ed. Margaret Macmillan and Francine McKenzie (Vancouver: UBC Press, 2003).

48 W.L.M. King memorandum, 15 April 1942, NAC, RG25, vol. 2152, file 149.

49 Canadian Chiefs of Staff (hereinafter COS) minutes, 161st meeting, 29 May 1942, Queen's University Archives (hereinafter QUA), Charles Gavan Power Papers, box 69, file D-2019; Air Marshal G.L. Johnson memorandum, 29 May 1942, ibid.; and Air Marshal L.S. Breadner to Air Commodore L.F. Stevenson, 29 May 1942, ibid. Stevenson was willing to send two squadrons to Alaska if a crisis arose; Stevenson to Air Force Headquarters (AFHQ) Ottawa, 14 May 1942, DHH, Kardex File 181.009 (D3583); and Stevenson, "Memorandum Regarding R.C.A.F. Reinforcing Alaska in an Emergency," 14 May 1942, NAC, RG24, vol. 11765, file PC 010-9-20.

50 A.D.P. Heeney to Hugh Keenleyside, 16 May 1942, DHH, Kardex File 314.009 (D17); CWC minutes, 14 May 1942, Privy Council Records, Minutes and Documents of the Cabinet War Committee, RG2 7c, vol. 9; G.O. Johnson, "Memorandum of telephone call from Lt. Gen. Stuart, Victoria, at 2340 Hours, May 30th, 1942," 1 June 1942, QUA, Power Papers, box 69, file D-2019; minutes of conference in Minister's office, 31 May 1942, ibid.; and Power memorandum, 31 May 1942, QUA, Power Papers, box 69, file D-2019.

51 Colonel Stanley W. Dziuban, *Military Relations between the United States and Canada 1939-1945* (Washington, DC: Department of the Army, 1959), 253; Pope to Stuart, no. MP40, 1 June 1942, DHH, Kardex file 314.009 (D67); diary entry, 1 June 1942, NAC, Maurice Pope Papers, vol. 1; Air Commodore F.V. Heakes, "Report of telephone conversation – Lieut. General Embick, U.S. Army, and Air Commodore Heakes, R.C.A.F.," 1 June 1942, QUA, Power Papers, box 69, file D-2019.

52 Heakes to Embick, no. A80, 1 June 1942, QUA, Power Papers, box 69, file D-2019; and W.A.B. Douglas, *The Creation of a National Air Force: The Official History of the Royal Canadian Air Force*, vol. 2 (Toronto: University of Toronto Press, 1986), 413-14.

53 Douglas, *The Creation of a National Air Force*, 412; WDC to U.S. Liaison Officer, Pacific Command, 18 May 1942, NAC, RG24, vol. 13823; Commander W.J.R. Beech to Naval Services Headquarters, no. 2304Z/23, 23 May 1942, NAC, Privy Council Records, RG2, vol. 32, file D-19-1 (1942); and Stevenson to AFHQ, no. X463A476, 1 June 1942, QUA, Power Papers, box 69, file D-2019. See also Galen Roger Perras, "'The Defence of Alaska Must Remain a Primary Concern of the United States:' Canada and the North Pacific, May-June 1942," *The Northern Mariner* 7 (October 1997): 29-43.

54 H.V. Evatt to John Curtin, no. ET30, 28 May 1942, NAA, files of Copies of Cables 1942-1943, series A4764, item 2; Skelton, "Canadian War Policy," 24 August 1939, NAC, W.L.M. King Papers, Memoranda and Notes, vol. 228; COS appreciation, 10 December 1941, NAC, RG2 7c; and Galen Roger Perras, "Who Will Defend British Columbia? Unity of Command on the West Coast, 1934-1942," *Pacific Northwest Quarterly* 88 (Spring 1997): 59-69.

55 Diary entries, 9 and 11 December 1931, NAC, W.L.M. King Papers; Grant Dexter memorandum, 28

February 1942, QUA, Grant Dexter Papers, box 3, file 21; and Stuart quoted in C.P. Stacey, *Arms, Men and Governments: The War Policies of Canada 1939-1945* (Ottawa: Department of National Defence, 1970).

56 King to C. Mortimer Bezeau, 21 April 1942, NAC, W.L.M. King Papers, Correspondence, vol. 321, file Babbage to Blackmore.

57 Garfield, *The Thousand-Mile War*, 16.

58 James Russell quoted in Cloe, *The Aleutian Warriors*, 91; and William S. Hanable, "Theobald Revisited," in *Alaska at War, 1941-1945: The Forgotten War Remembered – Papers from the Alaska at War Symposium, Anchorage, Alaska, November 11-13, 1993*, ed. Fern Chandonnet (Anchorage: Alaska at War Committee, 1995), 75.

59 Cloe, *The Aleutian Warriors*, 101.

60 Stark, "Unity of Command over Joint Operations," December 1941, NARA, RG165, file WPD 2917-35; Marshall to General Delos C. Emmons, 20 December 1941, HI, Delos C. Emmons Papers, vol. 1, file Gen. George C. Marshall; Buell, *Master of Sea Power*, 174-5; Morton, *Strategy and Command*, 249-50; and Ronald H. Spector, *Eagle against the Sun: The American War with Japan* (New York: Vintage Books, 1985), 144.

61 Theobald, "Alaska," 17 February 1942, HI, Theobald Papers, vol. 12, file War Estimates; Theobald to Nimitz, no. 280114, 28 May 1942, NARA, RG165, OPD, Exec. file 8, book 5; and Theobald, "Operation Plan No. 1-42," 27 May 1942, HI, Theobald Papers, box 10, file Comtask Force No. 8, No. 1-42, May 27.

62 Theobald memorandum, January 1942, HI, Theobald Papers, box 12, file War Estimates; and Theobald to Task Group Commanders, 29 May 1942, HI, Theobald Papers, box 7, War Diaries, May 1942. Theobald's criticism of American intelligence is accepted by Edwin T. Layton, Nimitz's chief intelligence officer; Layton et al., *And I Was There*, 185-7.

63 Parker, *A Priceless Advantage*, 47; William Butler to Arnold, 16 June 1942, Air Force History Support Office (hereinafter AFHSO), William Ormond Butler Papers, reel A1838; entry for 27 May 1942, NHC, CINCPAC Command Summary; Lieutenant Colonel L.V. Castner, G-2 periodic report, 27-8 May 1942, NARA, Adjutant General's Office (hereinafter AGO), RG407, World War II Operations Reports 1940-48, American Theater, file 91-DC1-2.1; and Castner report, 30 May 1942, NARA, AGO, RG407, World War II Operations Reports 1940-48, American Theater, file 91-DC1-2.1.

64 Donald M. Goldstein and Katherine V. Dillon, *The Williwaw War: The Arkansas National Guard in the Aleutians in World War II* (Fayetteville: University of Arkansas Press, 1992), 140; Colonel S.H. Sherrill to Marshall, "Status of Alaskan Defense Command," 1 June 1942, NARA, RG165, OCS, box 107, file Alaska; Conn et al., *Guarding the United States and Its Outposts*, 261; and Cloe, *The Aleutian Warriors*, 105.

65 Mikami, "Aleutian Naval Operations," 2-3 and 7; Center for Military History (hereinafter CMH), "Submarine Operations Dec 41-Apr 42," *Japanese Monograph No. 102*, 10; and Prange et al., *At Dawn We Slept*, 431.

66 Interrogation of Captain Ito Taisuke, "Aleutian Campaign, Planning and Operations through November 1942," in United States Strategic Bombing Survey (Pacific) (USSBS), *Interrogations of Japanese Officials*, vol. 1 (Washington, DC: Government Printing Office, 1946); Cloe, *The Aleutian Warriors*, 109; interrogation of Commander Hashimoto Shigefuso, "Aleutian Campaign and Defense of the Kuriles – Planning and Operations from November 1942 to August 1945," in USSBS, *Interrogations of Japanese Officials*, vol. 1; and CMH, "The Aleutian Islands Campaign," *Japanese Studies in World War II, No. 51*, ch. 3, 3.

67 David C. Evans and Mark R. Peattie, *Kaigun: Strategy, Tactics, and Technology in the Imperial Japanese Navy, 1887-1941* (Annapolis, MD: Naval Institute Press, 1997), 420; CMH, "Submarine Operations in Second Phase Operations, Part I April-August 1942," *Japanese Monograph No. 110*, 20-3; Mikami, "Aleutian Naval Operations," 29-31; and Garfield, *The Thousand-Mile War*, 9-10.

68 Cloe, *The Aleutian Warriors*, 109-33.

69 Prange et al., *Miracle at Midway*, 35.

70 Fuchida and Okumiya, *Midway. The Battle That Doomed Japan*, 245; Morison, *History of the United States Naval Operations in World War II*, vol. 4, *Coral Sea, Midway, and Submarine Actions*, 77-8; and Spector, *Eagle against the Sun*, 167 and 177-8.

71 Dull, *A Battle History of the Imperial Japanese Navy*, 170-2 and 179; interrogation of Captain Ito, in USSBS, *Interrogations of Japanese Officials*, vol. 1; interrogation of Vice Admiral Omori Sentaro, "Operations of the First Japanese Destroyer Squadron," in USSBS, *Interrogations of Japanese Officials*, vol. 2 (Washington, DC: Government Printing Office, 1946); and "Japanese Aircraft Carrier Operations, Part III. Carrier Attack on Dutch Harbor," 9 and 10 October 1945, AFHSO, USAF Records, reel A7339. Kiska's invasion commander told American interrogators in 1945 the Adak plans had been scrapped two weeks before Midway; interrogation of Commander Mukai Nifumi, "Japanese Occupation of Kiska, the Kiska Garrison, and Operations in the Kuriles," in USSBS, *Interrogations of Japanese Officials*, vol. 1.

72 Interrogation of Commander Mukai Nifumi, "Japanese Occupation of Kiska, the Kiska Garrison, and Operations in the Kuriles," in USSBS, *Interrogations of Japanese Officials*, vol. 1; and Mikami, "Aleutian Naval Operations," 51-8. See Henry Stewart, "Aleuts in Japan, 1942-1945," in *Alaska at War, 1941-1945: The Forgotten War Remembered – Papers from the Alaska at War Symposium, Anchorage, Alaska, November 11-13, 1993*, ed. Fern Chandonnet (Anchorage: Alaska at War Committee, 1995), 301-4.

73 Bix, *Hirohito*, 449.

74 "MAGIC Summaries," 16 June and 8 July 1942, University Publications of America (hereinafter UPA), The MAGIC Documents: Summaries and Transcripts of the Top Secret Diplomatic Communications of Japan, 1938-1945, reel 1; Mikami, "Aleutian Naval Operations," 53; interrogation of Commander Mukai Nifumi, "Japanese Occupation of Kiska, the Kiska Garrison, and Operations in the Kuriles"; and "Report on the Aleutians," *Reader's Digest*, May 1943.

75 Army Headquarters Intelligence Summary No. 146, "The Aleutian Islands," September 1941, NAA, series A981/1, item ALA1.

76 WDC telegram, no. 4-C, 4 June 1942, FDRL, Roosevelt Papers, MRF, box 79, file MR 300 Alaska-Sec. A-1-Warfare May 1942 thru December 1943; Castner report, 3-4 June 1942, NARA, RG407, AGO, American Theater, file 91-DC1-2.1; Castner report, 5-6 June 1942, NARA, RG407, AGO, American Theater, file 91-DC1-2.1; Castner to Military Intelligence Service (MIS), 8 June 1942, NARA, RG165, OCS, box 107, file Alaska; Theobald to Nimitz and King, no. 052040, 5 June 1942, NARA, Dispatches and Records from the Chart Room of the Commander in Chief U.S. Fleet, RG38, box 89; and Theobald to Nimitz, no. 081830, 8 June 1942, HI, Theobald Papers, box 10, file Comtask Force No. 8, No. 1-42, May 27.

77 Major Joe E. Golden to Assistant Chief of Staff G-2, "Army-Navy Cooperation in Alaska," 15 July 1942, NARA, RG165, file OPD 384 WDC.

78 Theobald, "Written But Never Sent," 6 November 1942, HI, Theobald Papers, box 10, file Navy Department Correspondence and Orders, 1940-9; Hanable, "Theobald Revisited," 79; King to Theobald, 28 September 1942, NHC, C.W. Nimitz Papers, series XIII, folder 20; and Foster Oral History, NHC, 268.

79 Theobald to Butler, Parker, and Captain L.E. Gehres, "Notes on Operations of Task Force Eight," 3 June 1942, HI, Theobald Papers, vol. 10, file Report from HQ 11th Air Force Striking Group; CTF8 war diary, 4 June 1942, HI, Theobald Papers, vol. 7, War Diary June 1942; Cloe, *The Aleutian Warriors*, 130-5; and Theobald memorandum, 2 July 1942, HI, Theobald Papers, box 10, file Memoranda – Situation in Alaska.

80 Conn et al., *Guarding the United States and Its Outposts*, 266; Theobald to Buckner, no. 82000, 8 June 1942, HI, Theobald Papers, box 10, file Comtask Force No. 8, No. 1-42, May 27; Nimitz to Buckner, 10 June 1942, NHC, SPD, series XII, box 175, file Command – Alaska; and Gruening to Roosevelt, 20 June 1942, NARA, RG348, M939, reel 291, file 49 Unified Command.

81 CTF8 war diary, 11 June 1942, HI, Theobald Papers, vol. 7, file War Diary June 1942; Rear Admiral C.M. Cooke to King, "Despatch to Cincpac 091240," 9 June 1942, HI, Charles M. Cooke Papers, vol. 22, file Military Operations and Planning Pacific Theater; Cloe, *The Aleutian Warriors*, 153-60; and

interrogation of Commander Mukai Nifumi, "Japanese Occupation of Kiska, the Kiska Garrison, and Operations in the Kuriles"; and *Army Air Forces in the War against Japan 1941-1942*, Alfred F. Simpson Historical Research Collection, Maxwell Air Force Base, Army Air Force Historical Study No. 34, June 1945, AFS, 161-3.

82 Talley quoted in Lisa Mighetto and Carla Homstad, *Engineering in the Far North: A History of the U.S. Army Engineer District in Alaska 1867-1992* (Seattle: Historical Research Associates, 1997), 97.

Chapter 4: All Commanders on Minor Fronts

1 Carl von Clausewitz, *On War* (Princeton: Princeton University Press, 1984), 95 and 204.

2 Theobald memorandum, 2 July 1942, Hoover Institution on War, Revolution, and Peace (hereinafter HI), Theobald Papers, box 10, file Memoranda – Situation in Alaska; and Castner report, 6-13 June 1942, National Archives and Records Administration (hereinafter NARA), RG407, Adjutant General's Office (hereinafter AGO), American Theater, file 91-DC1-2.1.

3 DeWitt to Marshall, no. 121745, 12 June 1942, NARA, RG165, file OPD 320.2 Western Defense Command; Freeman to King, no. 121751, 12 June 1942, NARA, RG38, Chart Room, box 89; and Parker to Buckner, "Future Defense of Umnak and Cold Bay," 6 June 1942, NARA, RG338, Alaskan Department, file 370.26.

4 Advanced Intelligence Center, North Pacific Area, "Aleutian Campaign," AIC NorPac No. 880, 15 December 1944, Naval Historical Center (hereinafter NHC), Combat Narratives, 27; Edward T. Layton, with Roger Pineau and John Costello, *And I Was There: Pearl Harbor and Midway – Breaking the Secrets* (Old Saybrook: Konecky and Konecky, 1985), 448; Nimitz to King, no. 110929, 11 June 1942, NARA, RG38, Chart Room, box 92; King and Rear Admiral C.M. Cooke to the Joint Chiefs of Staff (JCS), "Estimate of Situation in the North Pacific Area June 13, 1942," 14 June 1942, NARA, RG218, JCS Geographic File 1942-1945, file CCS 381 North Pacific Area (6-13-42). Cooke was "highly regarded by navy, army, and State Department officials as an extraordinarily able strategist"; Robert William Love Jr., "Ernest Joseph King," in *The Chiefs of Naval Operations*, ed. Love Jr. (Annapolis, MD: Naval Institute Press, 1980), 146; and Thomas B. Buell, *Master of Sea Power: A Biography of Fleet Admiral Ernest J. King* (Boston: Little, Brown and Company, 1980), 142 and 250.

5 Extracts of Gruening to Ickes, 18 June 1942, in Ickes to Assistant Secretary of War John J. McCloy, 25 June 1942, Library of Congress (hereinafter LC), Harold L. Ickes Papers, box 93, file Alaska (2); diary entry, 7 June 1942, Yale University Library, Henry L. Stimson Papers; and PWC minutes, 7 April 1942, National Archives of Canada (hereinafter NAC), RG2, vol. 14, file W-29-1.

6 Admiral James S. Russell Oral History, NHC, September 1976, 107-11 and 155-7; and Admiral Paul F. Foster Oral History, NHC, June 1966, 254-8 and 265-8.

7 Diary entries, 5 and 9 June 1942, in *The Price of Vision: The Diary of Henry Wallace 1942-1946*, ed. John Morton Blum (Boston: Houghton Mifflin, 1973), 87-8; Leighton McCarthy to W.L.M. King, 17 June 1942, NAC, RG25, vol. 2152, file 149; minutes, 11th PWC meeting, 25 June 1942, NAC, RG2, vol. 14, file W-29-1; diary entry, 25 June 1942, NAC, W.L.M. King Papers; and PWC minutes, 25 June 1942, Franklin Delano Roosevelt Library (hereinafter FDRL), Roosevelt Papers, Map Room Files (hereinafter MRF), box 168.

8 Roosevelt to Joseph Stalin, 17 June 1942, LC, Arnold Papers, box 39, file Russia; and Hayes, *The History of the Joint Chiefs of Staff*, 133-5. See Baker B. Beard, "The Bradley Mission: The Evolution of the Alaska-Siberia Air Route," in *Alaska at War, 1941-1945: The Forgotten War Remembered – Papers from the Alaska at War Symposium, Anchorage, Alaska, November 11-13, 1993*, ed. Fern Chandonnet (Anchorage: Alaska at War Committee, 1995), 311-18.

9 Stetson Conn, Rose C. Engelman, and Byron Fairchild, *The Western Hemisphere: Guarding the United States and Its Outposts* (Washington, DC: Department of the Army, 1964), 264-5.

10 Ibid., 265; and Buckner to DeWitt, 23 June 1942, NARA, RG165, Records of the Office of the Chief of Staff (hereinafter OCS), box 101, file Alaska.

11 Edward P. Flynn, "A Bombardier at Heart, Kuter Must Fly a Swivel Chair," *New York Post*, 5 February 1942; "Strictly for Merit," *Army Times*, 7 February 1942; and Forrest C. Pogue, *George C. Marshall: Ordeal and Hope, 1939-1942* (New York: Viking Press), 291. Another study suggests that Kuter was Arnold's most important adviser from 1943 until the end of the end; Perry McCoy Smith, *The Air Force Plans for Peace 1943-1945* (Baltimore: Johns Hopkins University Press, 1970), 9.

12 DeWitt to Marshall, 23 June 1942, NARA, RG165, Records of the OCS, box 101, file Alaska; Marshall to Buckner, 23 June 1942, NARA, RG165, Records of the OCS, box 101, file Alaska; DeWitt to Marshall, 2 July 1942, NARA, RG165, Records of the OCS, box 101, file Alaska; DeWitt-Arnold telephone transcript, 3 July 1942, LC, Arnold Papers, box 189, file Telephone Conversations 1941-2 Dec 8-Aug 14; Arnold to General Thomas Handy, 28 June 1942, NARA, RG165, file OPD 384 ADC; and Arnold to Marshall, "Air Units for Alaska and Siberia," 24 July 1942, LC, Arnold Papers, box 125, file 452.1 Alaska.

13 "US Fliers Lash Japanese in Aleutians Despite Dense Fog and Rain, Says General Kuter," War Department Press Release, 5 July 1942, USAFA, Lawrence Kuter Papers, box 3, part 2. Clippings from dozens of newspapers carrying this press release can be found here as well. See also Samuel Eliot Morison, *History of the United States Naval Operations in World War II*, vol. 3, *The Rising Sun in the Pacific 1931-April 1942* (Boston: Little, Brown and Company, 1948), 256.

14 Nimitz to King, no. 290409, 29 June 1942, NARA, RG38, Chart Room, box 89; "Notes for the Commander in Chief for Conference with CINCPAC about 1 July," 29 June 1942, NHC, CINCPAC Command Summary; King to Nimitz, no. 291810, 29 June 1942, NARA, RG165, Office of the Director of Plans and Operations (hereinafter OPD), Exec. file 11, item 13; and Conn et al., *Guarding the United States and Its Outposts*, 265-6.

15 Diary entries, 8 and 28 July 1942, in *The Price of Vision*, ed. Blum, 94 and 100; Samuel P. Huntington, *The Soldier and the State: The Theory and Politics of Civil-Military Relations* (Cambridge: Belknap Press of Harvard University Press, 1957), 321; Handy to Marshall, "General DeWitt's Plan for Operations in Alaska," 27 July 1942, NARA, RG165, file OPD 381 ADC; Colonel Rufus S. Bratton to Colonel Joseph Smith, "Japanese Capabilities in the North Pacific," 10 July 1942, NARA, RG165, MID, file Alaska 6800; Foster to Vice Chief of Naval Operations (CNO), "Possibilities for Construction of landing fields in the Aleutians west of Fort Glenn, Umnak Island," 16 July 1942, NHC, SPD, series III, box 74; and T.H. Robbins to Cooke, 17 July 1942, NHC, SPD, series III, box 74.

16 JCS to Roosevelt, "Pacific Operations," 12 July 1942, HI, Charles M. Cooke Papers, vol. 22, file Military Operations and Planning Pacific Theater; Mark A. Stoler, "The 'Pacific-First' Alternative in American World War II Strategy," *The International History Review* 2 (July 1980): 439; Marshall interview by Forrest C. Pogue, in *George C. Marshall: Interviews and Reminiscences for Forrest C. Pogue*, ed. Larry I. Bland (Lexington: George C. Marshall Research Foundation, 1991), 593; Roosevelt quoted in Warren F. Kimball, *Forged in War: Roosevelt, Churchill, and the Second World War* (New York: William Morrow and Company, 1997), 152; and Mark A. Stoler, *George C. Marshall: Soldier-Statesman of the American Century* (Boston: Twayne, 1989), 99.

17 Michael Schaller, "General Douglas MacArthur and the Politics of the Pacific War," in *The Pacific War Revisited*, ed. Gunter Bischoff and Robert L. Dupont (Baton Rouge: Louisiana State University Press, 1997), 25.

18 Kimball, *Forged in War*, 150; and Maurice Matloff, "World War II: The Defensive Phase," in *American Military History*, ed. Matloff, vol. 2, *1902-1996* (Coshohoneck: Combined Books, 1996), 97-8.

19 Mark A. Stoler, *Allies and Adversaries: The Joint Chiefs of Staff, the Grand Alliance, and U.S. Strategy in World War II* (Chapel Hill: University of North Carolina Press, 2000), 101; McNarney to King, "Occupation of Tanaga or Adak Islands (Aleutians) and Construction of Landing Field Thereon," 23 July 1942, NARA, RG165, file OPD 580.82 Alaska; and Russell Wilson to McNarney, "Occupation of Tanaga or Adak Islands (Aleutians) and Construction of Landing Fields Thereon," 25 July 1942, NARA, RG165, file OPD 580.82 Alaska.

20 Theobald, "The High Command Situation: December 1941 – January 1943," November 1943, HI, Robert A. Theobald Papers, vol. 1, file Theobald, Robert A. Jr; Handy to Marshall, 27 July 1942, NARA, RG165, file OPD 381 ADC; John Haile Cloe, *The Aleutian Warriors: A History of the 11th Air Force and Fleet Wing 4* (Missoula, MT: Pictorial Histories, 1990), 190-1; Eleventh Air Force Headquarters, "Special Intelligence Report and Summary of Enemy Situation on Kiska," 3 August 1942, NARA, RG407, AGO, American Theater, file 91-DC1-2.1; Joint US Intelligence Committee report, JCS 78, "Japanese Capabilities in the Aleutians," 1 August 1942, NARA, RG218, JCS Geographic File 1942-1945, file CCS 381 Japan (4-23-42); notes on 26th JPS meeting, 5 August 1942, NARA, RG165, OPD, file ABC 381 Japan (5-7-42); Streett to Marshall, "Tanaga Island Development," 18 August 1942, ibid., file 580.82 Alaska; and Marshall to DeWitt, 21 August 1942, ibid., Exec. file 10, item 14.

21 Theobald to King, 19 August 1942, HI, Theobald Papers, vol. 10, file Navy Department Correspondence and Orders 1940-9; Theobald to Buckner, 20 August 1942, HI, Theobald Papers, vol. 10, file Navy Department Correspondence and Orders 1940-9; and Buckner to Theobald, 26 August 1942, HI, Theobald Papers, vol. 10, file Navy Department Correspondence and Orders 1940-9. Buckner's poem, attached to Theobald to Admiral King, 19 August 1942, HI, Theobald Papers, box 10, reads as follows:

> "In far Alaska's ice spray, I stand beside my binnacle
> And scan the waters through the fog for fear some rocky pinnacle
> Projecting from unfathomed depths may break my hull asunder and
> Place my name upon the list of those who made a blunder.
> Volcanic peaks beneath the waves are likely any morning
> To smash my ships to tiny bits without the slightest warning
> I dread the toll from reef and shoal that rip off keel and rudder
> And send our bones to Davey Jones – the prospect makes me shudder.
> The Bering Sea is not for me nor my fleet headquarters
> In mortal dread I look ahead in wild Aleutian waters
> Where hidden reefs and williwaws and terrifying critters
> Unnerve me quite with woeful fright and give me fits and jitters."

22 Forrest C. Pogue, *George C. Marshall: Organizer of Victory, 1942-1945* (New York: Viking Press, 1973), 152; and Marshall to DeWitt, 3 September, NARA, RG165, OCS, box 10, file Alaska. When King reopened the navy's postgraduate school in 1919, he chose Theobald as his executive officer; Buell, *Master of Sea Power*, 48.

23 DeWitt to Marshall, 23 September 1942, George C. Marshall Library (hereinafter GCML), George C. Marshall Papers, box 64, folder 17; Louis Morton, *Strategy and Command: The First Two Years* (Washington, DC: Center for Military History, 1989), 424; Marshall to King, "Command in Alaska," 28 September 1942, NARA, RG165, OCS, box 10, file Alaska; "Conference Notes," 7 September 1942, NHC, CINCPAC Command Summary; E.B. Potter, *Nimitz* (Annapolis, MD: Naval Institute Press, 1976), 187; and Marshall to DeWitt, 2 October 1942, in *The Papers of George Catlett Marshall*, ed. Larry I. Bland, vol. 3, *"The Right Man for the Job," December 7, 1941-May 31, 1943* (Baltimore: Johns Hopkins University Press, 1991), 379-80.

24 Foster to Vice CNO, "Unity of Command in Alaska," 30 July 1942, NHC, SPD, series XII, box 175; and Handy to Deputy Chief of Staff, "Army-Navy Cooperation in Alaska," 8 August 1942, NARA, RG165, file OPD 384 WDC.

25 Robert L. Reynolds speech, 13 July 1942, in *Congressional Record: Proceedings and Debates,* 77th Congress, 2nd Session, 1942, 88, pt. 5: 6083-74; Reynolds speech, 25 February 1942, in *Congressional Record: Proceedings and Debates,* 77th Congress, 2nd Session, 1942, 88, pt. 2: 1625-6; and Roland Young, *Congressional Politics in the Second World War* (New York: Da Capo Press, 1972), 149.

26 Chandler quoted in Cloe, *The Aleutian Warriors,* 189; Robert L. Johnson Jr., "Aleutian Campaign,

World War II: Historical Study and Current Perspective," MA thesis, United States Army Command and General Staff College, Fort Leavenworth, 1992, 169; and Handley Cantril, ed., *Public Opinion 1935-1946* (Princeton: Princeton University Press, 1951), 265.

27 Diary entry, 21 July 1942, Amherst College Archives, John McCloy Papers, box DY4, folder 80; McNarney to King, 4 August 1942, NARA, RG165, OCS, box 197, file Alaska; and Senate Subcommittee report, JCS 100, "Military Establishments in Alaska," 7 September 1942, NARA, RG165, OPD, file ABC 680 Alaska (9-7-42).

28 Cloe, *The Aleutian Warriors*, 190; War Plans Division (hereinafter WPD) to Marshall, "Creation of an Alaskan Department," May 1941, NARA, RG165, file OPD 384 WDC; Brigadier General Carl Spaatz to WPD, "Creation of Alaskan Department," 4 August 1941, NARA, RG165, WPD, file 4480; Colonels Frank M. Kennedy and Harold L. Clark to Arnold, "Report on Alaska," 5 September 1941, NARA, RG18, file 333.1 Alaska Inspection; and Representative Jack Nichols to Under Secretary of War Robert P. Patterson, 9 June 1942, LC, Robert P. Patterson Papers, box 111, file Alaska.

29 Marshall to DeWitt, 3 September 1942, NARA, RG165, OCS, box 10, file Alaska; and DeWitt to Marshall, 11 September 1942, NARA, RG165, file OPD 384 Alaska.

30 Marshall to DeWitt, 11 September 1942, NARA, RG165, OCS, box 10, file Alaska; and DeWitt to Marshall, 13 September 1942, GCML, Marshall Papers, box 64, folder 17. Marshall had informed senior commanders that indiscreet talk about poor army-navy relations was stirring up "bad blood"; Marshall memorandum, 11 September 1942, HI, Robert C. Richardson Jr. Papers, box 60.

31 Notes on 34th JPS meeting, 9 September 1942, NARA, RG165, OPD, file ABC 680 Alaska (9-7-42); JPS report, JCS 100/1, "Military Establishments in Alaska," 28 September 1942, NARA, RG165, OPD, file ABC 680 Alaska (9-7-42); JCS minutes, 36th meeting, 6 October 1942, NARA, Joint Chiefs of Staff (JCS) Decimal File 1942-1945, RG218, file CCS 334 Joint Chiefs of Staff (6-23-42); Leahy to Roosevelt, "Report of Chandler Committee," 9 October 1942, ; and Roosevelt to Albert B. Chandler, 13 October 1942, FDRL, Roosevelt Papers, MRF, box 164.

32 Theobald to Nimitz, no. 150039, 16 September 1942, NARA, RG38, Chart Room, box 89; Commander North Pacific Force to Nimitz, no. 210001, 21 September 1942, NARA, RG38, Chart Room, box 89; Marshall to King, "Defense of Positions in Aleutian Islands," 1 October 1942, NARA, RG165, file OPD 381 ADC; DeWitt to Marshall, 5 September 1942, NARA, RG165, file OPD 320.2 Alaska Defense Command; Handy to the Adjutant General, "Air Reinforcements for Alaska," 25 September 1942, NARA, RG165, file OPD 320.2 Alaska Defense Command; and JCS minutes, 36th meeting, 6 October 1942, NARA, RG218, JCS Decimal File 1942-1945, file CCS 334 Joint Chiefs of Staff (6-23-42).

33 Maurice Matloff, "The 90-Division Gamble," in *Command Decisions*, ed. Kent Robert Greenfield (Washington, DC: Office of the Army, 1960), 366 and 374.

34 Marshall quoted in Schaller, *Douglas MacArthur*, 69. MacArthur's strategic parochialism is discussed in Stanley L. Falk, "Douglas MacArthur and the War against Japan," in *We Shall Return! MacArthur's Commanders and the Defeat of Japan*, ed. William M. Leary (Lexington: University Press of Kentucky, 1988), 1-22.

35 Richard M. Leighton and Robert W. Coakley, *Global Logistics and Strategy 1940-1943* (Washington, DC: Department of the Army, 1955), 393.

36 Herbert P. Bix, *Hirohito and the Making of Modern Japan* (New York: Perennial, 2001), 453-4.

37 Military Intelligence Service (hereinafter MIS), "Situations and Capabilities of the Enemy," 1 October 1942, NARA, RG218, JCS Decimal File 1942-1945, file CCS 350.05 (3-7-42); Jakuo Mikami, "Aleutian Naval Operations: March 1942-February 1943," in *The Naval Armament Program and Naval Operations (Part II)*, vol. 5, *War in Asia and the Pacific* (New York: Garland Publishers, 1980), 55; interrogation of Lieutenant-Colonel Fuji Kazume, "Japanese Army Garrisons on Attu and Kiska," 21 November 1942, in United States Strategic Bombing Survey (Pacific) (USSBS), *Interrogations of Japanese Officials*, vol. 2 (Washington, DC: Government Printing Office, 1946); and interrogation of Captain Arichika Rokuji, "Operations of the Japanese First Destroyer Squadron," in USSBS, *Interrogations of Japanese*

Officials, vol. 2. James Bush argued after the war that Japan had a small caretaker garrison on Attu after 17 September; Bush Oral History, Albert F. Simpson Historical Research Center, Maxwell Air Force Base, 7.

38 ADC G-2 periodic report, 24-5 September 1942, NARA, RG407, AGO, American Theater, file 91-DC1-2.1; interrogation of Mukai, in USSBS, *Interrogations of Japanese Officials*, vol. 2; diary entry, 8 August 1942, in *Fading Victory: The Diary of Admiral Matome Ugaki 1941-1945*, ed. Donald M. Goldstein and Katherine V. Dillon (Pittsburgh: University of Pittsburgh Press, 1991), 178; and Nimitz to King, "Amphibious Training of Army Troops for Operations in Kiska Area," 24 September 1942, NHC, CINCPAC Command Summary.

39 DeWitt to Marshall, 29 September and 5 October 1942, NHC, CINCPAC Command Summary; David C. Fuquea, "Task Force One: The Wasted Assets of the United States Battleship Fleet, 1942," *Journal of Military History* 61 (October 1997): 720; King to Marshall, 5 and 12 October 1942, NHC, CINCPAC Command Summary; and King to Captain Corn, "Possible Operations against Japanese Advance in the Aleutians," 7 October 1942, NHC, Future Plans Division Records, series XI, box 152.

40 DeWitt to OPD, "Plans for Reduction and Occupation of Boodle," 12 October 1942, NHC, SPD, series XII, box 175; Marshall to King, "Amphibious Operations against Kiska," 17 October 1942, NARA, RG165, file OPD 381 ADC; MIS, "Situation and Capabilities of the Enemy," 15 October 1942, NARA, RG218, JCS Decimal File 1942-1945, file CCS 350.5 (3-7-42); and DeWitt to Marshall, 19 and 23 October 1942, NARA, RG165, OCS, box 10, file Alaska.

41 Ronald H. Spector, "The Pacific War and the Fourth Dimension of Strategy," in *The Pacific War Revisited*, ed. Gunter Bischof and Robert L. Dupont (Baton Rouge: Louisiana State University Press, 1997), 53; and Oscar A. Badger quoted in Daniel K. Blewett, "Fuel and the U.S. Naval Operations in the Pacific, 1942," in *The Pacific War Revisited*, ed. Bischoff and Dupont, 58.

42 Captain C.E. Olson to Cooke, "Comment on Cincpac Series 02798 re: Amphibious Training of Army Troops for Operations in Kiska Area," 10 October 1942, NHC, SPD, series XII, box 175; Cooke to King, 15 October 1942, HI, Cooke Papers, vol. 22, file Military Operations and Planning Pacific Theater; Marshall to DeWitt, 15 October 1942, NARA, RG165, file OPD 381 ADC; DeWitt to Marshall, no. 172103, 17 October 1942, NARA, RG165, file OPD 381 ADC; and Lieutenant Colonel W.J. Verbeck, "Terrain of Amchitka," 4 October 1942, NARA, RG165, OCS, box 10, file Alaska.

43 Marshall to DeWitt, 29 October 1942, NARA, RG165, file OPD 381 ADC.

44 DeWitt to Buckner, 30 October 1942, NARA, RG165, OCS, box 10, file Alaska; and DeWitt to Marshall, 31 October and 5 November 1942, NARA, RG165, OCS, box 10, file Alaska; and Buckner to DeWitt, 5 and 7 November 1942, NARA, RG338, Alaskan Department, file 201.

45 Theobald, "A Study in Enforced Strategy," 2 September 1942, HI, Theobald Papers, vol. 12, file War Estimates; Theobald to Nimitz, no. 280215, 29 October 1942, NARA, RG38, Chart Room, box 89; and Cooke to King, "Comment on Comtask 8 280215 Regarding Concern over Alaska Garrison Plans," 30 October 1942, NHC, SPD, series XII, box 175.

46 Takahashi, "The Japanese Campaign in Alaska," 37; Mikami, "Aleutian Naval Operations," 62; "Central agreement between the army and the navy," 31 October 1942, in Kevin Don Hutchison, *World War II in the North Pacific: Chronology and Fact Book* (Westport, CT: Greenwood Press, 1994), 54-5; and Brian Garfield, *The Thousand-Mile War: World War II in Alaska and the Aleutians* (New York: Bantam Books, 1969), 170-1.

47 ADC, "Fragmentary Aerial Photo Intelligence Report No. 6," 8 November 1942, NARA, RG407, AGO, American Theater, file 91-DC1-2.1; and Castner report, no. 170, 10-11 November 1942, NARA, RG407, AGO, American Theater, file 91-DC1-2.1.

48 Phillips, "Possible Scale of Japanese Attack on the American Coast," COS (40) 970, 22 November 1940, NAC, RG24, vol. 3913, file NSS 1037-5-3; G.F. Hudson to M.E. Dening, 17 June 1942, plus handwritten comments by Foreign Office officials, 23 and 26 June 1942, PRO, Foreign Office Records, Japan Correspondence 1941-1945, FO371/31836; Joint Intelligence Sub-Committee, "Japan's Intentions," JIC (42)

339 (Final), 9 September 1942, PRO, FO Japan, FO371/31817; J.R.M. Butler, *Grand Strategy,* vol. 4, *August 1942-September 1943,* ed. Michael Howard (London: Her Majesty's Stationery Office, 1972), 79-80; CIC to CCS, "Memorandum for Information No. 25 Japanese Intentions," 8 November 1942, NARA, RG218, JCS Geographic File 1942-1945, file CCS 381 Japan (4-23-42); diary entry, 7 December 1942, in Goldstein and Dillon, *Fading Victory,* 298; and Akira Iriye, *Power and Culture: The Japanese-American War, 1941-1945* (Cambridge: Harvard University Press, 1981), 88.

49 DeWitt to Marshall, 13 November 1942, NARA, RG165, file OPD 381 ADC; Buckner to War Department, no. 1256, 14 November 1942, NARA, RG38, Chart Room, box 88; and Buckner to DeWitt, 15 November 1942, NARA, RG338, Alaskan Department, file 201.

50 Marshall to DeWitt, 20 November 1942, NARA, RG165, OCS, file Alaska; Office of Naval Intelligence, "The O.N.I. Weekly No. 43," 18 November 1942, Directorate of History and Heritage, Kardex File 112.3M1013 (D6); and War Department, "The Weekly Strategic Resume: The Western Hemisphere," 21 November 1942, NARA, RG165, OPD, Exec. file 1, item 10.

51 CINCPAC, "Summary of the Situation," 25 November 1942, NHC, SPD, series XII, box 175.

52 King to Marshall, "Amphibious Operations against Kiska," 15 November 1942, NARA, RG165, OCS, box 107, file Alaska; and Nimitz to Theobald, no. 171915, 18 November 1942, NARA, RG38, Chart Room, box 88.

53 Representatives John M. Coffee and Karl E. Mundt speeches, 8 October 1942, *Appendix to the Congressional Record,* 77th Congress, 2nd Session, vol. 88, pt. 10, A3607; Roosevelt Fireside Chat, 12 October 1942, FDRL, Roosevelt Papers, President's Personal Files (hereinafter PPF), series 1820, file 1st Carbon; diary entries, 21 October and 10 November 1942, in *The Price of Vision,* ed. Blum, 123 and 132; and James J. Cooke, *Billy Mitchell* (Boulder, CO: Lynne Rienner, 2002), 279. Roosevelt noted that three groups in the United States "say they want to win the war (a) if, at the same time, Russia is defeated, (b) if, at the same time, England is defeated, (c) if, at the same time, Roosevelt is defeated"; Roosevelt to Dr. Gallup, 2 October 1942, FDRL, Roosevelt Papers, PPF, file PPF4721.

54 Nimitz to King, no. 221041, 22 November 1942, NARA, RG165, OCS, box 107, file Alaska; memorandum for Acting Chief of Staff G-2, "Developments Pacific Area, November 26," 27 November 1942, NARA, RG165, OPD, Exec. file 11, item 4; Castner, G-2 periodic report, 28 November 1942, NARA, RG407, AGO, American Theater, file 91-DC1-2.1; and Buckner to DeWitt, 5, 15, and 25 November 1942, NARA, RG338, Alaskan Department, file 201. Theobald believed Japan was planning dual counterattacks in the Solomons and the Aleutians in late November; CTF8 war diary, 11 November 1942, HI, Theobald Papers, vol. 9, file War Diary November 1942.

55 King to Theobald, 28 September and 24 October 1942, NHC, C.W. Nimitz Papers, series XIII, folder 20; Gerald E. Wheeler, *Kinkaid of the Seventh Fleet: A Biography of Thomas C. Kinkaid, U.S. Navy* (Washington, DC: Naval Historical Center, 1995), 296; Embick to Marshall, "Garrisons in Alaska," 26 November 1942, NARA, RG165, file OPD 381 ADC; DeWitt to Marshall, 5 December 1942, NARA, RG165, OCS, box 107, file Alaska; and Morton, *Strategy and Command,* 425.

56 Nimitz to King, "Review of Alaska Situation," 8 December 1942, NHC, SPD, series XII, box 175; Olson to Captain R.L. Conolly, "Information Regarding Aleutians," 14 December 1942, NHC, SPD, series V, box 103; King to Marshall, 15 December 1942, NARA, RG165, file OPD 381 ADC; Colonel R.S. Bratton to Acting Chief of Staff G-2, "Developments Pacific Area," 15 December 1942, NARA, RG165, OPD, Exec. file 11, item 4; Handy to Marshall, "General DeWitt's Letters of 27 November and 5 December Concerning Employment of the 44th Division and the 184th Infantry in Connection with the Reduction of Boodle," 15 December 1942, NARA, RG165, OCS, box 107, file Alaska; Marshall to DeWitt, 17 December 1942, NARA, RG165, OCS, box 107, file Alaska; Conolly to King, "Operations against Amchitka and Kiska," 17 December 1942, NHC, SPD, series XII, box 175; and King to Nimitz, no. 181315, 17 December 1942, NARA, RG165, file OPD 381 ADC.

57 Talley quoted in Lisa Mighetto and Carla Homstad, *Engineering in the Far North: A History of the U.S. Army Engineer District in Alaska 1867-1992* (Seattle: Historical Research Associates, 1997), 123; and Cloe, *The Aleutian Warriors,* 251.

58 Theobald to Nimitz, no. 240115, 25 December 1942, NHC, SPD, series XII, box 175; Theobald and Buckner to Nimitz and DeWitt, no. 212238, 24 December 1942, NARA, RG38, Chart Room, box 90; and DeWitt to Nimitz, no. 252050, 26 December 1942, NARA, RG38, Chart Room, box 90.

59 Theobald to Nimitz, "Plan for Driving the Japanese Out of the Aleutian Area," 29 November 1942, HI, Theobald Papers, vol. 9, file War Diary November 1942; Kinkaid quoted in Wheeler, *Kinkaid of the Seventh Fleet*, 301; and Samuel Eliot Morison, *History of the United States Naval Operations in World War II*, vol. 4, *Coral Sea, Midway and Submarine Actions May 1942-August 1942* (Boston: Little, Brown and Company, 1950), 184.

60 Buckner to Brigadier General Lloyd E. Jones, 23 December 1942, NARA, RG338, Alaskan Department, file 201; Castner, Annex 3 to G-2 periodic report, 9 January 1943; Future Plans Division, "Plan for the Occupation of Amchitka and Semisopochnoi," 26 December 1942, NHC, SPD, series XI, box 151; and Cloe, *The Aleutian Warriors*, 257-8.

Chapter 5: Total Destruction Is the Only Answer

1 Carl von Clausewitz, *On War* (Princeton: Princeton University Press, 1984), 119.

2 Colonel John Weckerling, "Study of the Enemy Situation and Capabilities in the Western Aleutians," 18 December 1942, Naval Historical Center (hereinafter NHC), SPD, series XI, box 152; DeWitt to Marshall, no. 252, 22 December 1942, National Archives and Records Administration (hereinafter NARA), RG165, Office of the Director of Plans and Operations (hereinafter OPD), file ABC 381 Japan (5-31-42); DeWitt to Nimitz, no. 252050, 23 December 1942, NARA, RG38, Chart Room, box 90; OPD, "Offensive Operations in the Aleutians," 23 December 1942, NARA, RG165, OPD, file ABC 381 Japan (5-31-42); and Louis Morton, *Strategy and Command: The First Two Years* (Washington, DC: Center for Military History, 1989), 428.

3 Theobald to Nimitz, "Plan for Driving the Japanese Out of the Aleutian Area," 29 November 1942, NHC, SPD, series XI, box 152; A.E. Smith to Conolly, 21 December 1942, NHC, SPD, series XII, box 175; and Future Plans Division, "Plan for Occupation of Amchitka and Semisopochnoi," 26 December 1942, NHC, SPD, series XI, box 151.

4 Theobald to Nimitz, "Plan for Driving the Japanese Out of the Aleutian Area," 29 November 1942, NHC, SPD, series XI, box 152, file Kiska; Nimitz to King, "Plan for Driving the Japanese out of the Aleutian Area," 28 December 1942, NHC, SPD, series XI, box 152, file Kiska; DeWitt, "Plan for the Seizure and Occupation of Kiska," 12 December 1942, NHC, SPD, series XI, box 152, file Kiska; Nimitz to King, no. 090342, 9 January 1943, NARA, RG165, OPD, file ABC Japan (5-31-42); and Morton, *Strategy and Command*, 429.

5 F-1 to King, "F-1 Comments on C.T.F. 8 Plan for Driving the Japanese Out of the Aleutian Area," 12 January 1943, plus handwritten comments by Admiral R.S. Edwards, NHC, SPD, series XII, box 176.

6 Williamson to Arnold, "First Partial Report of Alaskan Inspection – Organization and Morale Problems of the Provisional Bomber Command, XI Air Force," 10 November 1942, Hoover Institution on War, Revolution, and Peace (hereinafter HI), Frederick L. Anderson Papers, vol. 89, file Alaska Inspection 1942; and Williamson to Arnold, "Second Partial Report of AFDRB Alaska Inspection – Conduct of Aleutian Action," 27 November 1942, NARA, RG165, file OPD 333.1 ADC.

7 Thomas B. Buell, *Master of Sea Power: A Biography of Fleet Admiral Ernest J. King* (Boston: Little, Brown and Company, 1980), 252.

8 King to the JCS, "Campaign against Japan via the Northern Route," 21 September 1942, attached as Enclosure A to JCS 182, "Campaign against Japan via the Northern Route," 1 January 1943, NARA, RG218, JCS Geographic File 1942-1945, file CCS 381 Japan (8-25-42); Military Intelligence Section, War Department, "Survey of the Kurile (Chishima) Islands," Summer 1942, NARA, RG38, Chief of Naval Operations Records, Office of Naval Intelligence, East European Section, box 51; and JPS, Enclosure B to JCS 182, "Campaign against Japan via the Northern Route," 1 January 1943, NARA, RG218, JCS Geographic File 1942-1943, file CCS 381 Japan (8-25-42).

9   Massey to Brooke Claxton, 20 March 1942, National Archives of Canada (hereinafter NAC), Brooke Claxton Papers, vol. 56, file Vincent Massey; Dill to Churchill, 7 March 1942, PRO, PREM3/478/6; Richard Overy, *Why the Allies Won the War* (London: Pimlico, 1995), 250; Mark A. Stoler, "The 'Pacific-First' Alternative in American World War II Strategy," *The International History Review* 2 (July 1980): 447-8; and JCS minutes, 49th meeting, 5 January 1943, NARA, RG218, Joint Chiefs of Staff (JCS) Decimal File 1942-1945, file CCS 334 Joint Chiefs of Staff (11-10-42).

10 Brian P. Farrell, "Symbol of Paradox: The Casablanca Conference, 1943," *Canadian Journal of History* 28 (April 1993): 22-40.

11 Churchill to the Chiefs of Staff Committee, "Memorandum on the Future Conduct of the War Part IV – Notes on the Pacific," 20 December 1941, in *The Churchill War Papers*, ed. Martin Gilbert, vol. 3, *The Ever-Widening War 1941* (New York: W.W. Norton, 2000), 1649-53; British Chiefs of Staff (hereinafter COS), "American-British Strategy," 7 November 1942, HI, Cooke Papers, vol. 24, file Strategic Policy for the Conduct of the War 1942-1945; and British COS, CCS 135/2, "American-British Strategy in 1943," 3 January 1943, HI, Albert C. Wedemeyer Papers, vol. 72, file 72.9

12 Sir Ian Jacob and Lieutenant General Sir Hastings Ismay quoted in Buell, *Master of Sea Power*, 256-7; diary entry, 9 February 1942, in *War Diaries 1939-1945: Field Marshal Lord Alanbrooke*, ed. Alex Danchev and Daniel Todman (London: Weidenfeld and Nicolson, 2001), 228.

13 Diary entry, 14 January 1943, in *War Diaries 1939-1945*, ed. Danchev and Todman, 359; and CCS minutes, 14 January 1943, NARA, RG218, JCS Decimal File 1942-1945, file CCS 334 Com Chiefs of Staff (10-30-42).

14 JPS, CCS 153 (Revised), "Situation to Be Created in the Eastern Theater (Namely Pacific and Burma) in 1943," 17 January 1943, NARA, RG218, JSC Decimal File 1942-1945, file CCS 334 Com Chiefs of Staff (10-30-42); CCS minutes, 59th meeting, 17 January 1943, NARA, RG218, JSC Decimal File 1942-1945, file CCS 334 Com Chiefs of Staff (10-30-42); British Joint Staff Planners, CCS153/1, "Situation to Be Created in the Eastern Theater (Pacific and Burma) in 1943, 17 January 1943, NARA, RG218, JSC Decimal File 1942-1945, file CCS 334 Com Chiefs of Staff (10-30-42).

15 Forrest C. Pogue, *George C. Marshall: Organizer of Victory, 1942-1945* (New York: Viking Press, 1973), 27; and diary entry, 20 January 1943, in Danchev and Todman, *War Diaries 1939-1945*, 360.

16 CCS minutes, 60th meeting, 19 January 1943, NARA, RG218, JCS Decimal File 1942-1945, file CCS 3334 Com Chiefs of Staff (10-30-42); CCS, CCS 155/1, "Conduct of the War in 1943," 19 January 1943, NARA, RG218, JCS Decimal File 1942-1945, file CCS 3334 Com Chiefs of Staff (10-30-42); Pogue, *Organizer of Victory*, 29-30; and Warren F. Kimball, *Forged in War: Roosevelt, Churchill, and the Second World War* (New York: William Morrow and Company, 1997), 272.

17 OPD, "Occupation of Kiska Island," January 1943, NARA, RG165, OPD, Exec. file 6, item 7; JCS minutes, 58th meeting, 22 January 1943, NARA, RG218, JCS Decimal File 1942-1945, file CCS 334 Joint Chiefs of Staff (1-14-43); JCS, CCS 168, "Conduct of the War in the Pacific Theater in 1943," 22 January 1943, Wartime Conferences of the Combined Chiefs of Staff, reel 1; and CCS 170/1, "Report to the President and Prime Minister," 23 January 1943, Wartime Conferences of the Combined Chiefs of Staff, reel 1.

18 Brooke quoted in Alex Danchev, "Great Britain: The Indirect Strategy," in *Allies at War: The Soviet, American, and British Experience, 1939-1945*, ed. David Reynolds, Warren F. Kimball, and A.O. Chubarian (New York: St. Martin's Press, 1994), 5; and Wedemeyer quoted in Maurice Matloff, "Grand Strategy," in *American Military History*, ed. Matloff, vol. 2, *1902-1996* (Coshohoneck: Combined Books, 1996), 106. Field Marshal Sir John Dill had told Brooke the Americans were very conscious that Britain had imposed its strategy on them; Danchev, "Great Britain: The Indirect Strategy," 6. By September 1943 the American army had twenty-six divisions overseas, thirteen in the Pacific, thirteen in Europe. As 1943 closed, almost 1.88 million Americans were in the Pacific compared with 1.81 million in Europe; Russell F. Weigley, *The American Way of War: A History of American Military Strategy and Policy* (New York: Macmillan, 1973), 271. By 1 April 1945 the figures had altered dramatically. Over 3 million soldiers were in Europe, while just 1.2 million were in the Pacific; Matloff, "Grand Strategy," 124.

19 Roosevelt quoted in Michael D. Pearlman, *Warmaking and American Diplomacy: The Struggle over Military Strategy, 1700 to the Present* (Lawrence: University Press of Kansas, 1999), 255; diary, 18 June 1943, Yale University Library (hereinafter YUL), Henry Stimson Papers; King to Nimitz, no. 042000, 4 February 1943, NHC, SPD, series XII, box 152; and Nimitz to Kinkaid, 5 February 1943, NHC, Thomas C. Kinkaid Papers, box 8, file Aleutians Correspondence 1943.

20 Ray S. Cline, *Washington Command Post: The Operations Division* (Washington, DC: United States Army, 1985), 303; OPD memorandum, 22 February 1943, NARA, RG165, file OPD 370.5 Alaska Defense Command; and Colonel Ray T. Maddocks, to Assistant Chief of Staff OPD, "Aleutian Operations" plus "Outline Plan of an Operation against Attu Island," late February 1943, NHC, SPD, series XII, box 180.

21 Handy to DeWitt, "Air Reinforcements to Meet Aggressive Requirements," 25 February 1943, NARA, RG165, Records of the Office of the Chief of Staff (hereinafter OCS), box 10, file Alaska; SPD memorandum, 3 March 1943, NHC, SPD, series XII, box 176; and JIC 80/1, "Japanese Strategy, 1943," 5 March 1943, NARA, RG218, JCS Geographic File 1942-1945, file CCS 381 Japan (2-12-43).

22 Richard B. Frank, *Guadalcanal: The Definitive Account of the Landmark Battle* (New York: Penguin Books, 1990), 614. See also Ronald Spector, "American Seizure of Japan's Strategic Points Summer 1942-1944," in *From Pearl Harbor to Hiroshima: The Second World War in Asia and the Pacific, 1941-45* ed. Saki Dockrill (New York: St. Martin's Press, 1994), 78.

23 DeWitt to Major General George R. Pearkes, 25 February 1943, Directorate of History and Heritage (hereinafter DHH), Kardex File 181.002 (D433).

24 Kinkaid to Nimitz, 20 February 1943, NHC, Kinkaid Papers, box 8, file Aleutians Correspondence 1943; and Kinkaid to Nimitz, no. 070115, 7 March 1943, NARA, RG165, file OPD 381 Security. Nimitz's comments about Kiska being a tough nut are in Nimitz to Kinkaid, 5 February 1943, NHC, Nimitz Papers, series XIII, folder 20.

25 Buckner to DeWitt, 10 February and 9 March 1943, NARA, RG338, Alaskan Department, file 201; King to Nimitz and DeWitt, no. 111221, 10 March 1942, NARA, RG165, file OPD 381 Security; minutes of the 2nd meeting of the Pacific Military Conference, 12 March 1943, NARA, RG218, JCS Decimal File 1942-1945, file CCS 334 Pacific Military Conf.; Morton, *Strategy and Command*, 430; and DeWitt to Nimitz, no. 172239, 19 March 1943, NARA, RG165, OPD, file OPD 381 Security.

26 King to Marshall, 22 March 1943, NARA, RG165, OPD, file OPD 381 Security; War Department, "Operation against Attu," 22 March 1943, NARA, RG165, OPD, file OPD 381 Security; and King to Nimitz, no. 221939, 22 March 1943, NARA, RG165, OPD, file OPD 381 Security.

27 Colonel Henry A. Barber to Major General John E. Hull, "Landcrab," 23 March 1943, NHC, SPD, series XII, box 180; and DeWitt-Hull telephone transcript, 23 March 1943, NARA, RG165, OPD, Exec. file 8, item 8.

28 Herbert P. Bix, *Hirohito and the Making of Modern Japan* (New York: Perennial, 2001), 460.

29 Samuel Eliot Morison, *History of United States Naval Operations in World War II*, vol. 7, *Aleutians, Gilberts and Marshalls June 1942-April 1944* (Boston: Little, Brown and Company, 1951); interrogation of Lieutenant Colonel Fuji Kazume, in United States Strategic Bombing Survey (Pacific) (USSBS), *Interrogations of Japanese Officials*, vol. 2 (Washington, DC: Government Printing Office, 1946); "Army-Navy Central Agreement," 4 February 1943, in Kevin Don Hutchison, *World War II in the North Pacific: Chronology and Fact Book* (Westport, CT: Greenwood Press, 1994), 73-4; and John A. Lorelli, *The Battle of the Komandorskis* (Annapolis, MD: Naval Institute Press, 1984), 10-11.

30 W.J. Holmes, *Double-Edged Secrets: U.S. Naval Intelligence Operations in the Pacific During World War Two* (Annapolis, MD: Naval Institute Press, 1979), 132-3.

31 McMorris quoted in Jonathan M. Nielson, *Armed Forces on a Northern Frontier: The Military in Alaska's History, 1867-1987* (Westport, CT: Greenwood Press, 1988), 154; and Morison, *History of United States Naval Operations in World War II*, vol. 7, *Aleutians, Gilberts and Marshalls*, 8. John Lorelli claims that McMorris, anticipating "a walkover of some transports," failed to consult his captains about

tactics. And although many sailors resented McMorris for abandoning the *Salt Lake City*, Commander Ralph H. Millsap had ordered his vessels to regroup around the *Richmond* but the badly damaged *Salt Lake City* simply could not comply with that direction; Lorelli, *The Battle of the Komandorski Islands*, 154-5; and Commander Ralph H. Millsap, "Skill or Luck?" *United States Naval Institute Proceedings* 111 (March 1985): 87. See also Gary Candelaria, "Tin Can at War: The USS *Monaghan* and the War in Alaska," in *Alaska at War: The Forgotten War Remembered – Papers from the Alaska at War Symposium, Anchorage, Alaska, November 11-13, 1993*, ed. Fern Chandonnet (Anchorage: Alaska at War Committee, 1995), 113-23. Nimitz thought McMorris had demonstrated considerable skill in the face of a superior enemy; Nielson, *Armed Forces on a Northern Frontier*, 158.

32 Kinkaid to Nimitz, 28 March 1943, NHC, Nimitz Papers, series XIII, folder 20; Kinkaid to Nimitz, no. 310322, 31 March 1943, NARA, RG165, file OPD 381 Security; and Nimitz to Kinkaid, 20 April 1943, NHC, Kinkaid papers, box 8, file Aleutians Correspondence 1943.

33 DeWitt to Marshall, "Komandorski Islands," 5 April 1943, NARA, RG165, file OPD 381 ADC; and Marshall to DeWitt, "Komandorski Islands," 12 April 1943, NARA, RG165, file OPD 381 ADC.

34 DeWitt to Marshall, 1 April 1943, NARA, RG165, OCS, box 10, file Alaska; and Buckner to DeWitt, 5 January 1943, NARA, RG338, Alaskan Department, file 201; Marshall to DeWitt, 8 April 1943, NARA, RG165, file OPD 381 Security; and Kinkaid to Nimitz, 26 April 1943, NHC, Kinkaid Papers, box 8, file Aleutians Correspondence 1943.

35 DeWitt to Marshall, 1 April 1943, NARA, RG165, OCS, box 10, file Alaska; Kinkaid to Nimitz, 14 April 1943, NHC, Kinkaid Papers, box 8, file Aleutians Correspondence 1943; Kinkaid to Nimitz, 16 April 1943, NHC, Kinkaid Papers, box 8, file Aleutians Correspondence 1943; and Nimitz to Kinkaid, 29 April 1943, NHC, Kinkaid Papers, box 8, file Aleutians Correspondence 1943.

36 War Department, *The Capture of Attu As Told by the Men Who Fought There* (Washington, DC: United States Government Printing Office, 1944), 2.

37 Weckerling, G-2 periodic report, 27 March to 3 April 1943, NARA, RG165, file OPD 319.1 Western Defense Command; and Headquarters Landing Force, Task Force 51, "Field Order No. 1," NARA, RG407, Adjutant General's Office (hereinafter AGO), American Theater, file 91-TF4-3.4.

38 John Prados, *Combined Fleet Decoded: The Secret History of American Intelligence and the Japanese Navy in World War II* (New York: Random House, 1995), 474; and diary entry for 6 May 1943, NHC, CINCPAC Command Summary.

39 Kinkaid to Nimitz, 26 April 1943, NHC, series XIII, folder 20; Lieutenant General Robert E. Hogaboom Oral History, 1972, Marine Corps Historical Center, 158-66; and General Holland M. Smith, "The Development of Amphibious Tactics in the U.S. Navy," *Marine Corps Gazette* (January 1947), 57. Eareckson, sent to California by Buckner, had nothing but praise for the "hard-bitten" marines he worked with; William Eareckson to Butler, 3 February 1943, Air Force History Support Office, Eleventh Air Force Records, reel A4217.

40 Donald M. Goldstein and Katherine V. Dillon, *The Williwaw War: The Arkansas National Guard in the Aleutians in World War II* (Fayetteville: University of Arkansas Press, 1992), 284-6.

41 George L. MacGarrigle, *Aleutian Islands: The U.S. Army Campaigns of World War II* (Washington, DC: Government Printing Office, n.d), 20. Brian Garfield asserts that Japan learned of the attack when Walter Winchell advised radio listeners on 10 May to "keep your eye on the Aleutians." According to Robert A. Anderson, a Japanese submarine spotted TF51 on 30 April and relayed that information to Attu. Stetson Conn maintains that the Japanese believed Kiska would be the target; only when American aircraft bombed Attu and dropped surrender leaflets on 11 May did the enemy realize Attu was under attack; Brian Garfield, *The Thousand-Mile War: World War II in Alaska and the Aleutians* (New York: Bantam Books, 1969), 236; Robert A. Anderson, "Attu: WW II's Bloody Sideshow," *Army*, 33 (May 1983): 43; and Stetson Conn, Rose C. Engelman, and Byron Fairchild, *The Western Hemisphere: Guarding the United States and Its Outposts* (Washington, DC: Department of the Army, 1964), 287-8.

42 Lamar Tooke, *Infantry Operations in the Aleutians: The Battle for Attu* (Carlisle Barracks: United

States Army War College, March 1990), 11; Lieutenant Colonel Lynn Davis Smith, "Preliminary Report on Attu Landing," 30 May 1943, NARA, RG407, American Theater, file 91-DC4-0.30 (3646); and MacGarrigle, *Aleutian Islands,* 21.

43 Diary entry, 8 June 1943, Black Family private papers, J.L. Black Diary.

44 Verbeck, G-2 periodic report, 13 May 1943, NARA, RG338, Alaskan Department, box 3, file Daily G-2 Report May 1943; and USN HQ, "Aleutian Islands Action," 14 May 1943, Franklin Delano Roosevelt Library, Roosevelt Papers, Map Room Files, box 74.

45 Dwinnell and Paulson quoted in *The Capture of Attu,* 50-1 and 27-31; and Attu Landing Force HQ, "Narrative of Events of Landing Force 51.4," 22 June 1943, NARA, RG407, AG's Office, WWII Operations Reports, American Theater, box 45, file 91-TF4-0.3.

46 Verbeck, G-2 periodic report, 16 May 1943, NARA, RG407, AG's Office, WWII Operations Reports, American Theater, box 45, file 91-TF4-0.3; Colonel R.S. Bratton to Acting Chief of Staff, G-2, "Developments Pacific Area, May 15," 15 May 1943, NARA, RG165, OPD, Exec. file 11, item 5; Bratton to Acting Chief of Staff, G-2, "Developments Pacific Area, May 17," 17 May 1943, NARA, RG165, OPD, Exec. file 11, item 5; and "The Aleutian Campaign June 1942-August 1943," NHC, Combat Narratives.

47 Kinkaid to Nimitz, 21 May 1943, NHC, Kinkaid Papers, box 8, file Aleutians Correspondence 1943; Garfield, *The Thousand-Mile War,* 244; and Wheeler, *Kinkaid of the Seventh Fleet,* 325-26. A witness aboard the *Pennsylvania* stated Rockwell displayed a rare fit of temper when he heard Brown had been removed from command; Commander I.E. McMillian to Major General Albert E. Brown, 11 April 1944, Military History Institute Archives (hereinafter MHI), Albert E. Brown Papers, box Attu, file Personal Correspondence 1944.

48 War Department, *The Capture of Attu,* 38-9.

49 Ibid., 88-9.

50 Worrall Reed Carter, *Beans, Bullets, and Black Oil: The Story of Fleet Logistics Afloat in the Pacific During World War II* (Washington, DC: Government Printing Office, 1952), 77; Verbeck, G-2 periodic report, 23 May 1943, NARA, RG338, Alaskan Department, box 3; and John Haile Cloe, *The Aleutian Warriors: A History of the 11th Air Force and Fleet Wing 4* (Missoula, MT: Pictorial Histories, 1990), 287.

51 Japanese practices of booby-trapping their casualties and offering fake surrenders had led to an American tendency to shoot all Japanese, wounded or dead. Private Raymond V. Braun of the Seventeenth Regiment watched approvingly as his sergeant bayonetted a wounded and helpless Japanese soldier. An anonymous American lieutenant reports having seen "many cases of bayoneting of [Japanese] wounded," especially after the Seventeenth Regiment commander was killed by a Japanese sniper. Claiming to have taken the ears from a dead Japanese major, the lieutenant said he preferred to use a pistol on Japanese wounded "because I am a gent": John W. Dower, *War without Mercy: Race and Power in the Pacific War* (New York: Pantheon Books, 1986), 61-71; *The Capture of Attu As Told by the Men Who Fought There,* 31-3; and "Bill" to "Joe," 27 May 1943, NARA, RG165, Military Intelligence Division Correspondence 1922-44, file Japan 6910.

52 War Department, *The Capture of Attu,* 110-11; Anderson, "Attu: World War Two's Bloody Sideshow," 45-6; Kenneth Deacon, "Combat Engineers 43. Attu, May 1943," *The Military Engineer* 59 (January-February 1967): 25; Nebu Tatsuguchi diary, United States Military Academy Archives, Harold S. Rosenthal Papers, box 1; and Ronald M. May, "Battle at Attu – The Japanese Side of It," *Periodical* (December 1985): 7.

53 Garfield, *The Thousand-Mile War,* 256.

54 A.J. Waldrum, *The Aleutian Campaign: A Study in Cold Weather Survival* (Quantico: United States Marine Corps, 1976-77), 45.

55 Herbert B. Knowles to Kinkaid, "Report of Activities as SOPA, ATTU from 19 May to 27 May 1943, Incl.," 29 May 1943, Library of Congress (hereinafter LC), Herbert B. Knowles Papers, box 1, file Attu and Kiska May 25-June 5, 1943 Reports; Colonel Lynn Davis Smith, "Preliminary Report on Attu

Landing," 30 May 1943, NARA, RG407, AGO, American Theater, file 91-DC4-0.30 (3646); Major R.P. Bronson, "Report of Operations on ATTU," 25 June 1943, NARA, RG407, AGO, American Theater, file 91-TF4-0.3 (23374); Captain J. Grant Lemmon to Buckner, "Comments on Attu Operation," 7 June 1943, DHH, Kardex File 322.009 (D506); Castner, "Lessons Learned from Operations on Attu," 7 June 1943, DHH, Kardex File 322.009 (D506); and diary entry, 2 June 1943, YUL, Stimson Papers. Stimson had been briefed by Brigadier General William E. Lynd.

56 Vice Admiral William P. Mack Oral History, 1979, Naval History Institute Library (hereinafter NHIL), 126-7; Rockwell to Nimitz, 30 May 1943, NHC, Nimitz Papers, series XIII, folder 20; "The Aleutians Campaign June 1942-August 1945," NHC, Combat Narratives, 78-9; Smith, "The Development of Amphibious Tactics in the U.S. Navy," 56-7; and Nimitz to Kinkaid, 2 June 1943, NHC, Nimitz Papers, series XIII, folder 20.

57 Admiral Robert L. Dennison Oral History, January 1973, NHIL, 56; diary entry, 2 June 1943, YUL, Stimson Papers; and Lynd, "Performance of Maj. Gen. A.E. Brown during operations on Attu, May 11-16 1943, and preparations thereof," 3 June 1943, NARA, RG165, OCS, box 43, file Bro to Byr.

58 Brown to Brian Garfield, 27 December 1972, MHI, Brown Papers, box Attu, folder Correspondence and Reports Regarding MG Brown's Actions in Attu Operations; Brown, "Memorandum for the Record," 4 May 1948, HI, Brown Papers, box Attu, folder Correspondence and Reports Regarding MG Brown's Actions in Attu Operations; and Bush Oral History, Albert F. Simpson Historical Research Center, Maxwell Air Force Base, 12-13; DeWitt to Marshall, 18 May 1943, NARA, RG165, OCS, box 43, file Bro to Byr.

59 Nielson, *Armed Forces on a Northern Frontier*, 165; Brown to Marshall, 22 May 1943, NARA, RG165, OCS, box 43, file Bro to Byr; Lieutenant General L.J. McNair to Deputy Chief of Staff, "Major General A.E. Brown, formerly 7th Division," 2 June 1943, NARA, RG165, OCS, box 43, file Bro to Byr; D. Colt Denfeld, "The Battle of Attu," in *Builders and Engineers: U.S. Army Engineers in World War II*, ed. Barry W. Fowle (Fort Belvoir: United States Army Corps of Engineers, 1992), 371-2; and James Stokesbury, "Battle of Attu," *American History Illustrated* 14 (April 1979): 37. The claim that Brown acquiesced in his removal is found in Wheeler, *Kinkaid of the Seventh Fleet*, 327; and DeWitt to Marshall, 18 May 1943, NHC, Nimitz Papers, series XIII, folder 20.

Chapter 6: A Strong Alaska Means a Foot-Loose Fleet

1 Carl von Clausewitz, *On War* (Princeton: Princeton University Press, 1984), 548.

2 Handy to Marshall, "Personal Letter Dated 1 April, 1943 from General DeWitt to General Marshall Concerning Offensives in the Aleutians," 6 April 1943, National Archives and Records Administration (hereinafter NARA), RG165, file OPD 381 Security; Office of the Director of Plans and Operations (hereinafter OPD) memorandum, "Western Defense Command," 1 May 1943, NARA, RG165, Exec. file 6, item 13; and Kinkaid to Nimitz and DeWitt, tel. 192345, 19 May 1943, NARA, RG38, Chart Room Records, box 91, file Aleutians 22 May to 30 June 1943.

3 Canadian Chiefs of Staff (hereinafter COS) minutes, 12th meeting, 12 May 1943, National Archives of Canada (hereinafter NAC), RG24, vol. 11963, file MS 4-1.

4 JCS, CCS 220, "Strategic Plan for the Defeat of Japan," 14 May 1943, NARA, RG218, JCS Geographic File 1942-1945, file CCS 381 Japan (8-25-42).

5 CCS minutes, 21 May 1943, NARA, RG218, Joint Chiefs of Staff (JCS) Decimal File 1942-1945, file CCS 334 Comb. Chiefs of Staff (5-19-43); Robert William Love Jr., "Ernest Joseph King," in *The Chiefs of Naval Operations*, ed. Love Jr. (Annapolis, MD: Naval Institute Press, 1980), 163; and JPS report, CCS 339/1, "Operations in the Pacific and Far East in 1943-44," 23 May 1943, NARA, RG218, JCS Geographic File 1942-1945, file CCS 381 Japan (8-25-42).

6 Evatt to Curtin, tel. E104, 22 May 1943, National Archives of Australia (hereinafter NAA), series A4764, Item 3; Love, "Ernest Joseph King," 163-4; J.R.M. Butler, ed. *Grand Strategy*, vol. 4, *August 1942-September 1943*, ed. Michael Howard (London: Her Majesty's Stationery Office, 1972), 450; and CCS

report, CCS 244/1, "Implementation of Assumed Basic Undertakings and Specific Operations for the Conduct of War 1943-1944," 25 May 1943, NARA, RG218, JSC Geographic File 1942-1945, file CCS 381 Japan (8-25-42).

7 Colonel T.J. Betts to Wedemeyer, "Kiska," 31 May 1943, NARA, RG165, OPD, file ABC 381 Japan (5-31-42).

8 OPD memorandum, "Western Defense Command," 1 May 1943, NARA, RG165, OPD, Exec. file 6, item 13.

9 Lieutenant General Joseph T. McNarney to Handy, "First Special Service Force," 7 October 1942, NARA, RG165, file OPD 451 Plough Project; Handy to McNarney, "First Special Service Force," 12 October 1942, NARA, RG165, file OPD 451 Plough Project; and Handy to Marshall, "Employment of First Special Service Force," 14 October 1942, NARA, RG165, file OPD 451 Plough Project. See also Robert D. Burhans, *The First Special Service Force: A War History of the North Americans 1942-1944* (Washington, DC: Infantry Journal Press, 1947); R.H. Adleman and G. Walton, *The Devil's Brigade* (Philadelphia: Chilton Books, 1966); and Alastair Neely, "The First Special Service Force," in *Alaska at War, 1941-1945: The Forgotten War Remembered – Papers from the Alaska at War Symposium, Anchorage, Alaska, November 11-13, 1993*, ed. Fern Chandonnet (Anchorage: Alaska at War Committee, 1995), 87-95.

10 Colonel Robert T. Frederick to Handy, "First Special Service Force," 3 February 1943, NARA, RG165, file OPD 322.9 1st Special Service Force; Brigadier John R. Deane to the British COS, "Message to British Chiefs of Staff re operation against Kiska," 8 June 1943, NARA, RG218, JCS Geographic File 1942-1945, file CCS 381 North Pacific Area (6-13-42).

11 "General Staff Report on Greenlight Force Period From Inception to Despatch to Adak," July 1943, NAC, RG24, vol. 2921, file HQS 9055-1; and Major General George Pearkes to Stuart, 20 April 1943, Directorate of History and Heritage (hereinafter DHH), Kardex File 322.009 (D490). Pearkes had been relieved of command of the First Canadian Division on August 1942. According to McNaughton it was not "for inefficiency or anything," but because Ottawa had asked him to head Pacific Command. However, General Bernard Law Montgomery had judged Pearkes "unfit to command a Division in the field; admittedly he was "a gallant soldier without doubt" and "would fight his Division bravely till the last man was killed; but he has no brains and the last man would be killed all too soon"; Reginald H. Roy, *For Most Conspicuous Bravery: A Biography of Major-General George R. Pearkes, V.C., through Two World Wars* (Vancouver: UBC Press, 1977), 174; and General Bernard Law Montgomery to General H.D.G. Crerar, 25 April and 13 May 1942, NAC, H.D.G. Crerar Papers, vol. 2, file 958C.009 (D182).

12 Pope to Stuart, tel. CAW305, 10 May 1943, NAC, RG24, vol. 2919, file HQS 9055(1); and Hickerson to Embick, 11 May 1943, NARA, Department of State Records, Permanent Joint Board on Defense, RG59, box 10.

13 Cooke to King, 15 May 1943, Naval Historical Center (hereinafter NHC), SPD, series XII, box 175; and King to Marshall, 19 May 1943, NARA, RG165, file OPD 336 Security.

14 Hull to Marshall, "Canadian Troops in Aleutian Operations," 27 May 1943, NARA, RG165, file OPD 336 Security; Hull to DeWitt, tel. 3452, 21 May 1943, NARA, RG165, file OPD 336 Security; DeWitt to Marshall, tel. A-75DSH, 22 May 1943, NARA, RG38, Chart Room, box 91; and DeWitt to Marshall, tel. A-82DSH, 23 May 1943, NARA, RG165, file OPD 336 Security.

15 McNarney to Pope, 27 May 1943, NARA, RG165, OPD 336 Security; and DeWitt to Buckner and Pearkes, 27 May 1943, DHH, Kardex File 322.009 (D490).

16 McNarney to King, "Participation of Canadian Troops in Aleutian Operations," 27 May 1943, NARA, RG165, file OPD 336 Security; Edwards to Marshall, "Participation of Canadian Troops in Aleutian Operations," 31 May 1943, NHC, SPD, series XII, box 176; and DeWitt-Hull telephone transcript, 30 May 1943, NARA, RG165, OPD, Exec. file 8, item 10.

17 Pearkes to Stuart, tel. PCO2616, 20 April 1943, DHH, Kardex File 322.009 (D490).

18 J.W. Pickersgill quoted in J.L. Granatstein, *The Generals: The Canadian Army's Senior Commanders in the Second World War* (Toronto: Stoddart, 1993), 207.

19 Pope to Stuart, tel. CAW305, 10 May 1943, NAC, RG24, vol. 2919, file HQS 9055(1); Stuart to Pearkes, tel. CGS464, 11 May 1943, DHH, Kardex File 322.009 (D490); Stuart to Pope, tel. CGS465, 11 May 1943, DHH, Kardex File 322.009 (D490); and Stuart to Pope, tel. CGS475, 12 May 1943, NAC, RG24, vol. 2919, file HQS 9055(1).

20 Maurice A. Pope, *Soldiers and Politicians: The Memoirs of Lt.-Gen. Maurice A. Pope* (Toronto: University of Toronto Press, 1962), 215; and Pope to Stuart, tel. CAW317, 13 May 1943, DHH, Kardex File 314.009 (D49).

21 Pearkes to Stuart, tel. PCO2020, 25 May 1943, DHH, Kardex File 322.009 (D490); and Stuart to J.L. Ralston, 26 May 1943, NAC, RG24, vol. 2919, file HQS 9055(1).

22 CWC minutes, 26 May 1943, NAC, RG2 7c; A.D.P. Heeney to Admiral Nelles, 18 May 1943, NAC, RG2, vol. 35, file C-30 1939-43; and diary entry, 26 May 1943, NAC, W.L.M. King Papers.

23 A.J. Miller, "The Functional Principle in Canada's External Relations," *International Journal* 35 (Spring 1980): 311.

24 Robertson to King, 2 March 1942, NAC, RG2, vol. 48, file D-19-A (1942); and Robertson to King, 27 May 1943, NAC, King Memoranda and Notes, vol. 348, file WWII Aleutians 1942-43.

25 Robertson to King, 22 December 1941, in *Documents on Canadian External Relations*, vol. 9, *1942-1943*, ed. John F. Hilliker (Ottawa: Department of External Affairs, 1980). 1125-31; Robertson to King, 27 May 1943, NAC, W.L.M. King Papers, Memoranda and Notes, vol. 348, file WWII Aleutians 1942-43; and Malcolm Macdonald to C.R. Attlee, "Notes on Developments in North-Western Canada," 7 April 1943, Durham University Archives, Malcolm Macdonald Papers, file 12/5/1-61. See also K.S. Coates and W.R. Morrison, *The Alaska Highway in World War II: The U.S. Army of Occupation in Canada's Northwest* (Toronto: University of Toronto Press, 1992).

26 CWC minutes, 27 May 1943, NAC, RG2 7c.

27 PWC minutes, 20 May 1943, Franklin Delano Roosevelt Library, Franklin Roosevelt Papers, Map Room Files, box 168.

28 Diary entry, 27 May 1943, NAC, W.L.M. King Papers.

29 Diary entry, 28 and 30 May 1943, NAC, W.L.M. King Papers.

30 McNarney to Pope, 27 May 1943, NARA, RG165, file OPD 336 Security; diary entries, 26 and 27 May 1943, NAC, Maurice Pope Papers, vol. 1; Pope to McNarney, 27 May 1943, DHH, Kardex File 314.009 (D49).

31 Stuart to Pope, tel. CGS586, 27 May 1943, DHH, Kardex File 314.009 (D49); Pope, *Soldiers and Politicians*, 217; and diary entry, 28 May 1943, NAC, Maurice Pope Papers, vol. 1.

32 Pope to Stuart, tel. CAW353, 28 May 1943, DHH, Kardex File 314.009 (D49); Stimson to Ralston, 29 May 1943, Kardex File 314.009 (D49).

33 Stuart to Ralston, 31 May 1943, NAC, RG24, vol. 2919, file HQS 9055(1); CWC minutes, 31 May 1943, NAC, RG2 7c; and Ralston to Stimson, 3 June 1943, NAC, RG24, vol. 2919, file HQS 9055(1). "Stubborn in the extreme," Ralston "suffered from the terrible inability to delegate authority, a failing that chained him to his desk and gradually sapped his strength – and judgment"; J.L. Granatstein, *Canada's War: The Politics of the Mackenzie King Government, 1939-1945* (Toronto: Oxford University Press, 1975), 106. The fight to control Greenlight Force is discussed in Galen Roger Perras, "Canada As a Military Partner: Alliance Politics and the Campaign to Recapture the Aleutian Island of Kiska," *The Journal of Military History* 56 (July 1992): 423-54.

34 Diary entry, 1 June 1943, NAC, Maurice Pope Papers, vol. 1; DeWitt-Hull telephone conversation transcript, 30 May 1943, NARA, RG165, OPD, Exec. file 8, item book 10; and DeWitt-Hull telephone conversation transcript, 31 May 1943, NARA, RG165, OPD, Exec. file 8, item book 10.

35 DeWitt to Marshall, tel. CG0502, 27 May 1943, George C. Marshall Library (hereinafter GCML), George C. Marshall Papers, box 64, folder 20; and DeWitt to Marshall, 31 May 1943, GCLM, George C. Marshall Papers, box 64, folder 20.

36 DeWitt quoted in Michael S. Sherry, *In the Shadow of War: The United States since the 1930s* (New

Haven: Yale University Press, 1995), 64; diary entries, 8 and 13 December 1941 and 9 January 1942, in Theodore H. White, ed., *The Stilwell Papers* (New York: William Sloane Associates, 1948), 3, 5, and 23; Forrest C. Pogue, *George C. Marshall: Organizer of Victory, 1942-1945* (New York: Viking Press, 1973), 140; and Marshall to DeWitt, 8 June 1943, GCLM, George C. Marshall Papers, box 64, folder 20.

37 DeWitt and Nimitz to King and Marshall, tel. 292248, 30 May 1943, attached as Enclosure A to JCS 346, "Operation 'Cottage,'" 3 June 1943, NARA, RG218, JCS Geographic File 1942-1945, file CCS North Pacific Area (6-13-42); Major General Charles Corlett to Kinkaid, 1 June 1943, NHC, Thomas C. Kinkaid Papers, box 8, file Aleutians Correspondence 1943.

38 Wedemeyer to Hull, "Seizure of Kiska," 31 May 1943, NARA, RG165, OPD, file ABC 381 Japan (5-31-42); Wedemeyer to Hull, "Seizure of Kiska," 3 June 1943, NARA, RG165, OPD, file ABC 381 Japan (5-31-42); and Major General Muir S. Fairchild to Wedemeyer, 2 June 1943, NARA, RG165, OPD, file ABC 381 Japan (5-31-42).

39 Mark A. Stoler, *Allies and Adversaries: The Joint Chiefs of Staff, the Grand Alliance, and U.S. Strategy in World War II* (Chapel Hill: University of North Carolina Press, 2000), 104-8; and Brian L. Villa, "The U.S. Army, Unconditional Surrender, and the Potsdam Proclamation," *Journal of Military History* 63 (June 1976), 69.

40 JCS minutes, 91st meeting, 8 June 1943, NARA, RG218, JCS Decimal File 1942-1945, file CCS 334 JCS (5-21-42); Colonel John C. Blizzard to Handy, "Seizure of Kiska," 10 June 1943, NARA, RG165, OPD, file ABC 381 Japan (5-21-42); and JPS to JCS, JCS 346/2, "Operation Cottage," 11 June 1943, NARA, RG218, JCS Geographic File 1942-1945, file CCS 381 North Pacific Area (6-13-42).

41 General Order 58, "Assignment of units to Amphibian Training Force 9," 16 June 1943, NARA, RG407, Adjutant General's Office (hereinafter AGO), American Theater, file 91-TF2-0.3; Headquarters ATF9, "Composition of ATF No. 9," 21 June 1943, NARA, RG407, AGO, American Theater, file 91-TF2-0.3; and Rockwell, "Training Plan No. 4-49," 21 June 1943, NARA, RG407, AGO, American Theater, file 91-TF2-0.3.

42 Nimitz to Kinkaid, 2 June 1943, NHC, Kinkaid Papers, box 8, file Aleutians Correspondence 1943; Kinkaid to Nimitz, 11 June 1943, NHC, Kinkaid Papers, box 8, file Aleutians Correspondence 1943; and Buckner to War Department, "Garrison Ceiling, Alaska Defense Command," 18 June 1943, NARA, RG165, file OPD 320.2 ADC.

43 JIC 116, "Japanese Intentions," 25 June 1943, NARA, RG218, JCS Geographic File 1942-1945, file CCS 381 Japan (4-23-42); JIC 115, "Japanese Reactions to Certain Operations," 19 June 1943, NARA, RG218, JCS Geographic File 1942-1945, file CCS 381 Japan (4-23-42); CCS, "Memorandum for Information No. 110" containing CIC report, "Japanese Intentions," 5 July 1943, NARA, RG218, JCS Geographic File 1942-1945, file CCS 381 Japan (4-23-42); Weckerling, "A Study of Enemy Defensive Installations on Kiska Island As Known 5 July 1943," 5 July 1943, NARA, RG407, AGO, American Theater, file 91-DC4-2.18; and Pearkes to General H.F.G. Letson, tel. PCA1038, 10 July 1943, DHH, Kardex File 322.009 (D497).

44 Field Headquarters Eleventh Air Force, "Kiska Special Report," 17 August 1943, DHH, Kardex File 181.009 (D2756); "An Outline History of the Eleventh Air Force 15 Jan 42 to 31 Dec 43," 30 January 1944, Air Force History Support Office, Eleventh Air Force Records, reel A4214; Jonathan M. Nielson, *Armed Forces on a Northern Frontier: The Military in Alaska's History, 1867-1987* (Westport, CT: Greenwood Press, 1988), 144; "The Aleutian Campaign June 1942-August 1943," NHC, Combat Narratives, 117-22; Samuel Eliot Morison, *History of United States Naval Operations in World War II*, vol. 7, *Aleutians, Gilberts and Marshalls June 1942-April 1944* (Boston: Little, Brown and Company, 1951), 55-7; and "The Diary of Takahashi," *United States Naval Institute Proceedings* 106 (July 1980): 75.

45 Charles H. Corlett, *Cowboy Pete: The Autobiography of Major General Charles Corlett* (Santa Fe: Sleeping Fox, 1974), 64; First Special Service Force, "Field Order No. 5," 8 August 1943, DHH, Kardex File 595.013 (D2); Headquarters Landing Group 16.8, "Field Order Number 1," 1 August 1943, NARA, RG407, AGO, American Theater, file 91-TF2-0.3; Task Force 16, "Operation Plan no. 6-43," 6 August

1943, NARA, RG407, AGO, American Theater, file 91-TF2-0.3; General Paul D. Adams Oral History, undated, Military History Institute Archives (hereinafter MHI), Paul D. Adams Papers, folder Oral History Section 1; Kinkaid to Nimitz and DeWitt, tel. 030915, 3 August 1943, NARA, RG38, Chart Room, box 92; Marshall to DeWitt, no. 3946, 7 August 1943, in *The Papers of George C. Marshall*, ed. Larry I. Bland and Sharon Ritenour Stevens, vol. 4, *Aggressive and Determined Leadership, June 1, 1943-December 31, 1944* (Baltimore: Johns Hopkins University Press, 1996), 83; and Nimitz to Kinkaid, tel. 032211, 4 August 1943, NARA, RG38, Chart Room, box 92, file Aleutians.

46 Unknown source on Kiska to Kinkaid, tels. 152145 and 160911, 15 August 1943, DHH, Kardex file 322.009 (D878); Verbeck, "G-2 report," 16 August 1943, NARA, RG338, Alaskan Department, box 4; and Major S.E. Shoemaker, "S-2 periodic report," 18 August 1943, DHH, Kardex File 595.103 (D2).

47 Edward J. Drea, *In the Service of the Emperor: Essays on the Imperial Japanese Army* (Lincoln: University of Nebraska Press, 1998), 190; and Herbert P. Bix, *Hirohito and the Making of Modern Japan* (New York: Perennial, 2001), 464.

48 Masatake Chiyaya, "Mysterious Withdrawal from Kiska," *United States Naval Institute Proceedings* 84 (February 1958): 34-5; and "The Employment of Mobile Radio Intelligence Units by Commands Afloat during World War II," in *Listening to the Enemy: Key Documents on the Role of Communications Intelligence in the War with Japan*, ed. Ronald H. Spector (Wilmington: Scholarly Resources Inc., 1988), 83. Some Japanese submarines could carry ninety tons of cargo or several dozen passengers; Mark P. Parillo, *The Japanese Merchant Marine in World War II* (Annapolis, MD: Naval Institute Press, 1993), 175-6.

49 Chiyaya, "Mysterious Withdrawal from Kiska," 39-45; interrogation of Vice Admiral Omori, in United States Strategic Bombing Survey (Pacific) (USSBS), *Interrogations of Japanese Officials*, vol. 2 (Washington, DC: Government Printing Office, 1946), 306-7; interrogation of Commander Okumiya Masatake, in USSBS, *Interrogations of Japanese Officials*, vol. 1 (Washington, DC: Government Printing Office, 1946), 100-1; and Karl Kaoru Kasukabe, "The Escape of the Japanese Garrison from Kiska," in *Alaska at War, 1941-1945: The Forgotten War Remembered – Papers from the Alaska at War Symposium, Anchorage, Alaska, November 11-13, 1993*, ed. Fern Chandonnet (Anchorage: Alaska at War Committee, 1995), 121-3.

50 Entry for 25 July 1943, NHC, CINCPAC Command Summary; "The Employment of Mobile Radio," *Listening to the Enemy*, 83-4; Verbeck, "G-2 report," 24 July 1943, NARA, RG338, Alaskan Department, box 4; and Rear Admiral Bruce McCandless, "The Battle of the Pips," *United States Naval Institute Proceedings* 84 (January 1958): 50.

51 McCandless, "The Battle of the Pips," 51-6; and Morison, *History of United States Naval Operations in World War II*, vol. 7, *Aleutians, Gilberts and Marshalls*, 58-60. According to Garfield, a fishing boat captain had told him massive flocks of seabirds often showed up as single radar blips that appeared and disappeared as the birds took off and landed on the sea; Brian Garfield, "The Thousand-Mile War: World War II in Alaska and the Aleutians," in *Alaska at War, 1941-1945: The Forgotten War Remembered – Papers from the Alaska at War Symposium, Anchorage, Alaska, November 11-13, 1993*, ed. Fern Chandonnet (Anchorage: Alaska at War Committee, 1995), 31-2.

52 Nimitz to Kinkaid, 25 July 1943, NHC, Kinkaid Papers, box 8, file Aleutians Correspondence 1943; and Lt. Colonel H. McD. Brown to Colonel S.P. Collins, "Developments in the North Pacific," 19 August 1943, NARA, RG165, Military Intelligence Division Correspondence (hereinafter MID) 1922-44, file Alaska 9185.

53 "US Army-Navy Daily Intelligence Report No. 129," 4 August 1943, DHH, Kardex File 181.003 (D242); "S-2 Periodic Report No. 56," 5 August 1943, DHH, Kardex File 595.013 (D2); Headquarters First Special Service Force, "Periodic Report No. 1," 11 August 1943, DHH, Kardex File 595.013 (D2); "S-2 Periodic Report No. 57," 12 August 1943, DHH, Kardex File 595.013 (D2); "Western Air Command Weekly Intelligence Report Series No. 82," 12 August 1943, DHH, Kardex File 322.009 (D716); "US Army-Navy Daily Intelligence Report No. 140," 15 August 1943, DHH, Kardex File 181.003 (D242); Kinkaid

telegram, tel. 120953, 12 August 1943, NARA, RG38, Chart Room, box 92; diary entry, 8 August 1943, Black Family private papers, J.L. Black Diary; and Lieutenant Finn W. Roll SSF, "S-2 Estimate of the Enemy Situation," 12 August 1943, Hoover Institution on War, Revolution, and Peace (hereinafter HI), Robert D. Burhans Papers, vol. 1, file Telegrams Sent and Received at Amchitka.

54 H.M. Smith to the Commandant U.S. Marine Corps, "War Diary, Forward Echelon, Amphibious Corps, Pacific Fleet; Operations against Kiska," 27 October 1943, Marine Corps Historical Center (hereinafter MCHC), Marine Corps Records, Reference Section, file Alaska; and General Graves B. Erskine Oral History, 1975, MCHC, 298 and 305.

55 Lieutenant General John C. McQueen Oral History, 1973, MCHC, 72; and "War Journal of Forward Echelon, Amphibious Corps, Pacific Fleet; Operations for the Occupation of Kiska," 24 October 1943, NARA, United States Marine Corps Records, RG127, Geographic Area Files, Box 1, file A3-1.

56 Holland M. Smith and Percy Finch, *Coral and Brass* (Washington, DC: Zenger Publishing, 1948), 106; Kinkaid to Nimitz, 24 August 1943, NHC, Kinkaid Papers, box 8, file Aleutians Correspondence 1943; Major France Q. Wilson to Assistant Chief of Air Staff Plans, "Possible Partial Evacuation of Kiska by Japanese with Establishment of Such Forces on Adjacent Islands in the Western Aleutians and Possibility of Enemy Occupation of Russian Komandorskis," 14 August 1943, NARA, RG165, MID 1922-44, file Alaska 9185; and JCS minutes, 107th meeting, 14 August 1943, NARA, RG218, JCS Decimal File 1942-1945, file CCS 334 Comb. Chiefs of Staff (5-19-43).

57 Smith and Finch, *Coral and Brass*, 21; and Mack Oral History, Naval History Institute Library, 133.

58 Erskine Oral History, MCHC, 302.

59 "Interview with Ben C. Grey of Ottawa, Canada," 16 August 1963, HI, Robert Adleman Papers, vol. 12, file Interviews, and Lieutenant Colonel Charles R. Shrader, *Amicide: The Problem of Friendly Fire in Modern War* (Fort Leavenworth: United States Army Command and General Staff College, 1982), 91. Despite the fact far more Americans fell victim to mines and booby traps, Corlett argued the Canadians "apparently had not been well trained in the subject of booby traps ... Our men who had been very thoroughly instructed on these dangers were not hurt"; Charles H. Corlett manuscript, *One Man's Story: Some of It about War*, 1948, Charles H. Corlett Papers, MHI.

60 Captain Norman F. Fontes, "G-1 Report of Headquarters Amphibian Training Force 9 of Kiska Operation," undated (late 1943), NARA, RG407, AGO, American Theater, file 91-TF2-0.3; and Kenneth A. Ward report, undated (late 1943),NARA, RG407, AGO, American Theater, file 91-TF2-0.3.

61 Advanced Command Post Headquarters Alaska Defense Command, "Enemy on Kiska," undated (late 1943), DHH, Kardex File 595.023 (D1); and DeWitt quoted in USN Publications Branch, "The ONI Weekly," 25 August 1943, DHH, Kardex File 112.3M1013 (D6). Major Black had been told that ATF9 might suffer 10,000 casualties. Black diary, 14 June 1943.

Chapter 7: We Have Opened the Door to Tokyo

1 Carl von Clausewitz, *On War* (Princeton: Princeton University Press, 1984), 526.

2 "Extract from Air Intelligence Summary No. 132," 25 August 1943, Australian War Memorial, Defence Committee Records, series AWM123, item [334] F/2.

3 Brian Garfield, *The Thousand-Mile War: World War II in Alaska and the Aleutians* (New York: Bantam Books, 1969), 198.

4 DeWitt to Marshall, 27 and 28 August 1943, National Archives and Records Administration (hereinafter NARA), RG165, Office of the Director of Plans and Operations (hereinafter OPD), Exec. file 9, book 11.

5 JPS 67/5, "Strategic Plan for the Defeat of Japan," 26 May 1943, NARA, RG218, JCS Geographic File 1942-1945, file CCS Japan (8-25-42).

6 John Haile Cloe, *The Aleutian Warriors: A History of the 11th Air Force and Fleet Wing 4* (Missoula, MT: Pictorial Histories, 1990), 303-10; "The O.N.I. Weekly," 21 July 1943, Directorate of History and Heritage, Kardex File 112.3M1013 (D6); and Harry L. Coles, "The Aleutian Campaign," in *The Army Air*

Forces in World War II, ed. Wesley Frank Craven and James Lea Cate, vol. 4, The Pacific: Guadalcanal to Saipan August 1942 to July 1944 (Chicago: University of Chicago Press, 1983), 396-9. All Kurile raids are described in William A. Herold, History of the XI Bomber Command. Eleventh Air Force. Shemya Island, Alaska, 19 March 1943-31 March 1944, (1944), 15-21, Albert F. Simpson Historical Research Center, Maxwell Air Force Base.

7 DeWitt to Marshall, "Plan for Suggested Offensive Operations on the Northwestern Pacific," 30 July 1943, NARA, RG218, JCS Geographic File 1942-1945, file CCS 381 Northwestern Pacific Area (7-30-43).

8 John Ray Skates, The Invasion of Japan: Alternative to the Bomb (Columbia, SC: University of South Carolina Press, 1994), 34; Nimitz to Kinkaid, 25 July 1943, Naval Historical Center (hereinafter NHC), C.W. Nimitz Papers, series XIII, folder 20; Kinkaid to Nimitz, tels. 3100915 and 031115, 2 and 3 August 1943, NARA, RG38, Chart Room, box 92; and diary entry, 20 August 1943, Amherst College Archives, John McCloy Papers, box DY5, folder 25.

9 SPD, "Should the Objective of the Cottage Operation Be Switched to Paramushiru?" 5 August 1943, NHC, SPD, series XII, box 175; JPS, JCS 446, "Specific Operations in the Pacific and Far East, 1943-44," 6 August 1943, NARA, RG218, JCS Geographic File 1942-1945, file CCS 381 Japan (8-25-42); CPS 83, "Appreciation and Plan for the Defeat of Japan," 8 August 1943, NARA, RG218, JCS Geographic File 1942-1945, file CCS 381 Japan (8-25-42); and JCS to CCS, CCS 301, "Specific Operations in the Pacific and Far East, 1943-44," 9 August 1943, 8 August 1943, NARA, RG218, JCS Geographic File 1942-1945, file CCS 381 Japan (8-25-42).

10 JCS minutes, 107th meeting, 14 August 1943, NARA, RG218, Joint Chiefs of Staff (JCS) Decimal File 1942-1945, file CCS 334 (5-19-43); and Marshall to DeWitt, 14 August 1943, NARA, RG165, OPD, file ABC 384 Northwestern Pacific 16 Aug 43.

11 King to Hanson Baldwin, 12 June 1950, Hoover Institution on War, Revolution, and Peace (hereinafter HI), Charles M. Cooke Papers, vol. 4, file King Fleet Admiral Ernest J.; CPS to CCS, CPS 83, "Appreciation and Plan for the Defeat of Japan," 8 August 1943, enclosure to CCS 313, 18 August 1943, JCS Records, Part I: 1942-45, Pacific Theater, reel 4, University Publications of America (hereinafter UPA); and JCS minutes, 108th meeting, 19 August 1943, NARA, RG218, JCS Decimal File 1942-1945, file CCS 334 (8-7-43).

12 OPD, "Implications of the Immediate Movement of the 7th Division," 20 August 1943, NARA, RG165, OPD, file ABC 320.2 Alaska 15 Aug 43; and Hull to the Adjutant General, "Garrison Ceiling, Alaska Defense Command," 30 August 1943, NARA, RG165, OPD, file ABC 320.2 Alaska 15 Aug 43.

13 AAF planners, CCS 323, "Air Plan for the Defeat of Japan," 20 August 1943, NARA, RG218, JCS Geographic File 1942-1945, file CCS Japan 373.11 (8-20-43); Colonel M.A. Libby to Arnold, "Relief of Units From Alaska," 26 August 1943, Library of Congress (hereinafter LC), H.H. Arnold Papers, box 84, file 320.2 Alaska.

14 JPS minutes, 98th meeting, 1 September 1943, NARA, RG165, OPD, file ABC 384 Northwestern Pacific 16 Aug 43; Marshall quoted in Larry I. Bland, ed., George C. Marshall: Interviews and Reminiscences for Forrest C. Pogue (Lexington: George C. Marshall Research Foundation, 1991), 381-2; and JCS minutes, 113th meeting, 7 September 1943, NARA, RG218, JCS Decimal File 1942-1945, file CCS 334 (8-7-43).

15 Buckner quoted in Jonathan M. Nielson, Armed Forces on a Northern Frontier: The Military in Alaska's History, 1867-1987 (Westport, CT: Greenwood Press, 1988), 166; JPS minutes, 101st meeting, 15 September 1943, NARA, RG218, JCS Decimal File 1942-1945, file CCS 334 (3-24-43); JPS minutes, 102nd meeting, 20 September 1943, NARA, RG218, JCS Decimal File 1942-1945, file CCS 334 (3-24-43); and Nimitz to Kinkaid, "Directive for Preparation of Plans for Advance upon Kurile Islands," 21 September 1943, "Command History North Pacific Force" 14 August 1945, NHC, Combat Narratives.

16 Admiral John W. Reeves memorandum, 20 September 1943, attached to JPS minutes, 102nd meeting, NARA, RG218, JCS Decimal File 1942-1945, file CCS 334 (3-24-43).

17 Mark A. Stoler, Allies and Adversaries: The Joint Chiefs of Staff, the Grand Alliance, and U.S. Strategy in World War II (Chapel Hill: University of North Carolina Press, 2000), 105.

18 JPS, JCS 474/1, "Garrisons in Alaska," 21 September 1943, NARA, JSC Geographic File 1942-1945, file CCS 320.2 Japan (2-4-43).

19 Ibid.; and Grace Person Hayes, *The History of the Joint Chiefs of Staff in World War II: The War against Japan* (Annapolis, MD: Naval Institute Press, 1982), 484.

20 JSSC, JSC 474/2, "Garrisons in Alaska," 21 September 1943, NARA, RG218, JCS Geographic File 1942-1945, file 320.2 Japan (2-4-43); JCS minutes, 115th meeting, 21 September 1943, NARA, RG218, JCS Geographic File 1942-1945, file CCS 334 (9-14-34); JCS minutes, 116th meeting, 28 September 1943, NARA, RG218, JCS Geographic File 1942-1945, file CCS 334 (9-14-34); and JCS minutes, 117th meeting, 5 October 1943, NARA, RG218, JCS Geographic File 1942-1945, file CCS 334 (9-14-34).

21 Hayes, *History of the Joint Chiefs of Staff*, 486.

22 JWPC, "Operations against Paramushiru and the Kuriles," 30 September 1943, NARA, RG218, JCS Geographic File 1942-1945, file CCS 381 Northwestern Pacific Area (7-30-43).

23 Hayes, *History of the Joint Chiefs of Staff*, 486; JPS 291, "Operations against Paramushiru and the Kuriles," 15 October 1943, UPA, reel 10; and JPS 288, "Plans for the Defeat of Japan within 12 Months after the Defeat of Germany," 4 October 1943, NARA, RG218, JCS Geographic File 1942-1945, file CCS 381 Japan (8-25-42).

24 Marshall to Buckner, 8 November 1943, NHC, SPD, series XII, box 164; and McNarney to King, "Advance into the Northern Kuriles," 12 November 1943, NHC, SPD, series XII, box 164.

25 JPS, JCS 581, "Specific Operations for the Defeat of Japan, 1944," 9 November 1943, UPA, reel 3; JPS, JCS 581/1, "Specific Operations for the Defeat of Japan, 1944," 16 November 1943, UPA, reel 3; JPS, JCS 581/2, "Specific Operations for the Defeat of Japan, 1944," 3 December 1943, UPA, reel 3; CSP, CCS 417, "Overall Plan for the Defeat of Japan," 2 December 1943, NARA, RG218, JCS Geographic File 1942-1945, file 381 Japan (8-25-42); and JWPC 297, "Operations in the North Pacific," 20 November 1943, UPA, reel 10.

26 Richard B. Frank, *Downfall: The End of the Imperial Japanese Empire* (New York: Penguin Books, 2001), 123-8.

27 Maurice Matloff, *Strategic Planning for Coalition Warfare 1943-1944* (Washington, DC: Department of the Army, 1959), 374-5; King quoted in Christopher Thorne, *Allies of a Kind: The United States, Britain, and the War against Japan, 1941-1945* (Oxford: Oxford University Press, 1978), 295-6; and Handy quoted in Matloff, *Strategic Planning for Coalition Warfare 1943-1944*, 375.

28 CCS 407 (Revised), "Collaboration with the U.S.S.R.," 26 November 1943, in Department of State, *Foreign Relations of the United States: The Conferences at Cairo and Tehran 1943* (Washington, DC: Government Printing Office, 1961), 426-8; A. Clark Kerr to FO, no. 337, 24 November 1942, Public Records Office (hereinafter PRO), FO Japan, FO371/31847; and Roosevelt-Stalin meeting minutes, 29 November 1943, *Foreign Relations of the United States: The Conferences at Cairo and Tehran 1943*, 529-32.

29 Quoted in Marc Gallicchio, "The Kuriles Controversy: U.S. Diplomacy in the Soviet-Japan Border Dispute, 1941-1956," *Pacific Historical Review* 60 (January 1991): 75.

30 George Alexander Lensen, *The Strange Neutrality: Soviet-Japanese Relations during the Second World War 1941-1945* (Tallahassee: Diplomatic Press, 1972), 10-11.

31 Sumner Welles, *Seven Decisions That Shaped History* (New York: Harper and Brothers, 1950), 153 and 162-3; Sumner Welles, *Where Are We Heading?* (New York: Harper and Brothers, 1946), 299; Charles Bohlen, *Witness to History, 1929-1969* (New York: Norton, 1973), 195-8; Gallicchio, "The Kuriles Controversy," 73; and PWC minutes, 36th meeting, 12 January 1944, Franklin Delano Roosevelt Library, Roosevelt Papers, Map Room Files, box 168 (my emphasis).

32 Australian Legation Washington, DC, to Department of External Affairs Canberra, tel. 32, 12 January 1944, National Archives of Australia (hereinafter NAA), Correspondence Files of the Australian Legation, United States, series A3300/7, item 265; and JWPC, "Operations against Paramushiru and the Kuriles," 30 September 1943, NARA, RG218, JCS Geographic File 1942-1945, file CCS 381 Northwestern Pacific Area (7-30-43).

33 Benjamin Welles, *Sumner Welles: FDR's Global Strategist* (New York: St. Martin's Press, 1997), 328.

34 Post-War Foreign Policy Advisory Committee minutes, 12 August 1942, HI, Stanley K. Hornbeck Papers, vol. 350, file Post-War Foreign Policy Advisory Committee; and Akira Iriye, *Power and Culture: The Japanese-American War, 1941-1945* (Cambridge: Harvard University Press, 1981), 60 and 134.

35 Iriye, *Power and Culture*, 150.

36 Minutes of the Security and Territorial Subcommittee, 16 July 1943, LC, Cordell Hull Papers, box 85, file Postwar Planning – General; and George E. Blakeslee, CAC-302, "Japan: Territorial Problems: The Kurile Islands," 28 December 1944, in Department of State, *Foreign Relations of the United States: The Conferences at Malta and Yalta 1945* (Washington, DC: Government Printing Office, 1955), 379-83.

37 MAGIC Summary No. 419, 19 May 1943, UPA, reel 5; Weinberg, *A World at Arms*, 634; and Iriye, *Power and Culture*, 222-3.

38 Frank, *Downfall*, 90.

39 Roosevelt tended to ignore the State Department's "professional priesthood" of faceless bureaucrats; Warren F. Kimball, *Forged in War: Roosevelt, Churchill, and the Second World War* (New York: William Morrow and Company, 1997), 36-7. The department thus drifted on "without direction, composed of a lot of busy people working hard and usefully but as a whole not functioning as a Foreign Office. It did not chart a course to be furthered by the success of our arms, or to aid or guide our arms. Rather it seemed to be adrift, carried hither and yon by the currents of war or pushed about by collisions with more purposeful craft"; Dean Acheson, *Present at the Creation* (New York: W.W. Norton, 1969), 38.

40 Marshall to King, 23 October 1944, George C. Marshall Library, George C. Marshall Papers, box 73, file 73/28; and JCS, CCS 417/3, "Over-All Objective in the War against Japan," 11 July 1944, NARA, RG218, JCS Geographic File 1942-1945, file CCS 381 Pacific Ocean Area (6-10-43). E.B. Potter recounts the cribbage board story in *Nimitz* (Annapolis, MD: Naval Institute Press, 1976), 246.

41 JPS 562, "Operations in the North Pacific," 23 November 1944, UPA, reel 3; and JIC 231/1, "Estimate of the Situation in the Northwestern Pacific Area, Spring 1945," 7 November 1944, UPA, reel 10.

42 Cooke to Marshall, "JCS973," 30 July 1944, and Cooke to King, "Kurile Operations," 6 December 1944, HI, Cooke Papers, vol. 22, file Military Operations and Planning Pacific Theater; and King to JCS, JCS 924, "Operations against Japan Subsequent to Formosa," 11 July 1944, NARA, RG218, JCS Geographic File 1942-1945, file CCS 381 Pacific Ocean Area (6-10-43). King's battle with MacArthur over Formosa is described in Hayes, *History of the Joint Chiefs of Staff*, 603-24; and Robert Ross Smith, "Luzon versus Formosa," in *Command Decisions*, ed. Kent Roberts Greenfield (Washington, DC: Office of the Army, 1960), 461-77.

43 King to JCS, JCS 1176/2, "Operations in the Kuriles," 11 December 1944, UPA, reel 3.

44 Diary entry, 20 January 1945, National Archives of Canada (hereinafter NAC), Maurice Pope Papers, vol. 1; Nimitz to King, "Future Operations – North Pacific," 10 December 1944, UPA, reel 3; and JPS 1176/4, "Suitability and Feasibility of Operations in the Kuriles-Kamchatka Area," 6 January 1945, UPA, reel 3.

45 JPS, Enclosure A to JCS 1176/6, "Russian Participation in the War against Japan," 18 January 1945, in *FRUS: The Conferences at Malta and Yalta*, 388-93; JCS to CCS, CCS 417/11, "Operations for the Defeat of Japan," 22 January 1945, in *FRUS*, 395-6; and JCS to Roosevelt, 23 January 1945, in *FRUS*, 396-400.

46 W. Averell Harriman to Roosevelt, 15 December 1944, in *FRUS: The Conferences at Malta and Yalta*, 378-9; "minutes of meeting held in the President's Sun Room, Livadia Palace," 4 February 1945, UPA, reel 2; 2nd tripartite meeting minutes and minutes of Roosevelt-Stalin meeting, 6 and 8 February 1945, in *FRUS: The Conferences at Malta and Yalta*, 650-1 and 768-9; Attachment 1, "Draft of Marshal Stalin's Political Conditions for Russia's Entry in the War against Japan," 10 February 1945, *FRUS: The Conferences at Malta and Yalta*, 896; and "Agreement Regarding Entry of the Soviet Union into the War against Japan," 11 February 1945, *FRUS: The Conferences at Malta and Yalta*, 984. Anthony Eden had told State Department officials that there was no need to offer the Soviets "a high price for their participation" in the war with Japan; FSM (Argonaut) 1st Meeting (Draft) minutes, 1 February 1945, PRO, PREM3/51/6.

47 Sumner Welles, *Seven Decisions That Shaped History* (New York: Harper and Brothers, 1950), 205.

48 King to Senator William F. Knowland, 21 June 1951, LC, Ernest J. King Papers, box 12; Acheson quoted in Athan G. Theoharis, *The Yalta Myths: An Issue in U.S. Politics, 1945-1955* (Columbia, MO: University of Missouri Press, 1970), 41-2; Churchill to F.M. Forde, no. D1170, 5 July 1945, NAA, Frederick Shedden Papers, series A5954, box 577; John Lewis Gaddis, *The United States and the Origins of the Cold War, 1941-1947* (New York: Columbia University Press, 1972), 79; Russell D. Buhite, *Decisions at Yalta: An Appraisal of Summit Diplomacy* (Wilmington: Scholarly Resources Inc., 1986), 101; Marc Gallicchio, *The Cold War Begins in Asia: American East Asian Policy and the Fall of the Japanese Empire* (New York: Columbia University Press, 1988), 2-3; and John J. Stephan, *The Kuril Islands: Russo-Japanese Frontier in the Pacific* (Oxford: Clarendon Press, 1974), 79. Beset by anaemia, upper respiratory infections, and high blood pressure, Roosevelt had been taking digitalis since 1943 to combat congestive heart failure. Reduced cerebral blood flow also engendered occasional forgetfulness; Kimball, *Forged in War*, 339-41; and Robert H. Ferrell, *The Dying President: Franklin D. Roosevelt 1944-1945* (Columbia, MO: University of Missouri Press, 1998).

49 Diary entry, 23 April 1945, Dwight D. Eisenhower Presidential Library, Simon Bolivar Buckner Jr. Papers, box 1; Michael S. Sherry, *Preparing for the Next War: American Plans for Postwar Defense, 1941-45* (New Haven: Yale University Press, 1977), 45; Stimson to President Harry S. Truman, 16 July 1945, in Department of State, *Foreign Relations of the United States: The Conference of Berlin (The Potsdam Conference) 1945*, vol. 2 (Washington, DC: Government Printing Office, 1960), 1322-3; and Gallicchio, "The Kuriles Controversy," 79. Stimson had said the same thing to Joseph Grew, the State Department's pre-eminent Japanese expert; Stimson to Grew, 21 May 1945, NARA, RG165, OPD, file ABC 336 Russia (22 August 43).

50 UK COS, "Plans for the Defeat of the Japan," COS (44) 123 (O), 5 February 1944, PRO, PREM3/160/7; PHPS, "Security of British Commonwealth and Empire Interests in South-East Asia and the Pacific," PHP (44) 6 (O) (Final), 31 January 1945, NAC, RG24, vol. 20347, file 952.013 (D69); PHPS, "Future of the Japanese Islands in the Pacific," PHP (45) 12 (O) (Final), 23 March 1945, NAC, RG24, vol. 20347, file 952.013 (D69); Illarion G. Matveev, "The Kuriles – Strategic Island Stepping-Stones Lying Athwart Northern Trade Routes," *Foreign Commerce Weekly* (30 October 1943): 11; and Colonel Charles Bonesteel marginal comments on "U.S. Position with Regard to General Soviet Intentions for Expansion," 6 July 1945, NARA, RG165, OPD, file ABC 092 USSR (15 November 44).

51 George A. Lincoln to Colonel Herman Beukema, 20 May 1945, United States Military Academy Archives (hereinafter MAA), George A. Lincoln Papers, box 3; and Lincoln memorandum, 4 July 1945, MAA, George A. Lincoln Papers, box 6; and minutes of the meeting of the United States and Soviet Chiefs of Staff, 26 July 1945, in *FRUS: The Conference of Berlin*, 410-11.

52 JWPC report, 264/8, 8 August 1945, NARA, RG218, JCS Geographic File 1942-1945, file 386.2 Japan (4-9-45); JCS to MacArthur, "General Order No. 1," 15 August 1945, MAA, Lincoln Papers, box 6; Gallicchio, "The Kuriles Controversy," 83-4; "Basic Outline Plan for 'Blacklist' Operations to Occupy Japan Proper and Korea after Surrender or Collapse," 8 August 1945, General Douglas MacArthur Foundation (hereinafter GDMF), RG4, reel 607; and CINCPAC, "Joint Staff Study Campus," 9 August 1945, GDMF, RG4, reel 607.

53 McCloy – Byrnes transcript, 11 August 1945, NARA, Records of the Secretary of War, RG107, files 385-387; and Gallicchio, "The Kuriles Controversy," 84-6.

54 Stalin to Truman, 17 August 1945, in Department of State, *Foreign Relations of the United States: 1945*, vol. 6 (Washington, DC: Government Printing Office, 1969), 667-8; Truman to Stalin, 17 August 1945, *Foreign Relations of the United States: 1945*, vol. 6, 670; Stalin to Truman, 18 August 1945, *Foreign Relations of the United States: 1945*, vol. 6, 670; and Byrnes to Truman plus attached message to Stalin, 25 August 1945, *Foreign Relations of the United States: 1945*, vol. 6, 692.

55 Quoted in Ronald H. Spector, *Eagle against the Sun: The American War with Japan* (New York: Vintage Books, 1985), 553.

56 The Americans trained over 12,000 Soviets in amphibious warfare techniques in 1945 and presented 149 vessels to the Soviet navy; Richard A. Russell, "The Hula Operation: The Top Secret Soviet-American Naval Lend-Lease Operation in Alaska in 1945," in *Alaska at War, 1941-1945: The Forgotten War Remembered – Papers from the Alaska at War Symposium, Anchorage, Alaska, November 11-13, 1993*, ed. Fern Chandonnet (Anchorage: Alaska at War Committee, 1995), 345-9. The Soviet invasion of the Kuriles is described in Stephan, *The Kuril Islands*, 158-69.

Chapter 8: Stepping Stones to Nowhere

1 "Extracts from Army-Navy Monthly Intelligence Summary," 5 October 1943, Directorate of History and Heritage (hereinafter DHH), Kardex File 181.003 (D242); ADC G-2 reports no. 74 and 77, 23 October and 13 November 1943, National Archives and Records Administration (hereinafter NARA), RG338, Alaskan Department, vol. 4.

2 Handy to the Adjutant General, "Establishment of Alaska Defense Command As a Separate Theater of Operations," 7 October 1943, NARA, RG165, file OPD 384 ADC; Jonathan M. Nielson, *Armed Forces on a Northern Frontier: The Military in Alaska's History, 1867-1987* (Westport, CT: Greenwood Press, 1988), 168; Claus-M. Naske and Herman E. Slotnick, *Alaska: A History of the 49th State* (Grand Rapids: William B. Eerdmans Publishing, 1987), 123; Brian Garfield, *The Thousand-Mile War: World War II in Alaska and the Aleutians* (New York: Bantam Books, 1969), 299; and Dean C. Allard, "The North Pacific Campaign in Perspective," in *Alaska at War, 1941-1945: The Forgotten War Remembered – Papers from the Alaska at War Symposium, Anchorage, Alaska, November 11-13, 1993*, ed. Fern Chandonnet (Anchorage: Alaska at War Committee, 1995), 9-10.

3 Theobald, "Operations of Diversion," 31 March 1942, Hoover Institution on War, Revolution, and Peace (hereinafter HI), Robert A. Theobald Papers, vol. 12, file War Estimates; JPS 67/5, "Strategic Plan for the Defeat of Japan," 26 May 1943, NARA, RG218, JCS Geographic File 1942-1945, file CCS 381 Japan (8-25-42); JCS minutes, 106th meeting, 17 August 1943, NARA, RG218, Joint Chiefs of Staff (JCS) Decimal File 1942-1945, file CCS 334 (8-7-42); JPS, JCS 498, "Overall Plan for Deception Measures against Japan in 1943-1944," 13 September 1943, University Publications of America (hereinafter UPA), JCS Records, reel 8; and JCS minutes, 114th meeting, 14 September 1943, NARA, RG218, JCS Decimal File 1942-1945, file CCS 334 (9-14-43).

4 Katherine L. Herbig, "American Strategic Deception in the Pacific, 1942-44," *Intelligence and National Security* 2 (July 1987): 264-5.

5 Handy to Buckner, "Directive for Deception Measures against Japan in 1943-44," 3 November 1943, NARA, RG165, Office of the Director of Plans and Operations (hereinafter OPD), file ABC 381 Alaska (15 Apr 43); Alaskan Department, AD-Japan-44, "Deception Measure against Japan," 9 January 1944; Nimitz to King, "Propaganda Plans for FORAGER," 22 March 1944, General Douglas MacArthur Foundation (hereinafter GDMF), RG4, reel 589; and Herbig, "American Strategic Deception in the Pacific," 266-72.

6 Stephan, *The Kuril Islands*, 133-42; Herbig, "American Strategic Deception in the Pacific," 274; and interrogation of Major Shimada Masuda, United States Strategic Bombing Survey (Pacific) (USSBS), *Interrogations of Japanese Officials*, vol. 2 (Washington, DC: Government Printing Office, 1946).

7 Herbert P. Bix, *Hirohito and the Making of Modern Japan* (New York: Perennial, 2001), 470 and 479; diary entry, 20 May 1944, in *Fading Victory: The Diary of Admiral Matome Ugaki 1941-1945*, ed. Donald M. Goldstein and Katherine V. Dillon (Pittsburgh: University of Pittsburgh Press, 1991), 374; and Herbig, "American Strategic Deception in the Pacific," 274.

8 Joint Security Control, JCS 705/2, "Report of Conference Regarding Plan 'Wedlock,'" 24 August 1943, UPA, JCS Records, reel, 8; and Herbig, "American Strategic Deception in the Pacific," 275-81 and 295.

9 Roosevelt quoted in Nielson, *Armed Forces on a Northern Frontier*, 168-9; Alvarez, *Secret Messages*, 220; John Haile Cloe, "The Legacy of War," in *Alaska at War, 1941-1945: The Forgotten War Remembered –*

Papers from the Alaska at War Symposium, Anchorage, Alaska, November 11-13, 1993, ed. Fern Chandonnet (Anchorage: Alaska at War Committee, 1995), 396; and John Haile Cloe and Michael F. Monoghan, *Top Cover for America: The Air Force in Alaska 1920-1983* (Missoula, MT: Pictorial Histories, 1984), 157.

10   Steven T. Ross, *American War Plans 1945-1950* (New York: Garland Publishing, 1988), 4-6.

11   JCS 1295/2, "An Outline Plan for the Military Development of Alaska," 21 December 1945, NARA, RG218, JCS Geographic File 1942-1945, file CCS 660.2 Alaska (3-25-45); and James F. Schnabel, *The History of the Joint Chiefs of Staff. The Joint Chiefs of Staff and National Policy,* vol. 1, *1945-1947* (Wilmington: Michael Glazier, 1979), 390-1.

12   Ross, *American War Plans,* 34-5; and Naske and Slotnick, *Alaska,* 124.

13   Hal M. Friedman, "The 'Bear' in the Pacific? US Intelligence Perceptions of Soviet Strategic Power Projection in the Pacific Basin and East Asia, 1945-1947," *Intelligence and National Security* 12 (October 1997): 82-3.

14   John Whitehead, "Alaska and Hawaii," in *The Cold War American West, 1945-1989,* ed. Kevin J. Fernlund (Albuquerque: University of New Mexico Press, 1998), 195; Lincoln to General Howard A. Craig, 28 February 1946, United States Military Academy Archives (hereinafter MAA), Lincoln Papers, box 7; and Lincoln to Strategic Plans Section, 16 July 1946, MAA, Lincoln Papers, box 7.

15   OP-30F to OP-30, "Summary of Conference Between Real Admiral Ralph Wood USN and Representatives of OP-30," 19 April 1946, Naval Historical Center (hereinafter NHC), SPD, series III, box 67; OP-30 to OP-03, "Alaskan Bases, Missions of," 19 April 1946, NHC, SPD, series III, box 67; and J.H. Towers to the Chief of Naval Operations (CNO), "Pacific Bases," 26 September 1946, NHC, SPD, series III, box 67.

16   Cloe, "The Legacy of War," 396-7; Ross, *American War Plans,* 45, 60-1, and 110-11; McNarney to JCS, "Analyses of Force Requirements for Budget Estimates," 2 November 1948, Harry S. Truman Presidential Library (hereinafter HST), Harry S. Truman Office Files 1945-1953, Part 2 Correspondence Files, file Bradley, Omar N.; Eisenhower quoted in Nielson, *Armed Forces on a Northern Frontier,* 184; William L. Worden, "One Division Could Take Alaska," *Collier's* (2 August 1947), 30-1 46, 48, and 52; Fergus Hoffman, "Unguarded Airfields Invite Enemy Capture of Alaska," *New York Journal-American,* 26 June 1949; and Gruening cited in "Defences in Alaska," *The Times of London,* 2 September 1949.

17   "Gen. Eisenhower on U.S. Defences," *The Times of London,* 3 April 1950; Preparedness Subcommittee of the Committee on Armed Services of the United States Senate, *Report of the Alaskan Task Force* (Washington, DC: Government Printing Office, 1951), iii and 30-1; and JCS, "Review of Current World Situation and Ability of Forces Being Maintained to Meet U.S. Commitments," 1952, HST, Truman Office Files Part 2, file Joint Chiefs of Staff 1952.

18   Lieutenant Colonel J.R. Davis and Lieutenant Colonel T.J. Ebbert, "The Aleutian Option," Center for Advanced Research, Naval War College, June 1983, Marine Corps Historical Center, Reference Branch, file PSOT and Stations – Alaska Adak; and Lael Morgan, "The Rise and Fall and Rise of Adak," *Washington Post,* 16 December 1972.

19   Masatake Chiyaya, "Mysterious Withdrawal from Kiska," *United States Naval Institute Proceedings* 84 (February 1958): 31-2. Estimates of Japanese fatalities inflicted by bombing range from 268,000 to 900,000; see Michael S. Sherry, *The Rise of American Air Power: The Creation of Armageddon* (New Haven: Yale University Press, 1987), 413n43.

20   Edward J. Drea, *In the Service of the Emperor: Essays on the Imperial Japanese Army* (Lincoln: University of Nebraska Press, 1998), 27; and David C. Evans and Mark R. Peattie, *Kaigun: Strategy, Tactics, and Technology in the Imperial Japanese Navy, 1887-1941* (Annapolis, MD: Naval Institute Press, 1997), 488-91. H.P. Willmott agrees with Drea, asserting that the IJN "did not understand the nature of war, specifically the nature of the war that it began in 1941. It did not understand the difference between war and a war, between a war and a campaign, between a campaign and a battle, and it did not understand that a war in the Pacific would involve a naval war – between fleets and formations and

endowed with an amphibious dimension – as well as a maritime war in defence of shipping. All its attention was geared to battle, an obsession that over time obscured the distinction between battle and the other elements that relate to the nature and conduct of war." H.P. Willmott, *The Second World War in the Far East* (London: Cassell, 2002), 58-9.

21 Coox, "Japanese Military Education and Planning before Pearl Harbor," 74.

22 Gruening quoted in Claus-M. Naske, "The Battle of Alaska Has Ended ... The Japs Won It," *Military Affairs* 49 (July 1985): 148. The tabulation of Japanese losses in the Aleutians comes from: John Haile Cloe, *The Aleutian Warriors: A History of the 11th Air Force and Fleet Wing 4* (Missoula, MT: Pictorial Histories, 1990), 322-3; Karl Kaoru Kasukabe, "The Escape of the Japanese Garrison from Kiska," in *Alaska at War, 1941-1945: The Forgotten War Remembered – Papers from the Alaska at War Symposium, Anchorage, Alaska, November 11-13, 1993*, ed. Fern Chandonnet (Anchorage: Alaska at War Committee, 1995), 122; and James S. Russell, "The Aleutian Campaign," in *Alaska at War, 1941-1945: The Forgotten War Remembered – Papers from the Alaska at War Symposium, Anchorage, Alaska, November 11-13, 1993*, ed. Fern Chandonnet (Anchorage: Alaska at War Committee, 1995), 73. Japan lost over 30,000 men, 683 planes, and twenty warships in the 1942-3 Solomons campaign; Richard B. Frank, *Guadalcanal: The Definitive Account of the Landmark Battle* (New York: Penguin Books, 1990), 602-14. John W. Dower contends that two-thirds of Japanese military deaths resulted from illness or starvation rather than combat; *War without Mercy: Race and Power in the Pacific War* (New York: Pantheon Books, 1986), 297-300.

23 Spector, *Eagle against the Sun*, 10.

24 Brian McAllister Linn, *Guardians of Empire: The U.S. Army and the Pacific, 1902-1940* (Chapel Hill: University of North Carolina Press, 1997), passim; and Russell. F. Weigley, "The Role of the War Department and the Army," in *Pearl Harbor As History: Japanese-American Relations 1931-1941*, ed. Dorothy Borg and Shumpei Okamoto (New York: Columbia University Press, 1973), 166-7 and 186.

25 Diary entry, 21 October 1942, Amherst College Archives, John McCloy Papers, box DY5, folder 5.

26 Dennison Oral History, Naval History Institute Library, 62-3.

27 Naske and Slotnick, *Alaska*, 123.

28 Russell F. Weigley, *The American Way of War: A History of American Military Strategy and Policy* (New York: Macmillan, 1973), xiv; and Robert Endicott Osgood, *Limited War: The Challenge to American Strategy* (Chicago: University of Chicago Press, 1957), 34.

29 Marshall to MacArthur, 6 January 1944, GDMF, RG4, reel 594; and Maurice Matloff, "The 90-Division Gamble," in *Command Decisions*, ed. Kent Robert Greenfield (Washington, DC: Office of the Army, 1960), 380. By 1945, with 8.3 million men in uniform, the army had 2 million in ground combat units. Some 2.35 million men served in the air force, while the rest could be found in service forces, non-combat formations, or were classified as "overhead," or as McNair described, "the invisible horde of people going here and there but seemingly never arriving"; Russell F. Weigley, *History of the United States Army* (New York: Macmillan, 1967), 440.

30 Edward S. Miller, *War Plan Orange: The U.S. Strategy to Defeat Japan, 1897-1945* (Annapolis, MD: Naval Institute Press, 1991), 29; Roosevelt quoted in Robert Dallek, *Franklin D. Roosevelt and American Foreign Policy, 1932-1945* (New York: Oxford University Press, 1979), 440; and Knox quoted in Michael D. Pearlman, *Warmaking and American Diplomacy: The Struggle over Military Strategy, 1700 to the Present* (Lawrence: University Press of Kansas, 1999), 254.

31 Ronald H. Spector, "The Pacific War and the Fourth Dimension of Strategy," in *The Pacific War Revisited*, ed. Gunter Bischof and Robert L. Dupont (Baton Rouge: Louisiana State University Press, 1997), 51.

32 Garfield, *The Thousand-Mile War*, 6.

33 Cloe, *The Aleutian Warriors*, 321-2.

34 John H. Bradley, *The Second World War: Asia and the Pacific* (West Point: United States Military Academy, 1984), appendix 13, 282.

35 For a dissenting viewpoint, see Carol A. Wilder, "Weather As the Decisive Factor of the Aleutian

Campaign, June 1942-August 1943," MA thesis, United States Army Command and General Staff College, Fort Leavenworth, 1993.

36 A.C.P. Wavell, *Speaking Generally* (London: Macmillan, 1946), 78-9.

37 Richard M. Leighton and Robert W. Coakley, *Global Logistics and Strategy 1940-1943* (Washington, DC: Department of the Army, 1955), 733.

38 Ibid., 391.

39 David M. Kennedy, *Freedom from Fear: The American People in Depression and War, 1929-1945* (New York: Oxford University Press, 1999), 608.

40 Quoted in Kimball, Warren F. Kimball, *Forged in War: Roosevelt, Churchill, and the Second World War* (New York: William Morrow and Company, 1997), 12.

41 See G. Patrick March, "Yanks in Siberia: U.S. Navy Weather Stations in Soviet East Asia," *Pacific Historical Review* 57 (August 1988): 327-42; and H.S. Yoder Jr., *Planned Invasion of Japan, 1945: The Siberian Weather Advantage* (Philadelphia: American Philosophical Society, 1997).

42 DeWitt-Hull telephone conversation transcript, 30 May 1943, NARA, RG165, OPD, Exec. file 8, item book 10.

43 Brigadier P. Earnshaw memorandum, 31 May 1943, DHH, Kardex file 112.3M2 (D459); DeWitt-Pearkes meeting minutes, 5 July 1943, National Archives of Canada (hereinafter NAC), RG24, Greenlight War Diary, vol. 13, 831; Colonel G.S. Currie to Ralston, 19 July 1943, NAC, Ralston Papers, vol. 43, file Currie Col. G.S. 1943-4; Pearkes to Major General A.E. Potts, DHH, Kardex File 322.009 (D486); Pearkes to Stuart, 13 August 1943, DHH, Kardex File 322.009 (D482); and Stuart, "Reduction in Operational Troops in Canada," 30 August 1943, NAC, RG2 7c.

44 CWC minutes, 8 September and 12 October 1943, NAC, RG2 7c.

45 Diary entries for 5 January and 14 September 1944, NAC, W.L.M. King Papers; Galen Roger Perras, "Eyes on the Northern Route to Japan: Plans for Canadian Participation in an Invasion of the Kurile Islands – A Study in Coalition Warfare and Civil-Military Relationships," *War and Society* 8 (May 1990): 100-17; and Galen Roger Perras, "Once Bitten, Twice Shy: The Origins of the Canadian Army Pacific Force," in *Uncertain Horizons: Canadians and Their World in 1945*, ed. Greg Donaghy (Ottawa: Canadian Committee for the History of the Second World War, 1997), 77-99.

46 Major General Guy V. Henry, "Continental Defense Value of Canadian Northwest," 8 June 1945, NARA, RG59, Decimal File 1945-49, file 842.20 Defense/6-2745; Henry, "Canada – United States Post-War Collaboration," 8 June 1945, Military History Institute Archives, Guy V. Henry Papers, box 2; J.G. Parsons to Hickerson, 27 June 1945, NARA, RG59, Decimal File 1945-49, file 842.20 Defense/6-2745; and Pope, "Note on General Henry's Statements," 3 September 1945, DHH, Kardex File 314.009 (D17).

47 Louis Morton, *Strategy and Command: The First Two Years* (Washington, DC: Center for Military History, 1989), 250; Kimball, *Forged in War*, 149. See also Louis Morton, *Pacific Command: A Study in Interservice Relations* (Colorado Springs: United States Air Force Academy, 1961).

48 Spector, *Eagle against the Sun*, 144. See also D. Clayton James, "Introduction: Rethinking the Pacific War," in *The Pacific War Revisited*, ed. Gunter Bischof and Robert L. Dupont (Baton Rouge: Louisiana State University Press, 1997), 2.

49 Major Charles B. Breslin, *World War II in the Aleutians: The Fundamentals of Joint Campaigns* (Newport: Naval War College, 1994), 9; and Joint Board, *Joint Action of the Army and Navy 1935* (Washington, DC: Government Printing Office, 1935).

50 Breslin, *World War II in the Aleutians*, 8-21.

51 Lincoln quoted in Ray S. Cline, *Washington Command Post: The Operations Division* (Washington, DC: United States Army, 1985), 325.

52 Thomas B. Buell, *Master of Sea Power: A Biography of Fleet Admiral Ernest J. King* (Boston: Little, Brown and Company, 1980), 180 and 418-20.

53 Robert William Love Jr., "Ernest Joseph King," in *The Chiefs of Naval Operations*, ed. Love Jr. (Annapolis, MD: Naval Institute Press, 1980), 162-3.

54 Pearlman, *Warmaking and the American Democracy*, 232.
55 "Log of the President's Inspection Trip to the Pacific, July – August 1944," Franklin Delano Roosevelt Library, Samuel R. Rosenman Papers, box 14; and Samuel P. Huntington, *The Soldier and the State: The Theory and Politics of Civil-Military Relations* (Cambridge: Belknap Press of Harvard University Press, 1957), 320; and Roosevelt quoted in "Tough War Ahead," *Montreal Gazette*, 18 September 1944.
56 Pearlman, *Warmaking and the American Democracy*, 255.
57 William A. Jacobs, "American National Strategy in the East Asian and Pacific War: The North Pacific," in *Alaska at War, 1941-1945: The Forgotten War Remembered – Papers from the Alaska at War Symposium, Anchorage, Alaska, November 11-13, 1993*, ed. Fern Chandonnet (Anchorage: Alaska at War Committee, 1995), 17.
58 Naske and Slotnick, *Alaska*, 127.

Bibliography

Archival Sources
Air Force History Support Office, Bolling Air Force Base
William Ormond Butler Papers.
Eleventh Air Force Records.
"Japanese Aircraft Carrier Operations, Part III. Carrier Attack on Dutch Harbor,"reel A7339.

Alfred F. Simpson Historical Research Collection, Maxwell Air Force Base
Army Air Forces in the War against Japan 1941-1942. Army Air Force Historical Study no. 34, June 1945.
Colonel James Bush Oral History, 24 May 1982.
Herold, Major William A., *History of the XI Bomber Command. Eleventh Air Force. Shemya Island, Alaska, 19 March 1943-31 March 1944, 1944.*

Amherst College Archives, Amherst
John McCloy Papers.

Australian War Memorial, Canberra
Series AWM123, Defence Committee Records.

Center for Military History, Washington, DC
"The Aleutian Islands Campaign," *Japanese Studies in World War II*, no. 51.
"Submarine Operations Dec 41-Apr 42," *Japanese Monograph*, no. 102.

Directorate of History and Heritage, Department of National Defence, Ottawa
Kardex Files.

Duke University Archives, Durham
John Jackson McSwain Papers.

Durham University Archives, Durham
Malcolm Macdonald Papers.

Dwight D. Eisenhower Presidential Library, Abilene
Simon Bolivar Buckner Jr. Papers.

Franklin Delano Roosevelt Library, Hyde Park
Adolf Berle Papers.
Henry Morgenthau Jr. Papers and Presidential Diaries.
Franklin Roosevelt Papers, Map Room Files.
Franklin Roosevelt Papers, Official Files.
Franklin Roosevelt Papers, President's Secretary's Files.
Samuel R. Rosenman Papers.
Sumner Welles Papers.

General Douglas MacArthur Foundation, Norfolk
Records of the General Headquarters United States Army Forces Pacific, RG4.

George C. Marshall Library, Lexington
George C. Marshall Papers.

Harry S. Truman Presidential Library, Independence
Harry S. Truman Office Files 1945-1953 Part Two Correspondence Files.
Karl R. Bendetsen Oral History.
Stuart Symington Oral History.

Herbert Hoover Presidential Library, West Branch
Herbert Hoover Presidential Papers.

Hoover Institution on War, Revolution and Peace, Stanford
Robert Adleman Papers.
Frederick L. Anderson Papers.
Robert D. Burhans Papers.
Charles M. Cooke Papers.
Delos C. Emmons Papers.
Herbert Hoover Papers.
Stanley K. Hornbeck Papers.
John Sydney McCain Papers.
Robert C. Richardson Jr. Papers.
Robert A. Theobald Papers.
Albert C. Wedemeyer Papers.

Legislative Records
United States. *Congressional Globe.* 1867-8. Washington, DC.
–. *Congressional Record.* 1942. Washington, DC.
–. Congress. *Hearings before the Joint Committee on the Investigation of the Pearl Harbor Attack: Part 26, Hart Inquiry.* Washington, DC: Government Printing Office, 1946.
–. Congress. House of Representatives. Committee on Military Affairs. *Hearings on H.R. 6621 and H.R. 4130,* 74th Congress, 1st session, 11-13 February 1935. Washington, DC: Government Printing Office, 1935.
–. Congress. House of Representatives. *Report on Need of Additional Naval Bases to Defend the Coast of the United States, Its Territories, and Possessions.* 27 December 1938. Doc. 65. Washington, DC: Government Printing Office.
–. Senate. Preparedness Subcommittee of the Committee on Armed Services United States Senate. *Report of the Alaskan Task Force.* Washington, DC: Government Printing Office, 1951.

Library of Congress, Washington, DC
H.H. Arnold Papers.
Raymond L. Buell Papers.
Cordell Hull Papers.
Harold L. Ickes Papers.
Ernest J. King Papers.
Herbert B. Knowles Papers.
William Leahy Papers.
William Mitchell Papers.
Robert P. Patterson Papers.

Marine Corps Historical Center, Washington, DC
Davis, J.R., and T.J. Ebbert. "The Aleutian Option." Center for Advanced Research, Naval War
    College, June 1983, Reference Section, file PSOT and Stations – Alaska Adak.
General Graves B. Erskine Oral History.
Lieutenant General Robert E. Hogaboom Oral History.
Marine Corps Reference Section Records.
Lieutenant General John. C. McQueen Oral History.

Microfilm Records
Joint Chiefs of Staff Records, Part I: 1942-45, Pacific Theater, University Publications of America.
The MAGIC Documents: Summaries and Transcripts of the Top Secret Diplomatic Communications
    of Japan, 1938-1945, University Publications of America.
Wartime Conferences of the Combined Chiefs of Staff: Arcadia, Casablanca, Trident, vols. 1 and 2,
    (Dec. 1941-May 1943), Scholarly Resources Incorporated.

Military History Institute Archives, Carlisle Barracks
Paul D. Adams Papers.
Army War College Records.
Charles H. Corlett Papers.
Guy V. Henry Papers.

National Archives and Records Administration, Washington, DC
Adjutant General's Office Records, Administrative Services Division, Operations Branch, Special
    Projects-War Plans "Color" 1920-1946, RG407.
Adjutant General's Office Records, World War II Operations Reports 1940-48, American Theater,
    RG407.
Army Air Forces Central Decimal Files 1917-38, RG18.
Department of the Navy Records, Proceedings and Hearings of the General Board of the US Navy
    1900-1950, RG80.
Department of State Records, Decimal File 1930-39, RG59.
Department of State Records, Decimal File 1945-49, RG59.
Department of State Records, Diplomatic Post Files Canada, entry 2195A, RG84.
Department of State Records, Diplomatic Post Files Japan 1930-1941, Tokyo Embassy, RG84.
Department of State Records, Permanent Joint Board on Defense, RG59.
Dispatches and Records from the Chart Room of the Commander in Chief U.S. Fleet, RG38.
General Correspondence of the Alaska Territorial Governor, RG348.
International Conference Records, Conference on the Limitations of Armaments, entry 100, RG43.
Joint Board Records, RG225.
Joint Chiefs of Staff Decimal File 1942-1945, RG218.
Joint Chiefs of Staff Geographic File 1942-1945, RG218.
Office of the Chief of Naval Operations Records, Office of Naval Intelligence, East European Section,
    RG38.
Office of the Chief of Naval Operations, Selected Naval Attaché Reports Relating to the World
    Crisis, 1937-1943, series M975, RG38.
Office of the Chief of Staff Records, RG107.
Office of the Secretary of War Records, RG107.
United States Army Commands, Alaskan Department Records, RG338.
United States Army Continental Defenses, 1914-1940, RG394.
United States Marine Corps Records, RG127.

War Department Records, Military Intelligence Division 1922-44, RG165.
War Department Records, Office of the Director of Plans and Operations, RG165.
War Department Records, War Plans Division, RG165.

National Archives of Australia, Canberra
Series A981, Correspondence Files of the Department of External Affairs.
Series A3300/7, Correspondence Files of the Australian Legation, United States.
Series A4764, Files of Copies of Cables 1942-1943.
Series A5954, Frederick Shedden Papers.

National Archives of Canada, Ottawa
R.B. Bennett Papers.
Loring Christie Papers.
Brooke Claxton Papers.
H.D.G. Crerar Papers.
Department of External Affairs Records, RG25.
Department of National Defence Records, RG24.
Governor General's Records, RG7 G21.
C.F. Hamilton Papers.
W.L.M. King Papers, Correspondence.
W.L.M. King Papers, Diaries.
W.L.M. King Papers, Memoranda and Notes.
Ian Mackenzie Papers.
E.W.B. Morrison Papers.
Maurice Pope Papers.
Privy Council Records, RG2.
Privy Council Records, Minutes and Documents of the Cabinet War Committee, RG2 7c.
Escott Reid Papers.
O.D. Skelton Papers.

Naval Historical Center, Washington, DC
CINPAC Command Summary.
Combat Narratives, "The Aleutian Campaign June 1942-August 1943," 1945.
Command Narratives, "Command History North Pacific Force," 14 August 1945.
Admiral Paul F. Foster Oral History.
Glenn Howell Papers.
Thomas C. Kinkaid Papers.
C.W. Nimitz Papers.
Admiral James S. Russell Oral History.
Strategic Plans Division Records.
Future Plans Section Records.

Naval Historical Institute Library, Annapolis
Admiral Robert L. Dennison Oral History.
Vice Admiral William P. Mack Oral History.

Private Collections
Black Family private papers, J.L. Black diary.

Public Record Office, Kew Gardens
Cabinet Office Records, CAB122.
Foreign Office Records, Japan Correspondence 1941-1945, FO371.
Foreign Office Records, United States Correspondence 1941-1945, FO371.
Maurice Hankey Official Papers, CAB63.
Premier's Office Records, PREM3.

Queen's University Archives, Kingston
J. Sutherland Brown Papers.
John Buchan Papers.
Grant Dexter Papers.
Charles Gavan Power Papers.

Rasmussen Library, University of Alaska, Fairbanks
Anthony J. Dimond Papers.
Ernest Gruening Papers.

United States Air Force Academy Library, Colorado Springs
Lawrence Kuter Papers.
Leigh Wade Papers.
William Mitchell Papers.

United States Military Academy Archives, West Point
George A. Lincoln Papers.
Harold S. Rosenthal Papers.

University of Rochester Library, Rochester
William H. Seward Papers.

Yale University Library, New Haven
Henry L. Stimson Papers.

Newspapers
Army Times, 1942.
Montreal Gazette, 1941.
New York Herald Tribune, 1942.
New York Post, 1942.
New York Times, 1942.
The Times of London, 1856, 1949, 1950.
Washington Herald, 1934.

Other Sources
Acheson, Dean. *Present at the Creation.* New York: W.W. Norton, 1969.
Adams, D.K., ed. *British Documents on Foreign Affairs: Reports and Papers from the Foreign Office Confidential Print.* Series C, *North America, 1919-1939.* Vol. 8, *Treaties and International Negotiations, 1919-1921.* Frederick, MD: University Publications of America, 1991.
–. *British Documents on Foreign Affairs: Reports and Papers from the Foreign Office Confidential Print.* Series C, *1919-1939.* Vol. 10, *Cables and Mandates, 1920-1925.* Frederick, MD: University Publications of America, 1991.

–. *British Documents on Foreign Affairs: Reports and Papers from the Foreign Office Confidential Print.* Series C, *North America, 1919-1939.* Vol. 19, *International Competition and Naval Rivalry, 1929-1939.* Frederick, MD: University Publications of America, 1995.

Adleman, R.H. and G. Walton. *The Devil's Brigade.* Philadelphia: Chilton Books, 1966.

Agawa, Hiroyuki. *The Reluctant Admiral: Yamamoto and the Imperial Navy.* New York: Kodansha International, 1982.

Allard, Dean C. "The North Pacific Campaign in Perspective." In *Alaska at War, 1941-1945: The Forgotten War Remembered – Papers from the Alaska at War Symposium, Anchorage, Alaska, November 11-13, 1993,* ed. Fern Chandonnet, 3-11. Anchorage: Alaska at War Committee, 1995.

Alvarez, David. *Secret Messages: Codebreaking and American Diplomacy, 1930-1945.* Lawrence: University Press of Kansas, 2000.

Anderson, Robert A. "Attu: WW II's Bloody Sideshow." *Army* 33 (May 1983): 38-46.

Arnold, H.H. *Global Mission.* New York: Harper and Harper Brothers, 1949.

Asada, Sadao. "From Washington to London: The Imperial Japanese Navy and the Politics of Naval Limitation, 1921-30." In *The Washington Naval Conference, 1921-22: Naval Rivalry, East Asian Stability and the Road to Pearl Harbor,* ed. Erik Goldstein John Maurer, 145-91. Ilford, UK: Frank Cass, 1994.

Barnhart, Michael A. "Japanese Intelligence before the Second World War: 'Best Case' Analysis." In *Knowing One's Enemies: Intelligence Assessment before the Two World Wars,* ed. Ernest R. May, 424-55. Princeton: Princeton University Press, 1984.

Beard, Baker B. "The Bradley Mission: The Evolution of the Alaska-Siberia Air Route." In *Alaska at War, 1941-1945: The Forgotten War Remembered – Papers from the Alaska at War Symposium, Anchorage, Alaska, November 11-13, 1993,* ed. Fern Chandonnet, 311-18. Anchorage: Alaska at War Committee, 1995.

Bezeau, M.V. "The Realities of Strategic Planning: The Decision to Build the Alaska Highway." In *The Alaska Highway: Papers of the 40th Anniversary Symposium,* ed. Kenneth Coates, 27-30. Vancouver: University of British Columbia Press, 1985.

Bidwell, Bruce W. *History of the Military Intelligence Division, Department of the Army General Staff: 1775-1941.* Frederick, MD: University Publications of America, 1986.

Bix, Herbert P. *Hirohito and the Making of Modern Japan.* New York: Perennial, 2001.

Blair, Clay, Jr. *Silent Victory: The U.S. Submarine War against Japan.* Philadelphia: Lippincott, 1975.

Bland, Larry I., ed. *George C. Marshall: Interviews and Reminiscences for Forrest C. Pogue.* Lexington: George C. Marshall Research Foundation, 1991.

–. *The Papers of George Catlett Marshall.* Vol. 2, *"We Cannot Delay," July 1, 1939-December 6, 1941.* Baltimore: Johns Hopkins University Press, 1986.

–. *The Papers of George Catlett Marshall.* Vol. 3, *"The Right Man for the Job," December 7, 1941-May 31, 1943.* Baltimore: Johns Hopkins University Press, 1991.

Bland, Larry I., with Sharon Ritenour Stevens, eds. *The Papers of George C. Marshall.* Vol. 4, *Aggressive and Determined Leadership June 1, 1943-December 31, 1944.* Baltimore: Johns Hopkins University Press, 1996.

Blewett, Daniel K. "Fuel and U.S. Naval Operations in the Pacific, 1942." In *The Pacific War Revisited,* ed. Gunter Bischof and Robert L. Dupont, 57-80. Baton Rouge: Louisiana State University Press, 1997.

Blum, John Morton. *The Price of Vision: The Diary of Henry Wallace 1942-1946.* Boston: Houghton Mifflin, 1973.

Bohlen, Charles. *Witness to History, 1929-1969.* New York: Norton, 1973.

Boorstin, Daniel J., ed. *An American Primer.* Chicago: University of Chicago Press, 1966.

Borg, Dorothy. *The United States and the Far Eastern Crisis of 1933-1938: From the Manchurian Crisis Through the Initial Stage of the Undeclared Sino-Japanese War.* Cambridge: Harvard University Press, 1964.

Bourne, Kenneth, ed. *British Documents on Foreign Affairs: Reports and Papers from the Foreign Office Confidential Print.* Series C, *North America, 1837-1914.* Vol. 10, *Expansion and Rapprochement, 1889-1898.* Frederick, MD: University Publications of America, 1987.

–. *British Documents on Foreign Affairs: Reports and Papers from the Foreign Office Confidential Print.* Series C, *North America, 1837-1914.* Vol. 12, *North American Affairs, 1906-1907.* Frederick, MD: University Publications of America, 1987.

–. *British Documents on Foreign Affairs: Reports and Papers from the Foreign Office Confidential Print.* Series C, *North America, 1837-1914.* Vol. 13, *North American Affairs, 1908-1909.* Frederick, MD: University Publications of America, 1987.

Boyd, Carl. "Japanese Military Effectiveness: The Interwar Period." In *Military Effectiveness.* Vol. 2, *The Interwar Period,* ed. Allan R. Millett and Williamson Murray, 131-68. Boston: Allen and Unwin, 1988.

Bradley, John H. *The Second World War: Asia and the Pacific.* West Point: United States Military Academy, 1984.

Braeman, John. "Power and Diplomacy: The 1920's Reappraised." *The Review of Politics* 44 (July 1982): 342-69.

Braisted, William Reynolds. *The United States Navy in the Pacific, 1909-1922.* Austin: University of Texas Press, 1971.

Breslin, Major Charles B. *World War II in the Aleutians: The Fundamentals of Joint Campaigns.* Newport: Naval War College, 1994.

Brodie, Bernard. *War and Politics.* New York: Macmillan, 1973.

Brown, Jerold E. *Where Eagles Land: Planning and Development of U.S. Army Airfields, 1910-1941.* New York: Greenwood Press, 1990.

Buell, Thomas B. *Master of Sea Power: A Biography of Fleet Admiral Ernest J. King.* Boston: Little, Brown and Company, 1980.

Buhite, Russell D. *Decisions at Yalta: An Appraisal of Summit Diplomacy.* Wilmington: Scholarly Resources, 1986.

Builder, Carl H. *The Icarus Syndrome: The Role of Air Power Theory in the Evolution and Fate of the U.S. Air Force.* New Brunswick: Transaction Publishers, 1994.

Burhans, Robert D. *The First Special Service Force: A War History of the North Americans 1942-1944.* Washington, DC: Infantry Journal Press, 1947.

Butler, J.R.M., ed. *Grand Strategy.* Vol. 4, *August 1942-September 1943,* ed. Michael Howard. London: Her Majesty's Stationery Office, 1972.

Bywater, Hector C. *The Great Pacific War: A History of the American-Japanese Campaign of 1931-33.* Boston: Houghton Mifflin, 1925.

–. *Sea-Power in the Pacific: A Study of the American-Japanese Naval Problem.* Boston: Houghton Mifflin, 1921.

Candelaria, Gary. "Tin Can at War: The USS *Monaghan* and the War in Alaska." In *Alaska at War, 1941-1945: The Forgotten War Remembered – Papers from the Alaska at War Symposium, Anchorage, Alaska, November 11-13, 1993,* ed. Fern Chandonnet, 113-23. Anchorage: Alaska at War Committee, 1995.

Cantril, Handley, ed. *Public Opinion 1935-1946.* Princeton: Princeton University Press, 1951.

Carter, Worrall Dean. *Beans, Bullets, and Black Oil: The Story of Fleet Logistics Afloat in the Pacific during World War II.* Washington, DC: Government Printing Office, 1952.

Challener, Richard D. *Admirals, Generals, & American Foreign Policy 1898-1914.* Princeton, NJ: Princeton University Press, 1973.

Chandler, Alfred D., ed. *The Papers of Dwight David Eisenhower – The War Years: I.* Baltimore: Johns Hopkins University Press, 1970.

Chiyaya, Masatake. "Mysterious Withdrawal from Kiska." *United States Naval Institute Proceedings* 84 (February 1958): 31-47.

Christie, Loring C. "The Anglo-Japanese Alliance." 1 June 1921. Reprinted in *External Affairs* 18 (September 1966): 402-13.

Churchill, Winston S. *The Second World War.* Vol. 4, *The Hinge of Fate.* Boston: Houghton Mifflin, 1985.

Clausewitz, Carl von. *On War.* Princeton, NJ: Princeton University Press, 1984.

Cline, Ray S. *Washington Command Post: The Operations Division.* Washington, DC: United States Army, 1985.

Cloe, John Haile. *The Aleutian Warriors: A History of the 11th Air Force and Fleet Wing 4.* Missoula, MT: Pictorial Histories, 1990.

—. "The Legacy of War." In *Alaska at War, 1941-1945: The Forgotten War Remembered – Papers from the Alaska at War Symposium, Anchorage, Alaska, November 11-13, 1993,* ed. Fern Chandonnet, 395-8. Anchorage: Alaska at War Committee, 1995, 395-8.

Cloe, John Haile, and Michael F. Monoghan. *Top Cover for America: The Air Force in Alaska 1920-1983.* Missoula, MT: Pictorial Histories, 1984.

Coates, K.S., and W.R. Morrison. *The Alaska Highway in World War II: The U.S. Army of Occupation.* Toronto: University of Toronto Archives, 1992.

Coffey, Thomas M. *Hap, Military Aviator: The Story of the U.S. Air Force and the Man Who Built It, General Henry H. "Hap" Arnold.* New York: Viking Press, 1982.

Cohen, Eliot A. "The Strategy of Innocence? The United States, 1920-1945." In *The Making of Strategy: Rulers, States, and War,* ed. Williamson Murray, MacGregor Knox, and Alvin Bernstein, 428-65. Cambridge: Cambridge University Press, 1994.

Coles, Harry L. "The Aleutian Campaign." In *The Army Air Forces in World War II,* ed. Wesley Frank Craven and James Lea Cate. Vol. 4, *The Pacific: Guadalcanal to Saipan August 1942 to July 1944.* 359-401. Chicago: University of Chicago Press, 1983.

Conn, Stetson. "Between World Wars." In *American Military History,* ed. Maurice Matloff. Vol. 2, *1902-1996,* 63-80. Conshohocken: Combined Books, 1996.

Conn, Stetson, Rose C. Engelman, and Byron Fairchild. *The Western Hemisphere: Guarding the United States and Its Outposts.* Washington, DC: Department of the Army, 1964.

Cooke, James J. *Billy Mitchell.* Boulder, CO: Lynne Rienner, 2002.

Coox, Alvin. "Aleutian Islands." In *The Historical Encyclopedia of World War II,* ed. Marcel Baudot and trans. Jesse Dilson, 7-11. New York: Facts on File, 1980.

—. "Japanese Military Education and Planning Planning before Pearl Harbor." In *Military Planning in the Twentieth Century: Proceedings of the Eleventh Military History Symposium,* ed. Harry R. Borowski, 67-87. Washington, DC: Office of Air Force History, 1986.

—. "The Pacific War." In *The Cambridge History of Japan.* Vol. 6, *The Twentieth Century,* ed. Peter Duus, 315-82. Cambridge: Cambridge University Press, 1998.

Corlett, Charles H. *Cowboy Pete: The Autobiography of Major General Charles Corlett.* Santa Fe: Sleeping Fox, 1974.

Corn, Joseph J. *The Winged Defense: America's Romance with Aviation, 1900-1950.* New York: Oxford University Press, 1983.

Dallek, Robert. *Franklin D. Roosevelt and American Foreign Policy, 1932-1945.* New York: Oxford University Press, 1979.

Danchev, Alex. "Great Britain: The Indirect Strategy." In *Allies at War: The Soviet, American, and British Experience, 1939-1945,* ed. David Reynolds, Warren F. Kimball, and A.O. Chubarian, 1-26. New York: St. Martin's Press, 1994.

Danchev, Alex, and Daniel Todman, eds. *War Diaries 1939-1945: Field Marshal Lord Alanbrooke.* London: Weidenfeld and Nicolson, 2001.

Daniels, Jonathan, ed. *1942.* Vol. 19 of *Complete Presidential Press Conferences of Franklin D. Roosevelt.* New York: Da Capo Press, 1972.

Davis, Burke. *The Billy Mitchell Affair*. New York: Random House, 1967.

Deacon, Kenneth. "Combat Engineers 43. Attu, May 1943." *The Military Engineer* 59 (January-February 1967): 25.

Denfeld, D. Colt. "The Battle of Attu." In *Builders and Fighters: U.S. Army Engineers in World War II*, ed. Barry W. Fowle, 367-78. Fort Belvoir: United States Army Corps of Engineers, 1992.

"The Diary of Takahashi," *United States Naval Institute Proceedings* 106 (July 1980): 74-6.

D'Este, Carlo. *Eisenhower: A Soldier's Life*. New York: Henry Holt, 2002.

Dingman, Roger. *Power in the Pacific: The Origins of Naval Arms Limitation, 1914-1922*. Chicago: University of Chicago Press, 1976.

Dod, Karl C. *The Corps of Engineers: The War against Japan*. Washington, DC: Office of the Chief of Military History, 1966.

Dorwart, Jeffrey M. *Conflict of Duty: The U.S. Navy's Intelligence Dilemma, 1919-1945*. Annapolis, MD: Naval Institute Press, 1983.

Douglas, W.A.B. *The Creation of a National Air Force: The Official History of the Royal Canadian Air Force*. Vol. 2. Ottawa: University of Toronto Press, 1986.

Dower, John W. *War without Mercy: Race and Power in the Pacific War*. New York: Pantheon Books, 1986.

Dull, Paul S. *A Battle History of the Imperial Japanese Navy (1941-1945)*. Annapolis, MD: Naval Institute Press, 1978.

Dyer, George Carroll. *The Amphibians Came to Conquer: The Story of Admiral Richmond Kelly Turner*. Washington, DC: Department of the Navy, 1969.

Dziuban, Colonel Stanley W. *Military Relations between the United States and Canada 1939-1945*. Washington, DC: Department of the Army, 1959.

Emme, Eugene M. "The American Dimension." In *Air Power and Warfare: The Proceedings of the 8th Military History Symposium United States Air Force Academy 18-20 October 1978*, ed. Alfred F. Hurley and Robert C. Ehrhrat, 56-82. Washington, DC: Government Printing Office, 1979.

–. "The Employment of Mobile Radio Intelligence Units by Command Afloat During World War II." In *Listening to the Enemy: Key Documents on the Role of Communications Intelligence in the War with Japan*, ed. Ronald H. Spector, 77-129. Wilmington: Scholarly Resources, 1988.

Evans, David C., and Mark R. Peattie. *Kaigun: Strategy, Tactics, and Technology in the Imperial Japanese Navy, 1887-1941*. Annapolis, MD: Naval Institute Press, 1997.

Falk, Stanley L. "Douglas MacArthur and the War against Japan." In *We Shall Return! MacArthur's Commanders and the Defeat of Japan*, ed. William M. Leary, 1-22. Lexington: University Press of Kentucky, 1988.

Farrell, Brian P. "Symbol of Paradox: The Casablanca Conference, 1943." *Canadian Journal of History* 28 (April 1993): 22-40.

Ferrell, Robert. *The Dying President: Franklin D. Roosevelt 1944-1945*. Columbia, MO: University of Missouri Press, 1998.

–, ed. *The Eisenhower Diaries*. New York: W.W. Norton, 1981.

Fogelson, Nancy. *Arctic Exploration & International Relations 1900-1932*. Fairbanks: University of Alaska Press, 1992.

Foulois, Benjamin D., with C.V. Glines. *From the Wright Brothers to the Astronauts: The Memoirs of Major General Benjamin D. Foulois*. New York: McGraw-Hill, 1968.

Frank, Richard B. *Downfall: The End of the Imperial Japanese Empire*. New York: Penguin Books, 2001.

–. *Guadalcanal: The Definitive Account of the Landmark Battle*. New York: Penguin Books, 1990.

Friedman, Hal M. "The 'Bear' in the Pacific? US Intelligence Perceptions of Soviet Strategic Power in the Pacific Basin and East Asia, 1945-1947." *Intelligence and National Security* 12 (October 1997): 75-101.

Fuchida, Mitsuo, and Masatake Okumiya. *Midway. The Battle That Doomed Japan: The Japanese Navy's Story*. Annapolis, MD: Naval Institute Press, 1955.

Fuquea, David C. "Task Force One: The Wasted Assets of the United States Pacific Battleship Fleet, 1942." *The Journal of Military History* 61 (October 1997): 707-34.

Futrell, Robert Frank. *Ideas, Concepts, Doctrine: A History of Basic Thinking in the United States Air Force 1907-1964.* Maxwell Air Force Base: Air University, 1971.

Gaddis, John Lewis. *The United States and the Origins of the Cold War, 1941-1947.* New York: Columbia University Press, 1972.

Gallicchio, Marc. *The Cold War Begins in Asia: American East Asian Policy and the Fall of the Japanese Empire.* New York: Columbia University Press, 1988.

–. "The Kuriles Controversy: U.S. Diplomacy in the Soviet-Japan Border Dispute, 1941-1956." *Pacific Historical Review* 60 (January 1991): 69-101.

Garfield, Brian. "The Thousand-Mile War: World War II in Alaska and the Aleutians." In *Alaska at War, 1941-1945: The Forgotten War Remembered – Papers from the Alaska at War Symposium, Anchorage, Alaska, November 11-13, 1993,* ed. Fern Chandonnet, 27-32. Anchorage: Alaska at War Committee, 1995.

–. *The Thousand-Mile War: World War II in Alaska and the Aleutians.* New York: Bantam Books, 1969.

Gibson, James R. "The Sale of Russian America to the United States." In *Russia's American Colony,* ed. S. Frederick Starr, 271-94. Durham: Duke University Press, 1987.

Gilbert, Martin, ed. *The Churchill War Papers.* Vol. 3, *The Ever-Widening War 1941.* New York: W.W. Norton, 2000.

Goldsborough, W.L. "The Aleutians – Their Strategic Importance." *United States Naval Institute Proceedings* 67 (June 1941): 830-4.

Goldstein, Donald M., and Katherine V. Dillon, eds. *Fading Victory: The Diary of Admiral Matome Ugaki 1941-1945.* Pittsburgh: University of Pittsburgh Press, 1991.

–. *The Williwaw War: The Arkansas National Guard in the Aleutians in World War II.* Fayetteville: University of Arkansas Press, 1992.

Goss, William A. "Air Defense of the Western Hemisphere." In *The Army Air Forces in World War II.* Vol. 1, *Plans and Early Operations January 1939 to August 1942,* ed. Wesley Frank Craven and James Lea Cate, 271-309. Chicago: University of Chicago Press, 1948.

Graebner, Norman A. "Hoover, Roosevelt, and the Japanese." In *Pearl Harbor As History: Japanese-American Relations 1931-1941,* ed. Dorothy Borg and Shumpei Okamoto, 25-52. New York: Columbia University Press, 1973.

Granatstein, J.L. *Canada's War: The Politics of the Mackenzie King Government, 1939-1945.* Toronto: Oxford University Press, 1975.

–. *The Generals: The Canadian Army's Senior Commanders in the Second World War.* Toronto: Stoddart, 1993.

Green, Murray. "Hugh J. Knerr: The Pen and the Sword." In *Makers of the United States Air Force,* ed. John L. Frisbee, 99-126. Washington, DC: Office of Air Force History, 1987.

Greenfield, Kent Roberts. *American Strategy in World War II: A Reconsideration.* Baltimore: Johns Hopkins University Press, 1963.

Gruening, Ernest. *The State of Alaska.* New York: Random House, 1954.

Hanable, William S. "Theobald Revisited." In *Alaska at War, 1941-1945: The Forgotten War Remembered – Papers from the Alaska at War Symposium, Anchorage, Alaska, November 11-13, 1993,* ed. Fern Chandonnet, 75-80. Anchorage: Alaska at War Committee, 1995.

Harper, John Lamberton. *American Visions of Europe: Franklin D. Roosevelt, George F. Kennan, and Dean G. Acheson.* Cambridge: Cambridge University Press, 1994.

Haycock, R.G. "The 'Myth' of Imperial Defence: Australian-Canadian Bilateral Military Cooperation, 1942." *War and Society* 21 (May 1984): 65-84.

Hayes, Grace Person. *The History of the Joint Chiefs of Staff in World War II: The War against Japan.* Annapolis, MD: Naval Institute Press, 1982.

Heinrichs, Waldo. *Threshold of War: Franklin D. Roosevelt & the American Entry into World War II.* New York: Oxford University Press, 1988.

Hendricks, Charles. "Race Relations and the Contributions of African-American Troops in Alaska." In *The U.S. Army and World War II*, ed. Judith L. Bellafaire, 171-81. Washington, DC: Center for Military History, 1998.

Herbig, Katherine L. "American Strategic Deception in the Pacific, 1942-44." *Intelligence and National Security* 2 (July 1987): 260-300.

Hilliker, John F. *Canada's Department of External Affairs.* Vol. 1, *The Early Years, 1909-1946.* Montreal and Kingston: McGill-Queen's University Press, 1990.

–, ed. *1942-1943.* Vol. 9 of *Documents on Canadian External Relations.* Ottawa: Department of External Affairs, 1980.

Hillmer, Norman. "The Anglo-Canadian Neurosis: The Case of O.D. Skelton." In *Britain and Canada: Survey of a Changing Relationship*, ed. Peter Lyons, 61-84. London: Frank Cass, 1976.

Holmes, W.J. *Double-Edged Secrets: U.S. Naval Intelligence Operations in the Pacific during World War Two.* Annapolis, MD: Naval Institute Press, 1979.

Honan, William H. *Visions of Infamy: The Untold Story of How Journalist Hector C. Bywater Devised the Plans That Led to Pearl Harbor.* New York: St. Martin's Press, 1991.

Hone, Thomas C. "The Evolution of the U.S. Fleet, 1933-1941: How the President Mattered." In *FDR and the U.S. Navy*, ed. Edward J. Marolda, 65-113. New York: St. Martin's Press, 1998.

Hoyt, Edwin P. *Japan's War: The Great Pacific Conflict.* New York: McGraw-Hill, 1986.

Huntington, Samuel P. *The Soldier and the State: The Theory and Politics of Civil-Military Relations.* Cambridge, MA: Belknap Press of Harvard University Press, 1957.

Hurley, Alfred F. *Billy Mitchell: Crusader for Air Power.* Bloomington: Indiana University Press, 1975.

Hutchison, Kevin Don. *World War II in the North Pacific: Chronology and Fact Book.* Westport, CT: Greenwood Press, 1994.

Ickes, Harold L. *The Secret Diary of Harold L. Ickes.* Vol. 2, *The Inside Struggle 1936-1939.* New York: Simon and Schuster, 1954.

Ienaga, Saburo. *The Pacific War 1931-1945.* New York: Pantheon Books, 1978.

Ikeda, Kiyoshi. "Japanese Strategy and the Pacific War, 1941-5." In *Anglo-Japanese Alienation 1919-1952: Papers of the Anglo-Japanese Conference on the History of the Second World War*, ed. Ian Nish, 125-46. Cambridge: Cambridge University Press, 1982.

Inglis, Alex I., ed. *1931-1935.* Vol. 5 of *Documents on Canadian External Relations.* Ottawa: Department of External Relations, 1973.

Iriye, Akira. *Pacific Estrangement: Japanese and American Expansion, 1897-1911.* Cambridge: Harvard University Press, 1972.

–. *Power and Culture: The Japanese-American War, 1941-1945.* Cambridge: Harvard University Press, 1981.

Ito, Masanori, and Roger Pineau. *The End of the Imperial Japanese Navy.* New York: Norton, 1962.

Jacobs, William A. "American National Strategy in the East Asian and Pacific War: The North Pacific." In *Alaska at War, 1941-1945: The Forgotten War Remembered – Papers from the Alaska at War Symposium, Anchorage, Alaska, November 11-13, 1993*, ed. Fern Chandonnet, 13-17. Anchorage: Alaska at War Committee, 1995.

James, D. Clayton. "Introduction: Rethinking the Pacific War." In *The Pacific War Revisited*, ed. Gunter Bischof and Robert L. Dupont, 1-14. Baton Rouge: Louisiana State University Press, 1997.

Johnson, Robert L., Jr. "Aleutian Campaign, World War II: Historical Study and Current Perspective." MA thesis, United States Command and General Staff College, Fort Leavenworth, 1992.

Johnston, R.M. *Arms and the Race: The Foundations of Army Reform.* New York: The Century Company, 1915.

Joint Board. *Joint Action of the Army and Navy 1927.* Washington, DC: Government Printing Office, 1927.

–. *Joint Action of the Army and Navy 1935*. Washington, DC: Government Printing Office, 1935.

Kajima, Morinosuke. *The Diplomacy of Japan 1894-1922*. Vol. 3, *First World War, Paris Peace Conference, Washington Conference*. Tokyo: Kajima Institute of International Peace, 1980.

Kasukabe, Karl Kaoru. "The Escape of the Japanese Garrison from Kiska." In *Alaska at War, 1941-1945: The Forgotten War Remembered – Papers from the Alaska at War Symposium, Anchorage, Alaska, November 11-13, 1993*, ed. Fern Chandonnet, 121-3. Anchorage: Alaska at War Committee, 1995.

Kennedy, David M. *Freedom from Fear: The American People in Depression and War, 1929-1945*. New York: Oxford University Press, 1999.

Kennedy, Greg. "Depression and Security: Aspects Influencing the United States during the Hoover Administration." *Diplomacy & Statecraft* 6 (July 1995): 342-72.

Kimball, Warren F. *Forged in War: Roosevelt, Churchill, and the Second World War*. New York: William Morrow and Company, 1997.

–. *The Juggler: Franklin Roosevelt As Wartime Statesman*. Princeton: Princeton University Press, 1991.

Knapp, Harry S. "The Limitation of Armament at the Conference of Washington," *Proceedings of the American Society of International Law*, 1922, 16-19.

Krauskopf, Robert W. "The Army and the Strategic Bomber, 1930-1939." *Military Affairs* 22 (Summer 1958): 83-94.

LaFeber, Walter. *The Cambridge History of American Foreign Relations*. Vol. 2, *The American Search for Opportunity, 1865-1913*. Cambridge: Cambridge University Press, 1995.

–. *The Clash: U.S.-Japanese Relations throughout History*. New York: W.W. Norton and Company, 1997.

Lautaret, Ronald, ed. *Alaskan Historical Documents since 1867*. Jefferson: McFarland and Company, 1989.

Layton, Edwin T., with Roger Pineau and John Costello. *And I Was There: Pearl Harbor and Midway – Breaking the Secrets*. Old Saybrook: Konecky and Konecky, 1985.

Leighton, Richard M., and Robert W. Coakley. *Global Logistics and Strategy 1940-1943*. Washington, DC: Department of the Army, 1955.

Lensen, George Alexander. *The Strange Neutrality: Soviet-Japanese Relations during the Second World War 1941-1945*. Tallahassee: Diplomatic Press, 1972.

Lewin, Ronald. *The American Magic: Codes, Ciphers and the Defeat of Japan*. New York: Farrar Strauss and Giroux, 1982.

Liddell Hart, B.H. *History of the Second World War*. London: Cassell, 1970.

Linn, Brian McAllister. *Guardians of Empire: The U.S. Army and the Pacific, 1902-1940*. Chapel Hill: University of North Carolina Press, 1997.

Lorelli, John A. *The Battle of the Komandorski Islands*. Annapolis, MD: Naval Institute Press, 1984.

Love, Robert William, Jr. "Ernest Joseph King." In *The Chiefs of Naval Operations*, ed. Love Jr., 137-79. Annapolis, MD: Naval Institute Press, 1980.

Lowenthal, Mark M. *Leadership and Indecision: American War Planning and Policy Process 1937-1942*. New York: Garland Publishing, 1988.

–. "Roosevelt and the Coming of the War: The Search for United States Policy 1937-42." In *The Second World War: Essays in Military and Political History*, ed. Walter Laqueur, 50-76. London: Sage: 1982.

McCandless, Bruce. "The Battle of the Pips." *United States Naval Institute Proceedings* 84 (February 1958): 49-56.

McDougall, Walter A. *Let the Sea Make a Noise: A History of the North Pacific from Magellan to MacArthur*. New York: Basic Books, 1993.

McFarland, Keith D. *Harry H. Woodring: A Political Biography of FDR's Controversial Secretary of War*. Lawrence: University Press of Kansas, 1975.

McGarrigle, George L. *Aleutian Islands: The U.S. Army Campaigns of World War II*. Washington, DC: Government Printing Office, n.d.

Major, John. "William Daniel Leahy." In *The Chiefs of Naval Operations*, ed. Robert William Love Jr., 101-17. Annapolis, MD: Naval Institute Press, 1980.

Mangusso, Mary Childers. "Anthony J. Dimond: A Political Biography." PhD diss., Texas Tech University, May 1978.

March, George Patrick. "Yanks in Siberia: U.S. Navy Weather Stations in Soviet East Asia, 1945." *Pacific Historical Review* 57 (August 1988): 327-42.

Matloff, Maurice. "The 90-Division Gamble." In *Command Decisions*, ed. Kent Roberts Greenshield, 365-85. Washington, DC: Department of the Army, 1960.

–. "Grand Strategy." In *American Military History*, ed. Matloff. Vol. 2, *1902-1996*, 104-30. Coshohoneck: Combined Books, 1996.

–. *Strategic Planning for Coalition Warfare 1943-1944*. Washington, DC: Department of the Army, 1959.

–. "World War II: The Defensive Phase." In *American Military History*, ed. Matloff. Vol. 2, *1902-1996*, 81-103. Coshohoneck: Combined Books, 1996.

Matloff, Maurice, and Edwin M. Snell. *Strategic Planning for Coalition Warfare 1941-1942*. Washington, DC: Department of the Army, 1953.

Matveev, Illarion G. "The Kuriles – Strategic Island Stepping-Stones Lying Athwart Northern Trade Routes." *Foreign Commerce Weekly*, 30 October 1943, 11-15.

May, Ronald M. "Battle at Attu – The Japanese Side of It." *Periodical* (December 1985): 3-8.

Mead, Dana G. "United States Peacetime Strategic Planning, 1920-1941: The Color Plans to Victory Program." PhD diss., Massachusetts Institute of Technology, 1968.

Mighetto, Lisa, and Carla Homstad. *Engineering in the Far North: A History of the U.S. Army Engineer District in Alaska 1867-1992*. Seattle: Historical Research Associates, 1997.

Mikami, Jakuo. "Aleutian Naval Operations: March 1942-February 1943." In *The Naval Armament Program and Naval Operations (Part II)*. Vol. 5, *War in Asia and the Pacific*. New York: Garland Publishers, 1980.

Miller, A.J. "The Functional Principle in Canada's External Relations." *International Journal* 35 (Spring 1980): 309-28.

Miller, Edward S. *War Plan Orange: The U.S. Strategy to Defeat Japan, 1897-1945*. Annapolis, MD: Naval Institute Press, 1991.

Millsap, Commander Ralph H. "Skill or Luck?" *United States Naval Institute Proceedings* 111 (March 1985): 79-88.

Mitchell, William. *Winged Defense: The Development and Possibilities of Modern Air Power – Economic and Military*. New York: G.P. Putnam's Sons, 1925.

Morgan, Lael. "The Rise and Fall and Rise of Adak." *The Washington Post*, 16 December 1972.

Morison, Elting E., ed. *The Letters of Theodore Roosevelt*. Vols. 4 and 5. Cambridge: Harvard University Press, 1951 and 1952.

Morison, Samuel Eliot. *History of the United States Naval Operations in World War II*. Vol. 3, *The Rising Sun in the Pacific 1931-April 1942*. Boston: Little, Brown and Company, 1948.

–. *History of United States Naval Operations in World War II*. Vol. 4, *Coral Sea, Midway, and Submarine Actions May 1942-August 1942*. Boston: Little, Brown and Company, 1950.

–. *History of United States Naval Operations in World War II*. Vol. 7, *Aleutians, Gilberts and Marshalls June 1942-April 1944*. Boston: Little, Brown and Company, 1951.

–. *Strategy and Compromise*. Boston: Little, Brown and Company, 1958.

Morton, Louis. "Germany First: The Basic Concept of Allied Strategy in World War II." In *Command Decisions*, rf. Kent Roberts Greenfield, 3-38. Washington, DC: Office of the Army, 1960.

–. "Interservice Co-operation and Political-Military Collaboration." In *Total War and Cold War: Problems in Civilian Control of the Military*, ed. Harry L. Coles, 131-60. Columbus: Ohio State University Press, 1962.

–. *Pacific Command: A Study in Interservice Relations.* Colorado Springs: United States Air Force Academy, 1961.

–. *Strategy and Command: The First Two Years.* Washington, DC: Center for Military History, 1989.

Moy, Timothy. *War Machines: Transforming Technologies and the U.S. Military, 1920-1940.* College Station: Texas A&M University Press, 2001.

Munroe, John A., ed. *1936-1939.* Vol. 6 of *Documents on Canadian External Relations.* Ottawa: Department of External Affairs, 1977.

Murray, David R., ed. *1939-1941.* Vol. 8 of *Documents on Canadian External Relations.* Ottawa: Department of External Relations, 1976.

Murray, Williamson, and Allan R. Millett. *A War to Be Won: Fighting the Second World War.* Cambridge: Belknap Press of Harvard University Press, 2000.

Naske, Claus-M. "The Battle of Alaska has ended and ... the Japs won it." *Military Affairs* 49 (July 1985): 144-51.

–. *A History of Alaska Statehood.* Lanham, MD: University Press of America, 1985.

Naske, Claus-M., and Herman E. Slotnick. *Alaska: A History of the 49th State.* Grand Rapids: William B. Eerdmans Publishing, 1979.

Neely, Alastair. "The First Special Service Force." In *Alaska at War, 1941-1945: The Forgotten War Remembered – Papers from the Alaska at War Symposium, Anchorage, Alaska, November 11-13, 1993,* ed. Fern Chandonnet, 97-102. Anchorage: Alaska at War Committee, 1995.

Nielson, Jonathan M. *Armed Forces on a Northern Frontier: The Military in Alaska's History, 1867-1987.* Westport, CT: Greenwood Press, 1988.

Nish, Ian, ed. *British Documents on Foreign Affairs: Reports and Papers from the Foreign Office Confidential Print.* Series E, Asia, 1860-1914. Vol. 10, *North-East Asia after the Russo-Japanese War, 1905-1914.* Frederick, MD: University Publications of America, 1989.

Nixon, Edgar B., ed. *Franklin D. Roosevelt and Foreign Affairs.* Vol. 2, *March 1934-August 1935.* Cambridge: Belknap Press of Harvard University Press, 1969.

Odom, William O. *After the Trenches: The Transformation of U.S. Army Doctrine, 1918-1939.* College Station: Texas A&M University Press, 1999.

Osgood, Robert Endicott. *Limited War: The Challenge to American Strategy.* Chicago: University of Chicago Press, 1957.

Overy, Richard. *Why the Allies Won the War.* London: Pimlico, 1995.

Parillo, Mark P. *The Japanese Merchant Marine in World War II.* Annapolis, MD: Naval Institute Press, 1993.

Parker, Frederick D. *A Priceless Advantage: U.S. Navy Communications Intelligence and the Battles of Coral Sea, Midway, and the Aleutians.* Washington, DC: Center for Cryptologic History, 1993.

Pearlman, Michael D. *Warmaking and American Democracy: The Struggle over Military Strategy, 1700 to the Present.* Lawrence: University Press of Kansas, 1999.

Perras, Galen Roger. "An Aleutian Interlude: Canadian Participation in the Recapture of the Island of Kiska." MA thesis, Royal Military College of Canada, 1986.

–. "Canada As a Military Partner: Alliance Politics and the Campaign to Recapture the Aleutian Island of Kiska." *The Journal of Military History* 56 (July 1992): 423-54.

–. "'The Defence of Alaska Must Remain a Primary Concern of the United States': Canada and the North Pacific, May-June 1942." *The Northern Mariner* 7 (October 1997): 29-43.

–. "Eyes on the Northern Route to Japan: Plans for Canadian Participation in an Invasion of the Kurile Islands – A Study in Coalition Warfare and Civil-Military Relationships." *War and Society* 8 (May 1990): 100-17.

–. *Franklin Roosevelt and the Origins of the of the Canadian-American Security Alliance, 1933-1945: Necessary But Not Necessary Enough.* Westport, CT: Greenwood Press, 1998.

–. "Once Bitten, Twice Shy: The Origins of the Canadian Army Pacific Force." In *Uncertain Horizons: Canadians and Their World in 1945*, ed. Greg Donaghy, 7-99. Ottawa: Canadian Committee for the History of the Second World War, 1997.

–. "'The Parties with Whom We Have Been Estranged So Long Can Scarcely Be Brought into a Close Relationship at a Moment's Notice': Canada's Failure to Provide Military Aid to Australia, 1942-1945." Paper presented at the annual meeting of the Australian Studies Association of North America, Vancouver, British Columbia, 7-9 March 1996.

–. "'She Should Have Thought of Herself First': Canada and Military Aid to Australia, 1939-1945." In *Parties Long Estranged: Canada and Australia in the Twentieth Century*, ed. Margaret Macmillan and Francine McKenzie. Vancouver: UBC Press, 2003.

–. "Stepping Stones to Nowhere? The United States, Canada, and the Aleutian Islands Campaign, 1942-1943." PhD diss., University of Waterloo, Ontario, 1995.

–. "Who Will Defend British Columbia? Unity of Command on the West Coast, 1934-1942." *Pacific Northwest Quarterly* 88 (Spring 1997): 59-69.

Perret, Geoffrey. *Old Soldiers Never Die: The Life of Douglas MacArthur*. New York: Random House, 1996.

Pogue, Forrest C. *George C. Marshall: Ordeal and Hope, 1939-1942*. New York: Viking Press, 1966.

–. *George C. Marshall: Organizer of Victory, 1942-1945*. New York: Viking Press, 1973.

Ponko, Vincent, Jr. "The Navy and the Aleutians before World War II: The Story of a Flirtation." *The Alaska Journal* (Spring 1983): 128-31.

–. "Report on the Aleutians." *Reader's Digest,* May 1943.

Pope, Maurice A. *Soldiers and Politicians: The Memoirs of Lt.-Gen. Maurice A. Pope*. Toronto: University of Toronto Press, 1962.

Potter, E.B. *Nimitz*. Annapolis, MD: Naval Institute Press, 1976.

Prados, John. *Combined Fleet Decoded: The Secret History of American Intelligence and the Japanese Navy in World War II*. New York: Random House, 1995.

Prange, Gordon W., with Donald M. Goldstein and Katherine V. Dillon. *At Dawn We Slept: The Untold Story of Pearl Harbor*. New York: Penguin Books, 1991.

–. *Miracle at Midway*. New York: McGraw-Hill, 1982.

Preston, Richard A. *The Defence of the Undefended Border: Planning for War in North America, 1867-1939*. Montreal and Kingston: McGill-Queen's University Press, 1977.

Roskill, Stephen W. *The War at Sea 1939-1945*. Vol. 2, *The Period of Balance*. London: Her Majesty's Stationery Office, 1956.

Ross, Steven T. *American War Planning 1945-1950*. New York: Garland Publishing, 1988.

Rourke, Norman Edward. *War Comes to Alaska: The Dutch Harbor Attack, June 3-4, 1942*. Shippensburg: Burd Street Press, 1997.

Roy, Reginald H. *For Most Conspicuous Bravery: A Biography of Major-General George R. Pearkes, V.C., through Two World Wars*. Vancouver: UBC Press, 1977.

Russell, James S. "The Aleutian Campaign." In *Alaska at War, 1941-1945: The Forgotten War Remembered – Papers from the Alaska at War Symposium, Anchorage, Alaska, November 11-13, 1993*, ed. Fern Chandonnet, 67-74. Anchorage: Alaska at War Committee, 1995.

Russell, Richard A. "The Hula Operation: The Top Secret Soviet-American Naval Lend-Lease Operation in Alaska in 1945." In *Alaska at War, 1941-1945: The Forgotten War Remembered – Papers from the Alaska at War Symposium, Anchorage, Alaska, November 11-13, 1993*, ed. Fern Chandonnet, 345-9. Anchorage: Alaska at War Committee, 1995.

Sarantakes, Nicholas Evans. *Keystone: The American Occupation of Okinawa and U.S.-Japan Relations*. College Station: Texas A&M University Press, 2000.

Schaffer, Ronald. "General Stanley D. Embick: Military Dissenter." *Military Affairs* 37 (October 1973): 89-95.

Schaller, Michael. *Douglas MacArthur: The Far Eastern General.* New York: Oxford University Press, 1989.

—. "General Douglas MacArthur and the Politics of the Pacific War." In *The Pacific War Revisited,* ed. Gunther Bischoff and Robert L. Dupont, 18-40. Baton Rouge: Louisiana State University Press, 1997.

Schewe, Donald B., ed. *Franklin D. Roosevelt and Foreign Affairs, Second Series January 1937-August 1939.* Vol. 6, *July-September 1937.* Cambridge: Harvard University Press, 1969.

Schmidt, Hans. *Maverick Marine: General Smedley D. Butler and the Contradictions of American Military History.* Lexington: University Press of Kentucky, 1987.

Schnabel, James F. *The History of the Joint Chiefs of Staff. The Joint Chiefs of Staff and National Policy.* Vol. 1, *1945-1947.* Wilmington: Michael Glazier, 1979.

Seager, Robert, III. *Alfred Thayer Mahan: The Man and His Letters.* Annapolis, MD: Naval Institute Press, 1977.

Seward, Frederick W. *Reminiscences of a War Time Statesman and Diplomat, 1870-1913.* New York: J.P. Putnam, 1916.

Sherry, Michael S. *In the Shadow of War: The United States since the 1930s.* New Haven: Yale University Press, 1995.

—. *Preparing for the Next War: American Plans for Postwar Defense, 1941-45.* New Haven: Yale University Press, 1977.

—. *The Rise of American Air Power: The Creation of Armageddon.* New Haven: Yale University Press. 1987.

Sherwood, Morgan. *Explorations in Alaska, 1856-1900.* New Haven: Yale University Press, 1965.

Shiner, John F. "The Air Corps, the Navy, and Coast Defense, 1919-1941." *Military Affairs* 45 (October 1981): 113-20.

—. *Foulois and the U.S. Army Air Corps 1931-1935.* Washington, DC: Office of Air Force History, 1983.

—. "General Benjamin Foulois and the 1934 Air Mail Disaster." *Aerospace Historian* 25 (December 1978): 221-30.

Shrader, Charles R. *Amicide: The Problem of Friendly Fire in Modern War.* Fort Leavenworth: United States Army Command and General Staff College, 1982.

Skates, John Ray. *The Invasion of Japan: Alternative to the Bomb.* Columbia, SC: University of South Carolina Press, 1994.

Smith, Holland M. Smith. "The Development of Amphibious Tactics in the U.S. Navy." *Marine Corps Gazette,* January 1947, 55-62.

Smith, Holland M., and Percy Finch. *Coral and Brass.* Washington, DC: Zenger Publishing, 1948.

Smith, Perry McCoy. *The Air Force Plans for Peace 1943-1945.* Baltimore: Johns Hopkins University Press, 1970.

Spector, Ronald. "American Seizure of Japan's Strategic Points Summer 1942-1944." In *From Pearl Harbor to Hiroshima: The Second World War in Asia and the Pacific, 1941-45,* ed. Saki Dockrill, 75-86. New York: St. Martin's Press, 1994.

—. *Eagle against the Sun: The American War with Japan.* New York: Vintage Books, 1985.

—. "The Pacific War and the Fourth Dimension of Strategy." In *The Pacific War Revisited,* ed. Gunter Bischof and Robert L. Dupont, 41-56. Baton Rouge: Louisiana State University Press, 1997.

—. *Professors of War: The Naval War College and the Development of the Naval Profession.* Newport: Naval War College Press, 1977.

—. "The Triumph of Professional Ideology: The U.S. Navy in the 1890s." In *In Peace and War: Interpretations of American Naval History, 1775-1978,* ed. Kenneth J. Hagen, 174-85. Westport, CT: Greenwood Press, 1978.

Stacey, C.P. *Arms, Men and Governments: The War Policies of Canada 1939-1945.* Ottawa: Department of National Defence, 1970.

–. *Six Years of War: The Army in Canada, Britain and the Pacific.* Vol. 1 of *Official History of the Canadian Army in the Second World War.* Ottawa: Department of National Defence, 1955.

Steele, Richard W. *The First Offensive 1942: Roosevelt, Marshall and the Making of American Strategy.* Bloomington: Indiana University Press, 1973.

Stephan, John J. *Hawaii under the Rising Sun: Japan's Plans for Conquest after Pearl Harbor.* Honolulu: University of Hawaii Press, 1984.

–. *The Kurile Islands: The Russo-Japanese Frontier in the Pacific.* Oxford: Clarendon Press, 1974.

–. *The Russian Far East: A History.* Stanford: Stanford University Press, 1994.

Stewart, Henry. "Aleuts in Japan, 1942-1945." In *Alaska at War, 1941-1945: The Forgotten War Remembered – Papers from the Alaska at War Symposium, Anchorage, Alaska, November 11-13, 1993,* ed. Fern Chandonnet, 301-4. Anchorage: Alaska at War Committee, 1995.

Stimson, Henry L., and McGeorge Bundy. *On Active Service in Peace and War.* New York: Harper Brothers, 1948.

Stokesbury, James. "Battle of Attu." *American History Illustrated* 14 (April 1979): 31-8.

Stoler, Mark A. *Allies and Adversaries: The Joint Chiefs of Staff, the Grand Alliance, and the U.S. Strategy in World War II.* Chapel Hill: University of North Carolina Press, 2000.

–. *George C. Marshall: Soldier-Statesman of the American Century.* Boston: Twayne, 1989.

–. "The 'Pacific-First' Alternative in American World War II Strategy." *The International History Review* 2 (July 1980): 432-52.

Symonds, Craig L. "William Veazie Pratt." In *The Chief of Naval Operations,* ed. Robert William Love Jr., 69-86. Annapolis, MD: Naval Institute Press, 1980.

Takahashi, Hisashi. "The Japanese Campaign in Alaska As Seen from the Strategic Perspective." In *Alaska at War, 1941-1945: The Forgotten War Remembered – Papers from the Alaska at War Symposium, Anchorage, Alaska, November 11-13, 1993,* ed. Fern Chandonnet, 33-8. Anchorage: Alaska at War Committee, 1995.

Talley, B.B., and Virginia Talley. "Building Alaska's Defenses in World War II." In *Alaska at War, 1941-1945: The Forgotten War Remembered – Papers from the Alaska at War Symposium, Anchorage, Alaska, November 11-13, 1993,* ed. Fern Chandonnet, 59-65. Anchorage: Alaska at War Committee, 1995.

Tate, James P. *The Army and Its Air Corps: Army Policy toward Aviation, 1919-1941.* Maxwell Air Force Base: Air University Press, 1998.

Taylor, John M. *William Henry Seward: The Definitive Biography of Abraham Lincoln's Controversial Secretary of State.* New York: HarperCollins, 1991.

Theoharis, Athan G. *The Yalta Myths: An Issue in U.S. Politics, 1945-1955.* Columbia, MO: University of Missouri Press, 1970.

Tooke, Lamar. *Infantry Operations in the Aleutians: The Battle for Attu.* Carlisle Barracks: United States Army War College, March 1990.

Trotter, Ann, ed. *British Documents on Foreign Affairs: Reports and Papers from the Foreign Office Confidential Print.* Series E, Asia, 1914-1939. Vol. 13, *Japan, January 1934-December 1934.* Bethesda, MD: University Publications of America, 1992.

Troy, John W. *Annual Report of the Governor of Alaska to the Secretary Interior for the Fiscal Year Ended June 30, 1933.* Washington, DC: Government Printing Office, 1933.

United States. Air Force Museum. *World Flight Chronicle.* 1999. <www.wpafb.af.mil/museum>, (23 October 2002).

–. Department of State. *Foreign Relations of the United States: The Conferences of Berlin (The Potsdam Conference) 1945.* Vol. 2. Washington, DC: Government Printing Office, 1960.

–. Department of State. *Foreign Relations of the United States: The Conferences of Berlin (The Potsdam Conference) 1945.* Vol. 6. Washington, DC: Government Printing Office, 1969.

–. Department of State. *Foreign Relations of the United States: The Conferences at Cairo and Tehran 1943.* Washington, DC: Government Printing Office, 1961.

–. Department of State. *Foreign Relations of the United States: The Conferences at Malta and Yalta 1945.* Washington, DC: Government Printing Office, 1955.

–. Department of State. *Foreign Relations of the United States: Diplomatic Papers.* Vol. 4, *The Far East.* Washington, DC: Government Printing Office, 1948.

–. Department of War. *The Capture of Attu As Told by the Men Who Fought There.* Washington, DC: Government Printing Office, 1944.

–. Resources Commission. *Alaska, Its Resources and Development.* Washington, DC: Government Printing Office, 1938.

–. Strategic Bombing Survey (Pacific). *Interrogations of Japanese Officials.* 2 vols. Washington, DC: Government Printing Office, 1946.

–. United States Strategic Bombing Survey (Pacific). *The Campaigns of the Pacific War.* New York: Greenwood Press, 1969.

Utley, Jonathan G. "Franklin Roosevelt and Naval Strategy, 1933-1941." In *FDR and the U.S. Navy,* ed. Edward J. Marolda, 47-64. New York: St. Martin's Press, 1998.

Villa, Brian L. "The U.S. Army, Unconditional Surrender, and the Potsdam Proclamation." *Journal of American History* 63 (June 1976): 66-92.

Waldrum, Major A.J. *The Aleutian Campaign: A Study in Cold Weather Survival.* Quantico: United States Marine Corps, 1976-7.

Watson, Mark Skinner. *Chief of Staff: Prewar Plans and Operations.* Washington, DC: Department of the Army, 1950.

Wavell, A.C.P. *Speaking Generally.* London: Macmillan, 1946.

Weigley, Russell F. *The American Way of War: A History of United States Military Strategy and Policy.* New York: Macmillan, 1973.

–. *History of the United States Army.* New York: Macmillan, 1967.

–. "The Role of the War Department and the Army." In *Pearl Harbor As History: Japanese-American Relations 1931-1941,* ed. Dorothy Borg and Shumpei Okamoto, 165-88. New York: Columbia University Press, 1973.

–. *Towards an American Army: Thought from Washington to Marshall.* New York: Columbia University Press, 1962.

Weinberg, Gerhard L. *A World at Arms: A Global History of World War II.* Cambridge: Cambridge University Press, 1994.

Welles, Benjamin. *Sumner Welles: FDR's Global Strategist.* New York: St. Martin's Press, 1997.

Welles, Sumner. *Seven Decisions That Shaped History.* New York: Harper and Brothers, 1950.

–. *Where Are We Heading?* New York: Harper and Brothers, 1946.

Werrell, Kenneth P. *Blankets of Fire: U.S. Bombers over Japan during World War II.* Washington, DC: Smithsonian Institution Press, 1996.

Wheeler, Gerald E. *Kinkaid of the Seventh Fleet: A Biography of Admiral Thomas C. Kinkaid, U.S. Navy.* Washington, DC: Naval Historical Center, 1995.

–. *Prelude to Pearl Harbor: The United States Navy and the Far East, 1921-1931.* Columbia, MO: University of Missouri Press, 1968.

Whitehead, John. "Alaska and Hawaii." In *The Cold War American West, 1945-1989,* ed. Kevin J. Fernlund, 189-210. Albuquerque: University of New Mexico Press, 1998.

Wilder, Carol A. "Weather As the Decisive Factor of the Aleutian Campaign, June 1942-August 1943." MA thesis, United States Army Command and General Staff College, Fort Leavenworth, 1993.

Wilford, Timothy. *Pearl Harbor Redefined: USN Radio Intelligence in 1941.* Lanham, MD: University Press of America, 2001.

Willmott, H.P. *The Barrier and the Javelin: Japanese and Allied Pacific Strategies February to June 1942.* Annapolis, MD: Naval Institute Press, 1983.

–. *The Second World War in the Far East.* London: Cassell, 2002.

Wiltz, John E. *From Isolation to War, 1931-1941.* New York: Thomas Y. Crowell, 1968.

Wittels, David G. "Lieutenant General Simon Bolivar Buckner." In *These Are the Generals,* ed. Walter Millis, 71-83. New York: Alfred A. Knopf, 1943.

Wohlstetter, Roberta. *Pearl Harbor: Warning and Decision.* Stanford: Stanford University Press, 1962.

Woldman, Albert A. *Lincoln and the Russians.* New York: Collier Books, 1961.

Worden, William L. "One Division Could Take Alaska." *Collier's,* 2 August 1947, 30-1, 46, 48, and 52.

Yoder, H.S., Jr. *Planned Invasion of Japan, 1945: The Siberian Advantage.* Philadelphia: American Philosophical Society, 1997.

Young, Roland. *Congressional Politics in the Second World War.* New York: Da Capo Press, 1972.

Index

Japan: Aleutian strategy, 186-7; army (see Imperial Japanese Army); assessment of Japanese war strategy, 100-1, 186-7; attack by Soviets (1945), 176; on future US strategy, 100; Manchurian invasion (1932), 19-20, 28; Midway (1942), 67-9, 80-1, 121, 187; navy (see Imperial Japanese Navy); Pearl Harbor attack, 55-8; relations with US (early 1900s), 8-9; Sino-Japanese War (1937), 35; Soviet occupation of Kuriles (1945), 176-8; Soviet-Japanese non-aggression pact, 169-72, 192; Tokyo bombing (1942), 66, 68; US assessment of capabilities, 63; US deception campaign (1944), 181-2; US postwar plans for (1942), 170-1; Washington Naval Treaty (1922), 12-13, 28-9. See also Aleutian Islands, Japanese occupation; United States–Japanese relations

Johnson, Lyndon, 185

Johnston, R.M., 11

Joint Army and Navy Planning Committee (JANPC), 11, 18, 42-3

Joint Board: defence of Alaska (1919), 11; on Kiska, 9; on Pearl Harbor, 56; Plan Orange, 18-19, 21, 31-3; "Rainbow" plans, 43

Joint Chiefs of Staff (JCS): on Alaskan resources, 99, 138; Attu and Kiska invasions (1943), 99, 122, 137-8, 148; deception campaigns, 180-2; garrisoning in Alaska (1943 and later), 166, 183, 185; on Japanese in Aleutians (1942), 90, 94; on Kuriles offensive (1943), 114-15, 159, 162, 164, 166, 173-4; on Pacific vs European fronts, 118, 194; on seizure of Amchitka, 109; south Pacific offensive (1942), 92; on Soviet threat postwar, 183; on Soviet-Japan conflict, 64; as theatre commanders, 77, 195-6

Joint Defence Plan No. Two (ABC-22), 72, 73

Joint Intelligence Committee (JIC), 120-1, 149, 154, 172, 183

Joint Planning Staff (JPS): Adak-Tanaga debate (1942), 94; deception campaigns, 180-2; on Kiska's recapture, 98-9, 148; on Kuriles offensive (1942-4), 114-15, 159-60, 163-7, 172-4; on Soviet cooperation to attack Japan, 65, 167-8; on Soviet invasion of Manchuria (1945), 176; and war effort planning, 196; on war priorities (1943), 116-17

Joint Strategic Plans Committee (JSPC), 186

Joint Strategic Survey Committee (JSSC), 148, 166, 196

Joint War Plans Committee (JWPC), 165-8, 170, 176, 183-5, 196

Kakuta Kikuji, Rear Admiral, 79-80

Keenleyside, Hugh, 39

Kilbourne, C.E., Brigadier, 21-2, 29-30, 185, 229

Kimball, Warren, 118, 194-5

Kimmel, Husband E., Admiral, 60

Kimura Masotomi, Rear Admiral, 152-3

King, Ernest J., Rear Admiral: after Japanese occupation of Aleutians, 88-9, 92; on Alaskan defence, 33, 60; Buckner-Theobald feud, 95-6, 107; at Cairo Conference (1943), 168; on Canadian aid in final assault vs Japan, 193; and command unity, 77, 195; re Japanese plans for Midway, 69-70; on Kuriles offensive (1942-3), 114-15, 162-4, 166-7, 172, 173; naval advisor, 89-90; on Pacific security (post-1941), 62-3; "Pacific-First" policy, 93-4, 115; personality, 62, 196, 216n23; on recapturing Aleutians, 101-2, 106-8, 119, 122, 137, 140, 148; on war priorities, 116-18, 137; at Yalta (1945), 174

King, William Lyon Mackenzie, 35-7, 74-5, 141-5, 192-4

Kinkaid, Thomas C., Rear Admiral, 126(i), 161(i); Attu occupation, 121-2, 124-31, 134-5; Kiska invasion, 113, 119, 125, 137, 147, 149-51, 154, 155; on Kuriles offensive (1943), 158-9, 161-2, 164, 165; with MacArthur in south Pacific (1943), 180; and move against Amchitka, 107-9; victim of "localitis," 188-9

Kiska Island, Aleutians: Japanese occupation (1942), 82, 85-6, 100-1, 104; naval base (1900s), 9, 10-11; US debate on recapture (1942-3), 91-4, 112-13, 118-21, 138, 147-8; US recapture (1943), ix-x, 88-95, 98, 101-3, 106-7, 149-55; use of Canadian troops, 138-45, 146(i)

Klondike gold rush, 7, 8

Knox, Frank, 92-3, 190

Kodiak Island, 7, 34, 44, 185

Komandorski Islands, 59, 123, 124

Korean War, 185-6

Kurile Islands: concessions by US at Yalta, 173-5, 177; "containment" strategy, 170; demilitarization by Japan (1922), 12-13; Paramushiro Island, 160, 162, 171; Shimushu Island, 160, 171, 177; Soviet aid in possible US offensive, 114, 159, 160, 167-71, 191-2; Soviet take-over (1945), 176-8; and Soviet-Japanese non-aggression pact, 169-72; US attacks on northern islands (1943), 160; US debate re attack (1942-3), 113-15, 158-76, 194; US deception campaign (1944), 181-2; US plans for postwar disposition, 170-1

Kuter, Lawrence, Brigadier General, 91-2

Layton, Edwin T., 22, 60

Leahy, W.D., Admiral, 33, 34, 39-40, 41, 115, 208n20

Sperry, Charles, Admiral, 9
Stacey, C.P., x
Stalin, Joseph. *See* Soviet Union
Standley, William H., 65
Stark, Harold, Admiral, 48, 49-50, 56, 59, 77
Stephan, John, 68
Stevenson, L.F., Air Vice Marshal, 73
Stilwell, Joseph, General, 147
Stimson, Henry: Aleutians debate, 89, 90, 93, 119; re Canadian troops in Aleutians (1943), 144-5; garrisoning of Alaska, 52; on Soviet occupation of Kuriles, 175, 177
Stoler, Mark, 94
Strategic Plans Division (SPD), 33-4, 120, 161-2, 196
Strategy and Policy Group (SPG), 148, 175-6, 184
Stuart, Kenneth, Lieutenant General, 73, 75, 140-5, 192-3
Swanson, Claude, 33, 34

Takagi Sokichi, Admiral, 55-6
Takahashi Hisashi, x
Takijiro Onishi, x
Talley, Benjamin, Colonel, 49, 107-9, 135
Tanaga Island, Aleutians, 93, 94, 102, 103
Tanetsuga Sosa, Rear Admiral, 68-9
Task Force Eight (TF8), 70-4, 78, 83, 102, 104, 108
Task Force Fifty-One (TF51), 113, 125, 127, 128, 131, 147
Task Force Sixteen (TF16), 88-9, 147
Theobald, Robert A., Rear Admiral, 76(i); feud with Buckner, 75-6, 84, 95-6, 107, 224n21; and Japanese Aleutian expedition (1942), 77-8, 83-5; removal from command, 107-9; strategies re Attu and Kiska, 88, 94, 99, 103-9, 112; Task Force Eight, 70, 83, 104, 107-8
Thummel, G.F., Captain, 186
Towers, J.H., Admiral, 184
Trenchard, Hugh, 14-15
Trident Conference (May 1943), 137-8
Troy, John W., 20
Truman, Harry, 175, 176, 177
Turner, Richmond Kelly, Rear Admiral, 48-51, 62

Ugaki Matome, Admiral, 56, 67, 101, 105
Umnak Island (Otter Point), Aleutians, 48, 49, 66, 78-9
Unalaska Island, Aleutians: army-navy defence plan (1941), 58; Dutch Harbor, 44, 51-3, 70-4, 78-80, 81(i), 102; importance in 1880s, 8
United Kingdom. *See* Britain
United States Army: in Alaska and Aleutians (late 1800s), 6-8; Alaskan defence (1939),

43-5; Alaskan defence post-Pearl Harbor, 58-60; Buckner as commander (1940-3), 45-7; garrisoning of Alaska (1930s), 21; manpower (1920s, 1930s), 12; plans to recapture Aleutians *(see under* DeWitt); retaking Kiska, 112; unity of command problems, 76-7, 83-5; view of Japan as opponent, 188. *See also* DeWitt, John L., Lieutenant General; United States military
United States Congress: army funding problems (1939), 44; defence expenditures (1920s, 1930s), 12, 23, 29-31, 41; Dimond and Alaskan defence, 21-2, 33-4, 44; funding for Alaskan defence postwar, 185; garrisoning of Alaska (late 1930s), 35; Hepburn Board on defence needs (1938), 42; naval reservation on Kiska (1900s), 9; Senate review of Alaska/Aleutians (1942), 97-8; view of Alaska purchase, 6
United States military: Alaskan security, indifference to, 33-5, 41-2, 188; army air corps, 16-17, 22-6, 44, 47-8; coastal defence role, 23, 26, 51-2; command unity difficulties, 76-7, 83-5, 96-9, 194-5; divisions in Europe and Pacific (1943), 229n18; Hepburn Board and defence needs (1938), 42; men in uniform (1945), 189-90, 245n29; on north Pacific security (1930s), 22; re Plan Orange (1935-8), 31-3, 41-2; "Rainbow" plans for Alaska (1939), 43-4; on Soviet occupation of Kuriles, 175; on Soviet support, possible (1942), 64-5; Soviet threat postwar, assessment of, 182-5. *See also* United States Army; United States Navy
United States Navy: Alaska and Aleutians, ability to defend, 47, 51-2, 62-3; Alaska and Aleutians, proposed facilities in (1930s), 33-4; Alaskan defence role (1939), 43, 45; in Aleutians (early 1900s), 7-9, 11; Aleutians' military use, assessment of (1923), 13-14; central Pacific strategy, 14, 119, 120, 162, 188; north Pacific security, reassessment of (1930s), 22; Pearl Harbor as base, 10-11, 184; on plans to recapture Kiska, 102-4, 112; post-Pearl Harbor reaction, 56; on Soviet cooperation, idea of (1941), 59; and Washington Naval Treaty (1922), 12-13. *See also* United States military
United States–Japanese relations: early 1900s, 8, 9-10, 20; impact of US–China relations, 13, 20; sinking of USS *Panay* (1937), 38; US trade sanctions (1940), 49; US war plans (1920s), 18-19; Washington Naval Treaty (1922), 12-13, 28-9. *See also* Japan; Pacific theatre
USS *Hornet*, 66
USS *Panay*, 38

Verbeck, Colonel, 129-30, 134
Victory Plan (1941), 99, 189-90
Villa, Brian, 148

Wallace, Henry, 90, 92-3, 107
War Plans Division (WPD): after Pearl Harbor, 58; on aid to Britain (1941), 50; on Alaskan defence, 33, 41, 43, 47-8, 49; on vulnerability of Alaska and Hawaii (1934), 21
Ward, Kenneth A., 156
Washington Naval Treaty (1922), 12-13, 22, 28-9
Watson, Mark S., xi
Weckerling, John, Colonel, 112, 149-50
Wedermeyer, A.C., General, 119, 147-8
Weigley, Russell, 188
Weinberg, Gerhard, x
Welles, Sumner, 37, 38, 169

Western Defense Command (WDC), 58-9, 112, 149, 159
Whitehead, John, 184
Wilcox, Mark, 29-30
Wilcox National Defense Act (US, 1935), 30
Williamson, Charles G., Colonel, 113-14
Willmott, H.P., 55
Wilson, France Q., Major, 155
Wohlstetter, Roberta, 56
Woodring, Harry H., 21, 44

Yalta Conference (February 1945), 173-5, 177
Yamamoto Isoroku, Admiral, 55, 57(i), 67-8, 80-1, 82, 187
Yamasaki Yasuyo, Colonel, 128, 132

Zimmerman, Wayne, Colonel, 131